BRITAIN IN
THE EIGHTIES

Other Spectator books

BRITAIN IN THE EIGHTIES

The Spectator's View of the Thatcher Decade

Edited by Philip Marsden-Smedley

Foreword by Charles Moore

GRAFTON BOOKS

A Division of the Collins Publishing Group

LONDON GLASGOW
TORONTO SYDNEY AUCKLAND

Grafton Books
A Division of the Collins Publishing Group
8 Grafton Street, London W1X 3LA

Published by Grafton Books 1989

Copyright © The Spectator 1989

British Library Cataloguing in Publication Data

Britain in the eighties: the Spectator's view
of the Thatcher decade.
1. Great Britain. Social conditions, 1980–
I. Marsden-Smedley, Philip   II. The Spectator
941.085'8

ISBN 0-246-13395-3

Printed in Great Britain by
William Collins Sons & Co. Ltd, Glasgow

'Engineers' Corner' by Wendy Cope is reprinted by permission of
Faber & Faber Ltd from *Making Cocoa for Kingsley Amis*
by Wendy Cope

CONTENTS

5 THE RISING GENERATION

6 TOWN AND COUNTRY

7 FAITH AND CHARITY

FOREWORD

Charles Moore

A party is in progress. Most of the guests are wearing dark glasses or berets or other items of revolutionary chic. In the foreground stands the incongruous figure of a man in a three-piece suit. A young woman exclaims to him, 'Now I know where I've seen you. You're on our death list.' Seeing this cartoon by Austin in the spring of 1989, I assumed that it must have been new-minted. In fact, however, *The Spectator* first published it in October 1980. The terrorist is almost the only unchanging figure of the decade – always there, always threatening, but never wholly successful; always powerful, yet also pointless. In the 1980s, he added the Brighton bomb, the Enniskillen Remembrance Sunday massacre, the flight of Salman Rushdie and much more to his role of dishonour.

Yet Britain in the Eighties did not feel as if it lived in the shadow of the gunman. The great political development of the age was the crumbling of socialism (more marked still in the countries officially committed to that doctrine). The great, related, social change was the vast increase in most people's wealth. These did not seem very likely at the start of the decade. We find Paul Barker in 1980 (see p. 5) writing of this country as 'the new Spain', idly floating on the unearned wealth of North Sea oil. The British, he wrote, no longer wanted to do anything today which could be put off till tomorrow. He cited the decline of the Port of London and the failure to dig a Channel Tunnel. Eight years later, private money had created a dispiriting but successful new world in the wastes of the London docks and was digging deep beneath the white cliffs of Dover. People who had worried about endless decline were now alarmed by the boom.

The decade divides quite neatly between its first and second half. In the first came mass unemployment, Wet revolt, the formation of a new political party, inner city riots, the miners' strike, Greenham Common. The second brought Big Bang, Wapping, a third Conservative victory, yuppies, the house price explosion and the Greening of absolutely everybody. Indeed, it is safe to assume that when everyone turns environmental, prosperity has truly arrived. Greenness is the ultimate luxury of the consumer society. Britain became wealthy enough to worry whether she were also healthy and wise. The last year of the decade revealed a new obsession with illness, pollution, food, and a new disgust at our own dirtiness and greed.

On some of these matters, I can truthfully boast, you read about it first in *The Spectator*. Quite a good index of this is how often an article published in the magazine is subsequently bought by other publications or plagiarised by them. When Nicholas Coleridge introduced the New Young Rich (see p. 101), his words were snapped up by about ten newspapers and magazines. When Dominic Lawson revealed that Britain was the greatest importer of toxic waste (see p. 252), his information was shamelessly lifted by journalistic Johnnies-come-lately. I am particularly proud of the fact that our cook, Jennifer Paterson, disclosed on 5 November 1988 that 'there is a very big threat on the horizon . . . It is the terrifying threat . . . of salmonella poisoning coming from any egg yolk that has not been cooked through and through like a hard-boiled egg.' Nobody picked this up at the time, but a month later, a Mrs Edwina Currie said that 'Unfortunately, most of the egg production in this country is infected with salmonella', and the rest is history – or, rather, hysteria. As for broader trends, our writers often sniffed the wind more quickly and sensitively than conventional journalists. Auberon Waugh wrote for years about the growth of the Yob Society. After the Heysel Stadium, every writer in Fleet Street parroted his prophecies.

The magazine itself experienced the vicissitudes of the period. Previously owned by private individuals, *The Spectator* succumbed to the Australian invasion in 1985 when Mr Algy Cluff sold it to the Fairfax Group. The Fairfax ownership went swimmingly until its new young chairman indulged in the great Eighties folly of the takeover and bought the whole company himself, borrowing half a billion pounds to do so. The crash came in the same month and Mr Fairfax sold *The Spectator* to meet a week's interest charges. The new buyer was the Telegraph Group, risen Phoenix-like from the destruction of Fleet Street, and now owned by a Canadian, Mr Conrad Black. Through these changes and chances the magazine continued to grow. It began the decade with a circulation of 17,000 and ended it with over 40,000.

The lives of our own contributors were sometimes scarred by the times in which they lived. Charles Glass, our correspondent in the Levant, was kidnapped in Beirut. He subsequently escaped, with great ingenuity and courage. Roger Cooper wrote for us with distinction about Iran. At the time of writing, he is still imprisoned there.

Much was new in the 1980s. At one extreme was the Princess of Wales, an icon of youth and beauty. At the other was Aids, for some a judgement on decadence, for all an emblem of fear and death. The two, movingly, met, and the Princess made a point of meeting and touching those who suffered from the disease.

Mrs Thatcher was almost new when the decade began. Although she had led her party since 1975, she was not secure in her job until she routed the Wets in 1981 and the Argentinians in 1982. For most people in Britain, she came to embody either what was right or wrong, black or white, about modern times. Shades of grey were not permitted. In these pages, two doctors reveal that all lunatics have heard of Mrs Thatcher even if they recognise no other public figure. Patrick Marnham discloses that he dreams about the Prime Minister. For better or worse, richer or poorer, in sickness or in health, the Eighties belong to her. These pages help to explain how and why.

The Spectator
March 1989

EDITORIAL NOTE

In selecting material for this book it was not necessary to delve any further back into *The Spectator*'s archives than the second half of 1979, for the Eighties form a neater decade than most, and one which seemed mature by the middle years (1984–7). It is this period which provides the richest pickings, and from these years, the first of Charles Moore's editorship, come the essential pieces: those on the conspicuous new wealth, the effects of Mrs Thatcher's second term, and the early tremors of a new morality. Subsequent developments, the blooms of the ecology movement, seem, in terms of social history, the natural extension of what emerged from the struggles of the early Eighties.

The reporting of the decade's events, the news, has been largely confined to one section. This book is not a retrospective; the political commentary of a weekly is soon dated. Instead, focus has been put on those details of thought and habit, and the personalities, that best characterise the startling differences between 1980 and 1990. Articles have been arranged by subject (chronologically within each section), a choice that has meant some revealing juxtapositions. In all cases, *The Spectator*'s laissez-faire editorial policy has been maintained: the text has been left as it first appeared.

Philip Marsden-Smedley

Chapter 1
WHITHER BRITAIN?

'It's all right, officer, he was going to light up.'

BACKWARD INTO THE EIGHTIES

Christopher Booker

Ten years ago, at the end of the Sixties, I contributed to these columns an article called 'Backward into the Seventies', which I ended with the expression of hope that I should 'still be here to write the same article in ten years time'. Well, here it is – and looking back at those predictions as to the likely character of the Seventies, the most obvious comment to make is how unusually (but gratifyingly) predictable the decade just ending turns out to have been.

When I say how unusual it is for a decade to be predictable, I mean that decades in this century have generally turned out to have quite the opposite character from that predicted at their outset. At the end of the Forties, for instance, against the background of continuing austerity, financial crisis and a worsening Cold War (with Stalin just having exploded his first atom bomb), the prospects for the decade to come were generally advertised as unutterably gloomy. Few, if any, foresaw the astonishing transformation which was to come over Britain and the world in the Fifties – to such an extent that, by 1959, in the high noon of Supermac's affluence and the 'Khrushchev Thaw', most commentators looked forward to the Sixties with a greater degree of optimism than had been true at the end of any previous decade of the century.

'At the gates of the new decade', wrote the *Economist* in December 1959, 'the main peril, blinding our eyes to what we could achieve, seems to be smugness.' In *Esquire*, in January 1960, sensing the mood that was shortly to unleash his friend John Kennedy's 'New Frontier', Arthur Schlesinger Jr predicted that the Sixties would be 'spirited, articulate, inventive, incoherent, turbulent, with energy shooting off wildly in all directions . . . there will be a sense of motion, of leadership and of hope'.

Well, as we all know, the Sixties turned out to be rather more uncomfortably 'energetic, incoherent and turbulent' than the good Professor can have allowed for in his wildest dreams – and ten years of 'dynamism', permissiveness, youthful protest and Vietnam later, the mood could scarcely have been more different. As I wrote then in *The Spectator*, 'Everyone seems by and large agreed that the Sixties were a party which got rather out of hand, and that in the past year or so, as we look round the wasteland left by ten years of battered hopes, tired novelties and exploded illusions, there have been plenty of signs of a kind of shocked and exhausted hangover setting in.' After the 'dear, dead, foolish Sixties', in short, we could confidently look forward to the 'solemn, square, sane Seventies' – and so, by and large, give or take a few qualifications on the sanity-element, it has proved.

Of course not even Nostradamus could have predicted the surprises of the past decade in detail – Watergate and the resignation of a President, the full scale of the horrors which followed the Communist take-over in South-East Asia, the crystallisation of the long-predicted world energy crisis round the Yom Kippur War and the fall of the Shah, the election in Britain of a woman Prime Minister and the rise of 'Thatcherism', the range of victims falling to the worldwide wave of terrorism, from prime ministers in Spain and Italy to Airey Neave and Lord Mountbatten. But at a deeper level, all these things, like inflation and the newly aggressive mood of the unions, were merely expressions or culminations of trends which were already discernible as the Sixties came to an end.

What perhaps I got most seriously wrong in my assessment of the mood of the times ten years ago was simply to prejudge the extent to which the great reaction to the euphoria and follies of the Sixties had already taken place. It is quite true that, by 1970, there were already abundant signs that the wilder notions of those earlier years were being called into question. The great tide of 'dynamism' and 'permissiveness', of tower blocks and technology triumphant, was certainly, in the wake of such pointers as Ronan Point, E. J. Mishan's *The Cost of Economic Growth*, the rise of 'conservation' and the 'ecology movement', on the ebb.

But in my eagerness to see an end to the foolish neophilia of the Sixties, what I misread was just how long the great Sixties dream would be a-dying, and just how far the reaction would have to work through until it became more or less the prevailing orthodoxy of the late Seventies.

It was not until the end of the Wilson–Heath–Wilson era, as I have argued before in these columns, that one could look back to see how much those twelve years between 1964 and 1976 formed a kind of self-contained period in English life, dominated by a kind of trendy, imma-ture wishful thinking, and by a certain kind of 'boy hero' personality (Wilson, Heath, Thorpe, Frost, Jim Slater, George Best, the Beatles) whose day now seems very much over.

Similarly, I did not foresee just how many of the fashionable notions of the Sixties would have a kind of last, wild fling in the early Seventies – most notably, perhaps, the belief in the bulldozing of our cities into a brave new world of tower blocks and motorways, which collapsed so sud-denly in 1974–6, like so much else from those earlier years.

Who indeed could have foreseen just what a turmoil America would have to go through in the mid-Seventies, in order to purge the sickness which, after 1963, had just gone on getting worse and worse – or just how total and terrible in its consequences would be the otherwise predictable failure of America to keep South-East Asia from falling under communist rule?

For all these things it can nevertheless be said that the prevailing trend of the Seventies has continued to run pretty consistently in the same direction. Altogether it has been a decade when we have steadily continued to be stripped of our old illusions, when faith in the technological, political, social, artistic and moral progress of our civilisation has become harder to sustain than ever. And the most interesting thing has been the almost complete failure of any new body of illusions to rise to take their place. For this reason alone it has therefore been a decade with much to be said for it. If we came 'backward into the Seventies', so even more firmly do we travel backward into the Eighties. In view of the catastrophes and atrocities which have followed in our century from looking rosily into the future, it is perhaps the healthiest of all postures to adopt. I recall saying on the radio at the end of 1969 that I thought the Seventies would probably be 'a quiescent interlude' before the renewed horrors of the Eighties. The Seventies have certainly not been without their horrors. As for my premonitions about the Eighties, however, I hope I am even more wrong. Even more fervently than in 1970 do I hope that I shall still be here in ten years time, to write the same article yet again, and to wish all *Spectator* readers, as I do now, a happy new decade.

22 December 1979

ENGLAND'S MOOD FOR MANANA

Paul Barker

Stands the church clock still at GMT? Even though we're now nearly two months into British Summer Time, it very likely does. Now public clocks that work are as antiquated an idea as watch committees. I went into my local bank for some cash and wrote on the cheque the date on the large display calendar behind the counter. 'That's wrong,' the teller said, when

I pushed it under the grille. Their calendar was still at yesterday's date.

Newspapers were printed the other Monday; but because it was a bank holiday, many were not distributed. Of three replica locomotives designed to commemorate the Liverpool–Manchester line, one broke down and one got derailed; only one could run. Things in England now seldom happen *as* they should; even less often do they happen *when* they should.

Does it matter? Who cares anyway? Most people would probably say 'No' and 'No one', respectively. In the sunset years of the 20th century, England has become *mañana*-land: the New Spain. 'Never do today what you can put off to tomorrow' has always struck me as a reasonable guide to life. Don't sell procrastination short. But this is not a paradox any more: it is a truism.

All nations are scarred by the period when they were great. Till these last few years at least, Spain was scarred by the time when it ruled half the Americas and large tracts of Europe. The history of Spain has uncomfortable echoes for anyone in England now.

After the setback of the Armada (Philip II's Suez), Spain seemed to lose its nerve. Politically and economically nothing got done. Sectional interests were always and everywhere more powerful than national ones. Here is J. H. Elliott, the Cambridge historian, on the decline of imperial Spain:

'Seville itself never built the bridge it so badly needed over the Guadalquivir, and it failed to tackle the increasingly serious problem of the silting-up of the river, which was finally to destroy its commercial prosperity. The reasons were similar to those which had wrecked the [earlier] Tagus navigation scheme: a reluctance to invest money in public works; personal and municipal rivalries; and, ultimately, a deadening inertia, which crippled both the capacity and the desire to act.'

What English project does this remind you of? The list is almost endless. The decline of the Port of London; the failure to dig a Channel tunnel; the muddle over a new London airport. It is characteristic of our time that Tony Crosland was hailed as a statesman just for scrapping (or so it seemed then) those last two. This is a country which cannot even go metric inside a decade and a half. 'Already by the end of the 16th century', according to Elliott, 'many Spaniards seem to have been gripped by that sense of fatalism which would prompt the famous pronouncement of a Junta of theologians in the reign of Philip IV. Summoned to consider a project for the construction of a canal linking the Manzanares and the Tagus, it flatly declared that if God had intended the rivers to be navigable, he would have made them so.' Philip IV's Junta seem to have been ecologists before their time.

The worrying thing about attempting a detailed comparison between

England and Spain is not that it falls apart but that it stands up so well. If we were really discovering the sheer pleasures of pre-industrial idleness – such as Professor Le Roy Ladurie chronicles in the village of Montaillou – that would be fine. Unfortunately, we have an industrial system on our hands.

I borrowed the London Library's *Economic History of Spain* by Jaime Vicens Vives. It has a sadly familiar chapter, I found, on 'Demographic, Agricultural and Industrial Decline'. A quarter of a century has passed since Michael Young wrote his Fabian pamphlet, *The Chipped White Cups of Dover*, and set up the Consumers' Association. The cups on your local café table are perhaps not chipped any more. But they are unique among the utensils in being still Made in England. The stainless steel spoons and forks and knives are from Taiwan. The patterned plastic tablecloth is from France. The teapot is from West Germany. The café itself is part of an American franchised chain. You drive to it in a Japanese car, and walk across in your dumped Polish leather shoes.

In 17th-century Spain, also, business was increasingly dominated by foreign imports, and by foreign firms setting up locally. The Germans, the Genoese and the Flemish moved in first. The job was finished off by the Dutch and the English (from Harvey's sherry to Rio Tinto Zinc). At the lower end of the social scale, immigrants took on what Vicens calls 'the humblest trades, those which repelled the minds of the natives'. In England we give these tasks to people with black and brown skins; in Spain they were mainly done by immigrants from the South of France. But there were also the swarthier Moriscos, the descendants of the Moors. The Kings of Spain eventually expelled the Moriscos to North Africa – where they mostly died – in order to gain some quick popularity.

What inertia and overseas infiltration began, the guilds helped to complete. Guilds started up in all trades: tanners, masons, shoemakers, woolcombers, linen weavers, glass blowers, carters. This did not seem to matter so much when trade prospered. But when it declined, 'the guilds became organisations of resistance to the contraction of economic life'.

On the face of it this seems as reasonable as the TUC's objection to monetarism. But a curious symbiosis grew up between the guilds and the Spanish state – like that between unions and government in England. (Sir Geoffrey Howe's latest remarks clearly presage a return to this.) The tax demands of the Spanish state continued to grow. It could not do without the cooperation of the guilds. So it nourished them, like an apple tree supporting mistletoe. They neutralised each other.

Bacon and Eltis may have been wrong about some things in their economic analysis of our problems. But they were right about the lack of commitment to production. The crock of oil in the North Sea has deepened this lack of interest. The money is being used to lubricate things as they are, not how they might become. This was a classic Callaghanesque manoeuvre – the strategy of King Log. But it has been continued by Queen Stork. Mrs Thatcher may be as uncertain as he was about what she wants to do. But she is certain she wants the chance to be seen doing it.

For us, oil; for Spain, silver. 'Events', Elliott writes, 'had conspired to disparage in the national estimation the more prosaic virtues of hard work and consistent effort. The mines of Potosí (the vast silver deposits found near Lake Titicaca in Peru) brought the country untold wealth; if money was short today, it would be abundant again tomorrow when the treasure fleet reached Seville. Why plan, why save, why work? Around the corner would be the miracle – or perhaps the disaster. Prices might rise, savings be lost, the crops fail . . . The idle prospered and the toilers were left without reward.' With a growing burden of tax, the Spanish took refuge (like the English now) in a 'grey economy' of fraud and contraband and generally dodging the Revenue.

In the Habsburgs' Heartbreak House, the laws of God and economics were not suspended forever, any more than they will be for England. But in the meantime it was not a bad moment for art. Interesting times are better for literature than for people. (In France the tacky Third and Fourth Republics were more impressive culturally than the more prosperous Fifth.) And in Spain there were Calderón, Lope de Vega – and Cervantes. Don Quixote is the only book written by any of them that anyone now reads outside university. To its contemporary readers, the fable had a very sharp edge. Spain was a country that fought with old weapons, and used them only against windmills.

We need not fear the comparison. Listen to any speech by Sir Keith Joseph – a nice man, living in a world of his own – and you will see at once that we have our own Knight of La Mancha. Early 17th-century Spain, we are told, surrendered to an orgy of national introspection, 'desperately attempting to discover at what point reality had been exchanged for illusion'. This sounds very like Sir Keith.

7 June 1980

THE SPECTATOR POLL ON THE DECLINE OF BRITAIN

Michael Trend

Successful Britons see an end to decline

The Spectator *Poll is designed to elicit the opinions, not of the general public, but of those holding senior positions in Britain, those who take important decisions and whose views are likely to influence public policy. The 154 respondents to this poll were drawn from the City, business and industry, the trade unions, the press and television, the universities, the law, medicine, the arts, the clergy, the Civil Service and the Houses of Parliament. Field work was carried out by the Harris Research Centre between 9 and 16 January 1987. The survey was co-ordinated by CDP Waterhouse.*

If one had asked the questions that were put to our respondents about the state and condition of Britain today – its decline and prospects – only a few years ago, it is a reasonable guess that the vast majority would have given gloomier answers than are revealed here. Underlying many of the replies to our questions there was to be detected a hopeful strain: the overall view was on the whole more positive than negative. Only eight per cent described Britain as in a state of continuous decline while 58 per cent thought that while Britain has declined in some respects it has also improved in others; and overall 62 per cent said that they were 'fairly optimistic'. More hopeful still were the 27 per cent who believed that they could see signs of a major regeneration occurring, although it is perhaps not surprising that this latter group consists mainly of respondents who said that they were Conservative supporters, a group that also included more business people than non-business people.

But the fact of real decline in the recent past was recognised by all but four respondents. The poll looked at the reasons our respondents gave for the causes of decline. Given a choice of 'economic' or 'social' factors, 52 per cent said 'both equally', with 20 per cent replying 'primarily economic' and 22 per cent 'primarily social'. A number of different reasons were given: Britain's changed position in the world following the loss of Empire, unpreparedness for the ensuing competitiveness required to break into new markets, an inability to cope with industrial and economic change, the decline in the traditional manufacturing industries, wholesale social structural change and the breakdown of traditional values. More specifically, one Member of Parliament was of the opinion that 'if more went to Sunday school, there would be fewer in the courts during the week'.

The most frequently mentioned historic starting point of decline in Britain was the period after the Second World War, mentioned by over a third of the 92 per cent who acknowledged some decline in Britain. The 'Swinging Sixties' were also believed by many to have been a major watershed for both social change and decline as well as economic change, mainly in terms of the onset of the years of inflation and mass unemployment. Some of our respondents traced the onset of Britain's decline much further back into history: the earliest moment given was 'the Boer war – it was the first overseas event which suggested that Britain would not get its own way in the world'.

The poll revealed that it was behavioural standards that are believed to have declined most dramatically. This was shown by responses to certain specific areas of concern.

Have these standards in Britain improved, declined or stayed about the same in the past 40 years?

	Improved at all %	Declined at all %	Stayed the same %
Respect for law and order	2	88	9
Sexual morality	3	80	10
The use and development of the English language	20	59	18
Professional ethics	8	54	34
Educational achievement	33	47	13
Political integrity	5	42	50
Social integration	48	32	14
Industrial and economic efficiency	55	27	11
Reward for individual initiative	56	18	21
Cultural activities	73	7	17

Who, our poll asked, should bear the responsibility for the decline? We were told that successive weak governments and politicians in general were to blame above all. This feeling was only rarely aimed at a specific political party, and was one shared by supporters of all of them. In total 37 per cent blamed political mismanagement above all other factors, including 36 per cent of Conservatives, 40 per cent of Labour, 44 per cent of Alliance and 33 per cent of the politically non-aligned. In keeping with this prevailing judgement, Mrs Thatcher's government scored only mid-dling marks for achieving her aim of restoring Britain's economic and industrial strength, with an average success rating across all groups in the poll of 5.5 out of a possible 10. And among her own party's supporters she only achieved 6.3 out of 10, with a mere 14 per cent of Tories award-ing a mark of 8 or above.

The vast majority of respondents (88 per cent) believed, however, that Britain's decline is reversible, a group that included many who were to some extent pessimistic about the next 20 years. In view of these answers it was interesting to see what resources our respondents thought Britain was going to draw on. They told us that Britain has a basic stability and commitment to democracy; and this was coupled with a belief in the strength of national characteristics – thought of as tolerance, adaptabil-ity, pragmatism, a sense of humour, stoicism, common sense and an abil-ity to cope with a crisis.

Britain was also believed still to possess commercial and trading strengths: innate ingenuity and inventiveness, as well as general com-mercial ability (especially in the banking and financial sectors). One civil servant put it thus: 'political stability, social cohesion, overseas contacts and financial expertise'. It was in some ways touching to see so many old friends in the list of fundamental unchanging strengths, although per-haps more surprising to see that British patriotism, love of tradition and the monarchy were comparatively rarely mentioned.

By way of comparison, the poll asked its respondents to contrast Brit-ain's recent performance with that of other countries. The table shows the percentage of the respondents who mentioned various countries which, in their opinion, had done better than Britain.

Countries which have performed substantially better than Britain during the past 40 years

Germany	82%
Japan	71%
USA	59%
France	44%
Italy	12%
Switzerland	12%
Holland	10%
Sweden	9%

Respondents also gave their reasons for admiring or not admiring other countries. One peer of the realm picked the US because he 'liked the go-go atmosphere of getting things done there'. Another was against Germany because of its 'humourless philosophy of life', and a clergyman was less than enthusiastic for the custom in Japan of 'physical exercise in the morning'. The acid test, however, was whether or not our respondents would advise a young person to stay in Britain or to go elsewhere. Only 14 per cent would advise them to go, while 75 per cent would advise them to stay at home.

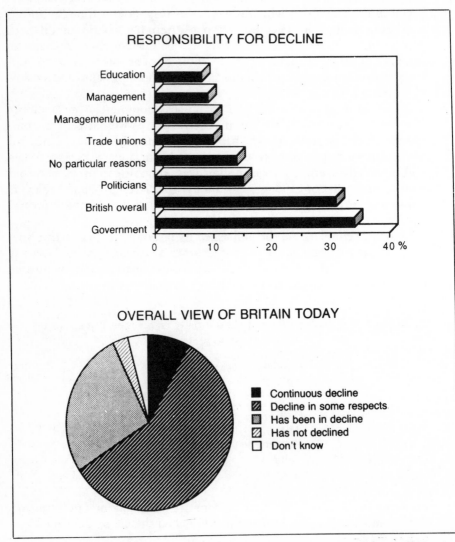

14 February 1987

ALL ANARCHISTS NOWADAYS

Ferdinand Mount

How the destruction of authority leads to totalitarianism
The paradox is by now so familiar that we take it for granted. The 'decay of authority' – or even the 'twilight of authority' – is a commonplace. Everyone mourns it or rejoices in it. Yet never has this country been so overflowing with authorities: local authorities, education authorities, health authorities, water authorities, broadcasting authorities, police authorities, transport authorities, aviation and airport authorities. The body politic seems to be overstuffed with authority. Recent name changes introduced by Whitehall have tended to dispense with any such suffix, as though this huge pile of claims to authority had become a little embarrassing. We now have simply 'British Coal', 'London Regional Transport', 'London Electricity'. Yet authorities they undeniably remain, just as a vicar without a dog-collar is still a vicar. They still have statutory monopolies, legal powers and privileges, often their own police forces and inspectors too.

Even this government and its supporters – supposedly so 'authoritarian' – seem reluctant to use the word. They prefer to talk of 'allowing managers to manage' or about 'parent power in schools', or about 'giving the trade unions back to their members' – although these are all clearly projects for the restoration of legitimate authority in one way or another.

It will, I think, become clear in retrospect to most people – is perhaps already clear – that Britain's history over the last two decades or so has been one of accelerating erosion of proper authority, culminating in near-collapse in the *annus terribilis* of 1974, then gradual and painful recovery of authority over the past ten years, at a quickening pace over the past five. This fall-and-rise of authority is most spectacularly visible in the coal industry and other industries such as steel, newspapers and the motor industry, but is beginning to become evident elsewhere, in schools and hospitals, for example, and also inside the Labour party and the trade unions. How far this recovery of authority is the work of government giving a lead to managers and other professionals, and how far it is a collective revulsion against anarchy, of which Mrs Thatcher is as much the beneficiary as the initiator, is not my theme here. The fascinating thing is that nobody much cares to talk about it, or not in quite those explicit terms.

The most fearless journalist would prefer to tackle almost any other subject – incest or sodomy certainly, perhaps even the Incarnation – rather than authority. One may refer to the dread topic, of course, in a sardonic spirit as Authority with a capital A or pejoratively by the epithet 'authoritarian'. But seriously to explore the nature of proper authority and the characteristics of authoritativeness, well, that is a risky undertaking. One cannot safely take the noun for a stroll without ostentatiously attaching a 'proper' to it. How handy it would be to have up one's sleeve a special word – 'prauth', say, or even a Welshified version 'prawdd', in order to indicate that we are dealing with an ancient and robust idea, something far wider than the mere consideration of who is to give the orders, wider even than the idea of law.

In fact, it is this shrivelled order-giving interpretation of authority which both corrupts authority-holders and helps to discredit the whole notion of authority, itself already weighed down by its battered and stained historical luggage. So much prauth is based on customs and habits which need involve giving no orders and which may have only a remote and ultimate connection with law in the modern, positive, statute-minded sense. The authority of a football referee, of a doctor, of a porcelain expert, of a priest, of an electrician, a schoolteacher, a policeman or a politician may or may not be, partly or wholly, set out in laws or regulations; he may or may not have powers to enforce some or all of his authority; that authority may or may not be backed by certificates of qualification. But the authority he exercises always has the same general character: that he is a proper person to carry out certain functions, a person whose authority must be respected in his field, because he is recognised by the appropriate body in that field, and so willy-nilly by the rest of us, as possessing that authority. We are not compelled to admire or to like or to listen to or even to obey such a person. All we are expected to do is to acknowledge that he is a proper person. As Michael Oakeshott points out in *On Human Conduct*, this authority may have little or nothing to do with justice or democracy or logic. It is conferred simply by virtue of our daily acceptance of it and of the rules and customs which define and limit its exercise.

The idea of authority has, it seems, always been pretty much like this: in Latin, in Old French, in Middle English, in more modern jurisprudence. Men have always used the same word to describe both legitimate power, him who wields it and the source from where he derives it (the source being animal, vegetable, mineral or abstract, depending on the circumstances). A man can be an authority or have authority or give authority. By using the same word, we show that what we are talking about is a continuous process of acceptance and acknowledgement, not a once-for-all contract, or Act of Parliament or passport stamp.

Another abiding feature: 'authority' still contains within it – though less obviously so in the naked, reductive terms of modern debate – the idea of augmentation or increase, like the cognate word 'author'. A person given authority is not simply licensed; he is added to, enriched, and so is the relationship between him and those who accept his authority; they have a new source of guidance, advice, instruction, justice – all of which imposes on him corresponding obligations and restraints, often codified, always fairly well understood by both sides even where neglected in practice. It is these relationships – starting with the acknowledgement of parental authority – which teach us or ought to teach us how to exercise authority ourselves, how to recognise it in others, when to challenge its excessive or illegitimate use.

Now to the Left all this sounds both pernicious and sentimental. For it is this network of authority-relationships which go to make up 'The System' that the Left must smash. This is the common aim of Trotskyist, communist, fascist, anarchist and revolutionary-feminist alike: first, to reduce authority to 'nothing but' the giving of commands, by de-mystifying it and shearing it of all its props, whether divine, or traditional, or professional, or electoral; to reduce all authority to Lenin's question 'Who? – Whom?' – who is exercising power on whom; then to demonstrate the harsh or illogical or unfair or vulnerable or contradictory aspects of those commands and the personal incompetence or callousness or corruption of those giving the commands; so to 'raise the consciousness' of people that they no longer take the old customs and practices for granted and thus to 'disorient' them so that, having no fixed standards of judgment, they may be brought to accept almost anything.

Mussolini was the first and most transparent master of this disorienting. In his innocently boastful way, he was quite happy to explain the tricks of his trade – in private. The public must not be allowed to *settle*, they must be kept on the hop; there must be 'a permanent revolution' (his phrase 30 years before Mao popularised it). Therefore, while showing the necessary brutality to frighten opponents and being quite willing to make use of any traditional means to power, the Duce must never let legitimacy accrue to any established organ of authority. The legends of 'the March on Rome' by 300,000 fascists and of '3,000 fascist martyrs' (in fact, there were only a fraction of that number involved in his accession to power and, much to his regret, only a dozen people were killed in the street fighting) were necessary to hide the fact that Mussolini had merely been asked to form a government by the King, for if the Fascist Revolution was brought into being by the King's authority, why then, it could be brought to an end in the same way – as it was, but, alas, not until 21 years had passed.

In just the same way, the Bolshevik régime and all its heirs and imitators have used systems of government and codes of law as hollow shells, called into being solely in order to dupe or entice Westerners. The only legitimate living political organism is the party, that lawless, anarchic impulse to power. 'All power to the Soviets' means precisely what it says. By reserving the monopoly of power for a 'democratic-centralist' party, communist leaders ensure not only that all power remains in their hands but also that no independent centres of authority are built up and thus that no political life as we know it in the West can emerge – that is, no transactions between independent institutions and individuals within a framework of known rules and conventions which may not be arbitrarily altered. This free play of ordinary life is at the heart of our liberties. By the same token, it is a fatal threat to the survival of any totalitarian régime.

Thus the 'long march through the institutions', as urged by Mussolini's victim, Antonio Gramsci, is not simply a means of building up revolutionary power bases in every significant institution, such as the TUC or the BBC or the BMA. It is also a means of eroding the independent existence of such institutions, of gradually squeezing the life out of them until their scrawny necks can be wrung with a single flick of the wrist. In this process, it may be necessary to mimic the language of 'democracy' and 'accountability' in order to show up existing practices as antiquated, oligarchic and irresponsible. This mimicry is calculated to deepen the confusion in the minds of existing authority-holders as to how and whence their authority is derived. All idea of proper authority as a bulwark against tyranny, fraud and brutality begins to be erased from their minds as well as from the minds of the general public.

Authority, as properly and traditionally understood, is in fact rather more than a guarantor of justice and fair dealing in social life. Again, the left-wing discreditors like to depict authority as, at best, a kind of dreary and grim headmaster who confines the flow of existence within the parameters of the status quo. But this cannot be a complete picture of the reality. Far from authority being the unswerving enemy of all change, it is scarcely possible to conceive of a society which is effectively open to change and which is not at the same time saturated in the understanding of authority. The discussion and testing of rival theories and devices – scientific, political, technical – demand a framework of rules and governing bodies for carrying out the tests, for judging their results, for agreeing and implementing change. A society lacking such arrangements must have its governing ideas dictated by force and fraud.

We have, of course, all experienced and read of many authorities which have become set in their ways and utterly resistant to reform or innovation. But this fossilisation is a perversion of proper authority, not its fulfilment, and is likely in the end to generate a refusal of consent and so to destroy the authority. Long-lasting authority is characterised by a willingness to respond, cautiously and appropriately, to changing circumstances, without succumbing to the paralysing fear that any change must be fatal. Yet here too the Left still manages to caricature as 'hidebound' or 'sclerotic' such constantly evolving and indeed sometimes over-flexible institutions as the British Constitution and the Papacy.

This discrediting of authority remains the most enduring achievement of the Left in the West, the most usable legacy of Marx's brilliant rhetoric. But the discrediting goes a great deal further than was consciously intended by the founding fathers of fascism and communism. Having shattered proper authority, they then utterly destroyed in the eyes of posterity the improper authority to which they laid claim. The disgusting consequences of their grand revolutionary projects have left succeeding generations, in the West at any rate, with a distaste for all authority and hence also for all efforts to distinguish the proper from the improper. Both legitimate authority in its traditional forms and its hideous parody in the form of totalitarian dictatorship are to be regarded with unyielding suspicion. Under the skin, we are all anarchists nowadays.

As a result, the Western media and most Western political scientists are to this day still estranged from the old conceptions of proper authority and remain quite easy to bamboozle or to inject with facile and often destructive enthusiasms.

They can, for example, be made to demand that every type of authority should be made subject to the methods of parliamentary democracy, when it is obvious that the politicising of scholarly or scientific institutions is almost invariably disastrous to their work. They can be made to swallow the constitutional fiction, so agreeable to MPs themselves, that 'Parliament can do anything' and that a simple majority has the authority to exercise unfettered power in all circumstances. In reality, there is a huge range of possible government actions which we would all agree that Parliament had no authority to sanction or demand, ranging from the slaying of the first-born to the sacking of any porcelain expert who had voted SDP. I am not concerned here with whether such restraints are to be described as 'moral' or 'constitutional', or whether they are to be justified by appeals to common law, to equity or to natural or divine law. They exist.

The intoxicating sense of omnipotence which has overcome Parliament has spread, with far less justification, to those Labour local authorities which appear to believe that any action which is not specifically forbidden to them by Parliament as *ultra vires* is fair game. Trade unions in hospitals and schools and elsewhere also came in the later

1970s to see their quest for justice as legitimising a limitless range of actions, regardless of the harm done to the public.

The consequences of this breakdown of proper authority became painfully familiar: hospitals in which crucial clinical decisions were made by the porters, schools in which the head teacher was buffeted between the NUT and the LEA and it was the caretaker who decided whether or not the school should open, newspapers run primarily to suit the printers. As some of these lunacies have collapsed, partly under the weight of their impracticality and partly as a result of remedial legislation, it is tempting to imagine that proper authority has thereby been restored. But in many instances, though not in all (the Wapping revolution is clearly irreversible, for example), the restoration is no more secure than that of the Bourbons in 1814. The pretensions of Labour local authorities remain only temporarily held in check by rate-capping. Until we are clear about what went wrong, about how and why proper authority collapsed, we shall be powerless to resist fresh demands which would lead to exactly the same thing happening again. Present Labour Party policy is crammed with such demands – all described as urgent priorities on grounds of social justice, industrial regeneration or local democracy.

The general outline of a programme for the restoration and maintenance of prauth is not obscure. First, authority must reside and be seen to reside where it is, in theory, supposed to reside. A headmaster should be allowed to act like one. A manager should be left to get on with managing. Trade union general secretaries should carry out the will of their members and be subject to periodic election by them. Secondly, authority should be clearly limited to the purposes for which it is appropriate. An education authority's function is to maintain or improve standards of education in its area; it is not an agency for socialisation or indoctrination. A brush company's purpose in life is to make brushes; an institution of learning's task is to uphold and advance scholarship; neither body is to be hijacked into serving as a getaway car for political or social causes. These limits on proper authority are in part a matter of self-limitation – of a true understanding of their calling by the members of the body in question – but also of precise and specific wording in statutes and other authority-defining rules. It is part of the burden of Lord Chief Justice Hewart's *The New Despotism* (1929) that Parliament was aiding and abetting 'the pretensions and encroachments of bureaucracy' by thoughtlessly granting ministers and statutory bodies such sweeping powers.

What we can see, 50 years later, is the curious result of having failed to heed Hewart's warning. We have got things back to front. These corporate authorities, governing water, coal, education and so on, have attracted such wide and vague powers as to offer a standing temptation to impose political foibles as public policy; they increasingly act like infantile, capricious *persons*. By contrast, the individual wielder of authority at coalface or chalkface – colliery manager, headmaster, hospital adminis-trator – has had his powers so hedged and clipped that his authority seemed to dwindle in the most visible and humiliating fashion. He became little more than a cog in a much bigger machine, almost less than a person.

The essential components of effective authority are that it should be direct, immediate, tangible, visible ('hands-on' management, in the mod-ern jargon). The essential limitations on authority – to minimise over-flow into domineering or exploitative relationships, to keep its harsher necessities consonant with our sense of justice – are that its exercise should be clearly defined and subordinate to both the letter and the spirit of impersonal forces such as law and custom, and that it should acknow-ledge the existence of higher authorities overarching its own sphere of activity. It is this dovetailing of the personal and the impersonal which makes for stability and continuity and hence for institutional strength and independence.

Can we see here the beginnings of an explanation of the authority par-adox? The wider the powers entrusted to the corporate authority, the more it will attract to membership ambitious, politically-minded people, and the more capricious and trend-blown its edicts are likely to become. The practice of its authority will become erratic and hubristic and so will begin to undermine itself. After all, customary acceptance is the founda-tion of all authority, whether backed by statute or not, and it is hard to accustom oneself to practices which seem to change every five minutes – whether they be approved methods of policing or approved methods of child-birth.

By adding this further trait – that proper authority ought to be slow to change its practices – we are not saying that all such change should be resisted to the last ditch. Many authority-bearing professions and insti-tutions are ossified or extortionate or both (the two qualities are closely linked). But proposed changes ought to be carefully tested, debated and phased before being irrevocably adopted. The case against overnight introduction of the obstetrics of Dr Wendy Savage or panda cars or the ordination of women is not that these things are necessarily wrong in themselves but that their instant universal adoption suggests a light-hearted abandonment of serious standards – and often hence an aban-donment of loyal congregations and colleagues who are accustomed to a different tradition of guidance and service. Proper authority must expect now and then to be denounced as 'stuffy' or 'sclerotic' or 'hidebound' or

'Establishmentarian'. Such accusations may only be signs that it is doing its job. To paraphrase Conquest's Law, most people are stuffy about things they know about.

25 April 1987

STANDING ROOM ONLY

Dominic Lawson

Britain now seems impossibly crowded: an investigation into the causes of the infuriating crush

As every zoologist knows, if you put enough animals in the same cage together, they will bite lumps out of each other. But in Britain today, it is not necessary to enter a mice-packed laboratory to observe the experiment. It is happening all around us. When the American journalist Bernard Nossiter returned this summer to Britain – and in particular London – after an absence of ten years, he detected 'a very sharp increase in incivility, even nastiness in the routine encounters of daily life'. Nossiter, who is what his fellow Americans like to call a 'liberal', blamed it all on Mrs Thatcher and her encouragement of an opportunist get-rich-quick society.

But no politician, not even Mrs Thatcher, can alter the way that humans behave towards one another. The two main examples of incivility chosen by Mr Nossiter are the behaviour of Londoners in their tube stations and on their roads. But he then fails to draw the obvious conclusion. It is simply that there are far more mice moving in the cage than there were ten years ago.

Let's visit some of the cages. Here is a tube-shaped one, so full that the mice seem to be chattering with rage. At Angel, the mice are in great danger of being pushed onto the tracks, and at Chancery Lane, none of the mice can enter at all in the morning rush hour.

Here is a much bigger cage, the rail cage. The professors who run this cage had promised that no mouse would have to stand up for more than 20 minutes, but they are now conducting experiments in which up to 400 mice in one cage have to stand for at least that length of time. That cage is labelled Croydon to London Bridge, but some mice have had to stand all the way from London to Newcastle.

Some of the mice on the train have cellular telephones but they cannot always get through to warn home that they might be delayed, because so many others are doing the same that the frequency has become overloaded. And they can *never* get through to Directory Enquiries.

If the mice get fed up with this experiment they could try to leave the country, and fly to one run by less sadistic scientists. But they will find that Gatwick, the world's second busiest airport, is just another cage with one rather old runway. The professors running this cage say there is little they can do, and very few of the mice know that these doctors make almost all their money, not by putting people on planes, on time, but through the purchases made by the bored mice at the duty-free shops. If the mice knew that, then they would get *really* angry.

Some of the mice in this cage do not behave according to the scientists' theory. They do not bite lumps out of other mice. They are philosophical. They tell the other mice, 'Don't get so angry. The air is so crowded, and there have been so many near hits (only humans call them near-misses) that we are far safer here on the ground.'

A few yards away, at the immigration cage, the scientists are thinking of putting up a new sign. It will say, 'Welcome to (overcrowded) Britain.'

The examples – or experiments – given above all have one thing in common. With the arguable exception of the telephone network, they all involve the infrastructure. And in the short term nothing can be done about the infrastructure. Roads cannot be imported, although cars – as last week's horrific trade figures reminded us – can.

The distinction may appear trite, but it illustrates the point that the overcrowding on Britain's railways and roads, and the record trade deficit are simply two sides of the same phenomenon, which is that domestic demand, whether it be for travel or for goods and services, is vastly outstripping our ability to satisfy it. But if British motor manufacturers cannot produce the cars we want – and foreign manufacturers for the first time have two-thirds of the market – then it is no problem for Citroën, or whoever, to fill the gap between demand and supply.

This exacerbates the underlying problem, which is that Britain already has more crowded roads than any Western country with the possible exception of Italy. As if to celebrate the achievement, this year, for the first time since the 1950s, not one mile of new motorway is being built.

At the moment the trade deficit is seen as a more pressing political and economic problem than the 'infrastructure deficit'. Yet it is not clear that this is a sensible attitude. With the almost simultaneous arrival of the single European market and the opening of the Channel Tunnel, businesses will have nothing to fear from trade barriers, and will begin to relocate in France, if its road and rail links continue to make ours appear primordial. So just as British consumers are increasingly prepared to buy French cars, so industries will ignore British roads and tracks, and 'buy' French ones.

If time is money, then the lost money implied by traffic congestion in Britain must be colossal. The Confederation of British Industry has calculated that congestion on the M25 alone costs companies – just in terms of vehicle and driver expense – more than £1.2 billion in a 200-day working year.

To some extent both industry and government – as the originator of infrastructure projects – have both been caught unawares by the rapidity of the growth in the economy in the past few years. And since, according to even the most ancient of economic textbooks, travel tends to grow at least one and a half times more than the underlying growth in an economy, this unpreparedness has had almost catastrophic consequences for the infrastructure's ability to cope.

In fact British industry has not been caught short in quite the way the Government has. Despite the remarkable and unpredicted five per cent growth rate, there is little bottlenecking in British factories, with more than two-thirds operating at below full capacity. British industry is now preparing to expand dramatically, planning this year to spend 15 per cent more on investment in manufacturing capacity than it did last year.

Yet the Government is only just beginning to authorise big new infrastructural projects – last month it finally announced the development of a new Thames crossing at Dartford and a desperately needed high-speed rail link to Heathrow. But still the typical new road project takes about 14 years from inception to completion, by which time the level of demand could render even the new infrastructure inadequate.

This was classically the case with the M25 orbital motorway, first mooted in concept in 1908 by the Royal Commission on Transport as the panacea for London's traffic problems. In 1944 the Abercrombie report recommended the creation of up to four orbital London roads. All but one were killed off, the survivor being the M25, which opened less than two years ago and is now congested for at least five hours a day. The planners wanted four lanes. The Government saved money by sticking at three ... and is now enlarging the motorway at greater expense per mile than it cost to build ten years ago.

Why should the Government have so underprovided for the infrastructure? The Government department responsible, Transport, is quick to disclaim responsibility, at least for the problems of rail and air. It points out that neither the Civil Aviation Authority, nor British Rail, nor London Transport has ever been turned down in any spending requests brought to the Department of Transport over the past ten years. These are the organisations which we trust to run the public transport network, argue the civil servants of the Department of Transport, and if their forecasts are too low, that is not our fault.

Naturally the buck is passed further down the line. British Rail, for example, can point out that its programme to scrap rolling stock which is now desperately needed stemmed from a report from the Monopolies and Mergers commission in 1981, which called for the action BR subsequently undertook.

Whoever is to blame, it is undeniable that transport has a lower political priority than virtually any other infrastructural project, whether it be hospital building or the electricity supply industry. The latter body has been ludicrously overfunded, leading to a surplus in generating capacity costing billions of pounds. Of course Mrs Thatcher would not have been able to see off Mr Scargill without all that 'useless' oil-fired capacity, so she probably regards it as billions well spent rather than billions wasted.

But the capacity was planned long before Mr Scargill was ever heard of. The point is that angry commuters on the Croydon train are not seen as an election-losing issue. But the lights going out, and little old ladies dying of hypothermia, is seen as an election loser.

Within the field of transport, governments, both national and local, show a strong preference for current rather than capital expenditure. This is partly because of the one-year funding cycle, which is so inimical to long-term planning, but also because the short-term political kudos to be gained from subsidising fares outweighs the value given by local politicians to the long-term benefits of a better network in ten years' time (when their opponents might be able to reap the benefits). A classic example of this sort of thinking was that of the now defunct GLC, when it gained local acclaim for its cheap fares policy which encouraged many more into an ancient system that the GLC had little inclination to modernise, less to expand.

The GLC at least was able to raise money for its own pet projects. The Department of Transport, however, has to ask the Treasury nicely for its money. And until recently the Treasury's overriding objective appeared to be the reduction of public spending. When the bright sparks at the Department of Transport tried to get round this with proposals for infrastructure projects financed by the private sector, the Treasury responded with the so-called Ryrie rules. First enunciated by a former Treasury official, Sir William Ryrie, in 1981, these stated that if an infrastructural project was worth going ahead with, it should be financed by government, since, as the only borrower that could borrow at base rate, it could finance such projects more cheaply than anyone else.

If this view was consistently held throughout the Treasury, then, logically, the Government should have nationalised all British private sector companies, rather than privatised the public sector ones. But until this year, with the start of the Channel Tunnel project, and the Dartford-Thurrock bridge financed by Trafalgar House, the Treasury block on such projects had been total.

Although the Treasury insists that it has thus successfully prevented private sector financiers from taking the taxpayer – as opposed to the commuter – for a ride, it does seem that value for money has been overstressed, to the detriment of the travelling public. This is seen clearly in volume two of the Public Expenditure White Paper which shows that new publicly funded road projects currently under way are expected to yield a benefit to cost ratio of 1.9 to one, broadly equivalent, says the White Paper, to an economic return of 15 per cent in real terms. This is over twice the real rate of return of seven per cent demanded by the Treasury of such projects.

If a private sector company found that its planned developments would average a rate of return of twice what it had targeted, it would – correctly – conclude that it was underinvesting the money entrusted to it by its shareholders. The Government ought to be able to draw similar conclusions from its own figures.

It is no longer possible, now that we have a Public Sector Lending Requirement, to come up with the argument of the early part of the decade, that 'there is not enough money'. We have already arrived at the moment wistfully forecast in the conclusion of the 1984 Treasury Green Paper, *The Next Ten Years: Public Expenditure and Taxation into the 1990s*: 'It would of course always be open to the Government to decide, once the virtuous circle of lower taxes and higher growth had been established, to devote some of these resources to improved public services rather than reduced taxation.'

The Soviet-style planner might observe that the bottlenecks in the infrastructure could be solved not so much by increased spending but by a little bit of migration here and a little bit of emigration there. The problem, after all, is hardly Malthusian. The British population is expected to increase only fractionally between now and the end of the century. If anything we shall just become older and slower. And while the South East is fit to burst, Burnley, or so the *Guardian* solemnly informed its readers last month, 'is disappearing'.

But as Alan Evans, professor of environmental economics at Reading

University pointed out in a pamphlet published last month by the Institute of Economic Affairs, the British town planning system is responsible for the overcrowding problem in and around the cities, because it enables bureaucrats to obstruct development in rural areas. It all reminds Professor Evans of Chapter VII of *Alice's Adventures in Wonderland*, 'A mad tea-party': 'The table was a large one but the three were all crowded together at one corner of it. "No room! No room!" they cried out, when they saw Alice coming. "There's *plenty* of room!" said Alice indignantly, and she sat down in a large arm-chair at one end of the table.'

3 September 1988

Chapter 2
THE PASSING PARADE: SCENES FROM THE EIGHTIES

'Now I know where I've seen you – you're on our death list.'

NOTEBOOK

Alexander Chancellor

'One might be able to live with Mr Nkomo, but there could be no compromise with Mr Mugabe.' This was Mr Ian Smith speaking hardly more than a month ago to an audience of white farmers in Matabeleland. 'Tell your workers that the Marxists will take everything they have: their cattle, goats and chickens. Tell them they will also take away their children.' This week Mr Smith has been talking to Mr Mugabe and, according to the Prime Minister Designate, they have 'agreed to cooperate'. Not only that, Mr Smith has said that he finds Mr Mugabe 'pragmatic' and better than he has been painted. During the Lancaster House talks, it is now suddenly revealed, Mr Smith found Mr Mugabe 'nothing like as bad' as the Marxists around him. One begins to feel sorry for those Conservative MPs like Julian Amery who in the past have accepted Mr Smith's analysis of the Marxist threat and still persist in sticking to it, while their hero himself now seems closer to Lord Carrington and Sir Ian Gilmour. But this is the extraordinary thing about Smith. He has managed to retain a reputation as a steely man of principle while holding himself ready to collaborate with what he has always portrayed as the forces of evil. His continuing presence on the political stage seems particularly strange to those, like myself, who met him in London during the Lancaster House talks. He seemed then to be seized with bitterness verging on despair. His contempt for Bishop Muzorewa was equalled only by the depth of his pessimism about the consequences of a Patriotic Front victory. He had the air of a man who had been outwitted and betrayed and who, having nothing more to lose, felt free to vent his frustration in public. Any suggestion that in a few months time he might be hobnobbing with Mr Mugabe and planning a new political career would have appeared ridiculous. But he was right about one thing. He told *The Spectator* last October that in any election in Rhodesia 'the Patriotic Front would walk it'. So they did.

8 March 1980

NOTEBOOK

Geoffrey Wheatcroft

The 'Council of Social Democracy' seems an awfully dull name. I was going to suggest that the Jenkins–Williams group should be called the League of Agweeable Fellows Incommoded by Tiresome Extweemism – or Lafite for short. Lafite have had a mixed press in the last few days. The critics concentrate on their nerveless dithering. It is true that the Gang of Four are in what might be called an ongoing poor cat i' the adage situation. But it is not their timorousness which I find depressing so much as the unimaginative dreariness of their ideas. Perhaps this is not surprising. There is, after all, something irredeemably second-rate about the Gang. None of them has the flair or the intellectual ability of Anthony Crosland. Compare *Face the Future* with *The Future of Socialism.* You may conclude that Dr Owen should stick to torturing rats. Mrs Williams is a charming woman but the received idea that she is a natural vote-winner is, like many received ideas, preposterous. It is an especially perverse thing to say of someone who has recently lost her Parliamentary seat. Mr Jenkins himself is possibly the most over-rated figure in British politics, a competent administrator but an uninspiring speaker and an irritating writer. He gave his political testament in the Dimbleby Lecture the November before last: 'You want the class system to fade without being replaced either by an aggressive and intolerant proletarianism or by the dominance of the brash and selfish values of a "get rich quick" society.' In other words, as Ferdinand Mount glossed at the time, you want to keep the yobs away from the best claret. Leave aside ad hominem jokes about a man who preaches the virtues of a get poor slow society from his garret at Morgan Grenfell (in between counting his coppers from an ungrateful European Commission); this does not sound election-winning stuff. The Labour Party will be in poor shape two years hence, but even when Lafite have steeled themselves (or Steeled themselves) to break ranks, I do not see their tired manifesto as posing a grave threat to Mrs Thatcher. Bookmakers are currently offering 11-10 against the Tories winning the next election. It must be a good price.

31 January 1981

NOTEBOOK

Alexander Chancellor

The terrifying riots in Liverpool this week have given rise to a predictable torrent of diagnoses from various quarters, mostly of the 'I told you so' variety. Depending on whom you prefer to listen to, you can blame the concentration of black immigrants, high unemployment, educational deprivation, parental irresponsibility, police brutality, or incitement by political extremists. The problem is that whether you accept any, or all, of these explanations, there is very little that can be done in the short term to prevent repetition of these disgraceful events other than make the police more effective in dealing with them. This Mr Whitelaw is trying to do. Some people plead that the deprived populations of places like Toxteth should at least be given 'hope'; but 'hope' can so easily mean nothing more than promises that are not fulfilled, and unfulfilled promises would guarantee worse violence in the future. Derek Worlock, the Roman Catholic Archbishop of Liverpool, claims (in *The Times*) that Liverpool will be spared further disasters because of its 'unfailing sense of humour'. Such ludicrous sentimentality must strike the police, at least, as in very poor taste. The only real hope for Liverpool, as for London and for a number of other British cities, lies in national economic recovery. May it come soon.

11 July 1981

THE TOXTETH AFTERMATH

Andrew Brown

Liverpool

What remains of Toxteth is cleaner, more brightly coloured, and a great deal less depressing than the centre of Liverpool, which is so squalid and run down at weekends that one cannot tell by looking at the rubbish, vomit, and orange peel on the pavement whether you are in Lime Street Station or a shopping arcade. The whole place has the pretentious shabbiness of something administered by British Rail. In the centre of the city everyone seemed furtive, resigned, or hopeless. On top of the hill, where the riots began last Saturday, everyone was simply frightened. Liverpool 8 has apparently always been an area where the police walked only in twos or threes. 'That's Nigeria, that is,' said a businessman, very drunk in the Press Club at six on Saturday evening, and added 'but you should have come here a few years ago, when things were really bad.'

This businessman was not the only man to have difficulty grasping that something historical had happened. The scale of the damage is immense, and a policeman I spoke to – he had been drafted in from somewhere miles away – simply refused to believe that the ruins of the Rackets club were not the result of a development scheme. I hope his faith steadied him, for Upper Parliament Street was a frightening place on Saturday night. It's a broad street. Judging from the photographs, five cars in line were needed to barricade it in the riots, and on Saturday evening it resembled nothing so much as a stage, around which we were all grouped, waiting for the 'incident', as the policeman called it, to begin. In the empty space in front of the burnt-out National Westminster bank and the burnt-down Rialto there were at least 50 policemen standing in groups of three or four within a radius of 100 yards. It was a fine summer evening, and the only other people in sight were three coffee-coloured children about eight years old playing on the pavement 200 yards away. And, of course, when I saw them, the first thing I wondered was how much they had managed to steal at the weekend.

This reflection would not have occurred on Sunday night, when it had become clear that the trouble was happening in other places this weekend. Across the Mersey, police attempting to keep order in one of the hideous purpose-built slums found themselves attacked from balconies.

Furniture, televisions, petrol bombs, and even a cooker were thrown down at the police, but the full scale of the trouble only became apparent later in the courts.

A priest, dressed apparently in jeans, remonstrated with policemen who were beating a youth with truncheons, and was of course charged with conduct likely to cause a breach of the peace, and duly convicted. One would have more sympathy with him if he had not described the rioting as 'a catalyst which has grown out of all proportions'.

Looking at the damage in Toxteth, one is tempted to ask why, if all this was caused by bad housing, there has been so comparatively little violence in the newly built council estates. In one of these, I was told, the tenants were offered their houses for as little as two thousand pounds, and still refused to buy them, on the reasonable grounds that they didn't want them even at that price.

On Sunday, at lunchtime, Toxteth still seemed a frightening place. On Lodge Lane you can walk for perhaps half a mile with shops on each side of you, and every single shop has been looted. Only two or three have re-opened, and the posters put up by a shopfitting firm – 'Can we help you to start again?' – have mostly been torn down. The pubs were gloomy but well-filled. Most people seemed to feel that if nothing had happened the night before, then trouble was inevitable now. 'They'll do the pubs next time. There's nothing else left for them to do' as a barmaid told her audience. They seemed to agree, though four West Indian youths drinking with a white, leant over and said they wouldn't do hers because it was such a nice pub. They roared with laughter at this. The barmaid winced, and the rest of the people in the pub just ignored them. That was the only evidence I saw that there were people living around Lodge Lane who were capable also of destroying it.

In the evening, as it became apparent that nothing was going to happen this weekend at all, the fear ebbed away, leaving the sediment of bitterness and rage. It was an extraordinary transformation. The crucially right thing that the police did was to change over from gathering in large groups to moving around in threes or fours. This not only enables them to cover a larger area, and to see any gatherings of youths before these reach the critical mass, but it makes them more approachable. The police stood in small groups every 30 or so yards down the whole length of Lodge Lane, and people kept coming up to them and congratulating them. All the conversations I heard had as their theme the marvellous job that the police were doing, and the bestial nature of the rioters. The pubs were full of middle-aged working-class people, their faces pinched into acuity. A sailor returned from Germany spoke with admiration of the methods of the Munich police. Many of the policemen had been drafted

in from Weybridge. They said the things one would expect: one constable, who could not possibly have been born at the end of the last war,
remarked over and over again that this was worse than the blitz. It was a
theatrical remark, but then this was a theatrical occasion: everyone
seemed conscious that they were taking part in an impressive, if quiet,
demonstration of the fact that the values of the traditional working
classes had been re-established in Lodge Lane.

Next day saw a more common sort of demonstration. By lunchtime,
the *Echo* had published the news that Mrs Thatcher was in Liverpool,
and a sizeable crowd had gathered outside the Town Hall. Some thought
they were waiting for her to arrive, some realised that they were waiting
for her to leave, and one man, a thin, malarial-looking Protestant priest,
who said he represented the African church, wanted to see her in order to
explain the answer to her problems. The answer was, apparently, that if
people have no conscience about moral issues, then they have no conscience about robbing and stealing either. The crowd, though large, was
reasonably good-humoured, and certainly pro-police. A few groups of
demonstrators chanted from time to time, but few people joined in. After
an hour or so, someone even struck up 'Why are we Waiting'. Then the
'community leaders' emerged to be interviewed.

'Who's that?' asks a woman. 'Nigger' said the man behind me quietly.
He was apparently part of the NALGO contingent; he was booing very
loudly later. Later when some American journalists appear, a voice
enquires 'Who's the coon?' The dirty words are spoken with real relish.

When Mrs Thatcher emerged, she paused for a moment, and walked
surprisingly slowly to the car. One had time to think 'Surely she doesn't
look like that in real life' before the crowd remembered what it had been

'Thank goodness they didn't bring back National Service – I'd hate to be attacked by
a trained army.'

waiting for. There were no chants, simply a terrible burst of inarticulate yells, mingled with very loud booing. For a moment you could feel what a mob is like, and then the car was pulling away, and a well-dressed man scooped something from the pavement she had crossed and lobbed it towards the crowd. It burst in the air, spattering the police cordon with tomato pulp. The well-dressed man was apparently a Tory councillor who is in danger of being charged for what he did. It is to be hoped that the magistrates make an example of him.

18 July 1981

LESSONS OF THE ROYAL WEDDING

Auberon Waugh

Languedoc, France
One would like to think the French had derived some permanent benefit from the Royal Wedding. So far as one can tell, the entire French nation watched it. Every Frenchman and Frenchwoman I meet speaks of it as one of the most emotional occasions of modern history, and it almost seems as if nearly 200 years after their abominable revolution, the French are beginning to have second thoughts.

Yet this same nation has just elected a socialist President and socialist Chamber of Deputies for the first time in 25 years. It may seem incomprehensible to us that anyone of the slightest intelligence or benevolence towards the human race can still profess to believe in socialism, seeing the miserable havoc and poverty it creates whenever it is tried. But the inescapable fact remains, to be explained as best one can, that this supremely intelligent and, in my experience, entirely benign race has chosen to express its contempt for all men by governing by this means.

So far, the only result has been to devalue the franc against the pound. With every day that passes, an extra frog's leg or snail lands on my plate without the slightest effort on my own part. The general conclusion must be that French socialists are not nearly so depraved as our own. Mitterrand, as a person, seems less objectionable than Giscard. I wonder if that half of what we laughingly call our Shadow Cabinet which boycotted the Wedding drew any conclusions from the fact that Mitterrand, who had actually won an election, attended. The week of the Royal Wedding cannot have been a happy time for socialist politicians waiting in the wings. No doubt, in time, national disgust at the Conservatives – at Mr Heseltine, for his horrible postures in Liverpool, at Mr Walker, for the spectacle of his naked ambition, or at Mrs Thatcher, for her mean and obstinate attitude towards Mr Worsthorne – will reassure them that the country is indeed ready for the exciting experience of civil war which they promise us. But it must have been a depressing thing to see all those happy, half-witted, cheering faces in the crowd.

Even in America, which has just elected the man who, I am convinced, will prove the greatest and best President of my own lifetime, and where our Wedding was also followed with rapt attention, the message does not seem to have got through. I cannot have been alone in noticing how Mrs Reagan, on being presented to the Queen at a polo match just before the Wedding, pointedly refused to curtsey. She is, of course, a woman of humble origins and may not have known any better. Or she might have been hinting that she was a Daughter of the American Revolution (which as a jumped-up chorus-girl she most certainly isn't). Or perhaps, like so many wives of even the greatest men, she is quite simply mad. But I prefer to think she was suffering from the same residual loyalty to her own country's revolution as the French evince when, on public occasions, they still pretend to believe that liberty and equality are reconcilable aspirations, or that either necessarily makes for happiness.

Something of this ancient, irrational urge may be understood by Englishmen when we analyse the extreme irritation we felt on learning – with this new concentration on the affairs of the Royal Family – that the children of Prince and Princess Michael of Kent have somehow been allowed to assume the style of younger son and daughter of a duke (or marquess). I do not know what pipsqueak in the Lord Chamberlain's Office or the College of Arms assured them that they had this right, but they don't. Mr and Miss are the proper styles, although after that they can call themselves anything they like. A special Royal ordinance authorising the practice would have been dubious enough, but for a junior member of the Royal Family to assume the style of a nobleman's younger son in this way is to spit in the face of Magna Carta. Possibly neither Prince Michael nor his bride has ever heard of Magna Carta, but if I were a baron, let alone a duke or a marquess, I should certainly take this usurping couple to Runnymede and dunk them both in the river which runs around that historic meadow.

Which may explain why intelligent and respectable Frenchmen still stand to attention for *La Marseillaise*, why Nancy Reagan refused to curtsey to the Queen. But the most sombre lesson of the Royal Wedding concerns the future, not the past. Ever since becoming a father, more than 19 years ago, I have tried to convince my children that if they neglect their studies they will end up as road-sweepers or lavatory attendants. If, on the other hand, they apply themselves diligently enough to all the absurd and humiliating subjects in the modern child's syllabus, achieving satisfactory 'A' levels in biology, physics, 'modern' mathematics, 'Nuffield' Latin, the theory and practice of positive anti-racialism, the political, philosophical and economic framework to a non-smoking policy, creative modelling in plasticine etc – then, if they are boys, they will become rich and famous like their father and grandfather before them; if they are girls, they will marry if not the Prince of Wales, at any rate a marquess, a duke or one of the better class of earls.

Even if I could think of a single unkind thing to say about our new Princess of Wales I would refuse to say it in deference to her beauty, birth and obvious amiability of temperament, but the fact remains that she has not got a single pass at 'O' level GCE and on that rock the whole ship of state looks like sinking. The Prince of Wales, in choosing such a mate, makes a statement of greater importance than if he had chosen to marry a girl of average educational abilities who was either black or working-class. What he is saying, in effect – and instructing all his dukes and marquesses down to the meanest citizen in the land – is that education is no longer of the slightest use or interest to the modern Briton.

In a sense, of course, he is right. In a society where the long-distance lorry driver earns more than the university professor, the ancillary technician in hospital more than the consultant surgeon, who needs education? A chimpanzee can be trained to perform most of the functions of the 'worker' in a modern factory, and would probably perform them with better grace.

The error in this is to suppose that education prepares people for employment rather than unemployment. Present figures for unemployment are not the product of a temporary recession, still less of the Government's non-existent 'monetarist' policies. They are the inescapable and permanent result of technological progress. The greatest challenge facing our civilisation – as opposed to the dragooned and regulated societies of the East – is the challenge of leisure. Even the lower classes grow intolerably bored with television after a time. Music is already surging ahead and literature, I feel sure, will revive once it has been taken away from the Arts Council and learned to address itself once again to its readers. Education is the key to everything. If the Prince is too busy himself he should appoint a tutor to instruct his young bride in music, dancing, poetry and all the gentler arts. If Lord Goodman's health is not up to the job, I will volunteer for it myself.

15 August 1981

PORTRAIT OF THE WEEK

Argentina successfully invaded the Falkland Islands, with the loss of about four men, possibly more, appointing a military governor of the renamed Malvinas Islands in the renamed capital of Puerto Rivero, formerly Stanley. The British garrison surrendered without sustaining any casualties. Mr Nott and Lord Carrington faced demands for their resignation at a special week-end meeting of Parliament. On Monday Lord Carrington resigned, taking with him Mr Atkins and Mr Richard Luce from the Foreign Office team. The UN Security Council condemned Argentina's action by ten votes to one. Mr Nott sent the greater part of the British fleet, including its only two aircraft carriers – one due for scrapping, the other already sold to Australia – vowing to take the islands back again, by force if necessary. Lord Carrington's letter of resignation gave no hint that he disapproved of military action to retake the Falklands, but British intelligence sources in Buenos Aires claimed that the Foreign Office had known of the intended invasion for at least ten days. Argentine assets were frozen in London, but more valuable British assets remain in Argentina.

10 April 1982

THE LAST ARMADA

Ferdinand Mount

A débâcle speaks for itself. All things that inescapably follow – the humiliation, the indignation, the ministers hurrying in and out of Cabinet, the spectacular sitting of Parliament on a Saturday, the calls for the resignation of Mr John Nott, Lord Carrington and anyone else standing in the line of fire – are not only themselves part and parcel of the débâcle; they help to explain why it happened.

The Falkland Islanders are the last victims of our refusal to be honest with ourselves; we have clung to the rhetoric of empire long after we have lost the desire or the ability to maintain its reality. The easy refuge in these circumstances is to blame the 'appeasers' in the Foreign Office. It was undoubtedly the Foreign Office which is to blame for the misreading of Argentina's intentions and for Britain being caught napping. Lord Carrington and his juniors had to go, and they duly went – in Lord Carrington's case, with remarkable candour and dignity – providing a respectable herd of scapegoats for a demoralised government. Mr Nott survives, I think rightly, but his survival surely depends on a successful outcome to what may be the last great naval task force Britain will ever launch.

This column has rarely found much to admire in Lord Carrington's style of diplomacy, except in Rhodesia. But apart from the immediate and crucial misjudgment over the Falklands, it would be unfair to pile all the blame on him or even on to the Foreign Office collectively for what has been the undeclared ambition of every British government for the past generation: somehow or other to disembarrass Britain of the Falklands.

Back in 1968, Lord Chalfont, then Minister for Peace and Disarmament, at the Foreign Office (one of Sir Harold's masterly fancies), was nearly debagged by the islanders when they gathered the impression that Britain intended to discuss a transfer of sovereignty with Argentina. Under this present government, Mr Nicholas Ridley had a scarcely less frosty reception from the islanders when talk of a 'leaseback solution' was in the air. The islanders were and are determined to stay British, and they know how to shame British politicians into giving pledges which they would rather not give.

After all, didn't the islanders have British public opinion firmly behind them? So they did, and do. But opinion is a relatively painless, cost-free commodity. When it comes to paying for the maintenance of a permanent naval force in the South Atlantic sufficient to deter any invader, British public opinion seems to be less ardent.

Year by year, for 20 years now, successive British governments have given Argentina the impression that they would not be prepared to pay for any major project which would help to secure the Britishness of the Falkland Islands. The runway was never lengthened to take direct flights from Europe. A commercial agreement was signed in 1971 which gave Argentina a virtual monopoly of air and fuel services. Britain gave up her nearest deep-water base, at Simonstown, because of apartheid. Almost more important than the lack of arrangements to secure the islands' defence was the absence of colonial enthusiasm. The Falklands were left to fend for themselves.

Most of the islanders are tenants of the Falkland Islands Company. Ultimate control of this company has changed hands several times. Recently, it belonged to the Charringtons Coalite empire; at one moment, it almost fell under Argentinian control, via Sir James Goldsmith. Since the islanders rarely own their own homes, many of them find themselves obliged to leave when they become too old for work; they tend to emigrate to New Zealand or Britain. The young often leave too. The result is that the population has dropped by about 15 per cent in 15 years. Whatever the final outcome now, many more will surely leave when and if they can.

Britain's contribution to the islands has been ancestors, a governor, a flag, a few marines, an occasional gunboat – and the rhetoric. Last Saturday it seemed that almost every British MP was personally prepared to shed his last drop of blood for the Falklands. Extremities of heroism were promised by all sorts, from Mr Patrick Cormack, doubtless to be remembered as Boy Cormack by readers of the next edition of the British Book of Heroes. 'The defence of our realm,' Mr Edward Du Cann told a hushed house, 'begins wherever British people are.' We should start, I suppose, by bombing Buenos Aires where there are ten times as many British people as there are in the Falklands.

How much would it have cost to protect the islands securely against Argentina in perpetuity? Mr Keith Speed, the Navy minister, who was sacked for disagreeing with Mr Nott, believes that it could be done for £20 million a year – on the analogy of what it costs for three British frigates to patrol the Straits of Hormuz. That sounds like an underestimate for patrolling waters 8,000 miles from home.

But even if his figures are correct, the costs of protection would come to £40,000 per island family per year. For half that sum, most of them would be quite pleased to emigrate to New Zealand. But if the safety of the islanders is not the sole concern, if British possession of the Falklands is militarily necessary and commercially valuable, then why have we not lengthened the runway? Why are we not busily drilling and leasing?

But Mr Speed is one of the few people in the whole business who is utterly honest. He believes that the Royal Navy ought to continue to patrol the world and the South Atlantic in particular and that if we will the end, then we must will the means.

The other form of honesty – and I think the preferable one – is to say that if we cannot provide the means, then we had better stop pretending that we can secure the ends. That was the logic behind Christopher Mayhew's resignation from the Navy ministry when Denis Healey – now the most zealous of gaucho-biffers – scrapped Britain's great aircraft carriers. A few years later, the next economic crisis proved Mayhew right by forcing the government to withdraw Britain's frontiers from the Himalayas, where Sir Harold Wilson in one of his most exuberant moments had drawn them, and redraw them distinctly West of Suez.

That sort of honesty comes hard to politicians. The cost of gunboat diplomacy increases at a prohibitively expensive rate. Even for superpowers, it has long lost the cheapness and effectiveness it had in the days of the huge technological gap between the imperial power and the natives, when whatever happens,

> 'We have got
> The Maxim gun and they have not.'

What they have now is our second-hand warships, plus some new French aircraft. In 1833 we gained the Falklands from Argentina with a single sloop. We are attempting to regain them with two-thirds of the Royal Navy.

In the case of the Falklands, the moral right is indisputably on our side. Is the British government really prepared to fight to regain its rights? Mr Enoch Powell insistently poses this question as the only one ultimately worth asking. But it is not the only question, and the answer to it is not settled by the despatch of this great British armada. How much force is to be used? At what point should Britain regard herself as having gained her point and retrieved her self-esteem? When the last Argentinian marine leaves the island? When Argentina begins to negotiate? Mrs Thatcher's undertaking to return the islands to British administration is less specific than it sounds, but it could not stretch to include total failure to dislodge the Argentinians.

The immediate causes of the débâcle are of the Government's own making. To despatch a task force to see what can be retrieved, by blockade or marine landings or both, is the only way to deter similar acts of aggression in other parts of the world. This last British Armada is a quixotic but necessary enterprise. The position of the British Government remains at best a highly undignified one. But then discarding an empire tends to be a succession of indignities.

10 April 1982

NOTEBOOK

Alexander Chancellor

I received a letter from a friend on Tuesday. 'What fun it all is!' he wrote. 'One must not get so pompous as to miss the fun.' That had been very much my mood over the weekend. It was a comfortable country week-end, spent in congenial company. As gales raged outside, we sat with our drinks in front of the television set, rejoicing – as Mrs Thatcher would have us do – at every new British success: the bombing of the airfields and the repulsion of Argentinian air attacks, all with no British lives lost. A few Argentinians seemed to have died, but not many. And there was so much else to enjoy. We had the extraordinary Mr Ian McDonald, the Defence Ministry's spokesman, reporting Britain's triumphs to the press in his unique manner, describing with such exaggerated clarity the events in places like 'Goooss Grreeenn' that the meaning was almost impossible to follow. (I had imagined Mr McDonald as a family man liv-ing somewhere in Surrey, but William Hickey revealed in the *Daily Express* on Tuesday that he is, on the contrary, 'a bachelor who collects exotic Indian pictures' and lives in a flat in north London.) We then had the equally diverting spectacle of the lugubrious General Galtieri addressing his hysterical nation with three motionless officers in uni-form standing immediately behind him. Indeed, there had been almost nothing but pleasure to be had out of the whole strange crisis since the task force set out weeks ago from England to the strains of Elgar. The almost bloodless recapture of South Georgia had been particularly satis-fying. It became a source of even greater pleasure when it was subse-quently learnt that the commander of the Argentinian garrison on the island, Captain Alfredo Astiz, who was given dinner afterwards aboard one of Her Majesty's ships, was a notorious torturer, wanted by the Swed-ish authorities for having shot a 17-year-old Swedish girl on a street in Buenos Aires five years ago. Oh, what fun it all was! But then, alas, came the news on Monday morning of the sinking of the Argentinian cruiser *General Belgrano*. This was something it was impossible to enjoy. First reports said there were 1,200 people on board, and it seemed as if few would survive. Luckily this turned out to be wrong. But it was clear that Argentina would now feel bound to take revenge, and that revenge came swiftly and effectively with the sinking of the *Sheffield* and the tragic loss of many British lives. The fun was now definitely over. We were faced with the reality of a nasty, bloody war and the problem of whether the ends could any longer justify the means. What are the ends? They are to recover British territory forcibly seized by Argentina and to restore to the 1,800 Falkland Islanders the right of self-determination. In pursuing these ends, Britain has undoubted right on her side. It is also clear that we would have little chance of achieving them without the threat of force. But we have now to consider the effects of escalating the war. Not only will many more lives be lost on both sides. The British Government will lose international support (in Europe it is already crumbling), it may lose popular support at home (an opinion poll last Sunday showed, even before the sinking of the *Sheffield*, that three in five Britons would not be prepared to lose one serviceman's life to regain the Falklands), it will stiffen Argentinian resolve not to negotiate, it will damage our relations with all the countries of South America, and it may not even achieve its purpose of saving the Falkland Islanders. We are caught in a horrible trap.

8 May 1982

NOTEBOOK

Alexander Chancellor

A little rejoicing is now in order, but only a little. We may rejoice that the Falklands war did not end in a bloodbath at Port Stanley, that the Argentinians did not stage a last doomed defence of the islands' capital. We may rejoice at the performance of our armed forces who have conducted themselves with great skill and courage and with as much humanity as is possible in war. We may rejoice that they achieved their objectives, for to have lost a war against the Argentinians would have been an unthinkable disaster. We may rejoice that the conflict has accelerated the decline of the British Labour Party. We may rejoice that the vain and indescribably stupid leader of the Argentinian junta, General Galtieri, has been frustrated in his imbecile plans of conquest and that Argentina may, as a result, find itself a worthier government.

But has the operation been worthwhile? Has, for example, the British

Government achieved the two purposes for which it said it was fighting –
that armed aggression should not be allowed to pay and that the Falkland
Islanders should be allowed to live under the government of their choice?
In a narrow sense, the answer is Yes. Argentinian aggression has certainly
not been allowed to pay; on the contrary, it has brought disaster to that
unfortunate country. But if anyone imagines that Britain's example in
the South Atlantic is likely to inhibit would-be aggressors anywhere else,
he must be of an agreeably optimistic disposition. Certainly Israel has not
felt inhibited. And did the Prime Minister really believe what she was
saying on Tuesday when she announced to a jubilant House of Commons: 'Let every nation know that where there is British sovereign territory, it will be well and truly defended'? Would we fight for Gibraltar?
Would we fight for Hong Kong? She has not, as she claimed, 'restored
once again the dominance of Britain'; she has shown – and this is already
quite impressive – that her Government is ready to defend British sovereign territory where this is possible: in the Falklands, in other words.

As for the Falkland Islanders, they are now once again under the sort of
government they prefer, namely a British one. But victory does not
ensure that this situation will continue in perpetuity. It would only
ensure this if the Argentinians were to drop their claim to the islands,
and all the evidence is that they are no more likely to do so now than they
were before. Rather the contrary. The islands' security and their economic development will continue to depend on some sort of deal with
Argentina, a deal that has become no easier to achieve. Already the British Government has tacitly taken the first tiny step towards admitting
this; the Governor is returning not as Governor, but as a 'civil commissioner'. One of the trappings of colonial rule has thus been removed. I
wonder what the kelpers feel about this. In fact, I wonder what they feel
about lots of things. What is in question is not their desire to remain British, but the quality of that desire. They would not, on the face of it, appear
to be the most passionate of patriots. They lead strange, lonely lives many
thousands of miles away from the mother country. Many of them are
only short-term workers, and the rest of them, according to Lord
Shackleton in his 1976 report, show 'lack of confidence and enterprise at
the individual and community level, and a degree of acceptance of their
situation which verges on apathy'. It is possible to imagine that, at the
end of the day, they would value more highly the right to carry on their
chosen way of life in security and tranquillity than the Britishness of the
Falklands administration.

In the meantime, they are clearly grateful that the British have
returned. They must be impressed by the amount of blood shed on their
behalf. I am impressed too. The casualties on both sides exceed the total

number of Falklanders. The deaths are more than half that number. Even
the British dead, mercifully few though they are, amount to one-seventh
of that number. Those who early in the campaign argued the moral significance of this equation may be relieved that it is not worse, but they
have no reason to feel that their anxieties were not justified. But, as was
predictable, the conduct and outcome of the war have assumed much
greater importance than the reasons for fighting it. Ironically, it was the
very shortage of Falklanders that made the war possible. Had those
remote islands been heavily populated, the risks of ousting the
Argentinians by force would have been too great for the British to contemplate. As it was, the Falklands provided an almost ideal environment
for a duel of honour between Mrs Thatcher and General Galtieri. Both
sides acquitted themselves well. The British achievement was brilliant,
but the Argentinians also performed great feats of courage – particularly
the airmen – and they did not succumb to the temptation of using the
islanders as hostages. Even the islanders themselves say that the
Argentinians did not treat them badly.

In Britain, the political consequences of the war have been considerable. Despite the horror of the modern weapons employed, it was a very
old-fashioned war, conducted in a limited theatre, with little danger to
civilians, and dependent to a great extent on the courage and skills of the
men involved. It has done a great service to the Conservative Party by
making conservatism seem respectable again. People can now finally see
the point of Mrs Thatcher and feel more comfortable with her. Set beside
the Falklands conflict, even her economic policies appear no longer
harsh but courageous. For a time the country looks set to be a more
united and more contented place. This is the real cause for which so
many people have died.

19 June 1982

PORTRAIT OF THE WEEK

The executive of the National Union of Mineworkers ignored appeals by
Mr Roy 'I stand by consultation now as I have done throughout this dispute' Hattersley and others to consult the rank and file, and voted to continue the pit dispute indefinitely. Two more people, this time teenage

boys, were killed mining coal from a railway embankment. Thousands of miners went back to work, including a senior NUM official in the Durham area, and NUM officials in the North Wales area said they no longer supported the strike, but the Coal Board abandoned its hope that the strike would be over by Christmas. It said that it would have no more talks with the union unless it received a written guarantee that Mr Arthur Scargill was ready to change his utterly intransigent position concerning pit closures. Mr Scargill went to the Russian embassy to ask for money and a blockade of fuel supplies from Eastern Europe. According to Mr Mick McGahey, the miners have received a million pounds from the Soviet Union. Mr Neil Kinnock left for a visit to Moscow.

24 November 1984

KINNOCK'S COP OUT BOOK

Charles Moore

As we know, Mr Neil Kinnock has such a full diary that he cannot manage to appear at any of the current NUM rallies. There are unbreakable dates with Sandwich Cooperative Society, the 77th anniversary dinner of the Amalgamated Society of Furniture Polishers (Leicester branch), receptions at the embassy of the People's Republic of Ruritania, all-day multi-racial rugby matches, and many more not-to-be-missed appointments now being confirmed and invented. According to spokesmen, the Labour leadership is conducting what is now always called a 'damage limitation exercise', in which it 'distances itself' from Mr Scargill.

Like many exercise regimes, this one seems rather questionable. If you think your politics need damage limitation, don't buy the *Neil Kinnock Cop Out Book*. Experts suggest that it only aggravates whatever problems you are already suffering from. For Mr Kinnock, burdened with first generation middle-class guilt about not going down the pit and with being the Member for Islwyn, supports 'the miners' with all that last drop of fibre and final ounce of breath that Mr Foot was always squeezing from his body in defence of socialism. According to Mr Kinnock, using the Shirley Williams trick of trying to sound tougher by swearing, the miners 'have a damn good case, and they must win'. He said this loudest when it rather looked as if they might win, and when he had to make speeches at the TUC and the Labour Party conferences, but he is still saying it, if rather more *sotto voce*, when he knows they won't. And he has not merely said that we should have a jolly large coal industry with lots of jobs: he has endorsed the NUM's demand that no pits should be closed on economic grounds. It therefore seems unsatisfactory that he does not want to go and speak in support of the damn good cause – he must know that the alternative to Mr Scargill's victory is acceptance of the Coal Board's offer, which he claims is unacceptable.

Make all these admittedly very obvious points to a Kinnockian, and he will fix you with a look of pitying scorn. Of course Neil must support the miners . . . he *does* support the miners; but he wants Scargill destroyed. Scargill is now clearly losing, but until he has all but lost, do not condemn him, just steer clear of him . . . 'It is a rule in politics,' one shadow spokesman said this week, 'never to kick a man until he is down.' In short, the strategy of all the mini-Machiavels who have got Labour where it is today is to sit quiet and let the miners, whom they 'support', work out their own salvation.

This is obviously a terrifically worldly and sly way to carry on, but as with many intensely pragmatic, feet-on-the-ground political exercises, one wonders whether it really is all that brilliant. After all, it has been inevitable from the beginning that the Labour leadership would be called treacherous by the Left unless, which it could never have done, it underwrote everything that Mr Scargill did and said. In recent weeks, the Left, having more or less spared Mr Kinnock during the party conference, has been working up the myth of betrayal. It is difficult to read the mind behind Mr Scargill's jabbering mouth, and so to know whether he yet realises that he will not win, but when he does realise, he will feel free to press on and lose poetically, confident that he can blame it all on the Judases.

Mr Kinnock has therefore done nothing to save himself from the ridicule and contempt of the people from whom he originally arose. But he has also done nothing to appeal to the larger set of people who tend to believe that a man ridiculed and condemned from such a quarter cannot be all bad. Judas he has not been; Pilate, perhaps, he has. Pilate's position, of course, was very understandable. He behaved just as a civilised, cowardly Foreign Office man would in a tight spot; definitely a man to condemn violence from whatever source it comes, Pilate. Perhaps by permitting the Crucifixion, 'regrettable' though it obviously was, Pilate succeeded in 'defusing the situation'. Nevertheless, the judgment of posterity continues to be that he did not do terribly well. In this distinctly lesser matter, it will be the same with Mr Kinnock. He could have led a party and a trade union movement whose most important members would have agreed not to countenance Scargillism: instead he washed his hands.

'No,' says the Kinnockian, 'you must understand what an emotional issue the miners are in the Labour Party. Labour must always support a miners' strike, never do anything to undermine it ... You'd be surprised how strongly my very moderate and reasonable constituency association feels on this point. You just have to let the tide of feeling run, and then try to clean up afterwards.' All of which is a way of saying that Labour's unity and morale depend on believing what is not true. It is bad for Scargill to win, but good for people to go around thinking that the fight which his union is fighting is a good fight; bad for industrial relations to be in the hands of militant ideologues, but good to pretend that it is only through the historic struggle of the vanguard of the working class that workers' emancipation can come; true that British coal is expensive and that tightly-knit communities are at one another's throats, also true that miners are lionhearts, men capable of killing ten Germans with their bare hands. In short, the Right offers a trade-off to the Left – let us win all the battles, and you can have all the good songs. If the Left ever was content with this offer, it certainly is not today. When Mr Scargill *does* appear on the same platform with Mr Kinnock on 30 November (for Mr Kinnock's 'too busy' excuse cannot be applied to rallies organised not by the NUM but by the Labour Party), he will surely make this clear.

It has been one of Mr Kinnock's themes that Labour has to modernise itself, that it has to appeal not only to the man on the dole but to the man with a mortgage, not only to a manual labourer, but to a computer expert; it has to redefine its idea of class to accommodate social trends. The miners' strike has been conducted by the NUM as the most old-fashioned of class wars, so that when the generals find that a third of their soldiers deserts them, they either heap abuse upon them or pretend that they do not exist. When Mr John Cunningham the elder, the NUM branch secretary at Ellington colliery, returned to work, his son, John Cunningham the younger, could only bring himself to refer to his father as 'him' or 'the former secretary'. It was as if the elder Cunningham was no longer really there.

But as the strikers treat those who disagree with them with a 'complete ignoral', the disagreers are busy. What might be called the Tebbit theory of union members is being borne out by events. This year there have been two abortive dock strikes, soon, I hopefully guess, one abortive coal strike, and the steady refusal of most workers to express anything resembling solidarity with Mr Scargill; and now we have a muddle at Austin Rover in which union practices are challenged by members, and, in the courts, by the company. Not only the Electricians, but the Engineers and even Mr Clive Jenkins's ASTMS seem to think that they could use the money which the Government has been setting aside for ballots. Trade union members are not just suspicious of Mr Scargill as being a bit extreme: they are coming to reject all his premises, let alone his conclusions. In doing so, they have no encouragement whatever from Labour. In relying on the law and the ballot, they have acted alone without their normal leaders. They must by now have found it an exhilarating, if dangerous, experience. Now that they know that they are not beholden to the people who claim to lead them, they despise those people's claims more and more. The men who cross the picket lines are just the sort of men that Mr Kinnock needs for his new Labour Party, but they are leaving Labour, and he does not dare to try to stop them.

24 November 1984

THE MINERS' STRIKE: BACK TO WHAT?

Andrew Brown

'We are not going to be constitutionalised out of this strike' (Mick McGahey, February 1984).
'No one in their right minds ever wanted this strike' (Arthur Scargill, February 1985).

Yorkshire

It's been a lot of fun. When all the other explanations have been tried and found insufficient, what remains to explain the miners' stubbornness must be the pleasure they took in the strike. Of course the fun was greater for the Loonies, to adopt the terminology of Mr Richard West. Their jobs, their wages, and their futures were not at risk. Bashing the police and encouraging others to do so was for them just an exciting, if rather pornographic diversion, the left-wing equivalent, perhaps, of calling the Nicaraguan *contras* 'freedom fighters'. Nor should the support given to the miners be overestimated. If 'Women Against Pit Closures' raised as much as £25 million (and I doubt they raised half that) this figure is still dwarfed by the £250 million which four per cent of the most

uneconomic capacity loses each year; or by the £2½ billion which represents the total subsidy to the Coal Board. These sums were not raised by
appealing to the finer feelings of the taxpayers. The Inland Revenue does
not recognise support groups.

But such mundane considerations were foreign to the strike from the
very beginning. 'The Miners United will never be defeated,' they chanted
in London and in Yorkshire, while in Nottingham they worked. It was a
mass flight from reality, a wonderful drunkenness, like that of a football
crowd. Only if the 'Miners United' are understood as a tribal or sporting
unity does that chant make sense. The last time I was in Hemsworth (9
February), I asked one of the pickets who showed me round Fitzwilliam
what difference it would make if Nottingham were expelled from the
union. He replied that it would only make the miners stronger. Clearly,
the miners were here considered as a mystical body, whose strength
depended on their unity and not on their economic worth. A 'miner' in
this sense was a man who did almost anything but digging coal, just as a
'woman' in a similar political usage is someone who has nothing to do
with either men or children.

Physical suffering would have been a lot easier to watch than the miners' struggles to come to terms with their defeat. Walking into the Blue
Bell pub in Hemsworth on Monday evening, the night before the men
were due to return to work, I felt as if I were intruding on a wake. A drive
around the local pits had shown not a single picket. The hut at the
entrance to Kinsley drift mine, which was sacked in the summer, where
the pickets had sheltered round a brazier the last time that I had seen
them, had now collapsed into a huddle of corrugated sheeting. Even the
brazier was gone, replaced by a garden incinerator; but the road up to the
pit was open. Three windows had been replaced in one building. The
scab's house now had a glass door and two windows replaced.

The faces in the Blue Bell were sick with grief, like men's at a bereave-
ment. When asked what he would feel when he returned, one miner
replied: 'Hate; hate for the Coal Board, for those bastards in Notts, for the
Government.' 'I only hope that if they shut ten pits, they shut them in
Nottingham. That will teach them. 'Cause they're not men. They're just
women.'

We were joined by a Nacods man, who seemed younger, plumper, and
bouncier than the miners, as well he might be. In a village like
Hemsworth, the wonder is not that Nacods came so near to striking, but
that any of its members ever crossed a picket line. Their wages were
referred to more than once as conscience money. He told me that the
miners had been sold down the river; but he told them that they should
have settled for the Nacods deal last autumn. No one seemed inclined to

dispute the point; but they argued from desperation. 'You might as well make this area a nuclear testing base if they shut the pits down.'

The men discussed with some relish the probable state of Kinsley drift mine, in Fitzwilliam. Since it is a new and modern mine, it needs a great deal of maintenance if it is to function effectively, and this it has hardly had over the last year, and it has been sacked above ground. 'Thousands and thousands of Maggie's money,' said one with relish. Since this was Hemsworth, the union's figures on the cost of the strike, and not the Government's, were believed. Several people pointed out that for the six billion pounds spent on breaking the strike the Government could have kept every uneconomic pit in the country going for years and years. They had no illusions about the magnitude of their defeat: this had been, said one, the last big battle between the Government and the unions in his lifetime.

But they had not been the aggressors in this battle. This is what it is almost impossible to remember in London. The Yorkshire miners, who seem to us insurgents, threatening the order of the state, see themselves as defending the proper order of things against a revolutionary and destructive government. At times this attitude leads them into absurdities; but it is completely sincere. Their wants are, after all, very conservative: enough money, a regular job, education and some future for their children, the preservation of traditional beliefs and social relations. (For example, that the union be more important and more powerful than the Coal Board.) The miners could be said to see themselves as a property-owning democracy, with their pit as their property. Whatever one may think of Scargill's generalship, it has been the most extraordinary feat of political education on the part of the 'Yorkshire Left' group in the NUM to convince such a conservative group as the miners of Hemsworth that their interests and aspirations are in fact socialist.

There was much talk in the pub that evening of an amnesty. 'We all came out together, and we're all going back together' was the slogan, spoken, as miners' slogans often are, in tones of quiet conviction, as if nothing could be more self-evident. I talked for a while with a man who had been sacked from Frickley Colliery for assaulting the police on a picket line in Notts, though he was still awaiting the results of his third trial, which might put him in jail for six months. He explained that there had been about 12 in his group, attacked by 'about 60 coppers. Though we had a go back at them, of course. You have to.' He seemed fairly resigned to his fate; what he found intolerable was the thought of marching back to work past men who had been sacked, and were to be abandoned by the union. That was the consideration that gave the flying pickets from Kent their moral force. To demonstrate that they would not cross picket lines, even when there were 2,000 would-be workers and only three pickets, was, on Tuesday, the only way left to the Hemsworth miners of showing that they still had their self-respect, and some sense of honour.

To know this threw an interesting light on 'media bias'. It was quite clear to the men I spoke to, and, to judge from their conduct, to all the other miners in the area, that the purpose of Tuesday's 'return to work' was to demonstrate the miners' unity, not to begin digging coal out of the ground. There was no intention to go to the pits if that involved crossing a picket line; and the pickets were confidently expected. Yet BBC reports spoke as if miners were being thwarted in sincere attempts to work. At Kinsley and Frickley at least, the men could only have been thwarted if no pickets had made possible a gesture of solidarity. At ten past eight the men had already been turned back from Kinsley. Six or seven large, squat men waited with a boy of about ten, on whose grubby sweatshirt a white ferret dangled upside down, regarding me with pink and baleful eyes. I asked what was happening: 'Maggie's f—ing crucifying us, that's what.' Then I was recognised: 'He writes for a f—ing Conservative magazine.' One of the kobolds advised me to f— off; another suggested that I photograph the ferret, call it 'nigger', and 'stuff it up Maggie's breeks', though whether he meant the ferret or the photograph was not clear. In any event, I decided to talk to the police instead. Two of them were waiting down the road in their car. They took the view that the picket was a private event; and they were wise to do so. Certainly, no one was being disturbed by it. The miners were to meet at noon to discuss the affair; in the meantime, a huddle of clerical workers waited down the road, and then dispersed.

At South Kirby, on the other side of Hemsworth, the miners were to have marched in with their banners. The last time I had seen the entrance to the mine, there had been about 100 pickets enfolded in 200–300 police as they tried to prevent 20 scabs from getting in. The pushing and the invective were ritualised, but sincere. This time there were about 2,000 miners, two policemen – and four pickets from Kent. The men took two of them into the pit yard: two more were left standing by their picket banner, which was strapped to an empty, crumpled paint tin, as the procession moved slowly, with banners, up the drive. They appeared in the yard, to show they were ready for work, and then they went home, to show that they wanted an amnesty. As I worked my way for the last time through the traffic jam outside the pit (here too the police were officiously ignoring the congestion) I found I was driving behind one of the miners' banners, hung from a scaffolding frame, and supported on wheels. Four young men pushed it homewards. 'Unity is strength', it said.

9 March 1985

AIDS IN THE BATHHOUSE

Tony Allen-Mills

... For more than 100 years, the gay bathhouse has provided American men with a convenient source of prodigious quantities of all-male sex. An odd combination of swimming pool, sex shop and short-stay motel, American bathhouses were until the Aids crisis the centres of indisputably the most intense sexual activity practised on the planet. In specially-padded orgy rooms, or in spartan private cells, homosexuals would gather to sodomise and masturbate at an awesomely energetic pace. 'What the baths sold was the opportunity for men to have an unlimited number of partners,' says Michael Callen, a young New Yorker who visited the baths regularly, until he contracted Aids.

Even without the Aids crisis, the baths presented a daunting health hazard. Quite apart from the venereal risks of frequent fellatio and the internal tearing caused by multiple buggery, bathhouse customers would regularly drink their partners' urine and even swallow faeces. So it was perhaps unsurprising that when the Aids epidemic exploded, it sparked off vigorous campaigns for the bathhouses to be closed.

Homosexual groups are badly divided over the bathhouse issue. Some complain that any official attempt to regulate homosexual behaviour is a denial of constitutional rights. Other gay activists doubt that the spread of Aids would be diminished by closing the baths, but feel they should close voluntarily anyway rather than encourage government restrictions on the gay community. A minority of gays now believes that the bathhouses are evil.

Into the last category falls Dr Stephen Caiazza, leader of a New York-based group of homosexual physicians. 'It is medically undeniable that if the baths close, some lives, how many we do not know, will certainly be saved,' he says. 'As a physician my primary and ultimate duty is to save lives and as far as I'm concerned right now the only good bath is a closed bath.'

Other gay doctors take the opposite view. Dr Dennis McShane of San Francisco argues that while baths might be a source of unsafe sex, 'so might be your bedroom'. Closing them, he believes, is pointless and discriminatory. His argument is supported by a Los Angeles Aids task force which studied the issue and concluded that 'closure would have no significant health impact inasmuch as the conduct which leads to infection can move to other locations and occur anywhere'.

The only American city to use the force of law to restrict bathhouse activity is San Francisco. Under regulations that are aimed at preventing 'unsafe' sex, bathhouse buggery has been banned. Employees with torches check dark corners to make sure the law is obeyed. San Francisco officials deny that this is a futile gesture, and scoff at suggestions that bathhouse activity is merely being transferred elsewhere.

'It is damned difficult to replicate the kind of sex you can have in a bathhouse in a cold and foggy park,' says Dr Mervyn Silverman, the city's public health director. According to Dr Silverman there is no disputing that gay bathhouses 'encourage and facilitate' the spread of Aids. He told the gay magazine *Advocate* that since the San Francisco clampdown on bathhouse activity the number of cases of rectal gonorrhoea in the city has dropped to its lowest level since records were started.

What is most unusual about this continuing debate is that there should be any homosexual demand whatsoever for facilities now so notoriously liable to transmit deadly disease. Yet in many cities bathhouse business is actually booming. At the Body Works Bathhouse in Indianapolis, owner Stan Berg claims record numbers of customers are passing through his doors, even though as a gesture to Aids he has closed down three of his four orgy rooms. At the Club Bath in Washington DC, one patron was recently quoted as saying that the orgy room was so busy 'you wouldn't know there was an Aids crisis'. And the personal columns of gay American newspapers make it abundantly clear that, Aids or no Aids, the search for intense physical gratification continues unabated in the homosexual world. To be sure, many of the ads are peppered with phrases like 'must be sincere and clean', or 'health-conscious'. But the overwhelming majority are of the 'man with big belly and sweet rear seeks gentleman's gentleman' variety, only far more explicit.

Given that the threat of disease does not seem to be discouraging many homosexuals from pursuing promiscuous sex, the current objectives of the majority of gay political activists are to promote healthier practices. Groups like New York's Gay Men's Health Crisis are distributing 'safe sex' posters to homosexual establishments urging men to use condoms during anal intercourse, to avoid swallowing human waste, and to switch to masturbation for mutual gratification. Bathhouse owners are being urged to make available free supplies of condoms, to keep the lights turned on, and to discourage orgies. In New York all this has reportedly helped bring about a 59 per cent drop in gonorrhoea cases among homosexuals. But elsewhere the effectiveness of such campaigns is in doubt.

Says Stan Berg in Indianapolis: 'Every time I put the safe sex poster up, somebody tears it down.' . . .

9 March 1985

BOMBED PARTY

Andrew Gimson

Brighton

On Wednesday night last week I arrived at the Conservative Conference and discovered a great pretence of boredom. Outside the Grand Hotel I ran into two friends. 'What's happening?' I asked. 'We've had dinner,' they said, full of the determined lack of interest which afflicts politicians at Tory conferences. 'What are you going to write about?' they asked. 'The Arts and Crafts exhibition at the Museum,' I replied. It isn't done to confess that you find a Tory conference of political interest, though you can concede that it is quite fun socially. To admit to liking the actual conference is comparable to saying that you like St Tropez. The most you are permitted to do is to look cheerful because you are seeing your friends.

After the bomb everyone had to admit that this Conference was interesting after all. It is un-Conservative, another sign of how horribly radical the party has become, to have two interesting conferences in a row. Mr Nigel Lawson knows that 20 years should elapse between one interesting conference and the next: he gave a heroic show of boredom, but was overborne, as Chancellors of the Exchequer invariably are, by forces outside his control.

Luckily my own experience of the bomb was as derisory as if I had been sent to Brighton by Thurber. On Wednesday night I stayed at the Grand until the bar closed, at about three o'clock, but on Thursday I went to bed early. In the middle of the night a bell half woke me, but I was not in the part of the Metropole to be evacuated, thought 'what a miserable joke', and fell asleep again, dreaming that the new *Spectator* cover was pale green, and that by a serious oversight it did not include the word 'spectator'. I awoke, feeling well rested, a little after eight o'clock, and heard about the bomb on the radio. Ferdinand Mount, staying in the same hotel, says that someone banged on his door (which often happens by accident at conferences, so he ignored it), but that beyond this, efforts to rescue him from the bomb reported to be at the Metropole were 'sketchy'.

Others had passed the most dangerous night of their lives, and at least two people had been murdered.

Talking to the haggard and unshaven survivors, however, it was clear that they had passed through an exciting adventure as well as a harrowing ordeal. Danger is exciting, danger survived is exhilarating. Othello was loved by Desdemona for the dangers he had passed. (This is not a justification of bomb attacks, murder or maiming, all of which are frightful, but an observation.) Mingled with fear about who might be dead or injured, there had been laughter. Mr Gordon Reece, the Prime Minister's adviser on self-presentation, had encouraged the refugees on the seafront by telling them that Sir Alfred Sherman, on learning at the height of the crisis that Mrs Thatcher was unhurt, offered to help her with her speech, an anecdote variously interpreted as showing Sir Alfred's insensitivity, his desire to amuse people, or his seriousness, much needed by a party of scoffers trying to fight the IRA. Horrified as I am by the failure of the British to take ideas seriously, I incline to the last explanation, though it could also be that one of the scoffers invented the anecdote. Some Tories laugh so much one would believe anything of them.

The Conference opened on time, in sober mood. Keeping to the established routine not only showed that the bombers had failed to destroy peaceful stage-managed debate, it was also less demanding than making a new set of arrangements. The morning went on with the utmost decorum.

Outside the hall rumours circulated about who had been hurt. The news about Mrs Wakeham was said to be very bad. Sir Anthony Berry was missing. Nothing at all had been heard about the Heseltines, which was unusual. I went to cash a cheque, in order to buy a drink for a grieving friend of Roberta Wakeham, found in front of me a titled Conservative from South Wales. He addressed the bank clerk in Battle of Britain tones. 'All our credit cards are inside the Grand Hotel,' came the terse revelation. 'We'll have to cancel them. And the cheques. There'll be a few disappointed people' – he gave a dry laugh – 'but there we are.' He and his wife were keeping incredibly calm, but soon I discovered why: 'Don't worry,' he added, 'I've still got my American Express card.' The IRA will never triumph while there are such unflappable morons on the other side.

The chairman of the party was giving interviews to television men. He had to do the same at Blackpool last year in the wake of catastrophe, and on both occasions he was excellent. Mr Gummer can handle adversity, saying sensible things off the cuff when to say anything much is admirable. It is in prosperity that he goes to pieces, starts fidgeting and overstating his case, repelling all but the zealots.

The sexual aspects of the affair were agreed, by those interested in such things (almost everyone), to be disappointing. There were more wives in Brighton on Thursday than earlier in the week: Wednesday would have produced a richer crop of people in the wrong rooms. As for the sartorial aspects of the matter, these have been too narrowly covered. Sir Keith Joseph's dazzling dressing gown blinded people to such minor pleasures as Lord Denham resplendent in a monogrammed shirt, Michael Spicer MP wearing, strange to relate, only a towel, and Richard Ryder MP, who has been looking a bit despondent lately, but cheered up a treat when he lunched with the Foreign Secretary wearing a green overcoat instead of a suit. For these gentlemen, and for Lord Gowrie, who achieved as mover of deckchairs the fame which eludes him as poet, a campaign medal should be struck. But the most splendid decoration should be reserved for the indefatigably hospitable Lord McAlpine, who gave the large quantity of champagne found in his room to the wonderful firemen, and who also arranged for Marks & Spencer to open early, to clothe the naked. Letters of thanks should be addressed to Mr Churchill, the manager of that branch.

Across the ocean in Connecticut, Mr Cecil Parkinson awoke, turned on the television, and saw a picture of a man resembling his friend Norman Tebbit being extricated from a pile of rubble. Can Miss Sara Keays have dreamt of the service she was doing him, by ensuring that he was not staying in the room at the Grand Hotel reserved for the Secretary of State for Trade and Industry? Miss Keays and Times Newspapers should share a medal.

Last but not least, the drink question. Mrs Thatcher was not drunk on Thursday night: instead of drinking, she works. It is one of the many ways in which she is untypical of her party. Nor was Tristan Garel-Jones MP drunk: he is a militant teetotaller. Most of the rest of the people in the Grand Hotel were drunk, or rather, had had a number of drinks. But the historian can only speculate about whether it is preferable to be blown up drunk or sober.

20 October 1984

PORTRAIT OF THE WEEK

Mrs Thatcher and Dr FitzGerald finally signed their agreement on the future of Ulster, at Hillsborough Castle outside Belfast. The treaty announces that the two governments affirm that any change in Ulster's constitutional position would only come about with the consent of a majority of people of Northern Ireland. It also provides for the establishment of a ministerial conference, with a permanent secretariat, which would allow the Republic's government to advise the British Government what to do about Ulster, though the British Government is not bound by this advice. Dr FitzGerald explained that this meant there had been no abandonment of nationalist aspirations, nor any threat to Unionist rights. The IRA murdered a policeman and a UDR man; Gerry Adams proposed an electoral pact between Sinn Fein and the SDLP, should the 15 Unionist MPs carry out their threat to resign and fight by-elections against the treaty. Mr Ian Gow resigned as a Treasury minister in protest against the deal.

23 November 1985

HER IRISH DREAM

The Spectator *Leader*

Both Mrs Thatcher and Mr Kinnock began their speeches on Tuesday, at the start of the debate in the Commons on the Anglo-Irish agreement, by deploring violence. 'There can be no such thing as an acceptable level of violence,' declared the Prime Minister. 'We must never give up the search for a solution,' added the Leader of the Opposition. Both of them attach the highest importance to defeating 'the men of violence', and both believe the new agreement will help, given time, to achieve that purpose. Neither of them alluded to the possibility that, given time, the same end might be achieved more successfully under the present arrangements for governing Northern Ireland. In 1972, the worst year of the present troubles, and the one in which direct rule from Westminster was introduced, 474 people were killed. In each of the four succeeding years, over 200 people were killed. Since then the annual figure has not exceeded 114, and last year it was 64, the lowest since 1970. But neither speaker mentioned this decline. In their insistence that something must be done, they overlooked the fact that things already are being done. They could not, perhaps, observe that many more people die in road accidents than are killed by bombs and bullets in Northern Ireland without sounding complacent, but they might have done opponents of the agreement the justice of admitting that there is a pragmatic case against the new arrangements. It is true that the Unionists do not always make their case sound very practical. Mr Enoch Powell is capable, in his less felicitous moments, of making his views seem exclusively theoretical, while his letter to Mr Molyneaux about whether or not he would resign his seat and fight a by-election, as the other 14 Unionist MPs have promised to do, sounded evasive and casuistical. Mr Ian Gow made a number of excellent and practical points in his speech on Tuesday, and was listened to by an attentively silent House, but was shortly afterwards dismissed by Mr James Prior as 'a romantic Unionist'. He might have done better to have omitted his reference to the feelings which Ireland first kindled in him as a young subaltern 30 years ago, and to have concentrated on his question: how will it be possible to proceed without the consent of the majority? The supporters of the agreement are being profoundly impractical – are, one might say, the victims of a romantic delusion – if they think that reconciliation can be forced on Northern Ireland. 'Reconciliation' is a new word for 'consensus'. Mrs Thatcher was thought to have discovered the limitations of 'consensus politics', yet now aspires to introduce them into the least receptive part of the United Kingdom imaginable. In this astonishing enterprise she carries with her the consensus politicians of all parties whose weak-minded wishful thinking she formerly spurned. She will use her formidable energy and courage to try to defeat, not some military, economic or political opponent such as General Galtieri, Arthur Scargill or Derek Hatton, but a million Unionist citizens. They will, she hopes, be forced to participate in power-sharing local government, which has failed time and time again in Ulster, because this will be the only way to remove their affairs from 'the purview of the intergovernmental conference'. But the Unionists differ in a vital respect from her other opponents. She does not merely need to defeat them, she needs to win their whole-hearted collaboration. She has gone a funny way about doing so. We hope Mrs Thatcher succeeds in bringing a greater degree of peace to Northern Ireland than direct rule has so far done, but cannot help thinking that in pursuit of this noble end she has adopted tactics likely to have exactly the opposite effect.

30 November 1985

PORTRAIT OF THE WEEK

Mr Heseltine was informed at a Cabinet meeting that all his future statements on the Westland affair would have to be approved by the Cabinet Office. He swept together his papers (history ignores his hair) and left the room, and his job. Within an hour, Mr George Younger had been appointed to his place; within four hours, Mr Heseltine had produced a spontaneous, yet enviably polished 3,500 words to justify his resignation and accuse the Prime Minister of a 'constitutional outrage'. After that, both sides in the dispute returned to their previous less flamboyant tactics of showing to selected journalists as many Cabinet papers and secret documents as seemed necessary to prove the other side guilty of bad faith and breach of confidence. Mr Brittan rose in the House to defend himself, and was immediately surprised by questions about a private and confidential letter to Mrs Thatcher. They were, however, inaccurately framed. He was enabled with perfect truth to deny that he knew of the supposed letter's existence, which gave the unfortunate impression that he knew nothing of the real letter. Being a man distinguished even among lawyers for his scrupulous honesty, Mr Brittan returned to the House that evening and apologised. Mr Kinnock rose to the house and spoke for the nation when he announced: 'Someone has been telling the truth and someone else has not been telling the truth.' The text of the letter, which contradicted Mr Brittan's account of a meeting with British Aerospace, was then released.

18 January 1986

PORTRAIT OF THE WEEK

Mrs Thatcher explained that this week's crucial letter in the Westland scandal, one sent on 6 January from the Solicitor-General to Mr Heseltine, had in fact been leaked by the Department of Trade and Industry, on Mr Brittan's orders, and that she fully approved of this, though she did not know it had been done. Mr Brittan, fortified by this expression of confidence, resigned, in order to satisfy the 1922 Committee, and was replaced by Mr Paul Channon. The question then arose: why had Mrs Thatcher, whose press secretary and principal private secretary had both approved Mr Brittan's action, remained in ignorance of what had happened for 16 days during which the newspapers had hardly talked of anything else? In the subsequent parliamentary debate this question was neither clearly put by Mr Kinnock nor answered by Mrs Thatcher. It did, however, emerge that she had known in advance that the famous letter would be written, and that the Solicitor-General himself had nearly resigned when his letter was leaked.

1 February 1986

WHY SHE NEVER ASKED
(AND WHY HE NEVER TOLD HER)

Ferdinand Mount

When going over a script, the late Alfred Hitchcock would often ask 'what's happened to the McGuffin?' By this he meant the device that was supposed to set the whole plot in motion, something which in itself might be quite trivial or irrelevant but which was needed to propel the film through all the chases and doubletakes and scary bits and which must never be quite lost sight of or the whole enterprise would begin to sag. The trouble with the Westland script is that it has never stuck to the same McGuffin. To start with, Mr Heseltine told us that it was a constitutional crisis, but, as Michael Foot pointed out in a delightful speech on Monday, 'he seems to have got over that pretty quickly'. Next, the question was who was telling the truth – Mr Brittan or Sir Raymond Lygo. That was patched up. Then it was 'who leaked the Solicitor-General's letter?' The answer to that was given, and the answerer resigned. So by the time the House of Commons was packed to the rafters on Monday afternoon, we were down to 'when did the Prime Minister know about the leak?' 'how much did she know?' and/or 'why on earth did she wait 16 days to find out the whole truth?' – all of which could be made to sound tolerably Watergate-ish but which had, I think, strayed a little too far from the original McGuffin.

Still, no credit should be taken away from Mr John Wakeham, the Chief Whip, who laid on a magnificent show, worthy not so much of Hitchcock as of Busby Berkeley. He had a huge, well-drilled cast of Tory MPs who chattered and giggled the whole way through the opening speech from Mr Kinnock (not quite as bad as it was reported, though certainly substandard). Mrs Thatcher was both stentorian and apologetic, not an easy combination. But the real *coup de théâtre* was Mr Heseltine's apology: no revelations, no accusations, just a dear little recognition of shared human frailty. By the end of the debate, in fact, we were knee deep in recognitions of human frailty.

All the same, you have to spare a thought for the dedicated scandal buff. Just as he has accumulated his expertise about the Real Questions – it's not the *meeting* of the seventh that matters, it's the discrepancy between the *letter* of the seventh and the meeting of the 21st when Haldeman told Mandy Rice-Davies that the *Belgrano* was heading north-north-west at the time – suddenly the steam goes out of the affair, and he is trampled underfoot by 400 Tory MPs singing 'Land of Hope and Glory'. And to have the instigator of the whole business saying he's extremely sorry and tremendously humble really is a bit much. It is rather as if, at the moment halfway through the car chase when the two cars are roaring along the Corniche side by side at 100 mph, the villain were to lean over and shout to James Stewart: 'I'm awfully sorry if you've got the wrong impression, but I was really only testing the acceleration.'

For that reason if for no other, the responsible political correspondent should resist the temptation to say 'well, any fool can see she's made the most frightful horlicks of the whole piffling business and she's lucky to get away with it. I think if we try the upstairs bar now, we should get a few in before the rush.' There are questions to be answered, and we must straighten up and answer them.

Is it credible that *for 16 days* Mrs Thatcher never asked her officials *point blank* – to use Dr David Owen's phrase – whether Mr Brittan was involved? Is it *credible* that she never asked Mr Brittan himself? Is it *credible* that Mr Brittan never came and told her off his own bat?

If one goes on gasping out these questions with a sharp intake of breath at each repetition, one develops a kind of asthma of incredulity. Thought and imagination alike tend to grind to a halt. Nothing seems to have any explanation.

But suppose we approach the business more like Alfred Hitchcock or, better still, like Hercule Poirot: employ the little grey cells and assume that there must be an explanation which, however bizarre or discreditable, is at least logical. Let us daringly start by assuming that virtually every word Mrs Thatcher uttered in her two statements was the literal truth, although not necessarily the whole truth.

She hears of the leak 'some hours' after it has occurred, like the rest of the nation (or those who bother to keep abreast of this increasingly complicated saga). She assumes, like the rest of the nation again, that the leak must have come from the Department of Trade and Industry and at a fairly senior level, since it was instantaneous. Conversation 'in general terms' with Mr Ingham and Mr Powell the next morning, Tuesday, confirms this impression. And there she leaves the matter. She asks no more questions. On Friday, Sir Robert Armstrong requests an enquiry. She agrees, but says nothing to him about her knowledge, fragmentary and vague as it may be. Why? Why does this energetic Prime Minister, dedicated to the pursuit of efficiency, fascinated by detail, not ask the question?

Because, *mon ami*, she does not wish to hear the answer. If she hauls Mr Brittan in and asks him the question point blank, he would have to say that he authorised the leak, and she would have to sack him. Well, would that not be the right thing to do, both to restore the good name of the Government and to ensure its survival? After all, it will all have to come out soon enough. The morning after, she has been told that the law officers are hopping mad. Sir Robert is bound to be forced to set up a leak enquiry. Why not take the initiative and act before she is forced to?

Why Mr Brittan never told her of his direct responsibility for the leak is a much simpler matter. Because he thought she already knew, or at any rate knew enough to summon him for a talk if she wanted to. In ordinary life, one does not burst in to the Employer to say: 'Oh by the way, Prime Minister, just in case you have forgotten, I'm the one who did it.' There is, after all, always the chance that the Awful Thing will go away. But why does she not haul him in?

Well, she does not want to lose Mr Brittan for several reasons – because she is fond of him, because he has supported her steadfastly throughout the whole Westland trauma, because he is, however clumsily, attempting to carry out her instructions to counter-attack against Mr Heseltine's letter to Mr Horne of Lloyds Merchant Bank – since that letter is a clear breach of collective Cabinet responsibility. She is reluctant to discard Mr Brittan at a stroke like that. Losing two ministers does look like carelessness.

Yet there is more to it than complicity and affection. And here I must bring in a piece of 'constitutional practice' which I think I have discovered – or rather rediscovered. At least, I have seen it referred to nowhere else.

Over the last 30 years, the circumstances in which ministers have resigned from the Cabinet have fallen roughly into three categories: either they have gone of their own free will because they are furious, bored or ill (George Brown, Heseltine, Prior, etc); or they have gone on grounds of inefficiency or age, as part of a reconstruction of the government (dozens of them); or they have been forced out after a prolonged campaign against their conduct in press and/or Parliament – Maudling, Parkinson, etc. The last occasion I can think of when the Prime Minister sacked a minister on the spot for a specific action was Attlee's 1947 sacking of Dalton for a Budget leak. That seemed a bit harsh even at the time, I think, and seems harsher in retrospect. Since then, Prime Ministers do seem to have felt the need to wait and gather some extra *collective* authority before getting rid of a colleague – either the pressure of a public hue and cry, or the imperative to reconstruct the government as a whole in order to improve its performance. Ex-Prime Ministers like to say 'of course, I'd have had him out of *my* Cabinet in five minutes' – but in practice they did not do it like that. Ministers do not get sacked quite like ordinary mortals. They are forced out by public outcry or reshuffled out. There is a difference, even if the discards may feel it comes to much the same thing. Propriety these days demands a period of reflection and a show of reluctance from the Prime Minister before disposing of a minister who has sinned or blundered. Thus she would not have found it easy either to sack Mr Heseltine as soon as he began to breach collective responsibility or to sack Mr Brittan until the press and Tory MPs had demanded it.

Suppose then that this is the explanation. She could not ask the question because, instinctively if not consciously, she knew she did not want to hear the answer, since the answer would have forced her to sack Mr Brittan on the spot – which would have not merely looked like disloyalty to her most loyal supporter but would have been against the modern constitutional fashion. Prime Ministers have to know when not to ask questions as well as when to ask them. Where she went wrong was surely much earlier on. I don't mean in putting up Mr Brittan to wheel on the Solicitor-General to give his view. That, after all, is what the law officers are there for, and very often their views turn out to be more illuminating or secure than Sir Patrick Mayhew's were. Her disastrous error lay in succumbing to the whole Westland hysteria in the first place, in joining the pursuit of the McGuffin, and so getting caught up in the hectic chase.

From now on, we are told, things are going to be very different.

Jolly Senior Ex-Minister (before the debate) to Junior Minister: 'Of course, all this means we're absolutely bound to win the next election.'

Junior Minister: 'Oh really. How so exactly?'

Jolly Senior Ex-Minister: 'Well, either she mends her ways and opts for consensus and collective responsibility, or she goes, and we get a consensus-minded leader. Either way, we can't lose.'

Many Tory MPs, weary of the hectic ride, are longing for the quiet life. They want an end to all this radical, dynamic stuff. Indeed, 'collective responsibility' is a code word for precisely that. If the Cabinet is not pretty hard driven, if the ideal of collective responsibility is allowed to flourish, then nothing contentious ever gets past it. The blockers gain in confidence and begin to obstruct even the most modest suggestions. It is a process which is most likely to occur in the second half of a parliament, fertilised by fatigue. If there is a legacy of this whole peculiar, occasionally enjoyable, sometimes ludicrous but mostly babyish saga, this is it.

Yet in practice, I suspect that 'the return of Cabinet government' and Mrs Thatcher's 'impaired authority' will amount to rather less than some fear and others hope. She has lost dozens of arguments in Cabinet before, and will lose dozens more. Many of the fiercest policy disagreements of her earlier years no longer apply. The niceties of Cabinet procedure may be more carefully observed in future. But Prime Ministers in good health with large majorities do tend to go on acting like Prime Ministers until they are thrown out – which is usually done by the voters, and not by their colleagues.

1 February 1986

WHAT WENT UNSAID

The Spectator *Leader*

This has been a depressing election. There have been no great speeches, few good jokes. There have scarcely been any interesting incidents. The chief excitement has come from watching a man who has passed his entire adult life only in politics trying to interest us in his character, background, family, smile, etc, and convince us that he is deep and crisp and even. He told us that he was the first Kinnock in 1,000 generations to go to university (Cardiff, pass degree in Industrial Relations) and expected us not to laugh. It was bold, to say the least, and more successful than it deserved to be.

What was dispiriting was the readiness of the participants to avoid any of the questions which make politics difficult. Very often, the television appeared to connive at this. Many have pointed out that in television-dominated elections parties concentrate on 'photo-opportunities'; no one has added that under the 'duopoly' system of British television the parties have a unique power to get the coverage they want. The strict rules of 'balance' mean that parties have to be given equal time. Television therefore has to report each day whatever the main parties do, no matter how inane. Political managers have at last understood and exploited this. The result is a sort of paradox: politicians are cocooned by publicity. A meet-the-people exercise means that very few people are met.

On the rare occasions when political questions have been discussed it has been with the same impoverished vocabulary and the same coward-ice and evasion that were apparent in 1983. Although the Conservatives produced a thoroughly workmanlike manifesto with several brave pro-posals, they soon gave up trying to discuss it. A couple of confusions about policy for schools and nothing more was heard of the entire docu-ment for the rest of the campaign. Labour speeded up the process by not putting anything at all in its manifesto in the first place. The Alliance programme gave no evidence that any moulds were going to be broken.

Arguments about public spending were conducted as if there were nothing whatever to be learned from the experience of the last ten years. On Tuesday, for instance, newspapers contained seven pages of advertisements placed by Labour and the Conservatives. All concerned the level of spending on 'caring' services. The competition between the two parties was simply about who was likely to spend more and how much had been spent already – the Tories boasted of their profligacy: Labour accused them of meanness. Before the campaign began, discussion about markets and the extension of choice had become semi-respectable. Dr David Owen talked a good deal about market virtues. But no sooner did politicians climb on the hustings than debate reverted to an exchange of bribes. A question like 'What are you going to do about the health service?' expected only the answer 'Spend much more.' Electoral convention permitted nothing else.

Yet, except for defence (some might argue, *including* defence), all the problems most hotly discussed were those arising from state provision. Pensions, health, social services, council housing, schools are all areas where there is huge discontent because of what the state has failed to achieve. Voters know how bad these services are and yet still seem to want to believe that money will cure their problems. Hence the extraordinary situation in which people flatly refuse to accept the statistics which show that the Conservative government has spent more than any of its predecessors in all major areas of provision. The idea that the health service is in a bad condition *because* it is guaranteed ever-rising amounts of public money was unsayable at this election, but not far from the truth.

The Tories can learn from all this. They will never be thanked for 'caring'. They would be associated with skinflint attitudes even if they doubled social spending. So long as the health and education services exist in their present form, Conservatives will always be attacked for not looking after them properly. Their craven boasts of high spending at this election have deserved the contempt which they received.

By the same token, the Tories are more or less invulnerable on those points where they have acted according to their beliefs. The reversal of council house sales is not remotely proposed by Labour. The renationalisation of British Telecom and British Gas is electorally disastrous, as is the repeal of laws against secondary picketing, as is a tax increase. If schools are ever granted the independence which the Conservatives have promised, any Labour government would find it almost impossible to take that freedom away. Even in health, a well-conducted policy over a long period, perhaps as much as 15 years, could make private care as entrenched and as widespread as home ownership is today.

An election ought not to be a time for the discussion of the distant future in calm, seminar voices. The clash of men is as important in the electoral battle as disputes over measures. There is even something to be said for plain insult. But an election should not be the time when the chief public questions are treated with the greatest evasion and stupidity. Anyone following the 1987 campaign without knowledge of the context of recent history would have learnt almost nothing about the political condition of Britain. Nothing happened in the campaign which will improve the government of the country. Ignorant armies clashed by night.

13 June 1987

STEEL SO SHARP HE MIGHT CUT HIMSELF

Ferdinand Mount

During the debate on the Queen's Speech, the Liberal leader alerted us to what sounded like a new form of social disadvantage. Mr Steel warned that 'if the run-down city areas are not to become the permanent sink of the affluent society, whose victims live shut away from the gays of the prosperous suburbs and the shires, except when they explode in resentment, what is needed is help and enablement'. Only the Liberals have had the compassion to understand the bitterness and frustration caused by the growth of a Two-Nation society. While country and suburban gays frolic at their tennis clubs and gymkhanas, the inner cities are, it seems, condemned to a grim future as a heterosexist underclass. 'Gay deprivation riots' will soon be commonplace on Merseyside, and in Greater Manchester social workers must be bracing themselves for new demands for Lesbian Access. Yet this urgent social problem is in danger of going totally ignored in the comfortable South, for, as usual, most MPs had fled the Chamber the moment Mr Steel began to speak, and Hansard even printed 'gays' as 'gaze'.

For those outside in the wider community, it may be hard to understand how little attention the House of Commons pays to Mr Steel or indeed to any of the Liberals. Now that Chancellor Jenkins is no longer with us, on the Alliance benches it is Dr Owen and only Dr Owen who commands attention. This is not because he is a brilliant speaker, though he is much improved, but because he appears somehow to engage with the politics of the day. Mr Steel, by contrast, embodies the irrelevance of the modern Liberal Party, its obsession with the issues of the 1960s, its lack of economic realism. None of this matters much on television, where his affable blandness is an asset. Nor is it a drawback in Liberal Party infighting, where his Lowland cunning always pops up when least expected.

This time, though, he has been so sharp I think he might cut himself. In theory, I suppose, Mr Steel does have the right to raise the question of merger without consulting Dr Owen, since it was he who originally hatched the idea of the Social Democratic Party in cahoots with Roy Jenkins. They had both always intended an eventual merger, and they could well argue that by now, to quote the Alliance's bathetic election slogan, 'The Time Has Come'. From his own career point of view, by raising the question so briskly after the election Mr Steel has both scotched any challenge from Paddy Ashdown to the leadership of his own party and much improved his chances of leading a merged party. Not bad for a man widely supposed to be suffering from post-campaign fatigue.

But it is a crude and counter-productive move, all the same. He knew not only Dr Owen's hostility to merger but also his prickliness and dislike of being bounced. The whole thing could have been managed much more gently. Above all, Mr Steel is wrong in regarding merger as a Grade-A priority. For most voters, it comes about 237th on the list of important questions. The two-headed monster was a disadvantage during the election, but not nearly such a disadvantage as having to confront two big parties in reasonable fettle. Mr Steel had, I suspect, built up unrealistic expectations on the basis of Michael Foot's 1983 campaign – a disaster without parallel in half a century. I really do not think the electorate would make much distinction between a totally merged party and an alliance of two parties with a single head and a single shadow cabinet and manifesto-making body. How far down the structure the merger reaches is really a matter of indifference to the outside world.

The public squabbling does matter, though. The media have been extremely kind to the Alliance so far, making very little of the scorn and derision most of its leaders continually express for one another. Perhaps it is the strain of being nice in public that makes them so obsessively vituperative in private. Now the slanging is out in the open. And David Owen's views about the Liberal Party as a whole seem to be even more contemptuous than his feelings about David Steel.

I find this arrogance unappealing. After all, the Liberal Assembly at Eastbourne was merely following his own refusal to 'fudge and mudge' on the Bomb – only in the opposite direction. Mr Steel has been slowly leading them away from their principles towards his. Just because they dig their heels in a few yards from the finish, there is no cause to deluge them with abuse.

Besides, Social Democrats and Liberals enjoy telling the rest of us how insular we are. In other countries, government is carried on very success-fully, they say, by all sorts of coalitions and alliances of parties. The point is that the precise mechanics – to merge or not to merge, for example – are irrelevant. What matters is the spirit of co-operation. That is what breaks the mould. And that is just the quality which has been conspicuous by its absence in the present imbroglio. Both Dr Owen and Mr Steel have been playing what they would normally condemn as 'the old politics'.

We have all praised Dr Owen for shedding some of his vanity and over-bearing manner since the days when he seemed so overpromoted at the Foreign Office. Yet as a party leader he has remained curiously one-dimensional. He seems unable to understand the uses of the Liberals, or how complementary the two halves of the Alliance could be. The SDP has the managers and the money; the Liberals have the enthusiasts and the membership (although their estimated members of 100,000 may not turn out in any contest to be as solid as the SDP's computer-based 60,000). Most Liberals are friendly souls, easily wooed with a kind word. No doubt it was Dr Owen's backbone that stiffened them throughout the Falklands War and the miners' strike. But people do not like being con-tinually told they have been stiffened. In any case, many prefer life as invertebrates. Dr Owen's formula of 'tough but tender' could with advan-tage be applied to the management of the Alliance.

True, life inside the Liberal Party on its own was not always milk-and-watery. The last contest for the Liberal leadership, in 1976, was an uproarious affair. The loser, John Pardoe, claimed that Mr Steel had con-ducted 'a carefully orchestrated character assassination campaign with the help of the press', including, according to some accounts, the allega-tion that Mr Pardoe wore a toupee. Cyril Smith declared that Mr Steel could not make a bang if he had a firework in each hand. Mr Smith and Mr Steel still sit side by side, sometimes, and Mr Pardoe re-emerged last month as the frustrated co-ordinator of the Alliance's election campaign. If he is wearing a toupee these days, it is a very grey one.

The whole business may yet blow over, and if it does not, it will be all their own silly fault. Who is most to blame? Six of one and half a dozen of the other, if you ask me.

4 July 1987

NOT THE SORT OF PARTY ONE WOULD BOTHER TO GATE-CRASH

Noel Malcolm

Blackpool

Whoever thought up the cumbersome and hypnotically unmemorable name 'Social and Liberal Democrats' has a lot to answer for. The obvious label, 'Liberal and Social Democrats', was turned down for even more obvious reasons; but at least 'the LSDs' would have stuck in the mind, and by now all the most facile jokes about hallucinogens or pre-decimal coins might have been exhausted.

My own guess, when the SLD label was announced, was that they would call themselves the SoLiD party, and that the Owenites would prefer to call them the SoLD party. But 'the Salads' sprang of its own accord into the political consciousness of the nation, and there it has stayed, with ghastly appropriateness. It is not just that salads tend to be rather miscellaneous, with chopped-up bits and pieces of various colours. The real point is that although we all vaguely feel that salad is good for us, and that we ought to like it, it never quite appetises in the way that a traditional meat-and-two-veg meal does. A 'salad' party sounds, then, as if it is destined to remain on the side-plate of history. It is a name which has supplied one good joke to Dr Owen, and one poignant parting shot to the former Liberal official, Mr Adrian Slade. Borrowing a line from his brother's hit musical, he told the conference on Monday: 'Let us leave our salad days behind.' Doubly poignant, in fact, when you think that the party might just as easily have been called 'the Slades'.

'Democrats' is a pretty meaningless name, and not just because of its lack (compared with the origins of the American party, for example) of any particular historical context. The term 'social democrat' had a real meaning originally, because the second word qualified the first: it distinguished the sort of socialist who would work through the democratic parliamentary process from the sort who wouldn't. To use the qualifying word on its own is to use a label which ought to apply equally to all the other parties which use the democratic system. Sir Russell Johnston pointed this out with surprising candour on Monday: 'To me, the word "Democrat" simply has no clear political meaning. Conservative and Labour politicians are democrats.' For this he was roundly booed and heckled.

But in the end the presence or absence of clear meaning is not the main thing. All that Mr Ashdown (or Ashford, or Ashley, according to my Blackpool taxi-drivers) really wanted was a short, snappy, memorable name. 'Donald Duck' would have done almost as well except that within a year the party would have been implacably divided into those who wanted to shorten it to 'Duck' and those who refused to abandon 'Donald'.

Image-conscious Mr Ashdown is doing his best to lead his party towards the future – that destination towards which, not surprisingly, most politicians claim to be travelling. 'Whatever you do,' he told them at their rally on Sunday, 'don't look back.' The debate about the party's name was meant to reinforce the sense of new identity which will render the SLDP more forward-looking; in the event it had precisely the opposite effect, encouraging an orgy of retrospection and introspection. It is as if a driving instructor, worried that his pupil was spending too much time looking in the mirror, told him first to concentrate on the road ahead and then to brush his hair and straighten his tie.

This may be part of the explanation of something which at first puzzled me at this conference. I was struck, I am afraid to say, by the lack of any sense of a new outward-going spirit; if anything, it felt more inward-looking, self-obsessed and semi-private than the last two Liberal assemblies. It may be a brand-new party, but it lacks that feeling (which the SDP had, exhilaratingly, in its first two years) that new members, and even people entirely new to politics, are just waiting to be drawn in right, left and centre. At the moment it doesn't look like the sort of party one would bother to gate-crash.

Nowadays no party can do without image-management, of course. But Mr Ashdown's obsession with his party's image is a special result of a process of mythologising which has gone on in the Alliance-SLDP since June last year. The party organisers have comforted themselves with two attractive theories about the reasons for the Alliance's poor showing in the general election. One is that they did badly because they said they were not expecting to replace the Tories as the party with an absolute majority. And the other is that they suffered from an 'image' problem: when it looked at the Alliance the electorate saw double and, in seeing double, saw nothing distinctly. All that is needed, therefore, is a snappy name, a single charismatic leader, and Paddy's (definitely not Bob's) your uncle.

The first theory is at best a half-truth. It is true that, in the British electoral system, nothing succeeds like success: many people fear that a vote for a minor party will be a 'wasted' vote. But it is not therefore true that a minor party automatically increases its support by making wildly unrealistic claims about its chances of an absolute majority. This is a point which could be made about any third party; but it is especially relevant to the SLDP. As Mr David Alton has observed, a political party which preaches co-operation and partnership, and attacks Dr Owen for his 'macho' tendencies, is under a special obligation to refrain from any boastful, go-it-alone machismo of its own.

Where the 'image' theory is concerned, the point about double vision last year may be true, but it is an unimportant truth. The overall image of the Alliance was clear enough: 'tough but tender', individualist but caring – the sort of fine-sounding dualities which Mr Ashdown is still churning out. (I quote from his word-processor, which must have a special program to generate these formulae: 'choice and opportunity, liberty and community, prosperity and sustainability'.) And at the humdrum, nitty-gritty level, the Alliance had no shortage of detailed policies.

But there is, in British politics, a level somewhere between detailed policies and overall image. It is the level where you can locate one or two major policy positions, on issues which matter enough to stick in, and sway, the mind of the voter: above all, on the economy and on defence. This is the field on which Labour and the Tories win or lose their battles. It is the area in which, crucially, the Alliance failed to take up clear, strongly defined positions at the last election. And there are few signs yet that Mr Ashdown either recognises that crucial failure, or would be able to remedy it even if he understood it.

1 October 1988

PORTRAIT OF THE WEEK

Eleven people were killed and more than 60 injured when a bomb planted by the Provisional IRA exploded in Enniskillen, Co Fermanagh, as crowds gathered for a Remembrance Sunday service. The Northern Ireland Secretary, Mr Tom King, described the incident as a 'monstrous and foul attack'. Ireland's Roman Catholic bishops strongly condemned those who perpetrated the outrage saying, 'It is sinful to support such organisations or call on others to support them.' Some observers believe that the political resolve of the British and Irish governments to make the two-year-old Anglo-Irish Agreement more effective will now have been strengthened.

14 November 1987

THE IRA'S 'MISTAKE'

Patrick Bishop

'A woman came out and the other man held her ... I just fired at the man in the hallway. I can't remember seeing that man's face but I killed him. I have prayed many times for that man since and for his wife. Why did it have to be me? I couldn't kill a dog but I killed that man. What is my wife going to think, what is my family going to think?' Looking for remorse from captured IRA men is rarely a rewarding experience. When sorrow is expressed it seldom lasts long. Within a few days of uttering the above words Kevin Barry Artt retracted his confession to the murder, on his front doorstep, of Albert Myles, the deputy governor of Crumlin Road prison in Belfast. Later he broke out of the Maze prison and is now on the run, suspected of involvement in numerous outrages.

It is possible that the perpetrators of the massacre at Enniskillen have felt some unease as a result of their actions but it will probably be as transient as Artt's. But there is genuine dismay among the pseudo-politicians at the head of the organisation, not so much at the loss of life but at the harm that has been done to Sinn Fein's pretensions. Hence Gerry Adams's expressions of regret and extension of sympathy to the families of the dead on the day after the explosion.

The blast that brought down St Michael's Reading Hall has also done severe damage to the rickety political edifice that Adams and his supporters have spent ten years struggling to erect. Even the dimmest Dutch liberal or the most cynical London Labour politico will have difficulty parroting the notion that the IRA is engaged in a legitimate struggle against the occupying 'Crown forces' and sees no distinction between Prod and Taig.

The electorate in the Republic, whom Sinn Fein's candidates struggled so assiduously to woo in the February election, will be surely revolted for years to come. From the point of view of the stated aims of Adams, which are shared by the bulk of the Republican movement, the episode is a disaster. How then did it happen?

The bombing at Enniskillen breaks every current IRA rule of engagement. These were revised ten years ago after another mass killing of civilians when a petrol bomb planted by the Provisionals at the La Mon House Hotel in the heart of Protestant North Down burned 13 people to death. The La Mon House massacre was a mistake. The fleeing bombers stopped to flag through a warning but the phone box was out of order. By the time they got to one that worked it was too late.

The revulsion that followed this incident led Adams and Martin McGuinness (who took over from him as IRA 'chief of staff'), who were already taking their first tentative steps down the political path, to impose new rules to avoid a repetition. Henceforth 'volunteers' must take care to avoid civilian casualties and cut out high risk bombings on buses, trains and hotels.

A brief glance at the civilian death statistics in the ensuing years shows how effective that instruction has been. Civilian casualties persistently outnumber those of the security forces in Northern Ireland. So far 60 have been killed this year alone against 37 in 1986. Nonetheless there has been a general acceptance in recent times that if you are in the ballots as well as bullets game, civilian massacres are bad for business.

The last occasion on which Gerry Adams was moved to express 'regret' was after the Harrods bomb which killed eight in 1983 and imposed a (temporary) *froideur* on the warm relationship springing up between Sinn Fein and the Livingstone London left. The Enniskillen bombing is special because it seems to go further than previous bombings in its wantonness. Unlike Harrods and La Mon House there was no attempt to phone a warning. The IRA have claimed that the bomb was intended for the security forces and went off by accident possibly triggered by an army radio scanner. Even if this is true it is impossible to see how such an operation could have been planned without envisaging civilian casualties, and Protestant ones at that.

Anyway the Provisionals have a long record of trying to wriggle out of responsibility for atrocities. After Bloody Friday which killed nine in Belfast in 1972, Sean MacStiofain made the fantastic claim that the security forces had deliberately ignored warnings in order to blacken the IRA's image. The incident is probably better seen as a fit of murderous frustration where the perpetrators' desire for revenge persuaded them to flout the existing rules.

This year has been a bad one for the IRA. After opening with a rich crop of assassinations, culminating in the murder of Judge Maurice Gibson and his wife Cecily in April, it has practically all been downhill. So far IRA men have been killed and at the end of last month more than 150 tonnes of weapons were seized by the French off the freighter *Eksund*. There have been equal reverses on the electoral front. In the elections in the Republic in February Sinn Fein managed to attract a pathetic 1.85 per cent of the first-preference votes.

The most painful setback came with the killing of eight of the IRA's most energetic terrorists in an ambush in the Armagh village of Loughall in May. This incident has created a powerful appetite for vengeance. An IRA team was despatched to Britain to redouble efforts to kill the Prime Minister or, failing that, Tom King. Their efforts have been frustrated. Nor have they been able to bring off an answering 'spectacular' in Northern Ireland. Enniskillen may well have been intended to be it.

In the light of Gerry Adams's discernible ambitions it is hard to believe that the operation – even in the form claimed for it in the IRA statement – had the leadership's blessing. Its nature – the setting, the Protestant crowd, the near certainty of civilian deaths – all give the lie to Sinn Fein's attempts to present Republican violence as accurate and apposite.

Instead Enniskillen may well be taken as an indication of the IRA chiefs' lack of control over their men in the field. The units that operate along the border have had a history of independence since the present troubles began. The South Armagh unit for example exempted itself from the 1975 ceasefire. This is partly the result of distance from Dublin and Belfast, partly to do with the fact that by going public Adams and McGuinness can no longer exercise direct control on events on the ground.

After the damage that Enniskillen has done to Adams's strategy we can expect an almighty row inside the Republican movement. Some attempt will undoubtedly be made to impose stricter discipline on those who plant the bombs and pull the triggers. The promised inquiry is unlikely to devote much time to the morality of the action. Nor should we expect the miscreants' punishment to be too harsh. Killing civilians is not a kneecapping offence in the IRA list of crimes.

14 November 1987

DIARY

Charles Moore

Surely no one really believes that the SAS had any intention of letting the
IRA bombing team come out of Gibraltar alive. There was ample opportunity to arrest or intercept the team and it was not taken. It may be true
that the terrorists reached for pockets that might have contained guns,
but it is hard to imagine *any* reaction to a challenge in that split second
which would have prevented the SAS from firing. Everyone should be
pleased, of course, that three terrorists are dead, but I would still argue
that the shooting reflects badly on British policy. The shooting happened
because policy is too liberal. Human rights arguments and international
pressure prevent the use of very strong security powers in Northern Ireland. And since the security forces have to operate without such powers
against implacable enemies, they act illicitly to get results. Killing
becomes a dangerously effective method, resorted to more quickly than
need be the case. The security forces know who most of the terrorists are
and often where they are. If internment could be introduced, preferably
on both sides of the Irish border, there would be less call for the horrible
histrionics of Gibraltar. Internment is not ideal, but it would be better
than the current policy – interment.

19 March 1988

ON HOW THAT NON-EXISTENT
GIBRALTAR BOMB MAY YET
FIND ITS MARK

Auberon Waugh

Perhaps it is only because I love money so much, but I am seriously
worried that if Mrs Thatcher and Sir Geoffrey Howe, not to mention

Nanny Hurd and every other pontificating oaf in the Government, plan
to use the Gibraltar killings (or executions) as the opportunity for an all-
out attack on the press and broadcasting media, they are going to end up
not only with egg all over their faces, but blood as well.

Their calculation was well set out by Sir Peregrine Worsthorne last
Sunday. Simultaneously with his own David Wastell on the facing page
and with Mr Brian Walden in the *Sunday Times* (who also happened to be
interviewing the Prime Minister that week), Sir Peregrine had been
struck by the thought that it might be a good idea to revise the mediaeval
concept of outlawry, whereby known IRA members could be shot at will
by the police and armed services (Worsthorne and Wastell) or imprisoned (Walden). In Worsthorne's prescription, Mrs Thatcher would be
awarding herself the much coveted 00 licence to kill, or at any rate to
organise murder gangs on the South American model.

No doubt the idea has something to recommend it, but I do not propose
to discuss it here. What worries me, as I say, is that the Government,
through talking only to itself and such elevated but like-thinking intellects as Sir Peregrine and Mr Walden, is going to get itself into really serious trouble. This was foreshadowed by the thug Bernard Ingham,
Thatcher's press secretary, in his attributable briefing to the *Observer's*
Richard Harris on Sunday, when he warned of the official government
view that television standards, as exemplified by interviews with
witnesses of the Gibraltar killings/executions, had 'declined to the point
of institutionalised hysteria'.

Mrs Thatcher's objective, we learned, is to try and create a climate of
opinion which will not tolerate the media overstepping certain bounds.
Well and good. It is a permanent desire of government to intimidate the
press and broadcasting (oh, all right, the media) whenever possible:
'Broadcasters and newspapers will be told that they operate within society and are obliged to uphold its institutions, notably legal proceedings.'
Fine. Go to it. There are already elaborate and oppressive laws of contempt. On this occasion, they were not infringed. Make them tighter.
Where the Government goes terribly wrong is in supposing that it can
use the Gibraltar killings for this purpose.

'Public opinion in this country does not give a button about whether
the SAS tried to arrest or warn three IRA terrorists before shooting them
down like dogs,' announced Sir Peregrine at the beginning of his rumina-
tion. Such a statement may ignore the diversity of public opinion, but is
borne out by opinion polls as well as by the general tenor of letters
received by the *Daily Telegraph*, and of conversations overheard in public
houses up and down the country. So far so good. Insofar as public opinion
exists, we might reasonably assume that it supports the wholesale shoot-

ing of IRA suspects out of hand. It is only when the Government plans to use this sentiment to whip television and the press, inevitably making sworn enemies of them both in the process, that I start trembling for my tax reductions: and only then that the spectre of a new Hattersley Terror looms.

Sir Peregrine goes on to argue that the SAS initiative may have been technically illegal, not to say criminal, but since both government and public opinion (not to mention high-principled thinkers like Worsthorne and Paul Johnson) support it, the time has surely come to change the law and make it perfectly legal for the army and security services to gun down suspected terrorists and other political wrong-doers. All this is at least arguable; at any rate, it is not my intention to dispute it on this occasion.

What it ignores is the rhetoric employed by Mrs Thatcher and Sir Geoffrey Howe to use this somewhat murky episode as an opportunity to stifle the media. Their talk is all of upholding the rule of law. Of course, it is balderdash. There is no law forbidding comment or speculation on an inquest to be held at some unspecified date in Gibraltar. The chances of a juryman in Gibraltar having seen a television broadcast on LWT or Ulster Television are in any case minute. So far as the Gibraltar episode is concerned, it would appear that the offending media are far more concerned to uphold the rule of law than is the Government. There was no similar complaint by Sir Geoffrey or Mrs Thatcher about the vicious smear campaign conducted by some newspapers against a key witness, Mrs Carmen Proetta, denounced by the *Sun* as 'The Tart of Gib', who claims she saw two unarmed men and a woman gunned down as they tried to surrender.

Public opinion might be prepared to let the Government get away with murder, under the circumstances, particularly if it is confused by rumours of a non-existent device in the terrorists' possession capable of exploding a non-existent bomb from many miles away. Certainly the media, well-disposed towards the Government and grateful for its tax cuts, would be prepared to play along for the most part. But everything depends on how the Government's case is presented by the media. A slight difference of emphasis in presentation and public opinion would quite simply *not* be prepared to condone the idea of unarmed civilians being shot down like dogs while they were concerned only to surrender. Neither Mrs Thatcher nor Sir Geoffrey Howe is popular enough to be entrusted with this degree of discretion.

The contradiction in their approach – between upholding the rule of 'law' against the media and ostentatiously flouting the rule of law in Gibraltar – is unimportant compared to the use which the media can make of this contradiction once it is sufficiently stirred. There is already an unease which is not confined to dedicated pilgerists, progressives and IRA sympathisers in the media.

By their actions to date, Mrs Thatcher and Sir Geoffrey Howe have already ensured that the Gibraltar cover-up will be subjected to a greater degree of hostile scrutiny than would have been the case. Only thugs like Bernard Ingham, used to handling the terrified poodles of the Parliamentary lobby, can suppose that press and media are capable of being publicly intimidated and called to heel. If they push their luck to use the Gibraltar cover-up as an excuse for disciplining the media, it will explode in their faces much more effectively than any IRA bomb yet sent by post.

14 May 1988

NON!

The Spectator *Leader*

So uninterested are the British in the politics of the EEC that few of us understood Mrs Thatcher's speech in Bruges for what it in part was – her first shot in the campaign for the elections to the European Parliament. The Prime Minister may not care much for the assembly in Strasburg, but she cares quite passionately about victory for her party in any contest. This accounts for the tough tone of the speech and particularly for the way in which it was presented to the press. She was said to have 'roughed up' the EEC, something which the British electorate likes.

Mrs Thatcher obviously hopes that the campaign began in Bruges will succeed in getting Tories of all descriptions to turn out for the European elections. Those suspicious of the Common Market will be reassured by her insistence on continuing national independence. Pro-marketeers will be able to find a commitment to staying in the EEC. She has covered the Tory flank. The strictest anti-marketeers (and the bored majority) may abstain. They will not vote Labour.

As a piece of electioneering, then, Mrs Thatcher's continental performance was skilful and unexceptionable. Why did so many people take exception to it? The Foreign Secretary, Sir Geoffrey Howe, was furious, as were the Euro-chancelleries.

One detects in the reaction the anger of an official class which had congratulated itself too early on having won round an awkward customer.

For years Mrs Thatcher employed an almost rhetorical device in her arguments with the EEC. Work towards a genuine common market, she said, and we shall raise fewer objections to your spending. Over the past two years, the Single Market of 1992 seemed to convince her that she was getting her way. Lord Young stuck lots of businessmen on posters to talk about it. Lord Cockfield frantically harmonised. Brussels began to believe that Mrs Thatcher would come quietly.

Just in time, however, she noticed the political implications of the reforms for which, in a rather vague way, she had been calling. M. Jacques Delors incautiously explained how he wanted to run virtually everything. Suddenly it seemed that the sort of control that she likes – frontier, immigration, her own – would disappear and the sort she hates – labour law, health and safety, exchange – would be imposed. The breaking down of barriers seemed to involve the erection of a fence of new regulations, regulations, what is more, that she could not alter.

So Mrs Thatcher is asking the EEC the question which it most dislikes: What do you mean by what you say? 'Europeans' will always deny, for instance, that they want a United States of Europe, and yet their ideas for the central direction of affairs from Brussels and the enlarging of the power of the European Parliament tend towards just such a conclusion. They always say how much they respect the diversity of European experience and culture, but never explain how that diversity could not be diminished by the downgrading of existing national institutions, the standardisation of weights and measures, the uniformity of rules. They proclaim their belief in free trade, yet support a ludicrous subsidy of agriculture, an extravagant regional policy and the creation of an EEC trade bloc that would be protection on a colossal scale.

And in asking these questions Mrs Thatcher was right to invite criticism of her tone. For it is the tone – evasive, generalising, vague – which is so maddening in so much discussion of the EEC. If the Prime Minister seeks to play the role of de Gaulle she is right to adopt his most successful method – a stiff-necked awkwardness that drives everyone else nearly to despair. Her tone should be insistent, strident, tiresome, which, after all, is the sort of tone she is best at.

Mrs Thatcher's speech at Bruges made clear the limits of her European ideal. She affirmed her belief in the unity of European civilisation, but rejected the idea of a community of political aspiration comparable to that of the United States. She talked of the 'Atlantic Community', not the EEC, as 'our noblest inheritance and our greatest strength'. She emphasised the need for economic liberty rather than the dissolution of the independent, sovereign state. All these are beliefs which are widely shared in Britain and it is interesting that many on the Continent should object to them. It will also be interesting to see whether Mrs Thatcher will be as firm in making practical British decisions about the EEC on the basis of these beliefs as she is in stating them in general terms. The story until now has been of stirring declarations, followed by actual results distressingly satisfactory to Brussels.

1 October 1988

DIARY

Jennifer Paterson

There is a very big threat on the horizon; in fact it is already here, lurking about, ready to pounce on any of us at any moment. Far worse than all the nanny-state warnings about meat, butter, all fats and anything delicious including alcohol being the way to dusty death, this is the real McCoy and we must all kick up a hell of a fuss with our MPs so that they will harry the Ministry of Ag. and Fish. It is the terrifying threat and actuality of salmonella poisoning coming from the consumption of any egg yolk that has not been cooked through and through like a hard-boiled egg. You may remember a large amount of people were felled at the House of Lords after a summer party which had included mayonnaise and mousses in the menu. Luckily everyone recovered after a very nasty bout of the illness, but if it is contracted by the very young or very old or already sick the poisoning can result in death, and as the versatile and much loved egg has always been a nutritious food for all these categories someone in authority should make some definite statement. Apparently the disease is endemic to large amounts of laying hens, especially those brought up in batteries, but no one seems to be sure where it has come from or why. Perhaps it is another sinister ailment produced from refuse, like the seals with their new distemper. It may be in the food they eat. The large producers are very worried, as well they might be. It will be farewell to all the hollandaise, béarnaise, mayonnaise sauces, all soufflés and chocolate mousses and all the other mousses. There is the dreadful thought we may all have to revert to powdered egg as in wartime. We used to make mayonnaise in the war with dried egg and liquid paraffin: it must have been horrendous but we thought it brilliant and certainly better than salmonella. So Ag. and Fish, what have you to say? I am still eating eggs, but for how long?

5 November 1988

'THE JEWEL IN THE CROWN OF INDIA'

Richard West

Bradford

There have been two newspaper photographs in the last 20 years which instantly took on an epoch-making significance. The first, showing the strikers at prayer in front of the Lenin shipyard in Gdansk, portended what we are seeing now throughout Eastern Europe and even the Soviet Union itself: the rapid decay of communism. The second photograph, of a Muslim burning Salman Rushdie's *Satanic Verses*, here in Bradford, seemed to illustrate the end of the Sixties era, what used to be called the Permissive Society, the liberal, free-thinking, sexually tolerant, multi-racial ethos preached to us over the years by the BBC, the *Guardian* and the *Observer*, the Church of England bishops, the Arts Council, the British Council and most of our authors, notably Salman Rushdie.

The photograph had a special poignancy because it was taken in Bradford, the home town of an author, Michael Wharton, who has for the last 30 years, in the *Daily Telegraph*'s 'Peter Simple' column, poured scorn and ridicule on the permissive ethic. The book was burned in the Town Hall Square, in front of what Wharton has called 'the vast smoke-blackened building with its bell-booming towers piercing the rainy skies and indeed, as some believed, actually precipitating rain'. The Town Hall was cleaned, 'when, not long ago, the beautiful smoke-blackened heart of Bradford was torn out to make way for cheap, cardboard skyscrapers'. The Muslim leader, shown burning the book, has more than a passing resemblance in spite of his colour to Wharton's illustrious Alderman Foodbotham, 'the 25-stone, crag-visaged, grim-booted, iron-watch-chained perpetual chairman of the Bradford City Tramways and Fine Arts Committee, and for many years Lord Mayor'.

My first response to that picture, before the Ayatollah had issued his blood-curdling threats, was pure and simple laughter. And I am glad to

find that some of the whites in Bradford saw the joke. 'I'd never heard of
the Rushdie fellow, nor had anyone else I know,' I was told by a man in a
pub near to the Town Hall. 'When I heard them creating, I thought to
myself it was just the Pakis playing silly buggers again. Then I looked at
the papers next day and found that Bradford was famous.' His amusement, and that of the other Bradford whites that I met, was mixed with a
bitter feeling of *Schadenfreude*. For 30 years now, Bradford has been, with
Birmingham, the city with far the highest number of immigrants, most of
them Muslims from Pakistan. Bradford has been the butt of innumerable
jokes: 'the capital of Pakistan', 'City of Mills and Minarets', 'On Ilkley
Moor baht turban . . .' It also had to endure the strictures and bullying
of the race relations industry, chiding the whites of Bradford for not
making the immigrants more welcome. The anger of whites in Bradford
came to a climax when some of the Muslims, backed by the left-wing
whites on the Council, sought and obtained the resignation of one of the
city's headmasters, Ray Honeyford, who had said in print that English
children were not getting a proper education in schools where Pakistanis
formed the majority.

In the Manningham district, where I am staying, the races are just as
separate as they were in the Fifties, when immigrants started to come
here in thousands. Many Pakistanis have little or no English. Asian girls
rarely form a romantic attachment to young white men. The whites and
browns are friendly enough on the surface, addressing each other as 'luv',
but they tend to stick with their own kind. The Pakistanis share with the
Yorkshire people a fierce love of cricket, but tend to support their own
side in test matches or matches against Yorkshire.

The one feature of Asian culture that Yorkshire people have taken to
with enjoyment is food. The whites have discovered that hot curry, rice
and chapattis soak up beer. At a very fine pub called The Ram's Revenge,
one of the customers told me where I could find just past the Alhambra
three good curry houses. He then showed me the *New Tyke Taverner* – a
Bradford and district real ale journal, which every month has an article
on an eating house, 'Curry Corner'.

One of the customers at another good pub, The Shoulder of Mutton,
has geared most of his social life to the curry house: 'I'll have five or six
pints of Smith's and maybe a couple of Theakston's and then I go off to a
curry house for a chicken vindaloo, rice and maybe six chapattis. I drink a
bottle of wine with the meal and then afterwards I get stuck into the
optics of whisky. They know when to put me into a taxi and home. My
wife likes her curry too and she knows now not to cook for me when I'm
out on the beer. I say to her, "Look luv, don't put nowt in t'oven till you've
seen the bloodshots of my eyes." I make my own beer at home and I

started to learn how to make curries. I got three of those Asian cookbooks but it seems they don't know how to make curry the way we like it in Yorkshire. Not hot enough. I think the English and Dutch invented curry.'

The Rushdie affair has given a great immediacy to Dervla Murphy's excellent *Tales from Two Cities*, a study of immigrant life in Bradford and Birmingham (Penguin). She knows the region of Kashmir from which most of the Bradford Pakistanis come. She understands their difficulties in coping with life in Bradford. She likes, but does not understand so well, the white people of Bradford. She tends to accept at their face value the whining complaints that the troubles of Yorkshire are all to be blamed on Thatcherism and cuts, rather than on the folly of politicians, Tory as well as socialist, during the previous three decades.

She says that there is no proof that white children do badly in largely immigrant schools, yet she herself relates that in one of these schools there were whites from 14 to 16 who could not read or write. She also concludes that some of the articles written by Honeyford 'indicated someone whose ethnocentricity operates unrecognised by himself (and many others) and influences many of his decisions and reactions'.

Although the great Alderman Foodbotham would not have 'taken cognisance' of a word such as ethnocentricity, he would have approved of the thing in himself and his fellow Yorkshiremen, perhaps the most ethnocentric people in these islands. The Bradford author J. B. Priestley carried his ethnocentricity to the point of what is now called 'racism', in his *English Journey*, published in 1936. He described Miss Murphy's countrymen in terms that would now have him hauled up before the Race Relations Board. Priestley thought of himself as a man of the Left and progressive opinions. He expressed the view, which was just as strong in the Labour Party as with Tories, that England should keep out immigrants.

The root of the present trouble lies in the hasty and catastrophic granting of independence to India as two, and eventually three, separate states. As part of a deal to make this acceptable to the Indian and Pakistani politicians, the British agreed that citizens of the Commonwealth should have the right to settle in Britain, a right which, incidentally, they did not reciprocate.

Soon British businesses were recruiting cheap labour to work in London Transport, the Midlands iron foundries, and Bradford woolmills. It is significant that the first politician to warn against immigration, Enoch Powell, also said that the Asians, not the West Indians, would prove the least adaptable, bringing with them political and religious differences. He said this from his own knowledge of India.

The British politicians who let in the immigrants then made Britain an unacceptable home to them. The first Pakistanis coming to Bradford during the 1950s found a society much like that they had left at home. The schools provided a basic education. A rigorous penal code made Bradford a safe place for women and children to live in without fear. There was nothing in books, newspapers, the radio or television that might offend anyone's moral or religious sensitivities. The English laws on divorce, homosexuality and abortion gave support to the family, which is the basis of Asian society. The permissive revolution during the 1960s was even more shattering to the Asians than to the old-fashioned English. Divorce and illegitimacy are rampant. Sex crimes and, allegedly, child abuse are epidemic in Yorkshire. This once law-abiding county produced the Yorkshire Ripper, the Black Panther and the Bradford Rapist. Daily newspapers such as the *Sun* provide a diet of crude pornography that 30 years ago could not be published even in books. People from countries like Pakistan, where even a kiss cannot be shown on film, have to bring up children with access to television full-frontal nudity.

A Bradford man who dislikes the Asians was furious at their wanting to burn Rushdie's book. 'After all it's a free country, isn't it? We've always been free to slag off our own religion, so why shouldn't we slag off theirs? It was only that silly old cow Mary Whitehouse who wanted to have a blasphemy law.' This man, who was in his thirties, was young enough to believe that there was, always, a right to 'slag off' religion, even in such repulsive ways as the homosexual poem on Christ, against which Mrs Whitehouse campaigns. Of course it was not always so. There was a time when even the Church of England bishops did not approve of blasphemy. And the British, of all people, knew that one should not insult the religion of others. The most ignorant Tommy in India had to respect the Hindu and Muslim customs, especially concerning food.

And this brings us back to Salman Rushdie. About six years ago, Mr Rushdie advanced the view that Britain had brought in immigrants from the Indian sub-continent in order to have a servile class on which to vent feelings of racial superiority. Two years later, he condemned the television series *The Jewel in the Crown*. It expressed nostalgia not for a lost India but for a lost England.

Nobody has expressed this better than Nirad Chaudhuri, the wise old Bengali who has set out to smash 'the myth that the decision to leave India was an act of wise and far-seeing statesmanship, ... that it replaced an evil imperial system with a free association of nations, and that it opened an era of sincere and real Indo-British friendship'. He calls the English decadent. In his latest book, *Thy Hand, Great Anarch!*, Chaudhuri says that even he, in 1947, had not predicted that as a result of independence millions of people would leave the three secession states to live in England, making her 'the Jewel in the Crown of India'.

4 March 1989

Chapter 3
RICH AND POOR

JOB HUNTING IN SOUTH WALES

Gerda Cohen

It's market day in Llanelli, clucking with damp cosy shoppers, the rain falling calmly on a Grecian Methodist Temple, a rinsed Tabernacle and a drowned rugby pitch. 'Bound to clear up soon.' The people are invincibly cheerful. Bound to save Duport Works, somehow. Privately-owned Duport have sold out to British Steel and declared closure of their plant at Llanelli. 'Duport's been here since 1907,' said one of the steelmen tramping out of the works gate, 'We shall put up a fight.' I had expected steelmen to be titans; not these short, blobby men with bad teeth and open, trusting faces. 'You can blame BSC and the bloody government for putting us out of business.' The company had just installed electric arc furnaces at a cost of £30 million to produce engineering steel from scrap iron. 'Funny notion, really; there's too much capacity anyhow.' Their voices wander up and down like the little hills of Carmarthen. 'I feel bitter,' one said, 'they let us down . . .'

In the town centre whole streets have been torn out and replaced by a pedestrian grid, formica forever, soaked litter and brave new shrubs among the chain-stores. 'You've no idea what an *improvement*,' hum the couple who share my café table. 'The town is so much nicer, it might be . . . Brighton!' 'Don't exaggerate, my dear, you never seen Brighton.' They're quite old, steaming away in Welsh tweed, feet close under the table. 'Enjoying it now?' They watch me try a bun like a kerb-stone, washed down by spoon-bending tea. 'Best tea in the world, that.' Past the bundled-up wives and the Penclawdd cockle stall, Army Careers have opened a smart new office. Dummy officers lean in the entrance, tight-lipped. Six lads are waiting inside, all with short hair-cuts and no O Levels. 'Truth is we're inundated,' the recruiting Sergeant told me, 'I've been sent here from Yorkshire to help out.'

Across the road Mr Edwards, Butcher, grieved over the departing lads. 'What a time to leave,' he said, his eye switching from boys to prime Welsh lamb. 'Llanelli is improving fast, never been better.' He arranged some petite Welsh legs in the window. 'We've got a full-back, you probably heard of him, Quinnel, most impressive. Bridgend had better watch out. Llanelli is on the up.'

      •   •   •

Swansea's slate roofs are sleek with wet; its soaked dog-biscuit chapels have been given over to bingo; and the defunct South Dock has been turned into an Industrial Museum. There are just two people trailing round the Museum, one young man, one old. Glyn Banks from Gorseinon, glad of a chat, said he took redundancy at 55. He made it sound like a strange and wonderful seaside resort, 'Rhedundd-on-Sea'. 'I'm getting used to Rhedundd-on-Sea, never thought I would.' Shyly he beckoned me over to a photographic display of people making tin-plate. 'That's me in thin vest and clogs, working in the Hot Mill.'

The faces stare out – blank, Thirties, thin and moustachioed. 'They're all dead', he said, letting out a treble laugh. 'I'm tee tee, never touch drink.' Glyn Banks explained that in Hot Mill, until modernisation, the intense heat of molten metal drove the workers to quench their thirst during the dinner-break. 'Dangerous', he said solemnly. We both gazed at the exhibits, brand-new machinery embalmed in oil. 'My grandson, now, lost his job at Velindre.' British Steel have made 1,200 redundant at their modern tin-plate works north of Swansea. 'Tins are old-fashioned,' said Glyn, as he traipsed over to the motor-bike display, 'peas is frozen. That's progress . . .'

British motor-bikes are lined up in the Museum ready to zoom across the carpet, and a young fellow inspected them, arms akimbo. He had a bright scornful smile and hair like anthracite, and was wearing a pink shirt bulging with rugby muscle. His name was Byron Price and he had no patience with his countrymen. 'Oh us Welsh – we're an English inven-tion.' Before I could get a word in, he urged me to go to the window. There was empty dockland out there, sodden soot, and a couple of tracked exca-vators, scooping out black slime from the South Dock bed. 'Swansea Marina,' he exclaimed with a grin, 'if the cash holds out. Typical Swansea, voting for a Marina when you can't afford a yacht!' Byron had been earning £60 a week as a factory cleaner until the firm went on short-time. 'I'd have had to move anyway,' he said. 'Father won't let me stay home. I'm a graduate, see, biology First Class at Cardiff. A whole crowd of us graduated last year, no jobs.' So what did they do? 'Went to a kibbutz,' he said, smiling hard, 'they hated it after a month.' Byron pouted, admir-ing his anthracite hair in the window. 'There's no hope for me here. It's London, join the London Welsh. Not a bad team.' He grinned. 'I hate bloody London.' Off he loped into the sloshing rain, tall and jaunty, alone.

It was St David's Day yesterday, and the bank clerks at NatWest were blushing in steeple hats and aprons whiter than best emulsion. The *Western Mail* mentions that of the 160,000 unemployed in Wales, half are under 25. It doesn't rate a headline. There are two Jobcentres in

Swansea, one for manual and one for clerical workers, and both as warm as a tumble-drier. People stand around, looking cheerful, flicking ash on to the new carpet. Men chat in snug armchairs, chain-smoking Embassy cigarettes. At first glance there seem to be jobs in plenty. But analysis proves otherwise. 'Star Job of the Week' proclaims a big board, 'Traffic Warden in London'. Or you are invited to join the Metropolitan Police, if you are over five foot six. This amused two jeering skinheads, their hands thrust in dirty jeans. 'You're a bloody dwarf.' 'You're a f—— midget.' No notice is taken by the girls, safe behind the Enquiry Desk. One is doe-eyed, a faraway miss. You can scent her 'Intimate by Revlon' drift over the cigarette smoke along with her dreamy look. 'Zimbabwe . . .' asked a man at the Enquiries, 'where would that be now?'

A special board announced that South Africa and Zimbabwe required contract electricians, *urgently*. 'Well I dunno about South Africa,' muttered the mild man. 'All them blacks.' He winked at me cautiously. 'But my earnings-related run out soon and my wife has got bad nerves.' He lit a stub. The girl came back to say that Zimbabwe was the correct name for Rhodesia. 'Fancy,' he said, laughing. 'Sounded a Welsh place to me.' A gentle titter ran round the Jobcentre. 'Anyway,' she told him kindly as he trotted out, 'you're over the age limit, over 35.' Leaflets lay on the wet pavement, offering Jobseeker tickets on South Wales bus routes.

At Swansea Leisure Centre, this rainy afternoon, the unemployed can avail themselves of free gym and a swim to follow. So do they? I wander into the wonderful garish Leisure Centre, its pool bobbing with livid green children, its glass dome covered with green and yellow plastic cow-

pats. Welsh notices abound; it could be Patagonia. 'Ni chaniater esgidiau bob dydd,' I read, as I wade into sub-tropical Swansea. 'Means you mustn't swim in your shoes,' gurgled someone coming out of a dive. Only three males in the water; the rest are recumbent with brown seaweed moustaches, talking their heads off on the make-believe beach. 'You from London? You got a Leisure Centre good as this?'

I readily admit that we haven't, but ask about the recession. Can people afford to use it? They tell me that Berwyn Price – 'the Olympic hurdler' – has introduced free recreation for the unemployed, despite doubt from the City Council. 'Oh they're *mean*, Swansea,' roars a burly fellow with ginger fuzz down to his navel. 'They charge 30p for swimming and 10p for spectating. The *cheek!*' All agreed, spectating should be gratis. 'We're from Aberafan, out of work,' said one. British Steel at Port Talbot had laid off 900 men – 'Oh months ago, we're living off our fat.' 'You are, Williams!' said another, and they piled into a scrummage. Blubbery, friendly, sad South Wales.

21 March 1981

THE OPPORTUNITY

John Stewart Collis

John Balfour aged 22, after two years' employment at an estate agent in the town of Westforth, received notice that his services were no longer required. In short, he was declared redundant.

Redundant. There's a word for you, thought Balfour. What's it really mean? He looked it up in the dictionary, and was struck with the word 'superfluous'. That's not me, he considered, I'm not superfluous. But he was 'unemployed'. Another word to conjure with. What did it mean? That he was not working, or 'out of work'. He decided to look up 'work' also in the dictionary and see what it meant exactly, and he was interested in the opening definitions – 'Application of effort to a purpose, force in action, doing something . . .' Am I incapable of doing something? he asked himself. No; that's not me either.

But he was now reckoned as 'one of the unemployed', a condition that was still regarded with a certain disdain not unmingled with pity. However, John Balfour was not in the least put out by this. He was in the highest spirits. He saw a great opportunity opening before him. If he was regarded as a sad object by society, that was not the attitude of the State. Far from frowning on his situation the State encouraged and even promoted it and paid him quite a handsome fee for not being employed. As an unmarried man he regarded himself as well off: in fact he had attained the status of a man of leisure. Here was his opportunity.

He had not done well at school, for he was not clever in the appropriate manner. Schooling had seemed to him a curious business. A man, called a schoolmaster, got hold of a pump, fixed it to his head, and pumped all sorts of facts into it – most of which were left to rot there, since they were not correlated. At one stage he had wanted to ask questions about things he wished to know, but he found that he was required to answer questions about things he did not want to know. He had heard of an eccentric Russian teacher of children, called Tolstoy, who had approved of a remark given by a mother, in a Russian comedy, complaining about the geography lessons – 'Why teach my son all the countries, the coachman will drive him where he may have to go?' Yes indeed, Tolstoy had declared, that was well said: 'What need was there for me to know where the river and town of Barcelona are situated, when for 23 years I have not once had occasion to use that knowledge?' John Balfour took the point; but such nonsense was soon knocked out of him and he had surrendered to the pumping system without protest, and had left school with some information but no comprehension of Knowledge.

Now came his opportunity: for he was not fundamentally a stupid man. He was aware that there was such an activity as real solid reading, that there was such a person as a reader, an artist in reading. The conditions at home with his parents, and a brother and sister, made privacy impossible, and he had put no effort into a serious attempt to read properly. Since in recent years illiteracy had made such rapid strides, his parents' house had no books (nor even any bookshelves) – for it was understood that radio and television could painlessly take their place.

Balfour could now put this matter right, and try himself out. Westforth was one of the ugliest towns in England, but it happened to possess a remarkably good library: that is to say it had that one little bit of actual communism which is only to be found outside the communistic regimes.

John Balfour entered the library. He was at first confronted with a room devoted to newspapers, weeklies and magazines, and to the depressing sight of listless men turning over the pages in a kind of stupor. But adjacent to this room was another which was devoted to books. From a shelf marked Literature he took down a volume. By good chance (for

luck favours the brave) it was a book by Quiller-Couch on various writers. He read a chapter on Thomas Hardy's *Jude the Obscure*. He asked the
librarian if that novel was on the shelves, and after he had filled in the
necessary form for book-vouchers, he was given it. The room was quite
spacious, and he found a chair in a corner where he could read in perfect
peace. The story gripped him at once, and he read on with growing excitement until the library was due to close – which seemed to come terribly
soon, for time had passed so quickly. He took the book home with him
without much intention of reading it there. Next day, and every day, he
resumed his place in the same seat in the library. He revelled in Jude, he
suffered with Jude. What a tragedy! But like all true tragedy its effect was
exhilarating. Jude had failed – but he would not fail.

After this he read more books by Hardy, then Dickens, then Charlotte
Brontë – evidently there was no end to this delirious joy. He had made the
discovery which comes to all who choose to educate themselves – that
one thing leads to another, one book to another, one subject to another.
He found himself launched into the classics.

The weeks passed as he sat entranced, while he gave himself up to this
new experience. He had not only discovered literature, he had discovered
in himself the faculty of imagination, and that imagination was a *tool*, it
was a key with which he could open doors, and he found that books were
doors leading into realms of excitement and beauty and alarm which he
could make his own. It soon occurred to him that literature was not con-

*'Will you stop saying that what goes up
must come down!'*

fined to story-telling. How about History? That should not be beyond him. He found H. G. Wells's *History of the World* (not the large *Outline*) and saw that it was the very thing he needed, a bird's-eye view of the whole. He decided to read one chapter a day.

He looked across, rather apprehensively, at the shelves marked Science, and, under A, took down a book on Archaeology. Heavens! – here were magicians in another guise: men who dug into the earth to excavate artefacts by which they could reconstruct cities lost in the jungle or buried in the desert; or, peering into dungeoned caverns, came upon relics of forgotten kings. He looked under the head of Astrophysics, and found ministers of another mystery, kings of infinite space who could interpret the radiations from the stars as if reading in a book! He looked up Geology and found the savants saying that fields are fallen mountains and mountains the seeds of future continents. He looked up Physics and was told that everything was chiefly composed of holes. Steady! he said to himself. Keep calm. Sort these things out quietly bit by bit. I have time in hand. Never need I use the word 'pastime' again, no thought of 'passing the time', I can never have enough of it to grasp these things which are as fantastic as any of the fantasies, as fabulous as the fables.

The Public Library of Westforth became the locus of a strange phenomenon. Throughout the day people came in and out; few stayed for long; many were stupefied in the torpor of a despairing lassitude. But in his corner sat John Balfour, quietly, with intense concentration, pursuing his way. He was 'gainfully employed' – in the use of that instrument which separates mankind from the animals, that birthright which if wrongfully used makes him lower than any of the creatures, if rightly raises him high above them. All unknowing, he was a model of that profound philosophy which holds that it is Spirit that *creates our condition*; it is Spirit that overcomes the world.

3 October 1981

THINK OF A NUMBER

Christopher Fildes

Those of us who can remember every number except the one we want – school boot-locker number, yes; S. G. Warburg's old telephone number, yes; Warburg's new number, not a hope – have found a friend at the

National Westminster Bank. The NatWest, like its competitors, hands out plastic cards which, tactfully handled, will cause the bank's cash-dispensing machines to dispense cash. But the machine will need to know your personal number, so as to stop thieves or pickpockets from using your card, and the bank urges you not to write the number down, for the same reason. So you are supposed to memorise it, and then forget it. All right, say NatWest, think of a number you can remember, and tell us what it is, and we'll give you that one. So NatWest, which is investing in electronic equipment at the rate of £120 million a year, has solved its most intractable problem – programming people to use it.

13 April 1985

DIARY

John Osborne

Those who were dismayed at the demise of the Flavour of the Week engagement photograph in *Country Life* were not reassured by its return when it was represented by Miss Kim Nevill. She was tasty enough, very, very, but her address was 47 Leigh Road, Westbury, and she was to be married to Mr Mark Young of 115 *Station Road*, also in Westbury. Could this aberration be what Mrs Thatcher meant by her own vision of a classless society? Might we look forward to the announced nuptials of Tracey, daughter of Cllr Sid and Mrs Wellfair of Bishop Boateng House, SE1? However, the following week's even fruitier flavour was the daughter of a neighbour. At the wedding, Brigade and Old Etonian ties were hanging from trees and I was the only guest in a lounge suit. High-rise Normans are not yet phoning for the fish-knives for Sharon's do at the Leisure Centre. We blessed reactionaries may breathe again.

3 August 1985

PRESENTS FROM THE UPPER CLASS
Simon Blow

Struggling through a crowded London department store the other day set me thinking about the attitudes of those who give. How much, for instance, do people really want to spend on each other at this Christian festival? Do the upper classes give more than the lower classes, or is it vice versa? I noticed husbands laden with large and bulging bags, and housewives equally laden and pushing babies. They were lower class people who looked careworn but determined. Then I heard a brisk voice chirp at a counter, 'My dear, too wonderful. Two shirts and frightfully cheap.' At this the lady turned with her companion, snapped her crocodile handbag shut, clasped the shirts, and dived back through jostling crowds.

The voice of this lady was unmistakably upper class. She was dressed in a brown check suit and wore dark brown patent leather high heels. I imagined that she would bus back to Knightsbridge where she stayed, but that soon she would be into her Volvo and back at her place – or might it not be 'seat'? – in the country. There she could heave a sigh of relief that her Christmas shopping had been satisfactorily and – more important – economically done. Watching her, confirmed for me a long-felt belief: that the upper classes do not like spending money. In fact 'far too expensive' and 'a dreadful waste of money' are phrases seldom off their lips. Perhaps it is a sense of economy that dates back to Victorian days, when the shadows of a profligate Regency still had not died away. But how well I recall the Christmas presents from my own rich and landed relations when an adolescent in the early 1960s. I remember nothing but socks, and ties, and hankies – and the £1 given by a particularly rich uncle, with the message that he hoped I would find something useful to do with it.

So, set against their land and other possessions, it must be said that the upper classes give far less by comparison with those further down the social scale. For the Christmas bags of the less well-off that I noticed in the department store were filled to swelling with gifts. And yet this seasonal upper-class thrift is not exactly meanness; it is a fear on the part of the rich member of a family that should he stand with all his wealth revealed, he will never see the end of begging relations. And he is probably right, for he knows that all that protects him from the cold outside is the accident of primogeniture. And at Christmas, surrounded by younger brothers, sisters and impoverished cousins, it is imperative that not a chink in the armour be seen. Thus these little Christmas suggestions of affection which help to keep up the protective wall. And though the relations may be silenced, they are certainly not deceived. The late John Fox-Strangeways, brother to the last Earl of Ilchester, was always peculiarly affected by the younger son, out-in-the-cold condition. He would be heard to suddenly boom across the floors of clubs in St James's: 'I'm a nobleman, I'm a nobleman.' This was soon followed by, 'I need a living, a living. My brother's got plenty, why doesn't he give me one?'

But a seemingly sound gesture of generosity is the invitation to relations or stray friends to stay at the family seat for Christmas or the New Year. Note that it is never Christmas *and* the New Year, for that would be too long. Yet at least for a few days the landless relations and other 'lame ducks' – as country house hostesses have been known to refer to their poorer friends – may enjoy a plentiful supply of food and wine, while possibly deluding themselves that their host would make them welcome forever. This is not the case. By Boxing Day the host is to be found staring hard at the lowering grey skies, fearing a heavy fall of snow. These people must be got off his hands before the roads are blocked; all the time he smiles nervously at them to indicate quite clearly that their stay is nearly up. They must now forget the large estate, the evening duck shoot, or childhood memories of frolics in haystacks and barns with more privileged cousins. They must return to their metropolitan dwellings or wherever, thankful for the brief glimpse they have had of those once-solid roots from which, now, beyond memory and blood, it is plain they are severed forever. And this, too, is intended as a present.

Of course, we must remember that the upper classes do not like showing off. Vulgar displays of wealth are unsettling to them. Whereas a working-class family who have made good may throw their cash around in every direction, for an upper-class family this would be unthinkable. And this reserve also influences their choice of gifts at Christmas time. There is nothing indiscreet about a half-dozen handkerchiefs, a silk tie, or a book. But the gift of a cocktail cabinet would be considered not only unnecessary, but distinctly odd. And then there is that upper-class fear of embarrassment. To give a present which the receiver cannot return in kind could prove distressing. So did my uncle think when he gave me the annual £1 that more would either have embarrassed or distressed me? I have to say now that it would not, but the upper-class rules of giving and taking are set, and you do not quibble or question. To do so would be to display signs of a dreadful waywardness of character.

And so, in the aftermath of the upper-class Christmas must come the Thank You letters. Oh, the memory of those letters. 'Darling, have you written to Uncle Bill? You must write at once', my mother would say, in tones not unlike those of the poor boy's mother in *Kind Hearts and Coronets* – a tale ever dear to this writer's heart. Into those letters had to go an emphasis of feeling as if you had been given a farm, a pair of Purdey guns, or a cool £5,000. 'Dear Uncle Bill and Aunt Mary. Thank you so very much for the lovely Christmas. The food was delicious and I did like all that thick cream. And thank you also for the wonderful socks. I know they will be very useful. It was so very kind of you . . .' 'Dear Uncle Edward. Thank you so much for the £1, which I will take great care of and not spend foolishly . . .'

One result of receiving over many years so many tactfully understated presents has been to make me doubt ever afterwards the sincerity of my own Thank You letters. But whether this is a fault in the system or signs that I was born with a waywardness of character, is not for me to judge.

21/28 December 1985

THE NEW CLUB OF RICH YOUNG MEN

Nicholas Coleridge

A couple of months ago I was billeted with strangers for a country dance. A stockbroker friend had been placed in the same houseparty, and he suggested we drive down to Dorset together in his new company BMW. Our destination was an old rectory near Sherborne and we were soon touching 110 mph on the A30. 'No need to contribute to the petrol,' said my friend as he filled the tank courtesy of Barclaycard Visa. 'It's company plastic.' There is nothing like fast motoring for turning the conversation to money, especially when it's a stockbroker behind the wheel, and the dual carriageway made him doubly confiding. 'I got another bonus last week,' he said. 'Third month running. So I should make £127,000 this year all in.' My stockbroker friend is 28.

Eventually we found the old rectory, a pretty stone house on the edge of a village. Outside on the gravel drive were parked three shiny sports cars and an ancient Morris Traveller. This, it emerged, belonged to our host, a genial country solicitor. The sports cars belonged to a variety of leading stock and commodity brokers, on permanent loan to our fellow guests, who could already be found in the drawing-room warming their designer-trousered bottoms in front of the one-bar electric fire.

Our host and hostess were generous and thoughtful. But they were rather badly off. The attic bedrooms of the old rectory were threadbare and chilly, and the brand new bottles of whisky and gin indicated that they did not normally keep spirits in the house. The dinner, while perfectly wholesome, did not feature inflationary out-of-season vegetables, which are the best you can hope for in London restaurants. The wine was filthy. My fellow guests, it must be stressed, were very polite. They were neither patronising nor disdainful of the hospitality. Nevertheless, as dinner progressed, their conversation revealed a host of assumptions about life and money, which clearly bewildered the genial country solicitor.

'I've just taken a ten-per-cent stake in a wine bar off Marloes Road,' said one. 'It's a spin-off from an Italian restaurant I was involved with in Olympia. I made my investment back on that in eight months.'

'I've arranged to be paid partly in deutschemarks,' said another, 'through our office in Bonn. It's more tax efficient for the German stockmarket.'

'Is anyone doing Philip's BES scheme for importing retsina? He raised the first £250,000 over three lunches at Sweetings, but they've still got to find another one-two-five.'

By the end of dinner it seemed that we had dipped in and out of every currency in the world, flirted with the Indonesian rupia, disparaged the yen, commiserated with some poor chap who'd signed his lease in dollars before the exchange rate recovered. We debated the advantages of buying wine in bond, property in Scotland, timber in Snowdonia, shares in Andrew Lloyd Webber, hotels near Bath, Land-Rovers in Stuttgart and driving them home. Diverse topics certainly, but all of them dependent on one thing: very large amounts of disposable income.

It is difficult to estimate the number of young investment bankers, stockbrokers and commodity brokers earning £100,000 a year. Perhaps there are only a couple of thousand, but they are so mobile and noisy that they give the impression of being far more numerous. Most are aged between 26 and 34, and two years ago they were being paid £25,000, in some cases even less, until the opening up of the City markets precipitated an epidemic of headhunting and concomitant salaries. In this respect they resemble the lucky winners on Leslie Crowther's television quiz *The Price is Right*, in which a random selection of wallies get the chance to win microwave ovens and Clairol foot spas. The young market makers were similarly in the right seats at the right time, with the right firms at the right level, but with no particular expectation of being singled out for big prizes. 'Investment bankers on the Japanese side,' Leslie Crowther might huzza. 'Come on down.'

A couple of the Sunday colour magazines have written about newly mega-rich commodity brokers, but these have tended to give a misleading impression. They featured naïve young men posing with their sports cars in Totteridge, the inference being that the lucky winners are chirpy *nouveaux riches*. This is erroneous because the majority of highly paid city boys are not *nouveaux riches* at all; they are traditional upper-middle-class pinstripes, who are banking the cheques as fast as they can while the going is good, and would never be so vulgar as to pose for a colour supplement. That is why one reads a good deal about commodity brokers (reliably contingent in Japanese or American banks) like Manufacturers Hanover, Bankers Trust, Morgan Guaranty and Merrill Lynch, or stockbrokers and jobbers like Rowe and Pitman, Grieveson Grant and Wedd Durlacher, where serious money is being distributed among the deserving young.

Money is the new club. In the early years of this decade it was narcotics that provided the focus and conversation for the aimless young rich. Now their more responsible and industrious cousins (some of whom felt rather left out during the drugs era, working away in their dull City offices) have a club of their own. Membership qualifications: a large salary, minimum £75,000. Club benefits: lively complacent conversation about tax avoidance, accountancy fees and how to spend what's left.

Spending it is rather a poser. A strange characteristic of almost all these young men is that they are not saving much. Certainly they are contributing to pension and life insurance schemes, but there is little evidence of capital accumulation, anyway in shares. Because they were not penniless in the first place, they often already own their house or flat. Their car, of course, is on the firm, as are their restaurant bills (regardless of whether they're entertaining clients or girlfriends), so there is no obvious stay on their cash flow. Consequently there are bags of surplus income to spend on holidays, paintings, wine and furniture. On the other hand, time is at a premium. The working day in the City, especially if you trade on the New York or Tokyo markets, has grown longer and longer. Twelve-hour days are commonplace.

One 30-year-old investment banker reckons that, on an hourly basis, he works two-and-a-half times harder than his father ever did in the same firm. (The son is paid 11 times more in real terms.) Month after month of arriving at the office by 7.30 a.m. and leaving at 8 p.m. makes him feel permanently exhausted. Every evening after work he drinks a whole bottle of claret in a City wine bar, before setting off home for pre-dinner whisky. Because he is paid so well, and what the hell, he never orders wine costing less than £17 a bottle. He takes four holidays a year of one week each, which is the longest he feels able to get away, always abroad: skiing, the Caribbean, Nepal, Morocco. Because he never knows until the last minute when he'll be able to go, he cannot buy Apex tickets, so air fares cost far more than they need. Because he's away for such a short time, he takes care to stay only in expensive hotels.

It would be wrong, however, to imply that young investment bankers are philistine. On the contrary, their backgrounds have often equipped them to spend with discrimination. Their holidays are enterprising: short assaults on Ladakh, visiting monasteries in Sinai, a week in Burma. They have a tendency to try to fit two destinations into one holiday, especially if this involves complicated and extravagant ticketing. They like to spend money on watercolours, Indian miniatures and African tribal masks. They give good parties.

The creation of all this new money is attracting resentment. Not from socialist sources (who are only beginning to grasp the scale of what's going on) but from the young men's contemporaries outside the City. Historically, of course, City jobs have always been better rewarded, because they are dealing in raw money. People in less well-paid professions like auctioneering, land agency and the wine trade did not really mind the discrepancy, because they knew that their own jobs were both more fun and more glamorous. Now this prejudice is being challenged. The new young rich have highlighted the plight of the educated, middle-class poor. A junior expert at Christie's, aged 27 with an Oxbridge degree, may earn £8,500. His City flatmate, quite probably stupider, may earn £116,000. Only a deeply philosophical or insane person could avoid a rush of panic and jealousy. Perhaps the Christie's expert should console himself by advising his richer friend on the formation of his picture collection. More likely he is indignant that the City boy is not only in a position to collect something he knows nothing about, but is also absolved from all future anxieties about paying school fees, when that moment arises. The bursar at a leading public school has remarked how surprised he is at the ease with which certain middle-class families are able to pay the fees out of income, while others are struggling more than ever, desperately spending capital. The difference, of course, lies in their choice of profession. One 34-year-old stockbroker claims to have made more money in the last six years than his father made in his entire career as a distinguished estate agent. I can think of several families that struggled a bit to put their children through public school, only to find that eight years later their standard of living is considerably lower than that of their sons. 'We only drink decent wine these days when we visit Benjy in Battersea,' moans one elderly sherry importer. 'He arrives back from his work with a carrier bag full of splendid claret. Shocking waste, because there's no time to let it breathe.'

More irritating still for the under-paid is the vogue for Business Expansion Schemes. Even I, with no inflated City income, am sent half a dozen prospectuses a month, inviting me to invest £5,000–£20,000 in new restaurants, wine clubs, theme parks and bloodstock agencies. These apparently tax-efficient enterprises have been catching on at such a rate that half the people I know seem to have a stake in one scheme or another. The vast majority of investors are, of course, from the City. Their motive, I suspect, is not tax relief, but a glamorous topic of conversation. At dinner parties these days boys are forever inviting girls to visit 'their' restau-

'ITV if you please, McGinty.'

rant or try a glass of 'their' wine from 'their' vineyard. Only later in the evening do they casually mention that, as well as being a partner in San Fellini's, they are also a junior director at Shearson Lehman.

The only good news, for those of us outside the winner's enclosure, is that the huge salaries will not last. They are largely contingent on performance and it seems unlikely that sufficient new business will be generated to justify the millions of pounds in overheads to set up quite modest operations. 'They're going to have to sweat to ratify their positions,' said an analyst in last week's *Financial Weekly*, cheerfully jumbling his metaphors. 'Unless the profits roll in, the screws will really be on.' Some commentators give the boom three years, others five to seven. After that we can look forward to a levelling (unless the Government does it first; there is wild pre-Budget talk of supertax for people earning more than £100,000). How the young market makers will adjust to reduced circumstances is hard to predict. Probably, by then, their wine bar ventures will be producing enough revenue to cushion the fall.

15 March 1986

INCENSED BY DWARFS

Taki

I first heard the rumours about six months ago. John Aspinall was going to throw a party in honour of the Torgamba Forest Sumatran rhinoceros, one of the rarest animals in the world, and now on the brink of extinction. (A catching expedition has been organised by Aspers to rescue some of the remaining rhinos whose natural habitat is being turned into a rubber plantation.) Knowing Aspinall as I do, it didn't surprise me. Normal people give parties for their daughter's coming out, or wedding, or even their son's coming of age. Although his 60th birthday passed unnoticed last month, Aspers has yet to celebrate a living human. It is either great kings of the past, or noble animals of the present.

This time rumour had it that 1,000 Mesopotamian midgets would be flown to Kent in order to *épater les bourgeois*. But as usual, the rumour mongers got it wrong. There were only 24 of them, and they all turned out to be dwarfs, and all holders of British passports to boot. The other thing the rumour reapers didn't guess was that the Torgamba party of last Saturday will probably do for future party givers what the Ligne Maginot did for French national pride in May 1940. Let me explain.

At the age of 48 I feel I've been around long enough to know about parties and balls as well as, say, Lord Elgin knew the importance of saving marbles from uncivilised environments and preserving them for posterity. Some of the great ones that come to mind were the Bestegui one in Venice, the Agnelli dance in the Bois de Boulogne, the last party the Rothschilds gave at their château at Ferrière, and the Patino blast in Portugal during the final years of Salazar. And although it may sound ungracious to compare, such was the spectacle Aspinall created last Saturday that I'm sure my hosts of the past will understand. This put them all to shame.

The ball took place at Port Lympne, Hythe, the Sir Herbert Baker-built mansion for Sir Philip Sassoon, now owned by Aspers. I arrived promptly at 8.45 and, as parking attendants took my car, we were greeted by the scarlet-tuniced Queen's Regiment band that struck up the kind of military marches that can inspire even a Lebanese to act nobly. Then it was about a mile's walk through what Russell Page has called the most beautiful gardens in England, and Rex Whistler the Virgin Forest. It was through stands of catalpa trees over 40 feet high, accompanied by wolves, Siberian tigers, and a snow leopard or two that one suddenly arrived at the Great Stairs that lead down to the house.

On either side of the Trojan stairway are cascading boxed hedges, or ziggurat, giving a pyramid effect. Five years ago Aspinall had chosen boy scouts to line the stairs and entrance. This time, the theme being the rhino, Michael Howell had created a Sumatran market scene that was, well, as real as any Sumatran market scene would be if directed by Cecil B. De Mille in the good old days of Hollywood. There were half-naked, exotically dressed 'Sumatrans', pelting us with rose petals, offering us food, while the dwarfs stirred their cups and produced the strongest smell of incense I've smelt outside the Greek Orthodox Church.

Down at the bottom of the Nuremberg-like stairway stood Aspinall and Sally greeting their by now rather open-mouthed guests. Every person there was known to the Aspinalls, all 432 of us, which is a rarity in itself. Hosts today invite people for what they are – especially in America – and the guests are the important element of the party. Not Aspinall. With him his guests serve as an audience, or necessary extras, to his creative megalomania. In fact he reminded me of a Renaissance prince, greeting the people who were paying homage to his genius for living well. Smallminded people like the Hartleys of this world may call it a waste, but that would be as wrong as calling Carter-Ruck an aristocrat.

Dinner, needless to say, was seated, and the tent had been transformed into a tropical rain forest by Michael Howell, who had spent four months planning the details. The seating followed a racist theme, or a racist aspect, rather. Better yet, it was vintage Aspinall. There were his Greek friends, their voices now lowered because of the crash of the shipping market, all seated together. Then there were the Sephardic Jews, happy to be once again making money in the countries of their choice, and the South African Jews, looking worried, but happy for a night. There was also the noisy racing owners table, with their acolytes, and the nob table, presided over by my cousin Sunny Marlborough, and including Lords Warwick and Suffolk. And there was the jailbird table, with Justin Frewen, Taki, and someone who almost made it but didn't.

Aspers never was a man to forsake old friends, whatever misfortune may have engulfed them, and they were there too. Last but not least was the homosexual table, headed by the octogenarian who survived the sinking of the *Titanic* by dressing up as a girl and screaming, 'Mommy, Mommy.' (There were eight poofters among the 432.) Oh, I almost forgot, there was also the Westminster table, headed by a government minister and the best looking MP in the Commons, both of whom showed interest in prison reform and questioned me closely.

After the cabaret we retired to the north lawn where Robert Tear, accompanied by the Philharmonic Orchestra, sang the favourite songs of another great tenor, Richard Tauber. I sat in front with my NBF, Benjy Fraser, and Natasha Grenfell and suddenly realised how Mrs Thatcher could do away once and for all with drug addiction, thuggery, Aids, and other diseases too ghastly to mention. All she has to do is ban rock music, jail every rock star except for Harry Worcester, and *c'est tout*.

Everyone's mood was so uplifted by the music that if somebody had offered anyone a snort, or a joint, they would have been as welcome as a Democrat in the Kremlin. Afterwards we danced to the Neal Smith band from Palm Beach, and the newest song they played was written before the war. I danced for the first time in 20 years, and danced non-stop for close to six hours. As always I was the last person to leave, and continued at the Imperial Hotel which Aspers had taken over for his guests. But Aspers told me that in five years he'll do it again, and knowing how preposterous and sumptuous he can be, I wouldn't put it past him.

19 July 1986

THE VAGRANTS OF LONDON

Paul Barker

Ratso lives in what he calls, wryly, Tennis Court Boulevard in Lincoln's Inn Fields. He has big eyes and a scarred forehead. He is 36 next birthday. Like all London's sleepers-out, he is a great reader. He questions me about the *Telegraph*'s editorial move to the Isle of Dogs.

The number of vagrants – the men (very few women) who sleep out rough – is growing, and they are getting younger. 'The old wino is no longer the right image,' I was told – though there remain plenty of old winos.

I suspect that many people think of them as an undifferentiated morass of misery. But it isn't so. Just because they have chosen, or been forced, to live unlike the rest of the world, sleepers-out have not abandoned all ideas of rules. They have their own tribal divisions, their pecking order and their own codes of morality.

Many are ex-soldiers, who learnt about rules in their military years, even if they learnt nothing else much, apart from how to prop up the Naafi bar. They are often fiercely independent. That is one reason for preferring Lincoln's Inn Fields, in the middle of London, to a hostel. There's camaraderie, if you want it. Ratso, however, says he avoids the little schools of drinkers, because they end in punch-ups.

Ratso has been 18 years in London, since he left home in Middlesbrough. He has been in and out of jail. 'I've not been in for two years now: they haven't caught me yet. I'll probably be in again. I was in last time for shoplifting. I was stupid. I got greedy. But the nick's just part of life. If you worried about it, you wouldn't commit the crime in the first place, would you? You just do your time, and think of the £61 you get when you get out.' In one Teesside philosophical side-swipe he thus demolishes the whole theory of deterrence.

These are the rules Ratso lives by. He has his geographical routine. 'I get up in the morning, about six, and then I wander over to the day centre.' This is in a Victorian building off the Marylebone Road, with a blue plaque to the philanthropist Emma Cons on the outside. She started it in the 1870s as a Temperance coffee house. Now it is presided over with amiable firmness by Derek White. He breaks off from time to time to don

Anglican white damask silk as curate of St Cyprian's Clarence Gate.

From the day centre, Ratso goes to 'the Dripping Factory', off Holborn. It's a church. 'If you ring the bell, they'll give you a sandwich. It was bread and dripping in the old days. Then I go back to the Fields. In this weather you can't get bedded down before eight or nine because of the tennis.'

Ratso is very chirpy, very knowing. But he will then slide off into a self-protective silence. Derek White banned him from the centre for eight years because he punched him to the ground. All the sleepers-out have a high mental fence round them. They only want other people to come so far. Many were brought up in care. The break-up of a marriage or the loss of a job precipitated them here. 'Forming relationships is *the* problem for them,' Derek White thinks, and not (say) drink. 'Being loved is something you have to learn – at a very early age. There's no substitute for a family.'

In the evening sunlight, the Fields look idyllic. Lawyers hurry to and fro with late briefs. A dozen young and youngish women play netball. But quickly the Fields are gathering themselves together for night-time.

Men drift into the ungated Fields. Friends joke together in Glasgow or Kerry accents. It is an open-air version of the old-style 'public bar', which pubs almost everywhere have merged into the 'saloon' or turned into a cocktail lounge.

Plastic sheets appear, draped down from sheds. They look like a moth chrysalis. Within each is a sleeping bag and a snore. Huge DIY cardboard double-cubes are balanced on the park benches. If you could not see the tremble of a sleeper inside, you would think it was the tidying-up of corpses after Hiroshima. Over by the tennis courts, some latecomers are still constructing their overnight coffins. They build them punctiliously. I am reminded of soldiers squaring off their blankets for barrack-room inspection.

At the day centre, a list gives 21 regular sources of free food. 'Nobody starves in London,' Ratso says. 'There's too many handouts. And it's surprising what you can get in a litter bin. Tourists, especially, throw things away. Not bad, is it?'

Surprisingly many sleepers-out have a watch. If you thought that time did not matter, you would be wrong. Many have a radio or a Walkman. Ratso has a little yellow 'wireless'. He likes LBC and Radio Four. Like newspaper-reading, radio-listening is an agreeable cocoon.

'I don't look bad, do I?' Ratso says. And he doesn't. Many sleepers-out – if you saw them walking about – would look like building labourers going home from work. Shabby, but neat. The catch is that there isn't much labouring work left on building sites anywhere, and in central London none.

I didn't see a single black or brown vagrant in my wanderings. There must be some. But generally sleeping-out is for poor whites.

Myths get wrapped around vagrants, as they do about Australian Aboriginals. They are invisible, most of the time, watching us, living by an older set of rules. When we notice them, we think they must have some secret. Are they gents down on their luck? Do they have hoards of gold? Sometimes. But you never know till they are found dead. For most of them, £100 in cash would be extreme wealth. This is less than the average take-home pay for a manual worker.

Fred Thrussell says it is not safe to have even £30 or £40 in your pocket in the Fields. 'They'll come at night and cut it out.' He is sitting on a bench under a hawthorn, trying to mend a radio. He is 57, and his mother is still alive up North at 94. He has stopped trying to spell his unusual name for most purposes. 'I call myself Michael Whitefield and get by like that.' There are a lot of more or less joky aliases among vagrants. When I sat in as receptionist at the day centre, I had to write down, unblinkingly, Jack Frost and Eamonn De Valera.

Fred has a friendly, impish face, long hair, and only one visible tooth. He came down to London in 1953. 'There was lots of work then, in the Fifties and Sixties. It was in the Seventies that the recession hit. It wasn't Mrs Thatcher's fault. It's the employers put on the restrictions. I vote Labour. I'm from that class, the labouring class. But I don't know if it's in my interest. I'd like to see the Alliance get a chance.'

He is remarkably unbitter. 'I don't blame the Government. There's lots of opportunities. You can start up a business. I had lots of opportunities when I was young – oh yes.'

He comes from Leith, the port of Edinburgh. He says he does casual work – kitchen portering, furniture removal. He claims unemployment benefit (when he is *not* working, he tells me carefully) at Mortimer Street. He has been sleeping out for three years.

Many vagrants do not, or will not, claim any state benefit at all. Alec is the classic old-timer. He used to sleep on the gratings of the Strand Palace Hotel, opposite an office I used to go to. I must have seen him every day. He has an oily overcoat in all weathers. He says almost nothing. The day centre looks after his old-age pension and doles it out to him. Till they persuaded him to draw his pension, he had never claimed. The day centre's success is a mixed blessing. He now drinks more than he did.

Vagrants always know of someone below them. They have their own pride. The 'ruralists' who live in and around the Fields think themselves a cut above the 'urbanists' in Cardboard City, who live under the arches of the Charing Cross railway bridge and whose lodging is now at risk from Charing Cross redevelopment. Here, in Embankment Place, the warm smell of chips drifts across from the fish bar. The rattle of the suburban trains overhead is somehow consoling. You can use the huge illuminated clock on the riverside Shell-Mex Building to tell the time.

Kipling lived round the corner in the 1890s. He would relish the scene now. Piles of garbage and packaging outside the fast-food restaurants give the sleepers their raw material. Up on the Strand, a little old woman stands talking to herself, next to her box for the night. The close-down of mental hospitals has given the street a new flood of recruits.

Jimmy has the cheerful, child-like face of 'Our Willie' from the Scottish comic strip. His yellow sweatshirt is labelled 'All American Wrangler'. He has a flat from a housing association. But he only goes back a couple of nights a week to clean himself up. 'Otherwise I sleep rough.'

He trembles with DTs. 'I'm a *very* hard drinker. I'll drink anything,' he says, in a serious Dundee voice. 'I was at the old Spike at Camberwell. I had three bottles of aftershave and a bucket. I went out and got some hair lacquer. I put it all in the bucket and I drank it. I was staggering about, bumping into walls. I was in the sick bay for three weeks.

'I don't know why I'm still alive. Lots are dead. There's only two reasons why people are on the street – alcohol and gambling. Alcoholism and perhaps drugs. I'm an alcoholic.'

He says he went on the booze when his marriage in Dundee broke up. 'I'd been to college there, training as a chef. I've got two City and Guilds. It's terrible the things you see on the streets. I was in a doorway once on Old Compton Street with two mates. Just us and a lot of cardboard. We'd been drinking. They'd also been taking the tablets for alcohol. You shouldn't do both. In the morning I woke up and lifted the wine bottle and gave them a prod. I looked and they were both brown bread. I went round the corner and was sick. I'd never seen a dead body before. I went to West End Central and came back in the van. The constable was sick, too. He'd just had his breakfast.'

'I see vast riches. Tie Rack shares and a job at TV-am.'

Jimmy sleeps where he collapses. Yogi has his own nest: a garden shelter outside a block of council flats. He looks like his old television cartoon namesake. He is chubby and brisk, with rosy cheeks and a close-cropped grey beard. Like Hemingway in his later years, too.

He has built a barricade of old mattresses and sofas. An oil drum is a brazier for wet or cold weather. A fluffy white toy poodle is a mock watchdog. On one sofa are a bottle of pink medicine and a packet of pills. A sheet of hardboard is painted with the words, 'DHSS ponces leave me alone.'

He asks me, in broad Yorkshire, if I can see his plastic bag of belongings. I find it for him. 'They steal 'em, you know. You'll see on the bench down there. They come up this way, begging. I see 'em and give 'em summat to remember.'

He gestures behind him. 'These flats are the worst. I remember them being built. They just take their dog for a walk, morning, dinnertime and night – and they get paid for it. They get their rent paid direct. It's this government's fault. Pay their rent all right. But you don't need to feed them.' Those are Yogi's rules.

He is 'very comfortable here – even Mrs Thatcher can't chase me off'. He claims his old-age pension but nothing else.

He was a miner, from Sheffield. He came to London, doing jobs like road sweeping, when he was demobbed from the Second World War. Then he put up market stalls. 'I retired from that at 74. I'm 77 now. It's easily worked out: 21 May 1910. My partner on the market stalls died at 55. It's the Special Brew that kills them off.' He makes a tippling motion with his hand, and reels off a list of the dead.

It is dark now in Lincoln's Inn Fields; two young men get out of their white Porsche and go over to the bright lights of the wine bar on the corner. A young couple stand in the middle of the Fields and kiss, paying no attention to the sleepers all around them. Each world to its own rules.

26 September 1987

WINTERHALTER ON THE FLOOR

Alexandra Artley

A Fancy-dress ball at the Reform Club

The Reform Club is always a wonderful place for a fancy-dress ball. With its subdued polychrome magnificence and wide staircase melting into huge rounded mirrors it calls for big people (or, at least, people in very big dresses) to fill Barry's opulent mid-19th-century spaces. On Saturday evening this vast 'frame for the people', as one dancer described it, held a dazzling succession of live portraits as 400 splendidly dressed guests arrived for the Winterhalter Ball. This very spirited and amiable event was arranged by Lady Harriot Tennant and Dr Malcolm Rogers of the National Portrait Gallery in aid of the gallery's Trust Fund. Including generous donations, over £12,000 was raised.

Dancing began at 8.30 in the long Coffee Room, whose windows over-look the club gardens between Pall Mall and Carlton House Terrace. It was chosen as the ballroom to provide a flat mile of polished parquet for the quadrilles (and one galop) which appeared on the programme of dances. The music, assembled by Oliver Davies (Director of the Prince Albert Ensemble), consisted of many ballroom rarities not much heard since their original performances.

Each dance was associated with a Winterhalter sitter. They included, for example, the *Alice-Polka*, composed by Johann Strauss for the sixth birthday of Princess Alice (and first performed at Buckingham Palace, on 30 April 1849). *Hommage à la Reine Angleterre*, again by Johann Strauss, turned out to be a waltz-time version of the National Anthem played at VR's first State Ball at Buckingham Palace on 10 May 1838. Many musi-cians in the band were drawn from the BBC Symphony Orchestra and the Royal Philharmonic. Conducting from the piano, Oliver Davies had the light, easy-going charm of the musician who genuinely enjoys playing for people to dance.

Winterhalter has always struck me as Easy Lookin' (the visual equiva-lent of what popular record labels used to call Easy Listenin'). But as direct evidence for the fashion historian or theatrical costumier he has his practical uses. The true 'Winterhalter Look' conveys a luxurious hot-house fragility, the much emphasised shoulders rising from a sea of pas-tel silk or tulle and with endless flowers worn in the hair (singly or in

wreaths) and attached to bodice, waist or skirt. Lace, fluttering ribbons
and veiling complete this most fully romantic of evening styles. After ten
years of fancy-dress balls and parties I have got crinoline fatigue. For a
complete change I took a tier off my pastel silk wedding dress, pinned
some full-blown silk roses to the bosom, dug out my white satin ballet
shoes and went as Carlotta Grisi, the ballerina who created the role of
Giselle and brought it to London in May 1842.

Dresses at the ball ranged from the youthful simplicity of white tulle
to the alarming flame velvet and gold lace of Olde Ruritania. At one end
of the colour range Ann Hodson-Pressinger and Jane Abdy dressed
entirely in white and wore long white veils cascading from the hair – a bit
like the Winterhalter portrait of Princess Metternich (1860). At the other
end of the spectrum, Anna Somers-Cocks (editor of *Apollo*) wore an enormous black silk crinoline with white flowers in her hair. Oriele Hawood
also wore black with a full wreath of red roses set over a black lace man-
tilla, rather like the Winterhalter portrait of Adelina Patti as Rosina in
The Barber of Seville. Both men and women had raided costume jewellery
trays for large 'diamond' stars like those which stud the loose hair of
Elizabeth, Empress of Austria, in a portrait of 1865. Boldly ignoring
the Winterhalter spirit, Margaret, Duchess of Argyll, appeared in a brilliant red sheath dress. As usual, most men looked immensely reliable in
boiled shirts (stiff enough to knock on) and white tie. Alan Powers and

Jonathan James looked particularly dashing as Prince Albert-like dandies.

To the pulse of Labitzky's *Sutherland-Waltzer* (1842) off we launched into the swift and dizzying turns of the Viennese waltz, which looks wonderful but requires immense concentration. (A little resin on the dance floor would have been a good idea.) In the great rounded mirrors at each end of the ballroom the chandeliers marched off in perspective, and as we whirled past, occasional soothing currents of sharp night air blew in through windows swagged with crimson velvet. 'Just like the Victorian dodgems,' said my partner cheerfully as he steered us firmly past hurtling young men and through satin shoals of high velocity twirling.

Quadrilles figured on the dance programme three times. These tortuous set-figure dances reduce me to giggles (I prefer waltzes, polkas and galops with a bit more go). Two quadrille classes had been held at Battersea Town Hall earlier in the week by Ellis and Christine Rogers of the Early Dance Circle. After these, some dancers gave a very good impression of knowing what they were doing. ('It's a bit like bridge except you're letting four people down instead of two.') At the end of each figure it was clearly a relief to return to Demi-Chaine Anglaise, a simple hand-clasping manoeuvre which gives dancers a sense of dance-floor geography again.

At ten o'clock the ball supper was unveiled on two vast buffet tables beneath the sombre gilded Corinthian columns of the club Library. Here dishes had been very elaborately presented by the chef, Alan Riddle, and sous-chef, Andrew McLay, in the manner of Alexis Soyer, the good-natured and eccentric Frenchman who became chef at the Reform in 1841. As in Soyer's enormous book, *The Gastronomic Regulator*, certain cuts of meat were crazily shaped like enormous fully-rigged galleons or men o' war, a style called 'the Dindoneau à la Nelson'. This was all done by sculpting turkeys and beef and setting them into carved pumpkins with wooden skewers for rigging and billowing sails made from linen napkins. These astonishing vessels were becalmed on a sea of two-tone (red and white) savoury tarts filled with cranberry jelly and horseradish sauce. Nearby, on shore, martello towers were carved from pumpkins and filled with melon crosses.

The historian-confectioner Alan Littlewood had also reconstructed dramatic *piéces montées* such as huge meringue cornucopias spilling fruit and enormous pyramids of profiteroles glazed with toffee. He also made white temples of royal icing in which sugar nymphs hid behind pillars iced with green ivy or looked down on votive offerings of coloured marzipan fruits. Feeding 400 guests at once is quite an enterprise, but was smoothly achieved. 'It's not a very long queue,' said Harriot Tennant as dancers waited to enter Soyer's food wax-works. 'It's just that the skirts are so big, it *looks* long.'

After supper, time flew, hastened by the *Patti Polka*, the *Prince of Wales Galop*, glasses of sorbet and the waltz, *Wiener Bonbons*. Shortly after midnight, an Orsini-like anarchist in a black cloak and wide-brimmed hat tossed a round fizzling 'bomb' into the ballroom as a reminder of what lay outside. Amid authentic screaming he fled down the back-stairs.

Well after two a.m. it was time to go home. 'I wish it *were* carriages, preferably with a foot-warmer,' said one girl as no taxis whatever appeared on Pall Mall. Gradually, as we queued down the stairs to collect our cloaks, the 'Winterhalter Look' was giving way to a sense of mere bovine encumbrance. Upstairs in the hall, post-ball reality took other forms. 'I've lost my car keys,' confided a young man, 'and worse than that, my house-keys are at the house where I changed and they're ex-directory....' Beyond him through the doors, the musicians packed up their instruments, the Soyer debris was patiently cleared away and with lowering lights the Reform Club looked inwards again, like a theatre sombre and waiting.

19/26 December 1987

'John and I have bought this wonderful old rocket silo.'

THE DEBTORS OF SMACK CITY

Dominic Lawson

He could not work it out, the Merseyside debt collector. And nor could I, accompanying him on the sort of biting winter evening that his profession relishes (the targets are more likely to be in). His card said that Mr Jones, owing £4,000 to two secured lenders, lived at number 30. But there did not seem to be a number 30. Where it should have been, laid back from the road, was the police station. Surely not . . . ? But as we advanced on the blue light, a mean little house, obviously attached to the station, revealed its number – 30. Yes, said Mr Jones, he was a policeman, but no, he did not want to discuss the matter at his front door. Why not come along with him to the station? And so it was that the debt collector, and the journalist pretending to be a debt collector, found themselves taking a statement from a police officer in his own interview room, both noticing with wry amusement the battered state of the chairs offered to them.

But if the circumstances of the meeting were bizarre, the predicament of the debtor was typical of the area. He had sold his house for less than the value of the mortgage he had incurred in its purchase, leaving the building society and a second secured lender – probably a double glazing firm – pursuing him for £4,000 he did not have. In the South-East, where property values have been regularly showing annual increases of over 20 per cent, such a withering of the home-owner's equity would seem incredible (though it may yet happen). But on Merseyside it is a commonplace.

And yet the Liverpool office of the Leamington Spa Building Society still has a smiling cartoon face in its window. '100 per cent mortgages to make you smile – 3½ × income,' it says, and I thought of all the other PC Joneses who had discovered that 'safe as houses' is, like all other investment advice, merely an opinion. The record number of mortgage repossessions in Liverpool is, of course, connected to the fragility of the employment market. Those who leap at the chance to turn a short-lived job into the base for first-time home ownership find out too late that for the first four months of their unemployment the state will not contribute to their mortgage interest bill.

Such worries of ownership and capital are most unlikely to afflict the residents of the Ford Estate – not the inhabitants of a car, but those 15,000 in what was once Europe's largest public housing venture. It is in Birkenhead, and, in Liverpool, just the other side of the Mersey, it is frequently referred to as 'Smack City'. Recently the authorities, in an effort to erase the drug-infested theft-ridden image of the Ford, changed its name to Upper Bidston Village. Similarly, another Birkenhead estate with a bad name (Cantrell) has had it changed to the rurally idyllic 'Stockbridge Village'.

As the debt collector sees it, these deceptions are not as purposeless as they seem. Many lenders operate – illegally – a 'red line' policy under which areas of known delinquency are denied credit en masse. But who could be so cruel to a little old lady hailing from Upper Bidston or Stockbridge Village? Those names, for the moment, have no past, even if they may not have much of a future either.

Liverpudlians raised their eyebrows when I told them I was to spend an evening knocking on doors on the Ford with a debt collector. But the experience did not match up to their lurid tales. The place is tidy in its bleakness, certainly a lot tidier than many roads in Islington or Camden in London, where the detritus of middle-class home improvements lies around in skips. On the Ford the deserted flats are neatly boarded up, like so many coffins. They are not the five-year-old architectural open graves that can still be seen in Toxteth.

Nor do the residents of the Ford, and other Birkenhead estates, show violence, or even aggression, to the debt collector and his well-padded accomplice. That may have been because the debt collector – let us call him Ian Smith – is solidly built, well over six feet tall, and sports a big black beard. But I doubt it.

Smith has never, in five years at the job, been physically assaulted. Indeed, he employs women to help out with the requests of almost 200 clients. On our rounds we were frequently made to feel almost welcome, particularly by the single person, bored to distraction, who regards even Nemesis as a pleasant change of company from the television (which object may well be the cause of the visit from the tall dark stranger).

If the debtor shows a surprising solicitude for the predicament of the collector, it may well be because he has done a spot of 'trade protection' himself. A two-and-a-half-hour shift of door-knocking on Merseyside will pay the financial canvasser about £20, on an averagely successful night, and is exactly the sort of moonlighting work which the over-borrowed factory worker can do with. It is also being sponsored, probably unwittingly, by the state. In his time Ian Smith has taken on young people from agencies operating under the financial umbrella of the Manpower Services Commission, and on odd occasions, even Youth Training

Scheme youngsters; it seems that the MSC 'trainees' see debt collecting as far more fun than travelling to the same estates with the idea of painting a house with one brush between five would-be decorators (a scene described to me by one rather disenchanted former MSC scheme organiser in Liverpool).

The most extraordinary thing that the trainee Scouse debt collectors will find – although they may not recognise how odd it is – is that none of the debtors ever asks the obvious question: 'How much do I owe?' On my rounds I never heard what self-preservation would suggest as an automatic response, and Ian Smith said that my experience was absolutely typical. All the Merseyside debtors say is: 'We can afford to pay £x a month' – presumably into the infinite future.

This attitude had a kind of weird logic in the days of Hire Purchase payments: they were in fixed instalments, and if you couldn't make them, then the Repo man would come and take the television, or whatever, away. But in these days of instant credit and Annual Percentage Rates the amount owed actually grows in the event of under-payment. The retailer does not want *your* television back, he just wants *his* money.

To walk around the shopping centre of Liverpool is to see how the retailer convinces those who should stay in the rental market to become owners. Every window seems to advertise 'instant credit'. Even Owen Owen, whose eponymous founder said, on his arrival in Liverpool in 1865, 'The guide to the harbour of best success is to give no credit to anyone for longer than two months,' is now offering 'up to £1,250 credit to spend immediately'. The repayment rate is a savage 34.4 per cent, or over three times the rate at which Messrs Owen Owen can themselves borrow on the open market.

At the time I was knocking on PC Jones's borrowed front door, the Rt Hon. Robin Leigh-Pemberton, Governor of the Bank of England, was lecturing the luminaries of the provincial newspaper industry on the dangers of the explosion in personal credit in Britain. Over the port and cigars the Governor noted that bank lending to the personal sector had grown by 50 per cent over the past two years, and that personal sector borrowing had for years been rising faster than personal incomes.

One does not have to be the Governor of the Bank of England – or indeed the Governor of the Bank of England's speechwriter – to observe that 'this may well lead to an increasing number of individual borrowers having difficulty in servicing their debt'.

It is equally clear that the British clearing banks, recoiling from the billions of pounds they have lost through filling their loan books up with South American debt in the 1970s, have decided that the safest way to make a turn on the money they borrow (or merely take) on Britain's high streets is to send it back whence it came, albeit at much higher rates and preferably secured on property.

But it is axiomatic that bankers – once described as marble brains upon marble floors – always stampede for the same fashionable business, and feel compelled by the force of that competition to make loans which subsequently do not bear the strictest examination.

Retailers such as Owen Owen doubtless judge that the rate of credit they charge amply compensates them for a high rate of default. For their methods of assessment are frequently irresponsible. Most will give credit to anyone displaying a valid credit card, with no means of knowing whether the person waving the Visa card is in fact the true owner of the plastic. If they do make a checking telephone call it will be to the computerised records of the list of debtors in the County courts. But these may well be out of date, and represent only the hard core of likely defaulters.

In Liverpool those financial delinquents are merely taking their cue from those they once elected to manage their affairs. The city is now struggling to find a way of meeting the £50 million shortfall between its rate-capped income and the expenditure needed to maintain services at their present levels. And about a quarter of next year's capital allowance from the Government of £46 million will go towards the repayment of some hair-raising financing incurred by Messrs Hatton and Byrne. They financed their improvements to the municipal housing stock by borrowing from Japanese and Swiss banks on the cute terms of a two-year moratorium followed by repayment over the next five (now). Even the Leamington Spa Building Society would not expect its Liverpool clients to buy that.

Gary Lane is an ex-merchant seaman who has lived in the former great seaport of Liverpool for 30 years and last year published *Liverpool: Gateway of Empire* (Lawrence and Wishart). He has summed up the character of the place: Liverpudlians, he says, have 'a cavalier disregard for money. This is a city with the habit of the seafarer ashore after a voyage – spend it while you can, because the world might end tomorrow. Strangers cannot help but notice the astonishing number of London-style black cabs on the streets. For where in the Metropolitan Police District of London there is one cab for every 522 persons, in Liverpool there is one for every 360. Such an elementary statistic encodes the peculiarity of Liverpool.'

'Don't look only for the bad things here,' the Conservative Party agent in Liverpool told me. 'Go down to the Albert Dock and look at what government support has helped to build.' So down the hill to the dock I walked, in the face of the kind of salty gale which explains why the waiting list for adenoidal surgery in the Mersey area is the longest in the country.

There, at Albert Dock, were all the accepted accoutrements of subsidised urban renewal, from art galleries to Mexican restaurants. By the edge of this Fulham-on-Mersey was a statue dating from the City's great days as the entrepôt of transatlantic capitalism. 'Enterprise', it said, and I followed its gaze across the Mersey to the Cammell Laird shipyard at Birkenhead. I could not make out any activity, because there was none. The 1,500 workers had been locked out, following their demand for more pay as a reward for clocking in with electronic tags rather than by the traditional manual method.

Easy to draw a vivid contrast between the entrepreneurial strivings at Albert Dock and the sullen self-destructiveness of the wage-slaves across the watery divide. But my first thought was of how many of the men at Cammell Laird had recently encountered my friend the debt collector, or one of his less scrupulous rivals, and that they were hoping to use the electronic identity tags as a means of meeting too-long-deferred payments for other state-of-the-art electronic gadgets at home on the Ford Estate.

27 February 1988

'HE USED TO GIVE ME ROSES'

Myles Harris

I stood looking at the long Georgian room. A discreet Cheltenham sun peered through the curtains. Two expensive cats lay curled in its rays on a small Bokhara. Books lay piled haphazardly on the shelves about an Adam fireplace. Outside in the long landscaped garden, behind wild shrubs and a weeping willow, somebody was mowing the lawn. There had been upper-class violence here. My hostess came back with the tea. She was about 30, blonde, thin-featured and nervous. The sort of woman who would talk about the SDP at a dinner party, or who mistaking one for a liberal would try and soften her husband's over-decided views on South Africa.

She had met her husband at Cambridge. She was reading history, he a classical tripos. He was witty, intelligent, the soul of the party and forth-right. If he disagreed with you he would tell you in no uncertain way. She liked that. It reminded her of her father, a tough, famous industrialist. But there was an odd side to him. He suffered episodes of fantastic jeal-ousy and would sometimes creep up to her bedroom window at three in the morning to see if she was in bed with somebody else. She passed her exams but he failed. I asked why. 'Probably because he was incapable of controlling his emotions over ideas. Once when I was 18 he gave me a black eye because he didn't agree with what I said.' They married after she came down. He went to work in a merchant bank. After the first child he began beating her. At first each beating would be followed by a box of roses. But that soon stopped and the attacks became involved with sex. There was a lot of drinking. She remembers the ringing in her ears going on for days after he hit her. He often locked her out. Once after he thumped her she miscarried. Afterwards he said, 'I don't have enough love in me for two,' and again, 'I want you to put my emotional welfare before the children,' – thump – 'will you?' I asked her if she ever defended herself. She said, 'I learnt that if you hit back it went on longer. I just stood there and took it.'

She took it for five years. I asked why. 'Because I couldn't believe that a well-educated, sensitive somebody like me could do this.'

In the final months she noticed he was using violence as a power play. That was different, it was cold-blooded – not, as she said, 'in the heat'. Finally he suggested moving a girlfriend in. For 24 hours she agreed. But then, for the first time, he hit her in front of one of the children. The child said, 'Mummy, what is worse, to live with somebody who is horrible or to be dead?' 'I stopped then,' she said, 'that was it.'

The next evening, before he came home, she called in a male friend for protection and hid all the carving knives. When she told him he had to leave, he managed to find a steak knife the au pair had left in the scullery and buried it quarter of an inch in the friend's neck. The friend fled. Mary called the police but they were reluctant to interfere and only did so when they found the house belonged not to him but to her. He was asked to leave. For months afterwards she had to have bars, burglar alarms and double locks. Often he would lurk outside between the cars, waiting to attack her. Then he drifted away.

We stopped speaking for a minute. She said, 'When you are in love with somebody you often want to imagine yourself inside their head – to be them – now I wouldn't be within a thousand miles of him.'

There are a lot of cases like Mary's. In London last year 100,000 inci-dents of domestic violence were reported to the police, 25 per cent of all violent recorded crime. Many marriages, some claim one in four, are violent. Very few assaulted women leave home even when the violence becomes established. Many cling on for months or years, some for ever, some only leave in death.

Why did Mary stay? Was she a 'murderee', the emotional key into which the murderer fits his lock? Are all women who stay and suffer murderees?

Dr Gillian Mazey is a psychiatrist at the Maudsley. She is young, personable, witty and specialises in treating raped and assaulted women. She thought there was an element of masochism in violent marriages but the evidence was wildly conflicting. Criminologists and the police, she said, talked rather grandly of 'victim precipitation' without much understanding of the complex nature of the relationship between a man and a woman.

One reason she thought that a woman might remain in a violent home is that frequent beatings can cause a condition known as learned helplessness. Learned helplessness is not exclusive to human beings. It can be induced in puppies by locking them in a cage wired to give random electric shocks through its floor and walls. When the dogs are first put in the cage they frantically search for a place where the current will not reach them. But the shocks are random and unpredictable and cannot be escaped. After a while the search gives way to passive acceptance and, ceasing all voluntary activity, the dogs lie on the floor and accept the current without resistance.

But this is more than just simply giving up. When the cage door is opened and attempts are made to encourage the dogs to leave they strongly resist and have to be dragged forcibly to the door of the cage several times before they regain their former desire to escape.

The puppies have learnt to be helpless. In beaten women, psychologists believe, a similar process takes place. The victim's experience, that of repeated random pain, becomes her only reality so that when shown the door out of her hell the victim refuses to walk through it unless dragged.

I asked why, having once escaped, some women return, or worse, marry another beater? Because, the psychiatrist said, some victims will try to relive a situation in order to master it, much as Vietnam war veterans volunteered to return to combat, or sexually abused children take up prostitution. Besides, many such women only know of life inside a violent family. They have no assurance that life in any other family is different. I asked about class differences. There were none, she said. (Social workers' offices merely have thinner walls and smaller rooms than those of Harley Street consultants.)

We know almost nothing about wife beaters, said Dr Mazey, except that they probably learn their aggression toward women from their fathers. She imagined they had a fragile sense of self-esteem, were frightened, feared prosecution, saw women as extensions of themselves and losing them a blow to their sexuality; and, of course, violence has the compulsive, addictive quality of a drug.

Sandra Horley is a tall and rather formidable lady in black who looks after a women's refuge in Chiswick. She has recently published a handbook on how to escape from violent marriage (*Love and Pain*, Bedford Square Press). Extremely charming on such subjects as the British (she is a Canadian), the weather, cars, religion and publishers, when we moved to the subject of men and women the conversation took on an uneasy note.

Miss Horley's passion is to control marital violence. Having seen what men can do to their wives and having been firebombed and stoned by violent husbands herself, she tends to see wife abuse more in terms of criminality, with the police ducking behind a screen of ageing myths to avoid the issue. Behind the police she believes lies that great lump of amorphous, self-conscious, backsliding guilt – English society.

All societies, she says, condone wife beating. Men learn very early that they can control the life, thoughts and behaviour of women by violence and that society will turn a blind eye to it. Beat up your neighbour, said Miss Horley, and you will soon find yourself in jail. Beat up your wife and nothing will happen.

Wife-beating comes festooned with myths. People believe that wife-beating is mainly a drunkard's occupation. Untrue, Miss Horley says. Drinking is not particularly associated with wife-beating, much of which is done in complete sobriety. She knows drunks who only beat their wives when sober. There is a widespread belief that a certain type of woman enjoys being beaten, and stays with her violent husband out of a sense of perverse pleasure. Wives, Miss Horley said sharply, stay because they are dependent on their husbands for money and, like most human beings, are surprised and cowed by violence and torture. In addition, taught by society to undervalue themselves, women often tend to blame themselves and stay, hoping to put things right.

Society, she says, is to blame for these myths. The only solution is for the police to put a stop to wife-beating by bringing criminal charges against men. When that was done in Canada, she said, domestic violence fell by two thirds. I do not know what this figure proves.

Miss Horley told me about a lady whose husband obliged her to make a cup of tea between the beatings he was administering, and of women so frightened they take 20 minutes to speak when they first contact the women's refuge on the telephone. Are these sorts of women going to shop their husbands? Miss Horley thinks they will if we can change attitudes, among them, among society in general and particularly among the police, who, she says, are not averse to a spot of wife-beating themselves.

There I fear what she proposes. Nature demands there should be an element of pursuit in all sexual relations. The chase, after all, hones the species. But while a chase implies conquest, it does not imply violence. Just because there are some men who are violent does not mean we should abandon the most basic of nature's prescriptions.

But radical feminists reject this. Men and women are the same. One cannot conquer the other – except males are sexually and almost universally violent. Therefore all men's sexuality must be altered through radical changes in society. But the new man that feminists are intent on producing may well be even more vicious and unhappy than the present model. Nature does not take kindly to tampering. One sexual revolution this century has already caused an epidemic of death. We should be careful.

11 June 1988

Chapter 4
THERE IS NO ALTERNATIVE . . .

WHY ME?

Patrick Marnham

Recently I have found myself dreaming about Margaret Thatcher; quite frequently. It requires a certain recklessness to admit to this. When the trouble first started I used to mention it to people with whom I regarded myself as being on a more or less friendly basis. In the early days it was just a sneaking admiration I felt for her. When the BBC first started to broadcast prime minister's question time Mrs Thatcher was usually on her feet, questioning Mr Callaghan. At first, nothing. Just Mrs Thatcher's familiar, precise enunciation. But then those terrible House of Commons background noises started up. On the radio it sounds like feeding time in Bedlam Hospital. And I realised with a growing feeling of frustration that Mrs Thatcher's voice was too *weak* to make itself heard. It seemed so terribly, terribly unfair.

Then she herself became prime minister and the real trouble started. Of course I knew what I was meant to think about Mrs Thatcher. Either she was the evil one or she was mildly embarrassing. I also knew what I had always really thought about her. Which was nothing at all. But now I found that when I did just occasionally think about her it was with a growing sense of warmth. She seemed rather gallant, dashing, attractive, witty even. I wondered if I was suffering from overwork.

Whenever I tried this new idea out on others there was a sort of stunned silence. 'What do you mean, "She's not *so* bad"?' they would eventually ask. Or, 'How can you possibly think that "She's really rather wonderful"?' And I asked myself the same anguished questions. How? Why? Why *me*? Before things got completely out of hand, and I lost all my acquaintances, I decided to pretend that it was just a joke after all. Oh very amusing; yes, yes, it's all right; go on talking among yourselves; nothing has changed . . .

But then these dreams started. The details are difficult to recall, but certain things remain constant throughout the series. Mrs Thatcher is always prime minister. I am always at her side. We are in public. Everything is entirely proper between us. The dreams would be quite suitable for family viewing. Around us there are large crowds who have come to see Mrs Thatcher. I am not quite sure whether I call her 'Margaret'. I think not. I call her 'Prime Minister'. She calls me 'Marnham'. My own role is not entirely clear. It seems that I am paid to advise her about the dangers of her position. I wear a suit. Mrs Thatcher, and this is rather odd, wears long flowing silk tea-gowns. Everyone else in the dream is dressed for work in the upper echelons of Whitehall. But she is all frills and ruffles and organdie, whatever that is. Very bold prints, dresses down to her ankles. She swishes when she walks and gives off an inner light.

The other thing that I recall from these dreams quite clearly is that she never listens to a word I say. In fact she seldom stops talking. I am not entirely alone as her Adviser. There are other men around – ambitious, ruthless, scheming – who seem to know more about economics than I do. That would not be difficult, but these sharks seem to know more about economics than anyone could, in all sanity, want to know. And Mrs Thatcher ignores everything *they* say as well. She just interrupts them, and when she starts to speak we all fall silent. None of us feels at all humiliated by this. On the contrary, we *like* her to interrupt. We are quite certain that if she has something to say it will be well worth listening to.

Normally we are grouped, me and these thrusting economists, around her in a motorcade. I am invariably standing in the back of the open car. She is raised slightly on a platform from which she can wave to the cheering crowds and also direct the conversation. She has uncannily good hearing and always gets straight to the point. Eventually the limousine draws to a smooth halt. She alights. We scramble out. The police close around our group and we struggle towards the sanctuary of whatever building it is that she has decided we must enter. In the middle of this teeming mob she again asks me for my opinion. I take the greatest care to express it as precisely as possible and begin to speak but she has already taken the point and disagreed. She is talking again. We struggle on towards the door. However many people call out to her from the crowd she remains completely calm.

I am not interested in any psychiatric interpretation of these dreams. You don't have to spend eight years dissecting hypothalami to trot out glib analyses of other people's dreams. It is apparently quite common for people to dream about the Queen. I have never dreamed about the Queen. I have no time to do so, apart from anything else, since Mrs Thatcher occupies so many of my unconscious moments. But if I did dream about the Queen, or if I did admit to thinking that the Queen was not *entirely* without merit, I do not think that it would arouse quite the same strangled and horrified reaction when I said so.

More than anyone else my secret life seems to outrage members of the Women's Movement. Why should that be? I have decided that until I can solve this mystery, and until I can control my dreams, I must stop writing this column.

7 February 1981

THE SKELETON AT THE FEAST

Peter Ackroyd

Kensington Town Hall does not, on the face of it, seem an ideal place to 'break the mould' of British politics but it has its virtues – neither too smart nor too tatty, neither humble nor imposing, a great deal of tasteful, modern brickwork. The kind of place a convention of hoteliers might pick.

But here are the SDP. A young man gets up and declares that 'we are committed to all forms of sexual orientation'. Everyone smiles and nods: yes of course, that's right, that must be high on our list of commitments. Roy Jenkins remains impassive. A few minutes before, William Rodgers, looking like the butler in a Charles Addams cartoon, had said something out of turn – I did not catch what it was. 'I apologise if I have hurt anyone's feelings . . .' More smiling and nodding – well, that's all right then. Mr Jenkins places his hand over his mouth and stifles a yawn. In fact, he becomes more interesting hourly: he is paying no attention to anything that is said, and sits reading the newspapers. He is like the mysterious stranger at a party who is about to deliver bad news.

'Sweetness and light' was an expression first used, I think, by Matthew Arnold as the distinguishing characteristics of those who were neither barbarians nor philistines – what we might now call the middle ground. The phrase never caught on, however, partly because it seemed peculiarly inappropriate in the energetic and squalid conditions of mid-Victorian England. Now sweetness and light are back. They are what the SDP stands for. It is in favour of everything nice – 'an open, classless and more equal society', 'competitive public enterprise', 'defence of human rights' – and opposed to anything nasty. The delegates are in the smiling and nodding business.

But Mr Jenkins isn't smiling. When the rest of the platform lean forward to appreciate a particularly telling point from the floor, he leans back or walks off the stage altogether. It is, of course, an old game: the 'good cop' and the 'bad cop'; the only difference, on this occasion, is that the good cops don't seem to know that a bad cop exists. The delegates have that look of niceness combined with bland optimism which one has seen before: the doctor's receptionist smiles and nods while unmentionable things are going on next door; the undertaker smiles and nods as the corpse is carried into the waiting limousine.

Where is the reality behind all the talk in Kensington Town Hall – where are the corpses and the pain? Somehow, as far as the delegates are concerned, they have ceased miraculously to exist. If someone had gone to the rostrum and suggested that the SDP was in favour of nuclear war as long as it was responsive to ordinary people's real needs and to openness in government, it would have passed without a murmur. Political parties were once a way of harnessing fear, resentment and self-interest but such emotions have no place here. The only passion generated is by points of order – they love their points of order, they rush to the microphone and think of new ones on the way. And if this is indeed a middle-class party, it is because it shares the one fundamental weakness of the middle class – the belief that the world will work perfectly if it can be organised properly, that other people will behave themselves if you explain patiently to them what is in their best interests, that you can, as one delegate put it, 'legislate against selfishness'. Social reality can be changed by a number of new year resolutions. One longed for a lady in a large hat to call for the hanging of immigrants, or a bearded youth to demand the nationalisation of launderettes – something inexplicable and horrid to break up the sweetness and light.

There were arguments, of course. How many units make up an area?

'Was it as bad as living under Mrs
Thatcher, Daddy?'

Should one use the term 'sex' instead of 'gender'? Should the delegates 'reject' discrimination or be 'regardless of' it instead? The delegates get excited about such matters: they rustle their newspapers and murmur to each other. They are neither old nor young, rich nor poor; in the intervals they stand in small groups and talk in that curiously flat English which comes from everywhere and nowhere. 'This is an historic moment,' one of the delegates tells them, but it is a discreet moment – as if history were a servant who has brought them a letter on a salver.

What is Mr Jenkins doing now? He looks inscrutable, large, ruddy in face, quite preposterously physical beside the pale, eager creatures who share the platform with him. When he gets up to speak, at the close of the convention, his body quivers with suppressed energy. He does not smile or nod. When he talks he clenches his fist, and prods the lectern with his finger when he speaks of 'battlefields' and 'struggle'. It comes as something of a shock: he is definitely not part of the sweetness and light, and does not bother to dissemble the fact.

There is a theory, propounded by Arthur Koestler, that human beings have evolved in schizophrenic fashion – with an 'old brain', reptilian, primitive, slowly being ousted by the 'new brain', rational, logical. Mr Jenkins is definitely the old brain making a comeback, set to defy the laws of evolution. If he can ride to power on the back of accountants and estate agents rather than coal miners or factory workers, so be it. He seems preoccupied because he is waiting for power.

Outside, two young men are selling SDP souvenirs. There are some particularly nice ties, at four pounds each. 'You can wear it tonight,' a wife tells her husband, 'at dinner.' It will be a talking point then, no doubt, and give the man a chance to explain why he has decided to join the SDP and 'break the mould'. He will wear it as a matter of principle. And it does look very tasteful.

20 February 1982

THE THREE FACES OF MARGARET

Ludovic Kennedy

Politicians can be divided into two categories: those whose public face is different from their private face and those for whom they are the same; put another way, those who feel it necessary in public appearances to put on an act, and those who manage to remain themselves. Among the latter are (or were) such disparate characters as Jack Kennedy, Willi Brandt, Jo Grimond, Edward Heath, Neil Kinnock; and among the former Adolf Hitler, Winston Churchill, Richard Nixon, Harold Wilson and Arthur Scargill (if you don't like that list, you are welcome to make your own).

Prominent among the last-named is our Prime Minister, but she is almost unique in having not two faces but three. The first is the semi-private one, worn when she is not on public display; the second is the House of Commons one, seen and heard at Prime Minister's Question Time; and the third is the one adopted for television interviews. We are all familiar with the last two, but there can be few of us who have been given the opportunity to observe the first. It did, however, happen to me the year after Mrs Thatcher first came to power.

The occasion was the making of a BBC drama-documentary, of which I was the writer and presenter, on the life of Airey Neave, the MP who had masterminded her campaign for the party leadership and was subsequently assassinated by the IRA when a time-bomb blew up his car as it was leaving the House of Commons. Mrs Thatcher had agreed to give us an interview for the programme between 10.30 and 11.30 a.m. at Ten Downing Street. She arrived on the dot, chic and elegant as one had expected but also delightfully relaxed – knowing, of course, that it was not controversial political views that she was being asked to give but reminiscences of a much loved colleague and friend. She knew exactly what was expected of her, and delivered it impeccably and on the first take; nor was there a moment when anything in her voice or manner distracted one from what she was saying. (Indeed the only distraction was a tiresome, buzzing fly which finally settled on the top of Mrs Thatcher's exquisitely coiffured head. Rather than interrupt an interview that was going so swimmingly, Ben Rea, the director, decided to carry on in the hope that on transmission nobody would notice it. Except for the two of us, nobody did.)

So flawless had been her contribution (I have deliberately eschewed the word 'performance') that by 10.55 the interview was over. I assumed that she would then shake hands all round and depart into the interior to attend to weightier things. Instead, looking at her watch, she said: 'I see it's just on eleven. I'm at your disposal until half past. Would you like me to show you round the house?'

For the next half-hour she took the eight of us on a tour of the public rooms, imparting with impressive assurance the history of this picture or that tapestry, anecdotes of what Pitt had done or Gladstone said. In the state dining-room with its rows of high-backed chairs, she said with a smile: 'You know I had Giscard here last week. Where do you think I put him?' We looked suitably baffled. 'Here,' she said, indicating a chair, and following her upward glance we saw on the wall opposite a full-length portrait of Lord Nelson next to a full-length portrait of the Duke of Wellington. Not once in that half-hour were we interrupted by a secretary with a message, not once did she give us anything but her undivided attention, not once was she anything but a charming and considerate hostess. We tottered into the street in a kind of glow.

Later came the Number Two face, that of Prime Minister's Question Time, which is now so different from the one we had experienced that you can hardly believe it is the same person. For a start the voice has dropped a couple of octaves into a sort of *basso profundo* so that you can imagine it belting out the Song of the Volga Boatmen or, in harmony with Paul Robeson, Ole Man River. Abrasive and corrective, it is the voice of the games mistress, the colour sergeant, the first mate. You can hear it bellowing below decks: 'Heave ho! Heave ho! Lash up and stow!' or, 'Call those boots polished, you horrible little man? I'll call them polished when I can see your ugly mug in them!'

To be fair, one does have to ask how much this voice has developed through the extreme (and, in any other context, ungallant) provocations of Neil Kinnock and what John Wells calls the smelly socks brigade. Women, it may be said, and particularly this sort of woman, are not accustomed to being spoken to in this way, and if they are, this is how they will react. Would a male prime minister take the insults less personally, make a cooler, less aggressive response? I put the question but am uncertain of the answer.

And finally there is the Number Three or television interview face, as different from Number Two as Number Two is from Number One. Safe in the knowledge that neither Brian Walden nor Robin Day will be trading Kinnock-style insults (and would be sacked if they did) she can afford to be gracious. Extreme femininity is the order of the day, and the blend of assumed intimacy with the interviewer ('*You* know that as well as *I* do, Sir Robin'), mild flirtatiousness, emphasis on the first person singular and finger-tip statistics, make for rum viewing. Words are stressed in a way they never are in ordinary conversation ('Of *course* I'm *deeply* concerned – how could anyone *not* be?'), giving an impression of someone not caring, when she probably does care quite a lot. In their artificiality and hollowness these performances rank with those of another quite different Prime Minister, Harold Wilson.

It is sometimes said of Mrs Thatcher that she is too partisan, too narrow in her outlook to heal the schisms in the country that she has largely helped to create, that while she is an able leader of the party which she represents, she can never speak for the country as a whole. Perhaps no prime minister can. Perhaps she sees that as a less desirable goal than pushing her policies through, regardless of dissent. In any case how can a prime minister hope to bridge the divisions within the country who has so many apparent divisions within herself? At the time of our visit to Number Ten back in 1980, this was not a question one ever thought to ask.

11 May 1985

DEMENTIA AND MRS THATCHER

Dr Ian Deary and Dr Simon Wessely

There are very few laws in psychology and it is not easy to break them. We have suspected for some time that Mrs Thatcher has been causing other people to break one of the sturdiest of psychology's laws, Ribot's law. It states that the most recent memories are the first to be lost, and is held to explain what everyone knows anyway: that we have little trouble in remembering the events of childhood, but we haven't the faintest idea of what happened on the way to work. In particular, Ribot's law is advanced as the reason why some sufferers from dementia appear to live in the past, able to recall events from the two world wars, but out of touch with contemporary life, be it what they ate for their breakfasts or the current state of the nation.

In our practice as psychiatrists we came across four patients who were suffering from dementia to the extent that they could not remember where they were or what the day or year was; indeed, they could not even remember their own names. Yet, these disoriented patients recalled one piece of information correctly – the name of the current Prime Minister. From a patient whose own name was lost we got the response 'Maggie Thatcher' or 'Mrs Thatcher'. In fact, this question is not asked in order to pass the time of the idle psychiatrist, it forms a part of the standard assessment of demented patients along with many other questions, one of which is to ask what the reigning monarch is called.

We could not believe that any other leader of the government had made such an impact in the minds of the severely demented and we set out to investigate what we had now dubbed the Thatcher Effect. Our results, published in the Christmas issue of the *British Medical Journal*, confirmed our suspicions. Neither Mr Macmillan nor Mr Wilson in their fifth year of office was recalled as often by the demented population as Mrs Thatcher. The search through the files of 1963 and 1968 revealed one other confirmation. In the years examined Queen Elizabeth was recalled more frequently than the two Harolds, but by 1983 Mrs Thatcher had exactly reversed this trend and was clearly more prominent in our patients' minds than the monarch.

We saw three possibilities in attempting to explain our results. It might be the case that Mrs Thatcher is seen more on television and achieves prominence by exposure. Also, we considered the hypothesis that she has created a more effective and memorable image than her predecessors. Third, we entertained the likelihood that there is something about Margaret Thatcher *per se* that makes her mental representation indelible.

Our correspondence with Mori and Gallup had provided evidence that it was more than wide media exposure that makes Mrs Thatcher memorable. In fact, more people were watching party political broadcasts in Mr Wilson's time than did so in 1983. Also, the mere fact of her being female was not a sufficient explanation; as Leader of the Opposition Mrs Thatcher was recognised more often in photographs than the then prominent Cabinet minister Shirley Williams. Similarly, we have shown Margaret Thatcher to be recalled more easily than the Queen, who has similar *ex officio* prominence and has been there longer.

But we were soon to notice a further clue in our own investigation. In the questionnaires we looked at there was another question which began to interest us, that of the previous Prime Minister. This is asked in the expectation that it will be a more demanding question than either the name of the queen or the name of the current Prime Minister. In the three periods we examined one name kept coming back as the name of the previous PM – Winston Churchill. What we now renamed the Churchill Effect was clearly a part of the Thatcher phenomenon. It was more than the mere creation of an image. Neither Mr Wilson with his pipe and Gannex, nor Supermac himself was a novice at image building, and both 'the pound in your pocket' and 'you've never had it so good' are just as closely associated with their authors as 'there is no alternative' and 'never in the field of human conflict'.

Just what makes Mrs Thatcher's personality so memorable is a moot point. In Hugo Young's 'The Thatcher Phenomenon' on BBC Radio it was clear that there was little disagreement with the assessment of her surprised civil servants at the Department of Education who found out that she was intelligent, tireless, never delegated and was ever-certain, 'the answer . . . springing from her character'. On the same programme Barbara Castle's estimation was that 'she is in love with power, success and with herself'. Strangely, no one considered that well-known psychological phenomenon of the 'figure' versus the 'ground'. In this view one could state that Mrs Thatcher achieves her prominence by default owing to the dreary lot that surround her. After all, a tree will always stand out in a desert.

But there is more to it than that. As Charles Moore, for example, has noted: 'She has almost become one of those perpetual characters with which the British stock their culture, expressive of elements of their national character. Just as we know what we mean when we mention Falstaff or Mr Micawber or Cromwell or Henry VIII, our descendants a century hence will know what they mean by Mrs Thatcher' (*Time and Tide*, Autumn 1985). This is Mrs Thatcher as Jungian archetype.

As scientists we eagerly await the end of Mrs Thatcher's reign. This will give us the opportunity to ask the question, 'Who was the previous Prime Minister?' and to obtain the correct answer, 'Mrs Thatcher'. If Mrs Thatcher can erase the Churchill Effect from our brains she will clearly have been Britannia.

21/28 December 1985

PLAYING WITH THE CASINO'S MONEY

John Mortimer talks to Norman Tebbit

A visit to Norman Tebbit arouses excited expectations. Should you take a long spoon, a bulb of garlic, or two twigs roughly bound into a cross? He has been variously described as a 'semi-house trained polecat' (Michael Foot), 'the Chingford Skinhead' (a Labour MP) and, since he acquired a cottage in Devon, 'The Hound of the Baskervilles'. Would he arise creakingly from a coffin in the basement of Smith Square in a crumpled suit of tails and a scarlet-lined opera cloak? Eager for the green limelight and the sound hissing from the wings I hurried down the backstreets of Westminster.

There was no smell of sulphur in the Conservative Central Office, only the flags of the United Kingdom, bust of Winston Churchill wearing his siren suit, large helpful girls hurrying back from lunch and a gentle, grey-haired man talking about his retirement. 'We have this big labrador dog and I think I'll devote my time to him.' And then, after a longish wait, I was ushered into the presence of the man whom the *Financial Times* could best describe as an enigma. If this were true I had only 45 minutes of the Chairman's time to find any sort of solution.

'My father was in the retail trade when I was born in the Thirties.' Mr Tebbit touched lightly on the story of his life. 'Which had the most influence on me, my mother or my father? Heaven only knows. I don't think either of them had! I think I had more influence on them. Were they Conservative? I don't think I ever asked. They weren't particularly religious. I don't think God ever came into my upbringing at all.'

'You've been very close to death at least twice.'

'My wife reckons I come close to death every time I drive a car, but I've got no convictions yet. Do go on.'

'Once when you were strapped into the cockpit of a burning Mosquito during your National Service and you had to break open the canopy to escape. Another, of course, at the time of the Brighton hotel bombing. Did you feel you came close to God on either of those occasions?'

'I would have to say, quite honestly, that I haven't met Him yet.'

'Did you learn anything about death itself?'

'I can't tell you that I saw it as a gateway to pleasure.'

'You wouldn't describe yourself as a religious man?'

'Well, I'm not an atheist. But Christ being the Son of God and so on . . . ? No. I can't believe that. But I do think there's a system of order in the universe.'

'So God's a paid-up member of the Conservative Party?'

'Oh, yes. Of course.' And the suppressed laughter which had been bubbling away behind Mr Tebbit's surprising answers was released like a jet of steam. 'I've never had the slightest doubt about that. After all, he couldn't be a socialist.'

'Why not?'

'Because of the process of evolution.'

'Tell me.'

'Well, as I've playfully pointed out, evolution meant getting rid of the dinosaurs and replacing them with some more efficient and up-to-date animals. Any socialist would have been dedicated to protecting the dinosaurs in the name of compassion or conservation or something. The dinosaurs would never have been allowed to go. So God can't be a socialist.'

'You mean to say that there aren't any dinosaurs in the Tory Party?'

'Of course there are.' Mr Tebbit was laughing openly now, almost blowing the lid off the kettle. 'And they've got to be got rid of too!'

We sat at a small, empty boardroom table in the Chairman's office. Mr Tebbit is smaller than I have been led to believe. His face is lined, his hair thin, he blinks a good deal and he has the pallor of actors or prisoners, persons who live by artificial light. He has the look of a sardonic conjuror, an illusionist without illusions. His eyes are very bright and he sits relaxed, with his hands folded. He has clearly emerged from his own ordeal, and the deep tragedy of his wife's injuries, with his sense of humour intact. What is curious is that he seems to find his own lethal brand of politics hugely entertaining. For a moment, and unexpectedly, I remembered my father who once told me that there was a great deal of harmless fun to be got out of the Divorce Court.

'This father of yours. When did he actually get on his bike?'

'In the Thirties. He'd lost his job as a shop manager and he went off round the building sites.'

'Round Edmonton?'

'He was looking for casual labour.'

I remembered that Mr Tebbit had made his famous remark as a riposte to Michael Heseltine (when they were shaping up as rival heirs apparent), who had suggested that more money should be spent on jobs in Liverpool. 'My father didn't riot but got on his bike to look for work.' It was perhaps more a bit of Cabinet in-fighting than serious advice to the hopelessly unemployed of northern England. In any event Mr Tebbit's father doesn't seem to have had a great effect on his son and at this point he departed from the interview, cycling hopefully.

'When did you become a Conservative?'

'At Edmonton Grammar School. When I first read Fred . . . Oh, what's his name again?'

'Hayek.' A grey-haired, red-faced, rather tweedy amanuensis had appeared silently and, sitting behind Mr Tebbit, supplied the name of the Austrian monetarist who seems to have exercised such a lasting influence on the boy from Edmonton. Even during his recent illness Mr Tebbit kept going by reading the work of the 'Two Freds, Hayek and Trueman'. 'I read *The Road to Serfdom*. I read history from 1830 to 1914. I knew that the centrally controlled state leads to unpleasant consequences. Socialism is bound to become authoritarian.'

'But you grew up in the years of the Attlee government. Wouldn't you agree that was a time of enormous political achievement?'

'Don't get me wrong. I'm in favour of the Health Service and equal educational opportunities.'

'And Attlee and Stafford Cripps were extremely well-intentioned and well-meaning people?'

'Well-meaning people are the most dangerous. You can't have socialism unless you control incomes and prices. So you go the way of Hitler and Mussolini.'

'But we lived through the Labour governments of Attlee and Harold Wilson and I never noticed many gauleiters around. I mean, not too many people got carted off by the Gestapo at dawn.'

'That's because those Socialist governments failed. You don't know what would have happened if they'd been a success!' Mr Tebbit fell into a happy silence, relishing the thought of the Fascist state England only seems to have avoided thanks to the clumsiness of Harold Wilson.

'So after school and Hayek you wanted to go into politics?'

'Like any other ambitious young man, I wanted to succeed.' Success came to Norman Tebbit after jobs in publishing and journalism, National Service, a long stint as an airline pilot (where he was an officer of Balpa, the pilots' union) and entry to the House as Member for Epping in 1970. On the back benches he emerged as the new style of abrasive, lower-middle-class, hardline and sharp-tongued MP who would herald the greatest and perhaps most vote-catching change in Conservative history. If Norman Tebbit hadn't existed, one perceptive old Tory was heard to say, it would have been necessary to invent him.

'When you got into the House of Commons, didn't you feel isolated among a lot of upper-class, old-public-school Tories?'

'To be quite honest with you, I don't think I noticed them. I did think a few of them were intellectually arrogant.' Norman Tebbit made an early impression by the savagery of his questions from the back benches. No doubt he was off on that strange quest for political power which has a fascination that has nothing to do with the free market economy.

'You talk a lot about monetarism, but money really isn't the most important thing in life, is it? I mean, you could presumably make a fortune in the City but you go on with this extremely thankless political task. It can't be for the money.'

For the first time in our conversation Mr Tebbit was silent, nor did he laugh.

'When Mrs Thatcher allowed the American planes to set off from our shores to bomb Libyans, did you expect such a hostile public reaction?'

'We thought that there might be some political repercussions. Yes.'

'Some newspapers, I think the *Daily Telegraph*, suggested that you weren't in favour of our giving permission for that. Were they right?'

'I'm in favour of everything which our Government has concluded it's in favour of.' Mr Tebbit chose his words with great care. They didn't seem to imply enormous enthusiasm for the Libyan adventure. 'The United States administration had supported us in the Falklands. It's best to be friendly with our allies.'

'I think some people find it hard to understand an American government which says it intends to fight terrorism over here but finances and supports some particularly brutal terrorism by the Contras in Nicaragua.'

'The Contra situation is a difficult area. Certainly the Nicaraguan government is not very democratic. I'm not prepared to say whether or not I think the United States is going about it in the right way.'

'Do you think that the British people resent our country being used as an American aircraft carrier?'

'Remember the captain of the ship is British and she had to give her permission.'

'You've said that anti-American talk is a sign of "cheap and dirty parties seeking cheap and dirty votes". But what's wrong with saying that we should be an independent force for moderation and common sense in the world and not become implicated in America's more thoughtless adventures? Is my vote dirty if that's what I think?'

'That's a perfectly reasonable position to take. I meant people who talk about Americans as they might about blacks who'd come to settle in the neighbourhood. The sort of people who chalked "Yanks Go Home" on walls during the war.'

'And perhaps we resent British businesses being sold off to America?'

'The United States don't mind us taking over their businesses, which we do quite a lot. And we never sold Westland to the Americans. It wasn't ours to sell, in spite of all they said on that terrible box in the corner.' Mr Tebbit nodded with deep disapproval at the expressionless, grey face of an unlit television set.

'Going on from what you said about "dirty votes". Is there really any future for you in abusing the other parties? I mean, to win the election you've got to capture the middle ground. Is there any sense in just saying things that'll only please the Party faithful? Presumably they'll vote for you anyway.'

'The faithful won't vote for you unless you're faithful to them. I've got to stand up for what I believe is right.'

'Didn't you emerge from the terrible ruins of that bombed hotel feeling that all the bickering and insults between political parties are rather trivial?'

'Oh no.' Mr Tebbit's eyes were twinkling and all his good spirits were restored. 'I think you come back from such experiences greatly refreshed and determined to carry on with the job in hand. And you may as well do all you can *while* you can. I feel I'm living on borrowed time anyway. I'm playing with the casino's money.'

'Why did you do so disastrously in the recent elections? And now you've sunk to third place in the polls . . .'

'I think people are pleased with what we've done. We've brought down inflation. We've seen off Galtieri and Scargill. Now they want us to do something else.'

'They want you to do something about unemployment.'

'Perhaps there's nothing that governments *can* do about unemployment. But the 80 per cent who're in work are benefiting from higher real incomes and pensioners are benefiting from lower inflation.'

'You can't expect a man suddenly thrown out of work in Middlesbrough to be much cheered up by the low rate of inflation.'

'Well, that's it. Our aims and objectives aren't being made clear to the public. Lower inflation should produce more jobs eventually, but they don't understand that.'

'Don't you think that people are quite willing to pay higher rates and taxes if it means proper education, less unemployment and better public services?'

'I believe they want all those things without having to pay for them. They want their cake and they want to eat it.'

'But if they decide they'll pay for a better sort of cake . . .'

'I don't think they've decided that. I think they agree with us about taxes but they're not clear what we mean to do next. And then there's the question of the Prime Minister herself . . .'

Mrs Thatcher, in full colour, smiled down on us from a large gilt photograph frame on the wall. Surely Mr Tebbit wasn't going to suggest that she might be an election liability?

'It's a question of her leadership when our aims aren't clearly defined. When people understand what she's doing there's a good deal of admiration for her energy and resolution and persistence, even from those people who don't agree with her. Now there's a perception that we don't know where we're going so those same qualities don't seem so attractive.'

'Isn't there also the boredom factor?'

'What?'

'Eventually we get bored with our politicians. We feel they've gone on too long. We got bored with Macmillan and Harold Wilson who were enormously admired in their time.'

'I'm not sure that people get bored. Journalists get bored. That's the trouble.'

Is that true? Or does the great British talent for boredom save us, even more than the free market economy, from the perils of dictatorship? I had another ten minutes before the Conservative Party Chairman had to rush away and see to the Duchy of Lancaster, and the enigma was still unsolved. Does he, for instance, believe his more extravagant opinions (that Labour Party government leads to dictatorship or that other political parties are 'dirty and cheap'), or has he, by his own choice of pungent words, come to convince himself? Both may be true; he has convinced himself therefore he truly believes. There's no reason to doubt his sincerity.

'You gave a Disraeli Lecture denouncing the Permissive Society. But surely there were some worthwhile reforms during the Roy Jenkins era. You wouldn't be in favour of us still imprisoning consenting homosexuals of full age, for instance?'

'I wouldn't imprison homosexuals *as such*, no.' What on earth did the 'as such' mean? For the first time Mr Tebbit sounded gloomy. Then he cheered up and went on. 'Don't get me wrong. I'm not intolerant or prudish. I'm nothing like Mizz Short of the Labour Party who wants to ban Page Three of the *Sun*. I mean, you can't ban all the naked ladies in the National Gallery, so I suppose Mizz Short thinks that the upper classes should be allowed to gaze at them in the National Gallery, but the workers shouldn't see them in the *Sun*. Unless she's against all paintings and statues like Cromwell, Michael Foot's favourite dictator.'

'You also talked about a return to Victorian values, but the greatest

Victorians, like Dickens, spent their time denouncing the injustice of Victorian society and the evils of uninhibited capitalism.'

'That's right! It's exactly what the Earl of Shaftesbury did. He was a Conservative MP. You see, the socialists talk a lot about compassion, but the Tories do something about it.' Mr Tebbit, having astutely snatched a party political point out of the horrors of Victorian England, found his cheerfulness quite restored.

'You don't give any recreations in *Who's Who*. Is that because you haven't got any?'

'Really because I regard my private life as private. It has been rumoured that I do a little gardening.'

'What do you read?'

'Mainly those horrible red boxes!'

'Do you think you'll win the next election?'

'If we can desist from shooting ourselves in the foot. I'm opposed to us constantly doing that.'

'And what have you done with Jeffrey Archer?'

Although I had seen that ebullient author's name on a door on the way up I thought that since he told the young unemployed that he solved all his problems with a best-seller he had been kept bound and gagged in the cellar.

'Jeffrey's doing a terrific job speaking to the faithful.'

'But he's not allowed to speak to the world at large?'

'Oh yes he is. We had him on *Question Time*.'

'Who do you admire on the Labour benches? I imagine you might have a bit of a soft spot for Dennis Skinner.' It was an appealing thought, a glimmer of fellow feeling for the 'Beast of Bolsover' from the 'Hound of the Baskervilles'.

'Yes. Except when he goes right over the top. The world needs a Dennis Skinner. I don't think the world needs a Hattersley.'

'Anyone else?'

'Oh, I'd hate to ruin their careers by naming them.'

My three-quarters of an hour had ticked away and Mr Tebbit was on his feet. I had time for one more question.

'If it became clear to you that by going on saying the things you've been saying you'd lose the next election, would you change them?'

'Of course not.' Mr Tebbit seemed only faintly amused by the suggestion. 'If the Conservatives wanted to change their policies they'd have to find another Chairman. I have to be true to what I stand for. And I shall go on expressing myself robustly.'

Although he has come in for more than his share of political abuse many people have experienced Mr Tebbit's considerable charm, and he is said to have earned the devotion of his Civil Servants, despite his habit of listening to Test Match commentaries during meetings. One MP called him a hard nut with a soft centre and even Mr Moss Evans, who Mr Tebbit would no doubt say is one of the 'cloth cap barons' of the trade union world, found him 'very scathing but without offence'. It seems clear that Mr Tebbit's particular brand of politics, by Friedrich von Hayek out of Edmonton County Grammar, is going out of style. Castigated by the electorate, the Conservative Party is now anxious to demonstrate its 'caring heart' and spend money, at least on education, which Mr Tebbit has called one of 'the soft issues'. He is probably too honest a man, and perhaps an insufficiently deft politician, to trim his sails to the prevailing wind. He may even feel, with one of his ironic little laughs, that he has, after all, nothing very much to lose. He is still playing with the casino's money.

24 May 1986

THATCHERISM: A MONSTROUS INVENTION

T. E. Utley

There is no such thing as Thatcherism. The illusion that there is in part a deliberate creation of Mrs Thatcher's enemies. They have proceeded on the age-old maxim that there is nothing (certainly not private scandal) more likely to injure the reputation of a British politician than the suggestion that he has an inflexible devotion to principle. This maxim is only partly true, but it is an unshakably established belief, a fact which helps to make it truer than it otherwise would be.

The illusion is in part also the creation of a coterie of admiring friends by whom Mrs Thatcher has been surrounded. Some of them, for cultural and sometimes ethnic reasons, have little sympathy with the English political tradition, which they regard as a fraud perpetrated on the people by an oppressive and incompetent political establishment. What the country needed, they argued, was someone who would sweep away all this rubbish about compromise and consensus and lead the country in a radical reconstruction of its habits and institutions. They easily identified Mrs Thatcher as their man.

The illusion, however, could never have achieved its present proportions without some assistance from its victim. Mrs Thatcher is not by temperament averse to the Messianic role. She also has a wish to be, and to be regarded as, something of an intellectual, and she has a passionate devotion to intellectual honesty. When she got into politics, she became an avid student of the writings of what is broadly and rather vaguely called the 'New Right'. In the press of public business, she still finds time to discuss at length such profound questions as why Britain 'lacks a free enterprise culture', and how this deficiency can be repaired.

At another level, however, she is an exceptionally astute politician and an accomplished party tactician. It is inconceivable that her devotion to doctrine would ever persuade her to do anything which was plainly politically suicidal.

Now, in all this, you may say, there is very little that is new. Many of her predecessors have had a taste for philosophy, and only a philistine would suggest that this taste has had no influence on their political conduct. All of them, like Mrs Thatcher herself, however, have been practical politicians with a sense of the status of principles as guidelines, not absolute and literal moral imperatives.

This is so, but somehow in the case of others the reflective and practical ingredients in their natures have blended more easily. It sometimes looks as though she lives a completely compartmentalised life. When talking to her friends or addressing a party conference, she is the philosopher-queen, although the impression, as far as her public oratory goes, springs rather from the manner of its delivery than from its actual content; listen hard enough and you will always hear the qualifying clauses, often uttered rapidly and with an almost palpable physical revulsion. Then something happens in the real world – the need to bring the Rhodesian crisis to an end, the need to avoid a miners' strike before the Government is ready to cope with it, the need to placate a divided Cabinet over trade union reform – and Mrs Thatcher yields to necessity, often swiftly.

Who can doubt, for instance, that Mrs Thatcher is convinced that the Welfare State needs radical reform, that she would like to introduce educational vouchers, student loans, possibly even to make the relatively rich contribute something directly towards their medical care? But most of these projects have been quietly dropped, or put into indefinite cold storage in obedience to supposed political necessity.

Consider, then, the 'ideology' in which Thatcherism is supposed to consist. Its chief plank is the advocacy of a free and competitive economy, but that simply represents one more or less permanent ingredient in modern Conservative philosophy. It was on that principle that Churchill fought the 1945 election, having just read Hayek's *Road to*

Serfdom; to judge from what is now said, one might suppose that Mrs Thatcher had 'discovered' the great Dr Hayek. What brought the Tories to 13 years of political supremacy in 1951 was the slogan 'Set the people free'. 'Under Labour there has been too much government interference in the day-to-day workings of industry . . . there has been too much government'; 'We will reduce and reform taxation, giving first priority to reducing income tax'; 'Our aim is to identify and remove obstacles that prevent effective competition and restrict initiative.' All those quotations are from Mr Heath's election manifesto in 1970.

Lord Bruce-Gardyne, in his admirable book *Mrs Thatcher's First Administration*, has suggested that the real difference between Mrs Thatcher and the rest (particularly Mr Heath) is the fact that whereas they regarded sound finance and free competition as means to an end, she regards them as moral absolutes to be applied whether they appear to work or not. For the reasons I have given above, I do not think this to be a wholly accurate description of her political behaviour; but the essential point, for the purposes of this article, is that there is absolutely nothing new about the doctrinal front that she presents on these matters., In 20th-century English Conservatism (I say 'English' because there are absolutely no authentically Conservative Scotsmen, Irishmen or genuine Welshmen) two schools of thought about the economy have existed side by side – the liberal school, to which Mrs Thatcher belongs, and the 'corporatist' school, to which Macmillan and (now) Heath belong. Sometimes one is in the ascendant, sometimes the other. Neither ever captures complete sway over the party. Neither is taken wholly seriously by any of its apostles who are seriously engaged in practical politics. That is all there is to it.

As for 'privatisation', Mr Powell proposed it in his famous 'Morecambe budget' speech in 1968. As for 'property-owning democracy', I believe it was Anthony Eden who coined the phrase.

There is an even stronger and more profound reason for supposing that Thatcherism does not exist: the Prime Minister likes to regard herself as an exponent of the 'politics of conviction', as distinct from the 'politics of consensus'. Now this is a silly dichotomy, invented by inferior journalists. Consensus politics is an intrinsic part of the art of government; one has to achieve a consensus with someone and no consensus embraces the whole of the community. But what this monstrous distinction implies is that Mrs Thatcher, unlike other politicians, is in no sense a product of history, that she is starting from scratch, that she is not putting her ear to the ground to hear what is going on in the world and to decide how she can (however slightly) influence it, but that she is deciding what is the good society and how she can create it. It is hard to imagine anything further from the truth.

Mrs Thatcher was produced by history. Her two major achievements – the control of inflation and the reduction of the trade unions to size – were simply the climax of a series of unsuccessful attempts by Labour and Tory governments alike to cope with what were increasingly seen as the two most important evils from which the country was suffering. When Chancellor of the Exchequer (1974–9), Mr Healey boasted that the government to which he belonged was 'perhaps the first in Britain for many years which has given monetary policy the importance it deserves'. In 1976 Mr Callaghan said to his party conference, 'Higher inflation followed by higher unemployment: that is the history of the last 20 years.' As for the trade unions, Mrs Castle had tried and failed to curb them in the late Sixties. Mr Heath tried again and failed in the Seventies. After 'the winter of discontent' Mrs Thatcher came to power on a wave of revulsion from trade union arrogance and oppression which had been steadily growing for ages. Bureaucracy and inflation were equally out. If she had not existed, it would have been necessary to invent her.

The other element in Thatcherism is supposed to be the wish to restore Britain as a great power in the world. By this Mrs Thatcher does not mean primarily a power devoted to the preservation of its own interests. She belongs to that militant Whig branch of English Conservatism which took over when Churchill became Prime Minister in 1940. This is to say that her view of foreign policy has a high moral content or, in other words, that she likes to devote herself to large and distant causes – the freedom of Afghanistan rather than the security of Ulster. She is suspicious about the Common Market, but seems prepared to swallow its consequences (e.g. the Single European Act) so long as the blame for them can be attributed to the Foreign Office. I believe that she went into the Falklands with reluctance and regret and that, having done so, carried it off with a courage and skill of which no other prime minister, possibly including Churchill, would have been capable. In terms of theory, however, she has contributed nothing new to the discussion of Britain's role in the world.

Margaret Thatcher is a great prime minister, great by virtue of her courage and by virtue of what ideologues would often, misguidedly, describe as her 'low political cunning'. We desperately need her; the greatest obstacle to our continuing to have her is the belief that she is the inventor of a 'political philosophy'. She will not get all she wants, as no politician can or should, but she will get more of it than others would and she will in the end be content with the deficiency. But, please, no more talk about Thatcherism.

9 August 1986

HOW CECIL PARKINSON DEALT WITH THE SCHOOLBOY'S QUESTION ABOUT HIS MORAL VALUES

Craig Brown

He had lost the top button of his shirt earlier in the morning, and was a little put out. 'Perhaps we'll be able to encourage someone to do a bit of sewing when we get there,' he said as we both got into the back of his small chauffeur-driven car. The cuffs on his well-cut blue-and-white striped shirt each had a third, spare button which, I thought, might come in handy later.

His family had been part of the strong Northern working-class Conservative tradition, he explained, as we smoothed our way away from the Tarmac building in Mayfair, but he had been a socialist at his grammar school. 'Socialism appealed to one's radical instincts but also to one's idealism,' he said. 'And it's easy now to forget what an idealistic concept nationalisation once was.'

Cecil Parkinson has a way of screwing up his eyes when talking, as if he is looking constantly at the sun. His hands, with their bitten nails, are rarely still. They smooth down his already neat hair; they run themselves up and down his tie; when cupped, they lend emphasis to a statement of political conviction; and, every now and then, they play anxiously with the buttonless collar.

'What was your early ambition?'

'Oh, I've been around this course many times before.'

'I'm sorry . . . I just wondered.'

'You know already, don't you?'

'No, I don't think I do.'

'I didn't realise that this would be a soul-searching interview. I didn't realise that those were the terms.'

'Well, I was just asking because I was interested.'

He pulled at his tie. 'It's been written before, but I was thinking of going into the Church. But that's old hat, it really is.'

We moved on to his Cambridge days. Reading English, he never missed a lecture by Leavis. 'He was so rigorous, you know, and his influence carried way beyond one's attitude to literature. He taught one to look for the difference between the imaginative and the contrived in one's daily life; between artificiality and conviction. And one can apply that attitude in the House of Commons too.'

'How?'

'Benn, for instance. He believes in what he says. It's not a charade. He may be deadly but he's earnest.'

'What about Kinnock?'

'I think most people would accept that he's the genuine article.'

'And Hattersley?'

'He's obviously a very able person with a wide range of interests. I think he's an exceptional writer, by the way . . .'

'But does he represent artificiality or conviction?'

'I think we'd better draw stumps on this one.'

He picked up his car telephone and punched out a number. 'Just getting some figures,' he said to me as it was ringing. It was the day after the council elections. '. . . Is that you, Paul? Have you got the figures? . . . Oh, I'm sorry. Could you tell me your number so I don't make the same mistake again? . . . Thank you.'

He turned to me as he was redialling. 'It was my father-in-law's number,' he explained, the right-hand side of his mouth smiling briefly before returning to place. He smoothed his tie. Paul answered. The figures were tremendously encouraging.

His head shakes very slightly while he talks. The surrounding demeanour of the rest of his face makes the scrunched-up, bewildered eyes sadder than they might appear on someone less manicured. Like many politicians, when he talks of others he talks of their personalities rather than their politics, but, on the subject of himself, he pooh-poohs what he calls 'soul-searching' questions, as if somehow one was being clumsy or naïve in asking them.

'What would you say were your faults, and what are your qualities?'

He looked straight ahead along the M3. There was such a long silence that I thought he might well not have heard me. Then he turned.

'That's for others to say.'

'But what would you say?'

Another long pause.

'I suppose some people would say that I was bland and that I lacked conviction, but others who know me better would say I have very strong political conviction.'

He could be harder on others, from all parties, than he was on himself, but never for quotation.

Throughout the day, he would say 'off the record' or 'I'd ask you not to put this in, though' with the almost flirtatious air people adopt when confiding the secrets of a circle they see as charmed, and as theirs. What would follow would be no more than a little off-the-record anecdote about Willie or Norman especially designed for affecting intimacy with journalists, for creating an air of complicity while actually establishing ground rules for superiority.

The Rt Hon. Cecil Parkinson was due to speak at a grammar school in Portsmouth. We had set off late and when we got to Portsmouth we lost our way. There were many people in the streets whom we could have asked the way without leaving the car, but, once the chauffeur had brought the car to a halt, Parkinson leapt out in his shirtsleeves and strode along the pavement to an elderly couple. I can't remember ever having seen anyone bothering to do this before. The chauffeur and I stared through the car window as Parkinson and the elderly couple talked animatedly and hands were shaken. 'He's made their day!' said the chauffeur, but the freshly contented look on his face made me feel that, in another way, they were making his. Before we found the school, Parkinson had leapt out of the car a second time, to be recognised by three businessmen.

In the headmaster's room before the lecture, Parkinson chatted with a select band of boys and staff over sandwiches. He obviously felt easy talking light-heartedly with groups of six or seven, drawing them into his stories of power, asking them for information about the school and about themselves.

He had something to say to everyone, and he was evidently going down well. A few minutes before we were due to climb the stairs to the lecture hall, there were words in the headmaster's ear, and, seconds later, a boy and three masters were ushered with a certain amount of bustle into the headmaster's study. The miscreant had let off a number of stink-bombs in the hall.

Meanwhile, a master told me that, on the whole, pupils these days were different from those he taught a decade ago. They were more interested in careers, in money and in getting on.

I asked the ambitious 17-year-old chairman of the Politics Society whether we could expect heckling. He looked a little sheepish and said that they'd all been told not to say anything they shouldn't.

Parkinson spoke about the fundamental differences between socialism and conservatism. As he speaks of all the achievements of the present Government, his chin thrusting to and fro, his hands gesticulating towards the ceiling, a sense of ease emerges that is rarely evident in ordinary conversation with him.

There is a refuge in public life and public issues, a refuge where everything is simple and certain, untinged with contradiction and desperation. 'That's all very well, you might say . . .'; 'The truth of the matter is . . .'; 'People want to stand on their own two feet . . .' Here, everything is momentarily straightforward. '"I don't want to play the fuddle-fiddle in the muddle-middle"', he recalls Roy Jenkins saying, years ago, '. . . and he got it right; absolutely ON THE BUTTON!' Everyone joined in the laughter.

At the end of his speech, there were questions. A girl asked, 'What motivates politicians: a lust for personal power, a desire to serve the people, or something else?' Parkinson seemed ruffled by this. 'I can't honestly claim that I had political ambition . . .' his reply began. 'Some people have a burning ambition to be Prime Minister. I can't honestly claim I had . . . then one day the Prime Minister asked me down to Chequers and asked me if I would be Chairman of the Conservative Party. I don't know who was more surprised – me or her!'

There were more questions, on defence and economics, and then: 'When the Conservative Party claims to be the party of moral values, how is it that some of its members fail to live up to these values in their personal life?' There was a feeling of embarrassment. Cecil Parkinson replied, 'We all have ideals which we can't always live up to as human beings, and I should guess that, by the way you're blushing, you're the same.' There was relief, and much applause.

As we were leaving the hall, the headmaster said, 'Not a very clever question, but a clever answer,' and, to Mr Parkinson, 'I thought you handled that one very well.' 'You won't mention that, will you?' said Parkinson to me. I said that he must get a lot of questions and heckles of that nature. He said, no, hardly ever. Sometimes at universities, maybe.

We went to tea with the Conservative agent for Portsmouth South, a seat at the moment held by the SDP with a 1,300 majority. In the drive there was a green Jaguar with a car telephone. In the sitting-room there was an abundance of scones and cream cakes, an upright piano and a local newspaper with the headline 'SOUTH TURNS DEEP SHADE OF BLUE'. 'Tremendous isn't it?' said the agent. 'Tremendous,' agreed Parkinson. Parkinson mentioned to one of the women in the room that he was afraid he'd lost his top button in the morning. She offered to mend it later. 'Oh, could you?' he said, smiling pleasantly.

Having lost to Paddy Ashdown in Yeovil, the Conservative candidate had been selected for Portsmouth on condition that he lived there. 'He lives in a good middle-style house in a middle-style road in a middle-style part of the constituency,' explained the agent. 'You've got to be careful in that respect.' While we had tea, Parkinson told stories of his dealings with Mrs Thatcher. Every time her name was mentioned, the women would hide their smiles with another sip of tea.

We moved to the study, where a journalist and a photographer from a local paper, *Street Life*, had an appointment for a brief interview. After talk of his time at the school – 'I was interested to hear from the headmaster that many of the pupils there were on the assisted places scheme' – and election prospects – 'very encouraging' – the journalist said, 'I must ask you this, Mr Parkinson: it was announced today that Gary Hart has given up being a candidate for the presidency.'

'Oh, really.'

'What are your feelings about that, Mr Parkinson?'

'I have no thoughts about Gary Hart.'

'Because his situation is very similar to the one you experienced yourself a few years ago.'

'I really have given no thought to Gary Hart.'

'So you've got nothing to say about him?'

'Nothing.'

'Because you also had a political career and a supportive wife and so on . . .'

'I have nothing to say, I'm sorry.'

'Well, if you don't want to talk about Gary Hart, perhaps we should move on to Trident . . .'

But after the first couple of sentences on Trident the photographer, who had been silent, said, 'You still talk like a Top Tory.'

'Do I?' said Parkinson. 'I can't tell. Do I?'

'Well, you're still one of Maggie's favourites, aren't you?'

'The Prime Minister is a friend of mine, yes.'

'Do you think you'll get back in the Cabinet then?'

'Whether she includes me or not is entirely a matter for her.'

'You must have suffered a lot of heart-ache and trauma, Mr Parkinson. How have you kept going?'

'I've done a great deal of public speaking. I think I can help the Party in numerous ways. I'm involved with a number of charitable organisations . . .'

'Would you describe yourself as a happy man, Mr Parkinson?'

'Yes,' he said. 'Yes. Very.' Though even the happiest of men would have found difficulty in smiling after those questions, Mr Parkinson smiled. 'You should be on television,' he said to his photographer-inquisitor as they shook hands. The photographer seemed gratified by the compliment.

After a photo-session over a bottle of coins on a Union Jack collected for a baby-care unit by local Conservatives, we went on to our final engagement, speaking to Conservatives at a Trusthouse Forte hotel. The full list of Mr Parkinson's posts was listed by the agent, including secretary and chairman of the Anglo-Swiss parliamentary group since 1972.

Elderly women beamed with admiration. Again the achievements of the Conservatives were listed with unaffected enthusiasm, again.

Roy Jenkins was pictured playing the fuddle-diddle in the muddle-middle, but now a reference to the coming election and Portsmouth: 'I believe we can win it back and we will win it back and we have just the candidate to win it back!' He pointed to the small, neat man in the Prince of Wales check who lived in the middle-style part of the constituency. The applause was vigorous. After polite calls for the return of the death penalty and for life to mean just that, the meeting was brought to a close.

In the car in the dark on the way back, Cecil Parkinson seemed to be pleased with the way in which the day had gone. He was matey and relaxed. His hands no longer fidgeted with such vigour. The lost button seemed forgotten. In the dark, the sad eyes in the executive face were less noticeable. 'I've had a song on my mind all day,' he said just before his chauffeur dropped me off. 'Very powerful song from *Paint Your Wagon*. D'y'know it? "I'm On My Way".'

The thought occurred to me later that, relaxed and matey as he was, he had mentioned 'I'm On My Way' because he thought it might be an optimistic note on which I could end my article, a catchy summary of the day's events. After all, everything looked tremendously encouraging, and prospects were excellent.

16 May 1987

THE INHERENT JUSTICE OF TAKING OCCASIONAL POT-SHOTS AT THE CLERGY

Noel Malcolm

There was a time when the denunciation of a major government policy by the Church of England would have sent shockwaves rippling through the political consciousness of the nation. Nowadays these things happen as a matter of course, and no one takes much notice. When the Right Revd Stanley Booth-Clibborn, Bishop of Manchester, attacked the poll tax as 'inherently unjust' this week, it made a small news item on page seven of the *Daily Telegraph*, sandwiched between 'Man cuts off his own ear' and 'Dearer cheese'.

The Bishop was only repeating the phrase used by the General Synod last year, so that news was a trifle stale. He was joined, however, by the president of the Baptist Union, who said that the tax was 'against Biblical teaching', and by the president of the Methodist Conference, who said it was 'contrary to Gospel values'. But somehow one feels that the only way for a churchman of any denomination to hit the headlines these days would be to preach a sermon exhorting people to render unto Thatcher the things that are Thatcher's. That really would make the front page.

The Government's reactions to clerical criticism are so tried and tested that there is little newsworthiness to be found in them either. The public response from Mrs Thatcher is invariably to trump them with a higher card of anguished indignation. How dare they preach to her about 'caring' for the poor, when more funds are made available for the relief of poverty under Conservatism than was ever possible under socialism? And in private, the reaction in the Tory Party can vary from irritation to barely concealed glee. Having an excuse to take pot-shots at the clergy from time to time is a pleasure to be relished, rather like being allowed an occasional open season on a protected species: these rare, slow-flying birds seem so unworldly and vulnerable, and one expects to hear a piteous fluttering of lawn sleeves as they drop out of the sky.

When preachers attempt to match government policies against Gospel values, they start with a tremendous disadvantage. The policies are concrete, detailed, and tied up with the social and economic conditions of life here and now. The guidance supplied by Scripture, on the other hand, is necessarily unspecific and timeless. The Bible may tell us to love our neighbours, but it does not tell us in detail how to do this – whether, for example, to do it by giving them enterprise allowances or employing them in nationalised industries. Even when specific examples are given (feeding the hungry, clothing the naked, etc.), a good deal of further interpretation is still required. How literally are these examples to be taken? If they are not intended as an exhaustive list, how do we extend the same principles to yield further examples? And so on. The general principles may be there, but in order to bring them down to the level of detailed applications, a mass of further assumptions must be brought into play, assumptions which cannot be founded with anything like the same degree of confidence on Scripture itself.

Take abortion, for instance. 'Thou shalt not kill' seems clear enough as a general rule – although most Christian churches, in most periods, have happily reconciled this with capital punishment and the killing of enemy soldiers. But how do we decide at what point the destruction of a potential human life becomes the killing of a human being? The Bible, unfortunately, does not go into that sort of detail. Christians may agree on fundamental truths, but the division of clerical opinion on abortion has largely matched the division of opinion on that subject among atheists and agnostics; and if Catholics have supported Mr Alton, most Protestants are inclined to feel that that does not really count, because they are only obeying orders.

So if the Church of England cannot offer clear, unequivocal advice on such non-political, 'conscience' issues as abortion, what hope is there that they can ever demonstrate the sinfulness of anything so humdrum and technical as a system of taxation? Has the Bishop of Manchester considered the use of a flat-rate charge for road tax or television licences? The average household pays £158 a year on these two non-redistributive charges, yet so far as I know the General Synod has not noticed even the tiniest stain of inherent injustice in them.

The Government can feel, then, that it is on solid ground when it fends off the assaults of the clergy. Religion is not a direct supplier of political programmes, and even where central moral issues such as hanging or abortion are concerned the same religious principles can often be used to back up completely opposite arguments. The churches have no monopoly of morality, and the Government should be willing to say so loudly and clearly.

But at the moment, while the Government says this out of one side of its mouth, it is busy affirming out of the other side that morality is uniquely dependent on religion. In the current debate about religious education, Conservatives have been falling over one another in the push to agree that religion is the sole source of moral values; and the Bishop of London's amendment to clause two of the Education Reform Bill, identifying religious education as first among equals in the basic curriculum, is

'And deliver us from the Prime Minister.'

the one piece of lordly tinkering with the Bill which the Government has shown itself most willing to accept.

When the Lords debated these amendments last week, the agreement that morality depends on religion was overwhelming in its unanimity and complacency. 'No religion, no morality', said Lord St John of Fawsley, and only a few brave souls dared to question this obvious untruth. One of them, Lord Sefton of Garston, somewhat weakened his case by questioning the Virgin Birth; the Bishop of London, in memorably unclerical language, told him not to 'rubbish' people's beliefs, and the motion was quickly passed 'that the noble Lord be no longer heard'. Speaker after speaker argued that morality could survive in our society only if children were indoctrinated with Christian beliefs at school, and then denied that they were advocating indoctrination. Nobody asked the obvious question about what happens to people who have been persuaded that morality cannot survive without religious beliefs, and then lose those religious beliefs.

There are, to be precise, two varieties of humbug at work here: the humbug of politicians, and the humbug of clergymen who give the impression that the sole reason for teaching religious doctrines is to improve public morality. A bit more old-fashioned hostility between church and state would do both politicians and churchmen a world of good.

14 May 1988

HYPERNATS AND COUNTRY-LOVERS

Ferdinand Mount

Are we seeing a serious revival of British nationalism? In right-wing circles, the quickening interest in the question of nationhood is undeniable. If you cast a glance at any of the mushrooming organisations in that region – the Salisbury Group, the Conservative Philosophy Group, the Claridge Press, the Committee for a Free Britain, the Freedom Association – the chances are not only that you will see Professor Roger Scruton's cheerful carroty mane in the thick of things but also that the Nation in one form or another will be under discussion. Twenty years ago, few people would have thought of founding or joining such organisations, certainly not in order to argue about Nationhood – then generally regarded as the most boring, taken-for-granted topic imaginable.

This may not be the first time we have come across the argument recently put by Professor E. J. Mishan in the *Salisbury Review* that the White Briton's 'sense of national wholeness' has been weakened by 'the omnipresence in his native land of peoples of Afro-Asian origin'. But it has not often been put so uncompromisingly by an academic. Nor have we often seen in British art magazines since the war a manifesto like Peter Fuller's declaration, in his effervescent new periodical *Modern Painters*, that the British art world ought to stick up for British artists and has dismally failed to identify itself with 'a common national culture'.

Professor Scruton, the indefatigable editor of the *Salisbury Review*, is an ally of Mr Fuller's on the aesthetic if not the political front and a frequent contributor to *Modern Painters*. And he lumps together 'race', 'nationhood' and 'culture' as 'pre-political forms of unity', which, he says, cannot be detached from political order and political stability. All this, we are given to understand, is the red meat which the wimps who cook up the menu of conventional politics leave out. The comfortable 'cosmopolitans' – a word now frequently used as a term of contempt – operate a conspiracy of silence which only a select few have the moral courage and the intellectual equipment to breach.

To the outsider, these discussions of Nationhood tend to be rather puzzling, unsatisfying affairs. The red meat is paraded before us, the maître d' sharpens his implements, the sauce is bubbling, but somehow we never get to taste the dish. The trouble is, I think, that it is so difficult to envisage any practical measures which would achieve the apparently desired results of racial or cultural homogeneity – or none which can be mentioned in the polite society we wish to keep one foot in.

We run into trouble as soon as we start talking about 'Britishness', for we know we really want to say 'Englishness', but know we must not, because of the Scots, and the Welsh and some of the Irish; as for 'Britons' and 'Britishers', the heart sinks at the first mention of such shatteringly bogus terms. To carry any kind of conviction, talk about nationhood must necessarily be vague, brooding, adumbrating; provocative thoughts can be dangled in front of the audience but not for long enough to be stripped down and examined. Spades may indeed be called spades – that is part of the thrill – but what precisely is to be done with them cannot be spelled out.

So we cannot really expect any sort of practical agenda from those whom I shall call the 'hypernationalists', meaning those who believe that 'the Nation' – sometimes they mean the Race or Tribe, sometimes the Nation-state, sometimes both – is the only political entity that matters and the only legitimate focus of loyalty. As an ideology, hypernationalism is opposed, often fiercely (it does most things fiercely), to other doctrines, such as liberalism or internationalism, but not necessarily to the hypernationalisms of other nations. The French may in fact be admired for being so cussedly French, the Russians for being so redbloodedly Russian. The gentler sort of affection for one's native landscape, province or nation I shall call 'country-love', in order to steer clear of 'nationalism' and 'patriotism' with their confusing, overlapping nuances.

But if the hypernats have no specific agenda to propose, why have they leapt into prominence at this particular moment? The reflex answer is usually that they are all 'Thatcher's children'. Yet many of these groups and magazines comfortably predate Mrs Thatcher's full-blown ascendancy. Clearly some of her triumphs – most notably the Falklands – have imbued her more hypernat supporters with fresh enthusiasm. With her at the helm, they feel a following wind at their back. The black-and-white way she likes to define and defend the national interest appeals to them.

Yet in some crucial ways, she does not quite seem to share their view of the world; she is keenly pro-American, they are often resentful of American influence; they are obsessed by the politics of race, she is not; she is much concerned with the rule of law, including international law – a subject treated with scorn and derision by the hypernat. A true hypernat would not write such gushing fan letters to President Reagan or welcome Nissan and Toyota to Britain so unreservedly or be happy to see British firms pass into foreign ownership.

What about Europe then? Is not Mrs Thatcher's Bruges speech the most resonant clarion call yet to hypernats? Does it not presage a great confrontation with the members of the Community?

Now it is true that the speech evoked considerable enthusiasm, mostly from those who had always been opposed to British membership of the Community. Many of them had, I think, more or less given up the cause as lost and were delighted, and not a little surprised, to receive what looked like a second chance – much as Gavrilo Princip and his fellow assassins were delighted to find the Archduke Franz Ferdinand coming round for the second time.

The Bruges Group, a newly formed collection of distinguished academics and journalists – Ralph Harris, Norman Stone, Patrick Minford et al – struggle manfully against the charge that they are 'anti-European' and protest that they are primarily interested in seeing that the causes of free enterprise and free trade dominate the new Europe. All the same one or two of them – I hesitate to single out Professor Scruton again – do give the impression that they are suspicious of all such foreign entanglements and are gleefully looking forward to a big bust-up.

By contrast, what the Bruges speech actually says is that 'our destiny is in Europe, as part of the Community', and this seems to be the direction in which public opinion, as measured by opinion polls and by random observation, seems to be moving in a sluggish sort of way. Grudging acceptance of membership seems to be shifting towards a more complaisant recognition that the Community is likely to develop, and so is our role in it, although not into a United States of Europe, or anything much like it, in our lifetime, if ever (although a recent poll showed over two-thirds of the sample as ready to accept a 'USE'). The Bruges speech was, I think, counter-productive, not because it annoyed Mr Heath and the federalists, but because its more caustic passages (largely provoked by M. Delors' antics at the TUC a fortnight earlier) encouraged unrealistic expectations among the hypernats, when the reality is that Mrs Thatcher is not about to engineer the break-up of the Community or the withdrawal of Britain from it.

Does the future of race relations offer any more encouragement to the hypernat? My impression is rather that the subject is noticeably less contentious than it was a decade ago, especially relations between the whites and the West Indians. I do not mean that relations are idyllic or that a riot will not break out tomorrow, but some of the edge has gone out of the topic. On the football terraces of North London, anti-black chants are less often heard these days, being sometimes replaced by anti-Semitic chants – no less repulsive but not what hypernationalists claim to be *the* problem of our times. Serious practical argument about repatriation schemes – whether voluntary or compulsory – seems to have dwindled to a trickle.

This does seem to be an odd moment for hypernationalism to be bubbling up among the intellectuals. Mr Enoch Powell's explanation remains unwavering: the coming confrontation with the Continental members of the Community – and with the non-white population of our cities – will be violent and painful, but confrontation is indispensable if we are to complete the business, so gloriously begun in the Falklands, of turning ourselves back into a nation.

To Mr Powell, being a nation is not simply an inert state, inherent in any collection of human beings. It is an *achievement*, something hard-earned, usually if not invariably purchased by copious donations of blood. Slothful, heedless peoples can mislay their nationhood – by signing away their independence, by careless immigration policies – but it is a recoverable treasure.

Yet are there any serious signs that we are about to recover it? Not
merely is there little prospect of the black or brown seven per cent of the
population diminishing. There seems every prospect of an ever-increas-
ing proportion of them anglicising in accent, dress, attitudes and birth-
rate. What happens if there develops an 'Anglo wedge' *within* the 'alien
wedge'? Would this diminish what Mr Powell calls 'the dignity and significance of tragedy' which resulted from the failure in the 1950s to
define British citizenship? Would hypernats then affably admit: 'OK, so
we got it wrong; it was a question of numbers, just as we said, but it
turned out we could assimilate more blacks than we thought'? Certainly
not. Such relaxed and informal manners would be foreign to their style,
which is normally what Mr Alan Watkins has dubbed Peterhouse Elevated. Hypernationalism has to be solemn, minatory, paranoiac. Fear is
the spur.

The puzzle remains. Hypernats seem to have so few grounds for
encouragement, in politics at least. Indeed, the fascination of so many
mainland hypernats with Northern Ireland looks like a kind of retreat.
How relieved they sound to have found the one last crag where the question of being British is being treated with proper seriousness. They seem
unaware of the difficulty which still troubles many of the mainland British, namely, that the Unionists appear so irremediably *foreign*, far more
alien, say, than Mr Lenny Henry or Mr Clive Lloyd. In championing the
Unionist cause, the hypernats felt they were at last among people who
had a passionately awakened understanding of the centrality of
nationhood, unlike their sleepy English compatriots.

If politics seem rather unpromising terrain for the hypernat, perhaps
we ought to look elsewhere and search some other recess of the British
psyche. Are there deeper cultural forces which presage some glorious
welling up of Britishness?

Peter Fuller, now in his early 40s, is a spirited polemicist and promoter of
polemics against fashionable art rubbish and the ninnies who push it and
profit by it. He is a champion of works by British artists; he was much
taken, as I was, by the 1987 Barbican exhibition of English neo-Romantics
– 'A Paradise Lost'; he is anxious to defend the traditional values and
techniques of painting and sculpture against commercialism, advertising and mass production. As a young man, he was a Marxist and a disciple
of the trendy Marxist critic, John Berger. He has seen through all that.

So far, so good. Alas, some of the fierce denunciatory sheep-and-goats
habits of his youth have stuck to him. The country-lover comes to look
alarmingly like a hypernat. Mr Fuller tells us to sweep away all foreign
rubbish and worship instead 'a uniquely *British* tradition, which has

always involved resistance to modernity'. Ourselves alone, in fact, or, as the Irish has it, *Sinn Fein*.

Now there are obvious oddities about this line of argument. Would one want to say that, for example, Turner, Ben Nicholson and Henry Moore were anti-modern exactly? Would one want to say that Epstein, Auerbach, Freud, Kitaj, Bomberg and Bacon were uniquely British? I don't just mean because they happen to have been born all over the place (do you know the Worcestershire Gaudier-Brzeskas?) but because as artists they are simply too diverse to be bundled together into a line of direct descent from Constable and Samuel Palmer; shared interests in the natural world and the human figure, which are sometimes advanced as the common denominators of their Englishness/Britishness, are really too large and loose to count. And what is to be done, say, with the Scottish colourists – Peploe, Cadell, and Fergusson? Are they to count as British because they painted flowers and Hebridean islands, or to be discounted as traitors because they were so heavily influenced by nasty foreign post-impressionist aesthetics?

Ever since the Middle Ages – in fact, especially in the Middle Ages – art has been soaking through and leaping over national boundaries. To embark at the end of the 20th century on the project of a nation-centred if not nation-bounded art seems not only barmy but morally dubious. It would fly in the face of what has always been regarded as the universality of artistic communication, and do so without acknowledging or justifying such a defection.

Mr Fuller has switched his allegiance from Berger to Ruskin – which is certainly a great improvement – and he likes to quote Ruskin's pronouncement that 'all great art, in the great times of art, is *provincial*'. Just so, let us repeat the underlining: *provincial* – or local, if you prefer – not national; that is, rooted to a time, a place, a group of artists, not to a continuous political entity like a nation-state. The Shoreham visions of Samuel Palmer and their fainter modern simulacra in the Barbican are provincial in just that way; they can, if you like, be said to represent a tradition, but it is a tradition which is far too broken, elusive, anarchic and variable in quality to be dragged up to London and made to stand to attention for the National Anthem.

Mr Fuller does say we must be careful not to be xenophobic. But the trouble with cultural nationalism, as with any other kind, is that it cannot help defining itself in terms of the hated Other. When Herder told his fellow Germans to 'spew out the ugly slime of the Seine', he thought he was only strengthening good German culture, just as Mr Fuller thinks he is only purifying the scene when he tells us to reject New York bullshit. But the xenophobia degrades standards of artistic achievement as fast as it corrupts standards of moral behaviour. Art in this country is already provincial enough in the worst sense without being deluded by hypernat flattery.

Most of the artists mentioned by Mr Fuller, in a recent *Sunday Telegraph* article on the painters who are patronised by Prince Charles, would be lucky to be described as second-rate.

Nobody is happier with the revaluations of, say, Lutyens, William Burges, Edward Lear, A. E. Housman and all the Nashes than the present writer. But we must be *exact* in estimating them. One of the great virtues of John Betjeman was that he knew his place – which is what sent him several places higher. Adding on marks for being quintessentially English (or any other nationality) is both a symptom and a cause of decline.

But the worst intellectual dishonesty of hypernationalists is the way they claim, with an air of injured innocence, that they are merely giving expression to human instincts which are enduring and ineradicable – and therefore natural and healthy. They often show a certain inconsistency in being strongly moralistic about most things – sexual conduct and obeying the law, for example – while being indulgently amoral towards manifestations of hypernationalism, however repugnant to any sense of decency or kindness. National feeling just *is*, we are told, and there is nothing much we can or should do to moderate it.

Only an idiot would deny that national feeling, when frustrated or forcibly suppressed, may unleash the most ferocious consequences. But it is also obvious that it is within the power of cultural forces – law, religion, tradition, education, art – either to moderate or to inflame the ferocity. When a politician invokes 'national identity', he is not referring to something fixed and 'pre-political'; on the contrary, he is helping to *make* something often by manipulation of the evidence of history or geography, and what he makes may have a momentous impact on events, for good or ill. There are moral responsibilities here which cannot be wished away. Would the Irish Troubles, either of the 1916 or the 1969 vintage, have been so savage and prolonged if Irish writers had not romanticised blood-sacrifice and if the churches had not damned one another's flocks? Yeats, in youth a hypernat as silly as any poet ever was, knew enough by the end of his life to ask himself:

> Did that play of mine send out
> Certain men the English shot?

The claim that nationalism is an unquenchable natural force sits oddly with the Powellite lament that the British sense of nationhood has gone to sleep. And it squares even less well with the arguments so tellingly put forward by a line of observers, stretching from Burke through Acton, Mill and Tocqueville to Kedourie and Minogue, that nationalism, of the hyped-up, obsessive kind which is all too familiar to us, is a *modern* phenomenon. Far from being a visceral, almost biological imperative, it is a deliberately fanned inflammation of those affections and loyalties that do come naturally to us. That is why, as some of these observers have noted, the wars of peoples are far more terrible than the wars of princes.

To see nationhood as an eternal, unaltering value is especially difficult for us in this country. We first have to ask ourselves which nationhood we mean – English, British, UK? And precisely where do we freeze the frame – at the defeat of Owen Glendower, or the Act of Union, or the Easter Rising? At what point was our nationhood achieved? And if we are to speak honestly of Englishness, does not that much abused concept include notions of tolerance and cultural restraint which look suspiciously like the abhorred liberalism? Is there not, in short, something frightfully unEnglish about Mr Enoch Powell and his dichotomous rigour?

Moreover, this rigour is not always as rigorous as it pretends. Sometimes, it seems that 'belonging' is merely a matter of legal classification, sometimes it appears to depend on cultural identity, sometimes on the colour of one's skin. What are minorities who do not fit the criteria to do – sit quietly indoors until the parade has gone past? Or can they hold their own parades? Does the good citizen merely have to obey the law, or must he pledge his soul to his country? Are half-castes and dual-passport-holders only half-people? The hypernat seems reluctant to answer such questions, since they would expose too rawly the terrible difficulties of trying to fuse civil obedience and cultural identity. Even Mr Powell's ultimate criterion of belonging – the willingness to die for one's country – has its difficulties. Even if we condemn pacifists to outer darkness, what are we to do about mercenaries?

The traditional alternative model of country-love does not face such difficulties since it is not concerned with excluding non-belongers. It may be called the Serial or Little-Platoon model, from Burke's formula: 'To be attached to the subdivision, to love the little platoon we belong to in society . . . is the first link in the series by which we proceed towards a love to our country and to mankind.' For Coleridge, cosmopolitanism – to him, a good thing – sprang out of and blossomed upon 'the deep rooted stem of nationality'; Balfour thought that 'some combination of different patriotisms is almost universal among thinking persons', and that the patriotisms ought to reinforce each other. Since conservatism teaches that human society demands structure and hierarchy, any creed which either concentrates all human energies and loyalties upon one institution or stops at national boundaries and scrawls over the rest of the world 'Here Be Tygers' cannot be conservative in the full Burkean sense.

The idea of any inherent incompatibility between patriotism and enthusiasm for membership of the European Community (or any other international institution) would have seemed peculiar to many great Conservative heroes of the past, despite the fact that they had little or no experience of membership of international bodies (there might, of course, be *practical* objections to membership, for example, a free trader's belief that the EEC was bound to remain protectionist). Why should this exclusive, sovereignty-hogging hypernationalism have sprung up at a time when we are so accustomed to every kind of sub-national and supra-national institution?

Perhaps a kind of answer may be found in Kenneth Minogue's little classic, *Nationalism* (1967):

> The formula that I find most convincing is to say that nationalism provides an escape from triviality. Implicitly or explicitly, men suffering a social upheaval put to themselves the question: what is happening to us? The nationalist answer is clear: our nation is struggling to be born, it is fighting for independence against its enemies. This answer is never the whole truth, and sometimes it has absolutely nothing to do with the truth at all. But that does not matter.

Minogue is talking here primarily of pre-industrial societies which are undergoing the bewildering shocks of modernisation and the breakdown of peasant life and traditional customs. Nationalism may help such societies to weather these shocks in all sorts of ways. In *Thought and Change*, Ernest Gellner points out that nationalism may be not an irrational, primitive force but rather a practical and relevant enterprise, aimed at securing jobs and political and social position for a tribal or linguistic group, and for its intelligentsia in particular; it may be not a sentimental but a defensive campaign. On the other hand, nationalism can also provide a substitute or a prop for a fading faith, a way of re-infusing the world with a sense of meaning and purpose – although few are as candid as Michelet was: 'It is from you that I shall ask for help, my noble country: you must take the place of the God who is escaping from us, so that you may fill within us the immeasurable abyss which the extinction of Christianity has left.'

Nation-worship is not a religion in the true sense of the word. But it is especially attractive to those who are or once were religiously inclined –

just as it is attractive to Marxists and ex-Marxists – because it offers the same disciplines: a jealous deity, monopolistic claims, the simplification of reality. It also offers the same benefits: a shapely picture of the world, a purpose in life, a set of guiding principles, feelings of self-esteem and self-confidence in dealing with strangers.

Looked at in this light, the British experience becomes a little less puzzling. If this country became industrial, urban and secular earlier than others, it did not thereby lurch into purposelessness as many others did. The Imperial mission, by a mixture of luck and design, offered the British a satisfying justification for what was happening to them. Factories were turning out goods, public schools were turning out engineers, clergymen and civil servants, parents were turning out children *for* the Empire. No doubt the Empire was mostly a matter of indifference to most of the population; but it was *there*, vast and shimmering, to console anyone afflicted by a sense of futility. It is, I think, no accident that the only organisation of my youth to be seriously concerned with nationhood was the League of Empire Loyalists.

Now all that has gone. Harold Macmillan's clumsy efforts to describe our entry into 'Europe' as a comparable mission did not wash for a minute. Clearly joining the EEC was the very opposite of a mission. It was the resumption of the Little-Platoon tradition, the abandonment of nationalism as a supreme value and its installation (or re-installation) as only one link, even if a dominant one, in Burke's chain of 'public affections', stretching from the family to the human race.

British hypernationalism may thus be a response to much the same stimuli as can be observed in Third-World countries today, or in First-World countries the day before yesterday. Although it may be fortified by recent events such as the Falklands victory and economic revival, its driving force seems to be the desire to construct, in the guise of re-constructing, a safe redoubt from which the world-as-it-is can be confronted with confidence.

Hypernationalism here as elsewhere in Western Europe seems to offer a beautiful single answer to all the multi-racial and multi-national perplexities and complexities of modern life.

But here I think we begin to catch a strong whiff of humbug. For the conduct of our leading hypernats shows quite clearly that the Nation is *not* their only god. Free speech, for example, is also in their bones; their journals and debates are conducted on impeccably liberal lines. They would, I am sure, deplore the burning of books, even Salman Rushdie's. And if put to it, they would also deplore racial harassment, even where the law had not been infringed. If challenged to produce a programme for the Nation's youth, it would probably go little further than the average

Tory's desire to see that British history is taught properly and that half-baked multi-cultural education is abandoned, not least because it handicaps immigrant children.

In short, when these great brooding clouds break over our society, they are to produce no more than a pleasant April shower. Our eyes were, it seemed, deceived by a playful mimicry of continental hypernationalism, designed to appal or thrill us, according to taste. That black, menacing shadow which bore such an unnerving resemblance to Fichte or de Maistre turns out to be jolly old Roger Scruton, after all. The more he goes on, the more we cannot help suspecting he only does it because he knows it teases.

18 February 1989

MARGARET THATCHER, HOUSEWIFE SUPERSTAR

Noel Malcolm

FOOD: NOW MAGGIE STEPS IN
Mrs Thatcher last night dramatically intensified Government action on food safety.
And pregnant women were warned not to eat ripe soft cheese . . .

This front-page story (from last Saturday's *Daily Mail*) is a true sign of our times. Drama, action, intensity – the sub-text, as they say, is telling us that we have a government here on red alert, perhaps even on a sort of permanent war footing. It is a government which responds instantly to dangers, issuing not information or advice but warnings. Above all, it is a government which does not merely administer or regulate or legislate, as other governments might: it *acts*.

Look a little closer, not at the sub-text but at the text itself, and you may feel rather more puzzled by what you see. 'Now' Maggie steps in: the date is 11 February, exactly nine weeks after the current series of food scares began. Read to the end of the story and you will discover, embedded almost in the last paragraph, the real nature of Mrs Thatcher's dramatically intense action: she has announced that she intends to set up a committee. The committee will monitor conflicting advice and information on food safety and draw up a more unified set of guidelines than has been available hitherto. This sounds rather less like the Government taking action about food and more like Mrs Thatcher taking action about the Government: the problem which it will solve is not food poisoning but contradiction and conflict between different ministries.

The one other new measure announced in this story is the Ministry of Agriculture's decision to use its powers to order farmers to destroy infected flocks. This had in fact been the subject of an argument for several weeks between that Ministry and the Department of Health, with the latter unsuccessfully urging the former to exercise its power. One gets the impression that the Prime Minister has not so much intensified government action as banged a few heads together to put an end to government inaction.

No doubt the popular press has always dramatised and personalised its stories, shifting the emphasis whenever possible from hesitation to decision. But the cult of decisive action which we are witnessing here is not just the sign of a popular (or popularising) medium. It is the hallmark of a self-consciously populist government. The traditional administrative and legislative roles of government lack popular appeal: they involve procedures which are slow, boring, arcane, clogged with specialist advice, weighed down by administrative practicalities, and often compromised by the need to resolve conflicting interests. A populist government is one which not only courts and appeals to the people (as all elective governments do), but which also pretends in some ways not to be a government. It wants to speak more directly to the people, to respond to their concerns, to act more immediately on their behalf. And since (like the people themselves, perhaps) it has little or no idea what their concerns are until it reads about them in the newspapers, a populist government has a peculiarly symbiotic relationship with the popular press.

The *Daily Mail*, for example, gives an extraordinarily accurate portrait of how this Government wishes to have its thoughts and actions understood: to say this is not to impute to that paper either gross subservience or uncanny journalistic skill. Just as its style of reporting reflects Government thinking, so the Government's style of thinking reflects the sort of reporting which it wants to get in papers such as the *Daily Mail*. (The quotations in this article are from that paper; but samples taken from the *Express* or the *Sun* would yield very similar results in the laboratory.) A news item creates 'public concern'; an editorial calls on the Government to end this shame or scandal; the Government faces 'mounting concern', and if it dallies too long it may even face 'mounting pressure'; till finally, however bland, timid or long-term in response, it does something. What it does may be no more than to hint at future measures. But to announce measures is to take measures – and to take measures is to *act*.

Mr Hurd acts at least once a month. In December it was 'Murder on Trains: Hurd Acts'. The thugs who terrorise Britain's underground and rail networks were 'facing a crackdown'. The Home Secretary was considering, it emerged, a vague string of possibilities: more video cameras, better lighting, New York-style 'safe areas' on platforms, and so on. In January it was 'Hurd Pledges Action on "Stupid Drinkers" ':

> A crackdown on 'stupid drinkers' was promised yesterday by Home Secretary Douglas Hurd.
>
> Employers, unions, entertainment and leisure industries, doctors and church leaders together with all local agencies will be asked to join the major new offensive. They needed to identify the extent of the problems locally and take joint action on the problems . . .

There you have the plight of a well-meaning, would-be but can-never-quite-be populist in all its pathos. Mr Hurd is an ambitious politician who knows that he must be seen to act. But he is held back partly by his corporatist, consensus-seeking political instincts, and partly by the responsibilities of real power: both of these factors require policies to be put into practice not by waving a wand but by going through all the humdrum procedures of consultation and committee-forming.

It is no coincidence, then, that the main sources of populism in this Government are to be found at the top and the bottom. In the middle you have the Secretaries of State and other senior ministers who, whether they like it or not, are prevented by the nature of their jobs from being true populists – however much the Whitehall publicity machine tries to dress them up in populist clothes. (Some of them, notably Messrs Ridley and Lawson, are enormously glad to be relieved of most populist duties: Mr Ridley because populism is vulgar, and Mr Lawson because it is intellectually feeble.) At the bottom you have a new breed of deliberately vulgarising, publicity-conscious junior ministers, whose role it is to troubleshoot, to 'spearhead' campaigns, to get themselves filmed and quoted. When Mr David Mellor poses with a television star sawing through a giant cardboard cigarette, he is getting the best of all possible populist worlds: voicing public concern, responding to it, symbolising 'real' action (none of your dreary White Papers or scientific documents – here is a man with a saw in his hand) and at the same time, *sub specie aeternitatis*, he is actually doing nothing, absolutely nothing at all.

And at the top . . . It is not surprising that Mrs Thatcher often seems so much fonder of her junior ministers than of her Cabinet colleagues. These are her best allies in the populist campaign. Their capacity to irritate people is construed by her as robust plain-talking; their constant appearance on radio and television is interpreted as constant action. And the Currie saga of the last three months has become a sort of political soap opera in which the Prime Minister can take a walk-on part whenever she wants it: either to tick off her erring children or to bring heart-touching comfort and solace.

> Mrs Thatcher asked the beleaguered Mrs Currie: 'Are you all right Edwina?'
>
> As the reply, 'Yes, Prime Minister', came, Mrs Thatcher uttered the words which not only kept Mrs Currie going, but told her she was right.
>
> The Prime Minister said: 'Good, I am sure you will be all right Edwina.'

The oddity of Mrs Thatcher's position, as a brief textual analysis of the 'Now Maggie Steps In' story has already suggested, is that she both is and is not the Government. Her personal brand of populism enables her to detach herself from government actions whenever it suits her to do so. Usually it is the Government's inactions from which she distances herself, so that when ministries actually do anything she can take the credit. In recent months the popular press has credited her with 'moving' to outlaw the sale of human kidneys, 'ordering' senior ministers to co-operate with Toyota in its search for a factory site (as if their policy up to that point had been one of non-co-operation) and demanding that the Foreign Office send aid to Afghanistan ('Maggie's Aid for Afghan Children'). The way these stories are presented reflects not only the stylistic requirements of vivid journalism but also the methods of her press secretary, Mr Bernard Ingham, who is happy to attribute all decisive action to the Prime Minister herself, symbolically detaching her from the Government and then blaming members of the Government for being 'semi-detached'. Many a Cabinet Minister has woken up on a Friday morning to find 'Maggie fury over minister's blunder' stories in the national press. Few have had the courage or recklessness to fight back like Francis Pym, who described such smears in 1983 as 'mischief-making by the Prime Minister's poisonous acolytes'. The poison still circulates: it is part of the life-blood of a populist Prime Minister.

Mrs Thatcher has been happy, in the past, to describe herself as a populist. Three years ago she spoke of her version of Conservatism as follows:

It is radical because when I took over we needed to be radical. It is populist. I would say many of the things I've said strike a chord in the hearts of ordinary people. Why? Because their character is independent, because they don't like to be shoved around, because they are prepared to take responsibility . . .

In 1984 she said that she hoped that she had 'shattered the illusion that government could somehow substitute for individual performance'. Populism is thus identified with being anti-government. This means that it is ideally suited to radical Conservatives when they are in opposition. But what are they to do when they *are* the Government? The answer, for Mrs Thatcher, is all too easy: she can disown the lot of them whenever it suits her.

But the problem goes deeper than this. Mrs Thatcher appeals to the idea of the individual who takes responsibility and gets things done. This is, indeed, the common-sense approach to human action: if there is a problem, get up and do something about it. Populist politics encourages people to think of the Government in exactly the same way: hence the cult of action, free from all the usual paraphernalia of policy-formation, consultation and legislation. Mrs Thatcher began by hitching her populism to a political philosophy of anti-statism: once in government, however, she found that those two forces were pulling in different directions. Populism may be hostile to systematic government intervention, but it is all in favour of sudden acts of intervening to solve problems, to make things happen, or (more commonly) to make things stop happening. And if the intervention is decisive enough, who cares whether it involves spending more money or making more unnecessary laws?

For years, political analysts have been trying to measure the public's attitudes on a scale which has collectivism and government action at one end, and individual action at the other. As John Rentoul shows in his study of public opinion published this week (*Me and Mine: the Triumph of the New Individualism?*, Unwin Hyman), it is difficult to find any evidence of a clear shift down the scale during the Thatcher years. Perhaps part of the explanation is that such a scale cannot measure the effect of a populism which favours both individualism in private life and a crude but powerful cult of government action.

There is, so to speak, an ideological schizophrenia at the heart of Mrs Thatcher's public performance. On the one hand we have Mrs T. of Finchley, Housewife; on the other the Right Hon. Margaret Thatcher, Superstar. The Housewife is the embodiment of sturdy market-town moral values, in favour of individual responsibility and hostile to all forms of government control. The Superstar, by contrast, is hostile to government (her Government) only when it fails to control things or get things done. Nothing is too difficult for her, whether it be sorting out food safety, taking action on kidneys or saving Afghan babies. 'Housewife Superstar' may be a formula for success in showbusiness – but it is no way to run a government.

25 February 1989

TIME TO TURN TO LABOUR

A. N. Wilson

English politics are excruciatingly boring, English politicians even more so. 'A plague on both your houses' has been my political creed for years; and when supposed alternatives to the Conservative or Labour Parties arose, I wished a plague on them as well. I am sure that this indifferentism is not unusual, and it partly accounts for Mrs Thatcher's extraordinary success. The thundering dullness of her Cabinet is matched by the greyness of the Shadow Cabinet. The choice between Mr Lawson and Mr Smith, or between Mr Hattersley and Mr Hurd is about as exciting as the choice on the menu at a McDonald's take-away.

Given this, it has been obvious who would win the last three elections. That is to say, it would be the party who fiddled the figures to provide the lowest rate of income tax. And it is these two facts alone, in my opinion, the dullness of the politicians and the apparently low rates of tax, which have allowed Mrs Thatcher to get away with her so-called social revolution.

But since the last election, I have changed my mind about the whole matter, and I suspect that I am not alone. It now seems to me quite essential, regardless of their personal unattractiveness, to support the leadership of the Labour Party.

The trouble with Thatcherism could be summed up in the words of the Duke of Norfolk when, on a notorious public occasion, he offered some reflections on the 'rhythm' method of birth control: *it doesn't bloody work.* The illusion has been that it is possible, or desirable, to dismantle the semi-socialist state set up by Attlee's administration and supported, more or less ineptly, by every government until 1979. Every civil servant and public administrator must have known from the beginning that this was an illusion, but Mrs Thatcher's public relations advisers have allowed the public to believe otherwise.

The illusion may be summarised in this sort of way. In an 'enterprise' economy, it will eventually be possible to reduce public expenditure and discard the notion of 'public' services. Taxes will be cut. There will be more money in the hands of private individuals. They will then be 'free' to choose whether they wish to spend their money on transport, motorways, airports, education, health, art, or any other desirable commodity. Nationalised industries will be sold off. The burden on the individual will be lifted and the socialist tyranny will have been destroyed forever.

The trouble is that none of these public services can actually be paid for by private individuals. All that happens when you privatise British Telecom is that for a publicly owned company, answerable (at least notionally) to Parliament and people, you substitute a hopelessly inefficient 'private' company answerable, it would seem, to nobody. The Government knows this really, and is therefore incapable of living up to its supposed convictions. It has therefore increased public expenditure in most areas, but done so in a mean-spirited way which has resulted in a decline in quality in almost every area of public life.

Anybody who travels regularly by rail is aware of the fact that the railways are markedly less efficient than they were a decade ago. Even allowing for the fact that 'engine failure', like Private Eye's 'tired and emotional', is a euphemism used by railway guards to cover the personal shortcomings of their colleagues, it is astonishing how many railway journeys are delayed by the creaking obsolescence of the engines. I would reckon that ten per cent of my extensive railway journeys in the last year have been delayed by the need to change engines in the middle of the journey.

This principle is extended by the Government into every area of life. They have not been prepared to make the necessary capital outlay to overhaul the railways. Speak to any librarian, museum curator, keeper of an art gallery or of a building in public ownership. Rather than allowing adequate funds to these bodies, the Government has relentlessly refused to increase the money as required. So, we have to face the prospect of artefacts falling into disrepair, books not being replaced or added to, museums closing off their exhibits. The classic 'monetarist' response to all this is that the idea of patronage should be reintroduced into the arts and 'heritage'. The simple fact is, that however generous rich patrons may wish to be to opera companies or museums, there is not enough money to keep these things going without government help. Insidiously, the argument turns from the rich patron to the less rich member of the public: museum charges, public library charges, and the exclusion of those who cannot pay.

The same is true of universities. Since Mrs Thatcher failed to become a Doctor of Civil Law at Oxford, we have witnessed a positive Ice Age as far as the 'freezing' of academic jobs is in question. Universities are kept going by the money placed in the Vice-Chancellor's begging-bowl by businessmen from Hong Kong or the United States. The oldest copyright library in the world, the Bodleian, is engaged in such a begging exercise, and it will almost certainly fail to raise enough even to repair its existing stock of priceless books, let alone expand to house the boundless flood of new ones. Oxford has been through a period of having no Professor of French and no Professor of German. There was even talk of 'freezing' the Regius Chair of Greek. In less famous universities the situation has been more parlous and the anti-intellectuals (right-wing dons among them) have been conspicuously gleeful at the prospect of reducing these seats of learning to a position in which they can no longer properly function. There is then the inevitable cry of 'close them down'.

If this has been true of the universities, it has been even truer of the National Health Service. And now we have a Secretary of State for Health who is only half committed to running the Health Service in the way that the vast majority of patients wish it to continue – and have paid for it to continue.

Wherever you choose to examine it, the Thatcherite idea has failed to work. It is not in a position to withdraw public spending altogether, though its extreme proponents would perhaps like to do so. Instead, it opts for the worst possible alternative, where bits of money are offered and everyone is in the red. Its attitude is that of a mean old friend of mine, now dead, who had the habit of 'taking' friends to meals. Everyone would eat their fill at his table. He would then airily offer a pound note to the waiter, and his 'guests' would be obliged to make up the shortfall out of their own purses.

It is an illusion to suppose that the Welfare State and the idea of a beneficent government committed to public spending are designed solely for the poor or the socially inadequate. They are meant for all of us. Trains, museums, operas, hospitals, universities cannot exist without public funding and those of us who pay high rates of tax have a right to expect something better than the present government offers.

Those who do not pay high rates of tax, or who pay no tax at all, or who are poor and depend on state assistance, are of course the worst affected of any of us by the Thatcherite experiment. And it is impossible to resist a feeling of distaste and shame at the sheer unimaginative meanness of this administration where the poor are concerned. It is all the more nauseating since the majority of the new Right would appear to come from modest backgrounds, and the likes of Mrs Thatcher and Mr Parkinson should be able to remember what poverty is like. One could mention their attitude to child benefit, their refusal to pay the dole to unemployed teenagers, their woeful record on housing. Two things which particularly outrage me, for some reason, are the introduction of charges for eye tests and false teeth, and the proposal for student loans.

If you are moderately well-off, it is possible to be persuaded that these schemes are fair, with ample provision for a means-tested poor. The reality of the situation is that by increasing dental charges the Government will deter the poor from ever visiting the dentist. We shall revert to being like our parents' generation, a nation of rotting gums and bad breath and people having false teeth by the time they are 40.

Similarly, the principle whereby higher education was freely available to anyone clever enough to take it, has now been altered. This will in effect remove the chance of a university or polytechnic career from anyone whose parents are not in a position to help with the repayment of the loan in later life. We shall also, almost certainly, be welcoming in an undesirable system such as that which obtains in the United States, whereby graduates flood into the more swindling and superfluous branches of professional life, such as the law, in order to command the salaries which will help them with their loan repayments. (There is a direct correlation between the absurd costs of American litigation and the need for pushy young graduates to repay their loans to the state.)

The unlikely spectre of a socialist state bossing our lives and confiscating our property gave Mrs Thatcher's Pooterite dream of the small shareholder buying his own council house a sort of quaint charm, though since the collapse of the stock market and the rise of interest rates the charm has lost its glow. Besides, as Auberon Waugh never tires of saying in these pages, this government is far more interfering and bossy than any previous British administration this century. Whether you are a broadcaster, or a motorist, or a trade unionist, your liberties are markedly more restrained than they were ten years ago.

We need to return to the simple idea that public services require public spending and it is the responsibility of governments to administer this spending. The Conservative Government does not display such a responsibility. Of all the parties on offer, only the Labour Party is fully committed to this idea of a government's role, and the fact that previous Labour governments were incompetent does not invalidate the principle of responsible government. Mrs Thatcher with her famous Gladstonian dictum that governments have no money (it all belongs to the tax-payer) has subtly evaded her fiscal and social responsibilities in almost every area until a crisis forces her to throw in money too late. It was truly scandalous, after two administrations of neglect, to watch her jumping on the

Prince of Wales's bandwagon in her announcement that she would make 'inner cities' her priority. In some inner cities it is already too late to repair the damage caused directly by the wilful negligence of Conservative governments from 1979 onwards, and their belief that it was more important to biff Labour councils than to look after the interests of the people.

How have they managed to get away with it? Not because a majority of voters have ever supported them, but perhaps partly because apolitical figures (myself included) were unwilling to align ourselves with the Opposition. They were also helped by the fact that the Opposition party chose this moment to fragment into absurd Lilliputian factions. It is quite obvious that Dr Owen and the Other Man, leader of the Whatever It's Called Party, will never be in a position to throw the Conservatives out. The only way to bring about the electoral miracle next time round is for everyone who sees the awfulness of this government to vote Labour. Greens. Tory Wets. Liberals. Everyone.

I think there should even be electoral pacts before the next polling day in which these other individuals stand down instead of the Labour Party. Cynics would say that there is no evidence that the Labour Party would do any better. But Labour are at least committed to the idea that they ought to govern, rather than allow a free-for-all in which we are dependent on whims of multi-national companies and the security provided by private insurance schemes. Unless we all decide to vote Labour – we the majority who are not committed to Conservatism come what may – we face a future with dud trains, dud libraries, dud museums, dud hospitals, and the poor getting poorer – sans eyes, sans teeth, sans everything.

11 March 1989

Chapter 5
THE RISING GENERATION

WITH THE HIPPIES IN WALES

Roy Kerridge

One bright afternoon, a few years ago, a friend was driving me along a mountain road in North Wales when suddenly he stopped and told me to look at an unusual view. I did so, and could scarcely believe my eyes. A field sloped down the hillside towards a swift-flowing stream, with a line of fir trees and a mountain range beyond, and right in the middle of the field was a 30-foot-high Red Indian wigwam, with a smaller one a little further away. I could have been in Canada. As I ran down the slope towards the wigwam, I was baffled by the fact that it seemed to have no entrance. At last I found a flap, pulled it open, and five tiny black puppies tumbled out, licking at my hand. Poking my head inside, I found another tent and inside *that*, as something of an anticlimax, were a circle of dopey-looking hippies sitting among filthy rags in a haze of cannabis smoke.

'Greetings to the Big Chief, and to his squaws and warriors, and may the buffalo herds ever prosper,' I said and tossed them some small pieces of chocolate. They scrambled for these eagerly and, as I left, seemed to be trying to smoke them.

Thus my host and I became aware of the hippies in Wales. The story has an unusual sequel, for the hippies lurched about in a drugged stupor, stealing, hitting people and alarming the postmistress who handed them their dole. Finally, when they were visited by mystery men in flashy cars, my friend, who was on the Bench, called in the police. Arrests were made, and evidence collected that was of some use to the Operation Julie investigation. So I have played some part in the development of hippiedom, which is now going through a post-drug puritanical stage, with 'dope fiends' being expelled from communes in disgrace, and the value of hard work, on hippie enterprises at least, lauded to the skies.

Later, farmers in Pembrokeshire spoke of losing lambs to the hippies, who presumably stole them under the impression that this represented living off the land. In North Wales, a hippie couple living rough made a herbal stew and, as they included hemlock among the ingredients, the girl died. It seemed as if Wales had to bear the brunt of the hippie exodus from the mainstream of English life. Those who could not get jobs in education, or Arts Council grants, simply headed for the hills in search of Utopia.

Yearning for Natural Man, living and loving in the Garden of Eden, is an essential part of the hippie myth. As I understand it, we cannot re-enter the Garden, for an angel with a flaming sword stands at the gate, and our attempts to evade him only land us in Hell, Soviet Russia, Jonestown or the Preachers' Commune, Llanaba. Most hippies deny the doctrine of Original Sin, and say that human shortcomings are merely the result of conditioning, caused by 'capitalism and the nuclear family'. In their mountain retreats, they hope to rear 'unconditioned' children, which can mean children who are either neglected or stringently conditioned by their parents' ideas instead. In towns, the children of hippies, often very earnest, worthy youngsters in their early teens, seek one another out with difficulty and can neither mix with non-hippie children nor make any sense of a bewildering world.

Hippiedom keeps pace with the Sixties and early Seventies generations, who are themselves trapped in a teenage cult world as they approach middle age. Teenage cults seem to be a shelter from the unknown and unnerving life of adult experience. In a cult the members' ignorance is never exposed because the rules preserve it. Tortuously, hippies are now trying to invent an alternative society which may, however, turn out to be a slipshod copy of the real world which they have never understood: different tasks allocated to different people, plenty of hard work insisted on, and Hell's Angels as an unusually dreadful 'police force'.

A few weeks ago, I went to Aberystwyth, where my wigwam-dwellers and many others in tents, caravans and buses had set up home on a stretch of river bank outside the normally peaceful village of Pontrhydygroes. There is another Tepee Community near Carmarthen, and the wigwams, or tepees, are made for the hippies by a commercial firm. The Aberystwyth settlement was called into being by badly printed circulars which found their way, passed from hand to hand, around most of the hippie flats and 'squats' of Britain. People who still had an interest in drugs were invited to a Psylocobin Festival. Psylocobin mushrooms, or Liberty Caps, have, when eaten, or boiled for their essence, an effect similar to the Julie-banished LSD, though I do not get the impression that they are quite so harmful. More to the point, from the hippie point of view, they are legal.

Tepee people still believe in drugs as a mystic road to salvation, unlike the new breed of 'farming co-operative' hippies, who regard narcotics as part of the capitalist world they reject. Evidently the authors of the 'free festival' pamphlet, one of many groups seeking to organise hippiedom, hoped to antagonise the real world by choosing a site where camping was forbidden. When the hippies arrived, they found that the landowner, Alun Davies, a 22-year-old carpenter, had, with council aid, dug a moat to prevent their expensive cars from getting through. After a fight with the police, the hippies and some very tough motorbike boys managed to fill in the moat, using logs stolen from a local timber yard. Instead of a short festival, with music and mushrooms, the hippies simply set up a township and stayed and stayed. For all I know, they are still there.

I walked over the hills to Pontrhydygroes from the Devil's Bridge, down by Moel Arther and its forestry plantations, and so to an enchanted spot where the Ystwyth river gleamed through the trees and buzzards soared over the crest of the hills. There I met a police road block, employed to prevent drugs getting to the hippies. Putting on an expression of moonstruck innocence, I walked by unmolested and then ran into a more formidable hazard – rain. Grey sweeps of rain, like giants from the *Mabinogion* marching the forested slopes, hurled by, drenching me to the skin.

Eerie in the half-light, for a yellow sunset now glimmered over the hills, river, tents and water-filled tyre-canals, Tepee Valley looked rather like a Victorian oil painting on a grand scale. Crows hopped along the grey stony shallows of the river, perhaps looking for mussels. The variety of vehicles, including buses, gave a hint of hippie wealth, and the variety of hippie was no less interesting. There were my old friends in their wigwam, now surrounded by fellow members of their tribe, while in tent doorways, brawny, whiskered young men watched me in amazement, for I wore a shirt, jacket and tie, and might have come from Outer Space for all they knew. Some of these young men still possessed the fierce arrogance of the first wave of Sixties hippiedom, with a touch of embitteredness added, while others were milder souls who played fondly with their children. Lank-haired girls drooped over pots of soup in the tents.

Some hippies who are greatly respected by the education-conscious Welsh are the Preachers' Community, as I shall call them, of Llanaba, North Wales. 'Barry of the Preachers' is a formidable local figure, a magnetic-eyed, shock-haired man in his forties, with a young flock of awestruck disciples, mainly female, who parrot his ideas with passion. These ideas, to judge by his pamphlets and conversation, owe something to Gradgrind, for he has carried the new hippie puritanism about drugs and the virtues of hard work to a terrifying extreme. As well as running an educational shop full of toys that aim to teach facts, with no fairy-tale characters allowed, Barry dabbles in computers, printing and bookbinding, and his commune, on a hilltop farm overlooking the town, is unique in making a profit of £120,000 a year. He seems to be seeking an ascendancy over all the other communes, who loathe him heartily, and he advertises extensively in almost every left-wing periodical, though he has less then 20 adult members, whose work and earnings he controls.

Here is the egregious Barry in conversation: 'We're called the Preachers, but I'm the enemy of all religion. We believe capitalist society to be basically inefficient, and we work a 16-hour day every day of the week. Hitler was a necessity, if you let society get as run down as it is today. The Welfare State has set the thick people breeding, and so the leaders will have to start a war to wipe them out. It should be a crime to protect the sick and weak. I'm the only one who can see a way out – I must take power of some sort – power over the child – it begins with children . . . But why are you asking me all this? Who are you? You've got a lot of confidence barging in here. Tell me about yourself!'

This put me in a spot, as I didn't want to say I wrote for *The Spectator*, and so could not explain myself. He swiftly concluded that I was an ex-convict who hoped to live on him 'parasitically', and I wondered, stuck as I was in his hilltop farm on a dark night, how I could get back to Llanaba. For a moment I thought I might be a one-man victim of a Dai Jonestown massacre. Pity for his child victims, for he could clearly run rings round any NSPCC inspector, changed to pity for myself.

'I don't mind criminals as long as they're not murderers,' one of his girl

*'Is that the cult that entices adolescents away
from their families?'*

friends remarked, and this seemed to ease the situation. He detailed this girl to drive me down the mountain, and on the way, a bat, intent on chasing a moth, hit the car – an omen if ever I saw one. Perhaps it heralds the end of the hippie idea, the closure of the communes and freedom for Wales.

29 August 1981

SHIRLEY'S ACHIEVEMENT

Auberon Waugh

Many middle-aged men nowadays must dream of revenging themselves on the young. It is not just that the young are so ignorant and rude. Their worst crime is to be so conceited. For two decades it has been fashionable to talk about the generation gap as if it sprang from some failure on their part. Weighed down by bourgeois and materialistic considerations, if not by simple snobbery, the middle-aged were unable to make the great imaginative leap necessary to communicate with the young.

Young people were by definition idealistic, uninterested in materialistic things, untouched by colour or clan prejudice. Their attitude to sex was healthy and natural, uncoloured by hypocrisy or religious guilt. They were interested in employment which gave them an opportunity to help other people – the old, or kiddies, or deprived folk generally – but they were definitely not interested in joining the wage-slave rat race, buying themselves a semi or equipping it with labour-saving devices. Wages were less important than fulfilment. If they drank at all, it was only in moderation. They preferred the subtler, more peaceful satisfaction of cannabis. Young people ruled the earth, and anybody over thirty must cringe before them.

As for the kids, they were if anything even better. They were never happier than when redecorating the home of some senior citizen, voluntarily, in their spare time. Of course they were too intelligent to be impressed by older people and, being naturally classless, they were sometimes slightly impatient of snobbery when they met it. But, by and large, kids were wonderful.

Then Shirley Williams arrived on the scene – or, to be more exact, the first Harold Wilson government arrived, with a huge apparatus of educational theory which had largely been thought up by Anthony Crosland. The primary purpose of state education was no longer to inculcate the rudiments of reading, writing and arithmetic in those whose natures made them unreceptive to anything more advanced. Still less was it to introduce a finer taste of the discipline necessary for any sort of social existence. The purpose of education was not even to prepare children for a classless society where nobody could look down their noses at anybody else – it was to create such a society. At whatever cost to the conventional values of education, the joys of engineering came first. Every valley must be exalted at whatever cost to the hills and mountains.

When Mrs Shirley Williams arrived at the Department of Education and Science it was already perfectly plain that the great Comprehensive experiment had been a disaster. Like socialism, it simply did not work. Huge schools, with little or no supervision of the teachers, let alone the pupils, were open invitations to truancy and violence. In the four years since the Labour government was defeated there has been plenty of time to take stock of the havoc which was wrought on an entire generation by this silly woman's opinions. For at least seven years I have been pointing out that a substantial proportion of young Britons – I would put it at about a third overall, perhaps a quarter in the south and a half in the north – are completely unemployable. They not only lack the discipline necessary to acquire the most rudimentary skills, they also lack the necessary will to please. They are a lost generation, without even the resources to amuse themselves.

My own observations, which must coincide with the experience of anyone prepared to take a look around, have generally been treated as a quirky, slightly perverse obsession of my own. Kids were still the kindly, idealistic people of *Blue Peter* and similar propaganda films. Now at last the truth is beginning to emerge, that the hopeless generation of louts and bores which Mrs Williams has produced is not only completely useless but also harmful to itself and deeply unhappy.

A brilliant series which ran all last week in the *Daily Mirror* was called 'Bloody kids! who do they think they are?' Put together by Keith Waterhouse, it echoes every sane person's awareness of what has happened and is continuing to happen to a substantial minority of Britain's youth. It is also, I fancy, to be read as a cry of pain from someone who is certainly the best and possibly the wisest commentator in the business. If the rest of my piece is taken up, for the most part, with quotations from his work, I hope he will interpret it as an act of homage rather than as one of simple plagiarism. I cannot, alas, reproduce the horrifying photographs which accompanied the text.

This is Heather Smith, 17, unemployed, of Gateshead, Tyne and Wear: 'I like being a skin because I like fighting . . . Sometimes they come looking for us, sometimes we go looking for them. We always beat them. There are about fifty of us in the SHAM (Skinheads Are Magic) Army and no one can beat us . . . I drink snakebites (lager and cider). They make me drunk quicker. I like getting drunk . . . I never had a job . . . I was supposed to go for an interview last year but didn't turn up. It doesn't worry me.'

Stacey Ottwell, 15, a schoolgirl of Derby, is more moderate in her approach to violence: 'Pointless violence, no. In a good cause, yes – like a demo for more jobs.'

No doubt Stacey is teacher's pet. Nigel Connelly, 19, unemployed, of Newcastle, may have been less pliable: 'It's just another game, isn't it? You can't let anyone push you around now, can you? . . . I've started fights a canny few times when I'm drunk . . . Mostly I have been provoked, but a couple of times it has been completely unprovoked. It doesn't give me a conscience. I'll do it again, probably.'

Most of them drink – 'I usually get into fights when I'm pissed up' (David Webster, 17, skinhead, Plymouth) – but there is a certain debate between drinkers and those who get their satisfaction elsewhere.

Darren Kemp, 16, Woolwich: 'I get £32.32 a week and spend £10 of it on drink. Cider – I just like it. Beer makes me sick. Got the money, can't spend it on much else.' Andy Butlin, 18, unemployed, Glasgow: 'I spend £16 a week on glue, it's £3 for a pint and I buy a pint and a half every other day. I sniff every day . . . I'm in the house all day – my dad drinks and he just annoys me.'

On sex, there was a healthy difference of opinion between members of the idealistic generation. Thus Ray Hillyard, an unemployed punk of Plymouth, says: 'Load of crap – not interested.' Wayne Munden, 17, also unemployed, of Worcester, says: 'I wouldn't get married. Girls are there to be used when you want them.'

Danny Newbury, 18, a fruitpacker of Bolney, Sussex, is more idealistic: 'I believe in sex. I was just over 14 when I started. You learn about it in school and that influences you a lot. They show you all these books and pictures and you think I'll try that. But I prefer spending time on my bike.'

Chivalry survives among the men – 'I've a lot of respect for them, especially if they don't drop their knickers for two or three weeks' (Jeff Strange, 19, unemployed, Bedwas, South Wales). Paul Higgs, 19, unemployed, of Mid-Glamorgan, carries his chivalry to extremes: 'I've never had sex with a girl friend, it would be too embarrassing like just to ask her.'

Above all, there is the perennial problem that teenagers are misunderstood. Thus Fiona Peace, 19, unemployed, of Leeds: 'Teenagers are misunderstood. Many people think we are all dreadfully promiscuous. I'm not easy to sleep with . . . I keep a list of boys I have slept with. I don't star-rate them – I don't think that's fair. My list has the boy's name, then how many times we have done it – not the exact number, but whether it was once or twice, numerous times or infinite.'

Perhaps the real difference is that we listen to their callow and idiotic opinions. That, too, I feel can probably be blamed on Shirley.

7 May 1983

ON THE GREENHAM BUS

Andrew Brown

Perhaps they're the last hippies. They're certainly the latest, and to understand them one must return to the first. 'The Merry Pranksters' were originally just a group of friends who liked to get stoned together, funded and to an extent led by the novelist Ken Kesey, who wrote *One Flew Over the Cuckoo's Nest*. They moved to a house in the countryside, and set about throwing the most memorable parties that they could, assisted by various psychedelic drugs. Eventually, they bought an old bus, and set out to drive from California to New York, with the vague aim of staging 'happenings' along the way, but in fact convinced that they were themselves the happening. They divided the world into people who were 'on the bus' and off it: the elect and the damned, if you like, but the criteria for election and salvation were vague and constantly shifting. Style, rather than conduct, was what they judged; and what united them most of all was the belief that having fun was the most significant thing that anyone could do.

This same belief makes the Greenham women immediately attractive. I don't remember what I had expected, but we might almost have been at Butlins. The sun shone; a naked woman with dyed red hair attended to her shining Citroën van; a woman shouted something about incest, but it was only part of a lover's conceit.

The women carried themselves with the cheerful hostility displayed by tourists towards natives, and with a similar conviction that they were far more important and interesting than their surroundings could ever be. They were, after all, 'on the bus'. Arlene, who had made the joke about incest, is a New Yorker, tanned until her wrinkles show up as little white lines when she smiles. She has the invigorating charm of someone who knows she will always land on her own feet – or on someone else's. She borrowed my pen, and scribbled telephone numbers and instructions all down the margins of a newspaper carried by a girl who was leaving the camp for the weekend; there was some business of a lawyer to be contacted. As she dismissed the messenger, she asked: 'D'you mind?' The girl, who had earlier complained that she couldn't keep a fact in her head, replied that she had a lot to do. 'Don't give me that crap,' said Arlene, restored at once to good humour.

Katarina sat by the roadside, waiting for a car to Newbury. She looked to be about 18, with long dark hair, and eyes full of kindness and ignorance set in the sort of face that aunts with pleasurable charity call plain. She wanted to know if I were for or against the Peace Camp. You could hear the capital letters in her voice. I said that I thought they were wrong, but that I was glad they were there. This reply puzzled her, so I explained that I would find it hateful to live in a country where everyone was right. Besides, I didn't *know* they were wrong. The future isn't knowable; you just have to consider the evidence and then decide what seems the best bet.

'Oh, but you can't let governments make moral decisions for you. You can't live without morality, because then there would be no rules. But the rules must come from within you. That's why people are strong. And you can *know* things in a moral way.'

The awaited car appeared, and Katarina lost interest in conversation as completely as an animal might. I decided that I needed an interpreter. Some of the language I could translate myself: 'People', to Katarina, obviously meant 'those who are on the bus'. The difficulty was to find 'people' who would talk at all. Politics – and even nuclear weapons – obviously played little part in their lives. Later, I was to discover that Katarina had no idea what an 'SS20' might be, while one woman asked me what the negotiations in Geneva were about; and another, what INF meant. No wonder they feel that the press is hostile. So the next day I returned with my sister and a small tape recorder.

We found Arlene, Katarina and some others sitting on a blanket and reading the *Guardian* women's page. A story on 'Women in the Van of Peace' had just appeared, and they were furious. None of them had been featured in it, but this fact by itself could not explain their fury. Arlene was good at anger. Later, reminiscing about psychiatrists, she said:

'Then I committed the worst crime of all. I went to the marriage guidance counsellor and I tried to talk about the thing that was troubling me. I was in a rage. The rage I was in was that my husband was taking no active role in terminating my marriage. He wasn't acting it out. He wasn't doing anything. He wasn't talking about anything. He was drinking all the time. He just wasn't available. So I sort of realised, right, that I was going to have to do it myself, right, and I was in this rage. Because the kids were going to stay with me, and it was going to cost him all his money. And I was working. I was making about as much as a woman can make; and I thought: "Why can't it be me that pays like 200 dollars a week?" And I went and I tried to talk about that . . . Oh my God!'

Her rage at the *Guardian* was of rather a different sort. The Greenham women seem obsessed by their image in the media. Such a preoccupation would be reasonable if their purpose really seems to be to change themselves. The image that they care about is their own in the eyes of each other. For the Greenham women, as for the Merry Pranksters, a shared experience is the only admissible reality. It must be shared: it cannot be

'What on earth do you mean, "No"?'

communicated. The *Guardian* has offended them far more than ever the *Daily Mail* could, by being sympathetic, and yet 'off the bus'. Such a position suggests the real existence of a world outside the camp – a prospect far more threatening than neutron bombs could be.

Their sublime incuriosity about the outside world went very deep indeed. Katarina talked with wonder about some soldiers she had met:

'They said all the soldiers who went out to the Falklands were prepared to die. I was shocked, because I thought: "How could they undervalue themselves so much? How could they undervalue their lives?" They have the right to life, and to a good life, and to be able to fulfil themselves; but they have such a low opinion of themselves that they are prepared to sacrifice themselves in that way. I just feel that's very sad.'

Later, we drove her to a camp outside Porton Down. 'I think what they're doing to the animals here is even worse than what they're going to do at Greenham,' she remarked as we drove up. A sign on the roadside announced 'Women for Peace and Animal Liberation' beside two faded caravans and a line of tents. A woman named Marion, alone in the camp, sat watching two kittens playing in the shade. If Arlene is easily imagined running her version of the Stritch Service, Marion had something of Tony Last about her: driven by a humourless, compulsive decency into the wilderness and squalor. The scents of wildflowers, and of Animal Liberator, blended richly. 'What a pity,' Katarina said, 'that these marvellous camps should have to be across the road from such horrible places.'

20 August 1983

KENTUCKY FRIED GEORGIAN

Alexandra Artley and John Martin Robinson

Conservation fogeys *love* expressing opinions. They bang on about COUNTY BOUNDARIES ('they can call Yorkshire what they like. I come from the NORTH RIDING and PROUD of it'); ABOLITION OF TELE-GRAMS ('I shall write to the Post-Master General'); OPEN-PLAN TRAINS ('the crack of ring-pull cans was DEAFENING!'); CENTRAL HEATING ('don't be so FEEBLE. It will split your mahogany'); FITTED CARPETS IN CHURCHES ('absolutely OUTRAGEOUS'); BUILDINGS

BY AGEING MODERNISTS ('meretricious TAT'); MODERN RC
CHURCH ('Father Banjo O' Marx'); THE ANGLICAN CHURCH
('Runcie-balls'); BRITISH TELECOM ('TeleCON more like'); HABITAT
('ha-ha-ha'); THE NATIONAL GALLERY ('a national DISGRACE');
NOUVELLE CUISINE ('had to eat a CHEESE SANDWICH on the way
home'); MICROWAVE OVENS (laughter in the house). Then, plop, *The
Spectator* falls through the letterbox and Mr Fogey sits in COMPLETE
SILENCE and reads it.

The flashing synapses of high-powered fogey brains burn food. Conservation fogeys are the world's greatest diners out. They have developed
the art of eating huge amounts while campaigning, SAVE-ing and talking
non-stop most convivially. THOSE OPINIONS boom out while roast
beef, boiled potatoes, cabbage anglaise, yummy, proper gravy in a hot
boat, rice pudding with skin, or failing that, crème brûlée, fly down the
fogey throat. With dinner they like little Knoxian jokes ('Do you take this
margarine for butter or worse?').

In winter, conservation fogeys often dine in Spitalfields, home of the
new Baroque. At nine, through the dark of the decayed vegetable market
they come in Suits, tweeds, grey wool scarves in plain but not purl, thick
corduroy trousers from the Bedford Riding Breeches Company, macs and
chestnutty brogues dull with dubbing. In the high art gloom, groups of
derelicts brawl with bottles round wild fires (very Joseph Wright of
Derby). Fire and gloom play a large part in the fogey temperament. When
a fogey is invited to dinner he arrives with wooden crates pulled off a skip
to fuel his host's huge hearths. Fires in fogey dining rooms are so fierce
that Mrs Fogeys often get burn marks between their shoulders from molten bra hooks.

Dinner in Spitalfields is a very *chiaroscuro* matter. Fogeys like dancing
shadows in panelled rooms and the smell of roast meat or Brick Lane
Indian take-aways wafting up from the basement. Then there is more
talk, campaigning, new strategies, DISGRACEFUL, large whiskies,
bashed silver candlesticks, strong beeswax candles bought by the pound
from church suppliers, eye-to-eye contact with canvas instant ancestors,
chipped cream-ware, dripping-wax sconces on the walls and the bong of
bones dropped on threadbare rugs for seething animals. In the candle-
light long fogey arms whip out for the eye-watering English mustard. At
three in the morning there are several feet of restless ash in the hearth
and a slim chance of taxis from Bishopsgate to other fogey haunts. Last
comes the lost cord: at night bachelor fogeys stride home to thick striped
pyjamas.

Conservation fogeys bounced off Sixties' property spivs and stack-a-
prole planners. They are the first English generation since the Thirties

(Robert Byron and friends) to be visually literate and to feel sorry for down-and-out things as well as people. The two are often connected. Buildings are pulled down and their vulnerable inhabitants moved on. Keeping philistines routed is quite time-consuming. Consequently, Mr Fogey consults a huge half-hunter worn on a watch chain and warmed by his chest. He never wears anything on his wrist (it stops him speaking off the cuff) but he likes plenty of clocks at home (boing, boing, boing). Other accessories include an old, very heavy bicycle for racing to conservation meetings. Sometimes, when cycling, he wears a pair of Thirties' leather motoring goggles. Fogeys cycle with an upright Edwardian posture and hang out like yachtsmen round Hyde Park. When Mrs Fogey sees this from a bus her heart gives a horrid leap.

The conservation fogey is an urban chevalier and his bicycle is his horse. He loves and understands the British city. When he is not cycling he walks long and purposefully across it like Dickens. The most time-consuming thing in Mr Fogey's life, apart from campaigning, is a house, or when he is a poor Very Young Fogey, a basement or garret flat in the right sort of house. Fogeys differ from young Sloanes in the way they look at London property. Sloanes choose the area they want to live in and then find a house. Fogeys find the perfect house to restore and don't give a damn about the area. They go where the architecture is and this is usually the rotting Georgian centres of big cities. Fogeys like places to be socially crunchy. This means a healthy mix of young, old, crims (criminals), Bangladeshis, clergy and council estaters. Whereas Sloanes treat everyone in a jolly way, they like to maintain class difference where they live because it feels safer. Conservation fogeys give the impression of being fierce, but they live in socially mixed areas because they like the *individualism* of different types of people. In grand circles this used to be called feudal familiarity.

Mr and Mrs Fogey like to live in decaying splendour with wonderful, slightly broken things. They love costly tatters, the aristocratic aesthetic of pleasing decay. Their walls of patchy bare plaster give the Crumbling Palazzo Look. It is like hanging pictures on the inside of a Stilton. To go with that they like old china repaired with brass rivets. (If they find a pretty mug in Woolworths, really mad fogeys break it and get repaired by a pro. Then it looks very interesting.) All fogeys love pink lustre china (sweet disorder on a shelf), English cream-ware and grisaille pieces. Fogey cats are encouraged to shred bits of silk to make them look like the cushions at Sissinghurst. For special occasions like weddings, christenings, house birthdays (250 YEARS OLD TODAY) or ordinary human birthdays, Mrs Fogey sits down at the kitchen table to splosh out pink lustre greetings cards with pinky-bronze ink. Meanwhile, Mr Fogey keeps obelisk culture alive. Obelisks mean I REPRESENT CLASSICISM, visual literacy, proportion in all things, restraint, the vanity of human wishes, and fogeys like them a lot. China obelisks are very expensive so fogeys make temporary ones from marblised paper, varnish them and letter them with the Roman numerals and greetings (A NUPTIAL OBELISK, A BIRTHDAY OBELISK, ANOTHER OBELISK). This is done on the theory of decoy obelisks – the cardboard ones might attract the real ones in due course.

To repair their houses properly, fogeys invented architectural salvage. Miles away when philistines are gutting an old house, fogeys pick up high-frequency distress signals. Suddenly, they are there, saving the bits if they can't actually stop the destruction. Cracked marble fireplaces, panelled doors masked by crude hardboard flushing, sash windows, shutters, Carron grates and strangely brilliant old glass are mourned over and carried home. Another good building RIP. When a demolition pickaxe shatters the work of the human hand, fogeys feel it is a blow against humanity. If an old house is modernised with a new crudely-panelled front door, fogeys call the style Kentucky Fried Georgian. The streets where fogeys live swirl with greasy boxes anyway. Like playing with Lego they swop building bits (one small Georgian reeded marble fireplace broken in three places equals a big cast-iron bath on claw feet).

To keep in touch with world fogeyism Mr Fogey hunts down big black telephones; heavy square Bakelite ones which do not move when his fingers are doing the walking. Fogeys letter them with the romantic names of old London telephone exchanges (EUSton, portal of the North, MUSeum, heart of Bloomsbury). Consequently, drunken guests have difficulty getting taxis late at night. Radio Cabs says, 'What is your number?' Drunken guest says, 'TERminus 2020.' The taxi never arrives and the guest slumps to the floor to be covered with blankets by Mrs Fogey.

Thomas Hope furniture springs eternal in the fogey breast and here fogey couples mildly disagree. Mr Fogey is a purist and he likes formal (that means rather hard) chairs and sofas while Mrs Fogey prefers squashy hippos in washed-out chintz. All over Bloomsbury the frilly hippos slowly emigrate upstairs. In Spitalfields, home of the guttering candle, fogey couples argue about light bulbs. Mr Fogey screws in 25-watters to maintain the Baroque gloom. After four o'clock on a winter's afternoon, this means Mrs Fogey needs a torch to fasten the tabs on her baby fogelet's Pampers.

England is a very masculine country and conservation fogeys have rather masculine views. (A woman is a – you know – funny sort of CHAP who steadies the bottom end of a ladder.) Fogey couples often meet at a SAVE lunch, on the first Friday in the month. They are drawn to each other, the lovely meat-paste sandwiches and grim photographs of a threatened factory in Bradford in the polychrome Egyptian style. Together they vow to save it. Fogey courtships take place on coach trips ('the chara') to see such things as glass cases of rotting taxidermy at Calke Abbey. The fogey lovers sit at the back of the bus and share a *Buildings of England*. The first sign of love is when Mr Fogey offers her a swig from his hip flask and says to her, 'Listen, WOMAN, your views are quite APPAL-LING.' The honeymoon must be somewhere architectural and is usually Rome, in a hotel five feet from the Pantheon. Rome is so wonderful, the fogey-weds think they must have been dropped head first into a box of chocolates. The honeymoon photographs rarely have Mr Fogey in them because he uses his bride to get *scale* into architectural photographs.

Back home Mrs Fogey wears a droopy skirt, three long sweaters and free-range earrings as she runs lightly through the conservation area. Quickly she learns that trying to ripen an avocado pear in front of a gas fire is useless. For years she saves the lead cappings from bottles of wine in case they can be melted down to repair the roof flashings. From good Spanish bottles she keeps the gold nets to make a little Rioja snood.

Fogey families believe in conservation heroics. They live with no roof, then no floors, then only a few walls, but lots of dry rot, Greek builders drinking Coca-Cola, collapsing ceilings, cold water, layers of filth, cellars full of old tights and tea-leaves, re-wiring by day, re-plumbing by fly-by-night and donating the drawing room as an emergency campaign office. Fogeys learned to rough it in the early Seventies. They trained as conservation commandos in squats and Direct Action against London's rapacious property developers. On any given evening, according to how the architectural battle is raging outside, Mrs Fogey can expect none or 14 people for dinner. Consequently, she depends on the flexibility of cottage pie and semolina. Down the stairs to stuttering candles and some soggy cabbage the convivial fogeys come: large whiskies, the smell of outdoors, DISGRACEFUL, clomp, clomp go the brogues, GRADE II I THINK. Keeping the best of the past is one way forward and fogey-land dines again.

22 December 1984

HOSTILITIES

P. J. Kavanagh

We were let off lightly, as far as junior teenage parties go. Everybody had had a good time, no one had disgraced himself, or herself, and there was the minimum of breakages. It was the younger brother's party, so we had left his older brother, with a couple of friends, to keep an eye on things and, not wanting to be wet blankets, had spent the evening out.

What was creepy was how we felt when we returned, a decent time past the appointed hour. The house was filled with cavorting young, most of whom we did not know. There was nothing wrong with them cavorting – the music, of course, was deafening – but that number of faces turned on you with lack of interest, or with disappointment, as you slink apologetically back into your own home, presents a serious problem as to how to behave. To join in, and cavort, was obviously inappropriate. To creep to bed was out of the question, quite apart from the din, because we had promised to ferry most of the guests home.

Not for the first time, as an adult confronted by the young, there seemed no way of doing the right thing; in fact, there seemed no right thing to do. But as I felt those young, indifferent eyes fall on my wrinkly mug – oh so well-meaning, oh so hoping they had had a good time (and would go home quickly) – and I sensed what my arrival and appearance signified: authority, ownership, the end of all the fun, *oldness*, it struck me for the first time that perhaps there really was a gap between young and old, in certain circumstances unbridgeable, and a kind of hostility; perhaps there are necessary hostilities built into the nature of things. But I do not believe this.

There are unnecessary hostilities of class, of course. We learned next morning there had been an attempted gatecrash, by 'mods', nobly averted by my older son who convinced them by the power of his eloquence that it was a rotten party they would not enjoy. We found the telephone wire had been cut and, less nobly, I suspected them. Later we discovered the culprit had been a larking guest and it was probably unintentional.

But this question of unnecessary hostility, between young and old, and between classes, gave me my first insight of 1985. If it has occurred to everyone else I apologise, but it has only just presented itself to me.

To begin at the beginning. When the Earl of Stockton made his memorable speech in the House of Lords deploring picket-line violence, and said in heart-broken tones: 'We can't have this sort of thing. These are the finest men in the world', he spoke for me and, I suspect, many others. But I discovered to my surprise that he did not speak for some articulate members of the generation younger than mine, the 25s to 35s who belong to the middle classes. They thought it was laying it on a bit thick and I could not understand why. Surely they could not imagine that the working class (clumsy term, but let it stand for now) was a set of undifferentiated yobbos, and be so unsympathetic at a time of such terrible unemployment? Then I realised they had never been in the army, or done National Service and had had little opportunity to meet people different from themselves. They had only middle-class schools, middle-class careers as their experience. But other generations of their kind had not been in the army, so that could not be the whole explanation.

Then it hit me, this famous insight. Not only had they never rubbed shoulders with different kinds of men in the Services, which is a powerful author of diffidence and respect, *they were the first generation of their kind who had no experience of the working class whatsoever.* Previous generations, of that affluence, were brought up by the working class; there were nannies, and servants, and gardeners. Today, with the advent of supermarkets and the Asian corner-shop, these young men had possibly not even become acquainted with so much as a shopkeeper. This ignorance led to the hostility. And that is the insight.

Is it true? Or, better, is it the explanation? I don't know. But what with the East hating the West, the young hating the old, and some of the middle classes hating all not of their number, we are clearly going to bash ourselves to pieces.

I was in Switzerland recently and noticed that, by law, every window is fitted with an anti-radiation shutter. When the big bang comes the Swiss shall inherit the earth, which could be worse, and is no more than we deserve.

19 January 1985

PRINCES OF THEIR OWN TIMES

Gavin Stamp

Fifty years ago next week, on 20 January 1936, King George V died:

Spirits of well-shot woodcock, partridge, snipe
  Flutter and bear him up the Norfolk sky:
In that red house in a red mahogany book-case
  The stamp collection waits with mounts long dry . . .

His successor immediately turned back all the clocks at Sandringham
from local time to GMT, thus setting, perhaps, the intended tone of the
new reign: modern, efficient, unstuffy. Edward VIII represented the spirit
of youth. Many looked to him in that troubled, messy decade to bring a
breath of fresh air into Britain, to inaugurate a new, forward-looking age
in reaction to the old-established ways associated with the dead King. In
fact Edward VIII was 41 when he became King, but he had, as the Prime
Minister, Mr Baldwin, declared, 'the secret of youth in the prime of age'.
    John Betjeman caught the mood in his poem 'Death of King George V':

. . . The big blue eyes are shut which saw wrong clothing
  And favourite fields and coverts from a horse;
Old men in country houses hear clocks ticking
  Over thick carpets with a deadened force;

Old men who never cheated, never doubted,
  Communicated monthly, sit and stare
At the new suburb stretched beyond the runway
  Where a young man lands hatless from the air.

The new King had flown from Sandringham to London. These lines
suggest – consciously? – the essential tawdriness and emptiness of
Edward VIII: a gilded, hatless youth of little substance, utterly uncritical
of the modern world, caught up by fashion and innovation, posing as
ordinary and casual, and, in the event, utterly unfitted to be King. His
reign, uncrowned, of less than a year was not glorious. He achieved little
except niggling economies in the royal household, and after the omi-

nously symbolic catastrophe of the burning of the Crystal Palace by signing the Instrument of Abdication concluded the farcical constitutional
crisis caused because a spoilt child of the 20th century could not live
without marrying an American divorcée. This seems a curious attitude
for one who tried so hard to be unconventional – why couldn't Mrs Simpson have remained his mistress?

The Abdication and the subsequent unedifying behaviour of the
Windsors have tended to overshadow Edward VIII's real achievements as
Prince of Wales. As heir to the throne he was a brilliant success. Glamorous and responsive, he helped to unite the Empire by his long tours in the
early 1920s. Unlike his grandfather, Edward VII, who as Prince of Wales
was little more than a drone, he took an active part in public affairs and
enhanced the prestige of the Crown by expressing his concern about certain aspects of national life. As he lent his name to charitable causes and
was not afraid to make controversial speeches, he performed a similar
role to his great-nephew, our own Prince Charles. As Princes of Wales
they seem comparable – or are they?

Frances Donaldson's fine biography of Edward VIII confirms that this
odd, lonely and melancholy man was really three separate personalities:
Prince of Wales, King and Duke of Windsor. But some of the more
unfortunate aspects of his character – his inconsiderate selfishness, fri-
volity and moodiness – were already evident in the 1920s. Even so, he
worked hard as a young man and was physically courageous. He was most
impressive during the Great War when he was so anxious to share the
sufferings of his generation in the trenches and was constantly –
understandably – thwarted in this resolve by the authorities. After the
war, he took an active interest in the welfare of ex-servicemen, in their
pensions, housing and employment – or, rather, the lack of it. He was
genuinely interested in ex-servicemen's associations like Toc H and in
working men's clubs, and was Patron of the British Legion. He once said:
'I feel more at home with the Legion than anywhere else.' As Frances
Donaldson remarks, 'Whether or not this was completely true, he succeeded in making the people of Britain feel it was.'

Travelling all over the country to the worst affected areas, there is no
doubt that the Prince was profoundly concerned with the welfare of the
unemployed, and he supported practical measures for helping them.
After the General Strike he contributed to the Miners' Relief Fund. In
1928 he became Patron of the National Council of Social Service which
encouraged voluntary action. He was instrumental in the founding of
the Feathers Clubs to help the unemployed, which were run by his first
mistress, Mrs Dudley Ward, even after he had cruelly dropped her in

favour of Mrs Simpson. In all this he anticipated our own Prince of Wales's work for unemployed youth, for the homeless and for the dispossessed of the inner cities.

Edward VIII's most celebrated intervention into social politics came during his brief reign. This was on 18 November 1936, when he visited South Wales and was appalled by the industrial dereliction and scale of unemployment. 'Something must be done to find them work,' he said to an official. To judge by a subsequent *Times* leader, the King's remarks, implicitly critical of the inactivity of the National Government, caused quite as much official annoyance as have Prince Charles's speeches about the neglect of inner cities. However, as Lady Donaldson notes, the King also announced in South Wales, 'You may be sure that all I can do for you I will', when he had no intention of doing anything at all, as he had already told the Prime Minister that he intended to abdicate. The unemployed were all very well but his own personal happiness came first: a dereliction of duty which appalled and confounded his family advisers. Indeed, Mr Baldwin found that arguments about duty, about the choice between Mrs Simpson and the throne, simply did not register with the King. His younger brother, the Duke of Kent, concluded – charitably, perhaps – that he was simply 'besotted'.

Edward VIII – unlike Prince Charles – seems to have had few wider cultural interests. He seldom read, had no interest in painting, music or architecture. It was not the Prince of Wales but his mother, Queen Mary, who was instrumental behind the scenes in preventing the Crown Commissioners from demolishing Carlton House Terrace in 1934 after the greatest preservation controversy of the decade. The Prince was involved with architecture but not in any informed manner.

When as King he wished to add a servants' hall and kitchens to Fort Belvedere in Windsor Great Park, his favourite and principal residence, he summoned Sir Giles Scott, past president of the RIBA and designer of Liverpool Cathedral: an odd choice for a kitchen extension. Scott naturally obliged and turned up at Fort Belvedere in full morning dress. He was, therefore, disconcerted to find the King in shorts rooting about in a hedge. This, of course, was typical of Edward VIII's self-consciously controversial casualness. Also typical was the fact that he never asked Scott to sit down or offered him any refreshment. There are many such stories about him: behind the outward progressive show, Edward VIII was arrogant and insensitive.

Edward VIII combined that contrived exhibitionism against authority, against the Establishment, with a tenacious enjoyment of its privileges which is characteristic of English liberalism or Whiggery. Never was this odious hypocrisy, which has done so much harm to Britain, more conspicuous than between the wars, when a whole generation gloried in their youth – the last resort of the young scoundrel – and traded on ridiculing their parents, whom they depicted as both sinister and absurd. Edward VIII was a perfect representative of this generation. Unfortunately, it had little with which to replace the values of Edwardian England other than self-conscious modernity, jazz, dancing and all things American, cars, aeroplanes and, above all, the ludicrous pursuit of sunbathing. Not for nothing has that generation been labelled the 'Children of the Sun'. Edward VIII was always bronzed. Addicted to open shirts and shorts – the uniform of the progressive 1930s man – Edward VIII's interest in dress, in casual clothing, was quite as obsessive as that of his father in correct formal dress.

Now nobody could accuse our own Prince of Wales of being obsessed with clothes or of indulging in a cult of youth. Indeed, he has been seen as representative of its antithesis, what has been given the odious but possibly useful label of Young Fogeyism. He looks old-fashioned. Unlike his great-uncle, having sown his wild oats he has married and has produced an heir to the throne. Like his grandfather and great-grandfather, he seems a model of pedestrian domestic virtue. Unlike his great-uncle, he does not look a day under his 37 years. It is hard to take seriously the account of Prince Charles's affinity with young people as described by Mr Pete Townshend of The Who, who noted how HRH had attended a pop concert by Status Quo and how 'it was the first time he's ever felt a true contemporary. He suddenly realised he was their age, part of a generation with shared problems.'

It is surely Prince Charles's strength that he has not been seduced by the cults and culture of many of his generation. He has been quite as serious and as practical as his great-uncle in his work for the homeless and unemployed, in setting up and supporting such bodies as the Prince's Trust. What is impressive is that his interests seem to be wider, that he has supported causes which are not conventional or fashionable. He is the first member of the Royal Family since George IV or Prince Albert to take an informed interest in architecture. Even if repeating ideas and criticisms which have been current for a decade, his 'carbuncle' speech which so annoyed the RIBA and his active support for the nebulous concept of 'community architecture' have brought architectural issues to a much wider public – just where they ought to be. If he meant it when he said that Ted Cullinan is 'a man after my own heart' then he is very well informed about the state of modern British architecture.

Now here I ought to declare an interest, or lack of it, before complimenting the Prince of Wales on agreeing with me. I have never met

Prince Charles and I seem to be one of the very few architects and critics around today who cannot claim to be 'Architectural Adviser to the Prince of Wales'. We are, however, near-contemporaries and we both went up to Cambridge to read history in the same year. Prince Charles was lucky. At that time the History Library was in the Old University Library, a superbly practical Neo-Classical building by C. R. Cockerell. He did not go on to spend a second year working in the new and notorious History Faculty Library by James Stirling, something which for me was a formative experience.

What I find interesting is that we share many of the same sympathies, and not just about architecture. All his causes seem to me to be the right ones: the hospice movement and the plight of the old; opposition to modern farming methods and support for organic farming; concern for the countryside and for wildlife; even his sympathy for vegetarianism and alternative medicine, and his open-mindedness about the paranormal. All these interests seem to me to be intelligent and necessary questionings of the sybaritic materialist assumptions of our parents' generation. Then there is his evident loyalty to the Church of England – shared by his mother – and his great respect for Roman Catholicism – perhaps not shared by his mother. In his interest in religion, Prince Charles is in marked contrast to his great-uncle, whose apparent indifference to his religious duties was the subject of the address by the Bishop of Bradford on 1 December 1936 which broke the self-imposed British press embargo on referring to the King's association with Mrs Simpson.

In all these interests, I suppose we both reflect the conservation-minded and anti-materialist attitudes of our particular generation. No doubt we are both subject to Sheldrakian morphic resonance in this respect. Similarly, Edward VIII's attitudes are often attributed to his upbringing, to his childhood with a martinet of a father and an unemotional, distant mother. Even so, his tough experience as a naval cadet at Osborne Naval College seems relatively no worse than Prince Charles's time at Gordonstoun. There is a story – I have no idea if it is true – that Prince Philip stopped his son learning to play the violin as it was an unmanly accomplishment for a King, but Prince Charles does not seem to have been scarred by his childhood experiences.

Perhaps the really important distinction between Prince Charles and his great-uncle is in his intelligence and understanding of his constitutional position. He is well equipped to be King. He is not sentimental; he well knows that cities cannot be regenerated, that better architecture cannot appear, without money. Hence his speech calling for an 'enterprise culture' and condemning the 'employee mentality' of the North which annoyed the left quite as much as his other speeches have annoyed Mrs Thatcher. He is not identified with any political party. Like his great-uncle, he believes in individual initiative and in old-fashioned concepts like leadership, but there is no danger of his becoming identified with a 'King's Party'.

In considering Edward VIII, who was, to say the least, politically naïve, it seems extraordinary that he was ever regarded as a radical and that the belief arose that he was forced to abdicate by a conservative Establishment fearful of his left-wing sympathies. Edward VIII was no liberal and no democrat, but he did have sympathy for one of the fashionable political ideals of his time: Fascism. We now know that both the Duke and Duchess of Windsor had a high regard for Hitler and not just because they thought he might put him back on the throne. Was it Baldwin who suggested that a statue of Mrs Simpson be erected in every town in the land in gratitude for her saving us from such a dangerous King?

In his book *The Thirties*, published in 1940, Malcolm Muggeridge noted how Edward VIII, in his failure to grow from Prince of Wales into King, shared 'the fate of many of his generation, who, youthful, were required to be mature, and in maturity persisted in being youthful . . . bricklayers, clergymen and kings betray the same restlessness in restless times, crave similarly to free themselves from the past's dead weight and let their egos thrive, and having freed themselves, are similarly forlorn. What befell King Edward makes the same pattern as what has befallen many of his subjects' (the late Christopher Isherwood?). If – as I believe he is – Prince Charles is a man of his time and not a 1960s survivor, just as Edward VIII was representative of his generation, that suggests that the 1980s are not half so bad as the 1930s, which makes me, as a fellow aging Young Fogey, for once rather optimistic.

18 January 1986

PART-TIME LOVERS

Nicholas Coleridge

Here is a modern tableau: six friends in their late twenties having dinner at Alastair Little's matt-black restaurant in Frith Street. The numbers are balanced: three men, three girls. So is the food: three escalopes of salmon in a chive *beurre blanc*, three tiny starters in lieu of main courses.

There are theatre programmes on the table, so we know they have come on from a play. Laugh and the restaurant laughs with you. The party is animated with fun and merriment and Muscadet sur Lie 1984.

The door opens and four girls come in from the cold and are shown to their reserved table. One of them, her name is Miranda, notices someone she knows in the theatre party. 'How was the play, Simon?' she calls across the restaurant as she draws her chair. 'So-so,' replies Simon. 'A bit overlong.'

Unless you happen to know that Simon and Miranda have been stepping out for five years, are universally regarded as a couple, take holidays together, are constant and monogamous in thought and word and deed, you might easily suppose they are acquaintances. They do not cross the room to greet one another, nor is any suggestion floated that the two parties should join up. This is not one of the evenings that Simon and Miranda spend together. The timetable of their romance is precise and meticulously adhered to: four evenings a week to see their own friends independently, two nights plus alternate weekends to pursue their romance.

There was an annoying pop record by Elton John called 'Part-time lover'. Annoying but prescient. Part-time love is becoming the predominant sexual suit of our times. Statistics show that, anyway among the *Spectator*-reading, restaurant-going classes, people are marrying later: approximately six years later for both sexes than was usual in 1956. This does not mean that they are being especially promiscuous. The notion that the older young of Britain lead the life of Riley is a false one. On the contrary, five different factors, some moral, some to do with work, have relegated the importance of sex several rungs down the ladder of desirable pastimes. By 1986, sex has become a leisure activity, enjoyed once or twice a week with a consenting partner at a prearranged time, just as two currency brokers might meet after work at the Lansdowne Club for a vigorous game of squash.

An important reason for the change, like so much else at the moment, is that people are working harder and longer. The protagonists of every modern love affair are yawning out their spare time against a backdrop of terminal exhaustion. Miranda, at 27 a Eurobond girl, is tired. Simon, at 29 a foreign exchange broker, is tired. It is never otherwise. Their love affair began, four years earlier, when they sleepwalked into each other's lives in a City winebar, collapsed onto the same bed and, hours later in the middle of the night, aroused by their mutual body heat, somehow summoned up the energy to make love. By the next morning they discovered they were in love. They have many interests in common, such as blue French cheeses and the minimum bank lending rate, and they talk once a day on the telephone or by fax. As time has gone by, however, they have seen each other less. After the hurly-burly of the first six months, they have become jealous of their spare time: not because they consciously wish to avoid one another, rather there is not enough time. This is not an excuse, there is actually *no time*.

The itinerary of modern romance does not allow for more than three and a half of these five options: *i*, demanding job with long hours including some evenings spent entertaining clients; *ii*, separate houses or flats with bills to pay; *iii*, both circles of old friends each partner wants to keep up with; *iv*, time-consuming girlfriend/boyfriend who likes to go out to dinner and talk to you from time to time; *v*, spending the odd evening at home with same, possibly with a view to sexual activity. The modern solution has been to split the week, officially or unofficially, into a series of fudged contingencies.

Miranda rolls up at her office behind Cannon Street Station at 8.15, Simon has arrived at London Wall 45 minutes earlier. There is no time to see each other over lunch. They leave their respective offices again in the evening at about seven o'clock. Usually one of them has a business drink on the way home. Both eventually head for their own flats, to read the post (which had not yet arrived when they set off for the office), turn the washing machine onto the drying cycle, and have a bath. By now it is already nine o'clock. They are shattered. Miranda cannot be bothered to iron and pack the clothes she'll need for the next day at the office, and cross London to Simon's flat in Ennismore Gardens. Instead she joins a couple of friends having dinner in a Thai restaurant. Before she sets off she rings Ennismore Gardens but Simon's answering machine is on. She has no idea, and certainly no concern, about where he is. (In fact he is kicking his heels in the American bar of the Savoy Hotel, listening to some highly speculative backchat about the deutschmark from two Swiss bankers.) Miranda knows there is no prospect of Simon deceiving her. She has learnt, to her occasional disappointment, that after a long day at the flickering electronic screens Simon's fund of passion is barely adequate for one Eurobond girl, let alone two.

That is not quite fair. If it were, then the host of two-day-a-week love affairs staggering on all over London could not continue. There is a theory, posed by my colleague Nicola Shulman, that girls who see their boyfriends only occasionally are more passionately involved with them, since the double bed, which in a formal live-in relationship would eventually become associated with sleep, is still correlated first and foremost with sex. As a secondary bonus, the girl is excused the emotional burden of actually living with a man. Women, runs the theory, worry more than men about the prevailing mood of their partners: whether he is happy, even whether he is enjoying a film. To see your boyfriend less is to worry about him less. Thus you have whole days free from anxiety.

Whole days to see other people. A consequence of marrying later is having more friends, each of whom needs regular servicing. It is impossible to generalise about how many friends other people have, but even if there were only eight people you wished to see, say, twice a month, then you are already tight on free evenings, not counting colleagues from work or satellite acquaintances. A girl involved in a part-time love affair explained the pressures on her diary. 'Once or twice a week I'm invited, quite a long time in advance, to a dinner party. Harry isn't generally asked too, since he doesn't usually know the people.' (It is now considered bad form, unless you are actually engaged to be married, to expect your lover to come along too.) 'Two evenings I go out to supper with old university or work friends who Harry doesn't know, and anyway finds rather boring. One evening I go to the cinema with a girlfriend. Which leaves two nights to see Harry. Either I stay with him or he comes over to my flat. This has been the routine for about three years. Harry did ask whether I'd like to move into his house, but I'm locked into a mortgage with a loan from my firm and it would be a waste to break it. I've no idea whether we'll get married, I hope so, I think so, but Harry might get sent to Hong Kong for a stint by the bank.'

In some respects the modern lover's dilemma resembles that of a lateral-thinking film critic: would the punter prefer to spend his £3 on this film or on a pizza? Would he prefer to devote Tuesday evening to having dinner with a longstanding friend, or to an overseas client who happens to be in town, which might lead to a commission, or to one quiet evening alone at home to ward off paranoia, or sleeping with girlfriend Annabel, which involves being on top form? (If you only see each other twice a week there is a certain social onus to amuse. Only the married can afford to be dull.)

Significant, too, is the rise of peer pressure. With later marriage, and the extended period of independence between leaving home and the altar, friends have usurped the traditional influence (and power of veto) of the family. A 27-year-old person may have 20 friends of both sexes who define the parameters of their social life. They have probably all known each other intimately for eight years. A new face in their midst is an intrusion, even a challenge, that must be assimilated into a sub-culture of private jokes, assumptions and nuances. This is tedious. It is more amusing to tell an anecdote about George's latest lunge at Mary than to subtitle the full sweep of their relationship. Thus the peer pressure to continue a flagging love affair, on a two-day-a-week basis, is considerable. Meeting the friends is the modern equivalent of meeting the mother-in-law.

Opportunities for breaking the part-time cycle become successively fewer. Even when you are out alone it is understood, anyway by your peers, that you are already spoken for. Nobody will 'muscle in': in a busy world, concern not to cause offence outweighs the sexual prize. The only prospect of change is the y factor; a stranger sweeps you off your feet on one of your free nights, and before you have time to stand up again, marries you. This is unlikely to happen. Unless the y factor is very decisive, there is a relapse into the comfortable pace of the truncated love affair, shored up by inertia and the security of the devil you know.

In a curious way, it is now considered less socially acceptable to end a well-established affair than it would once have been thought immoral to start such an affair in the first place. Morality has been supplanted by the Great God Sensibleness. 'Being sensible' is the unspoken rationale behind sex as a leisure activity. It is transparently sensible to get to know your potential spouse before marrying them. Similarly, it would not be sensible to marry until you have made a career and enjoyed life as a single

'While there's lifestyle there's hope.'

person. In order to make your career, it is sensible to work hard, which involves putting your love life sensibly on the back burner. However, if you have found a compatible companion, but are not yet ready to marry, then what could be more sensible than to see them twice a week?

An interesting, and perhaps disturbing, phenomenon at the moment is the high proportion of men in their late twenties and early thirties who, having baled out of a long-running affair, have decided not to bother to embark upon another. Work, money, food and friends salve the need for companionship. They are not lonely. If they feel a desire for sex, they buy it. The former deputy chairman of the Conservative Party is not the only workaholic in Britain accused of having a taste for emotion-free encounters. The proliferation of escort agencies advertising in the classified section of business magazines is symptomatic. In the Sixties, the fact that sex is 'free' was regarded as an advantage. Now, if anything, it counts slightly against it. With so much money swashing about in the City, 'only a skinflint', they say, 'would prefer a concerted bout of nookie to dinner in a decent restaurant'.

London is full of quite successful unwed 30-year-old girls. Because I am not a woman, I cannot say with any degree of certainty whether they are satisfied with the state of their affairs. If you feel happier seeing your boyfriend twice a week than seeing him every day, then the desirability of regularising your relationship is clearly not there. Nevertheless, most modern achieving women still expect one day to get married. The fact that, in a recent *Newsweek* survey, American women unmarried by the age of 25 were shown to have a 50-50 prospect of ever doing so, is only an unnerving spectre. A busy publisher tells me that when she was 16 she visualised herself wed at 24; now she is 28 and the target has shifted to 34. Her boyfriend, whom she adores, is so distracted by work that sometimes they don't speak for ten days at a stretch. If she could marry him just by snapping her fingers, she would; the hooha of a wedding appals her. It would be the last straw that breaks the camel's back. *There is no time.*

1 November 1986

GREEN POWER, YES PLEASE

Alexandra Artley

Child Green ('a child of the world') wears a rainbow-striped, Peruvian hand-knitted cap with ear-flaps, Osh-Kosh ('B'Gosh') dungarees, a jumper produced by Arran out-workers and faintly riddled with 'natural imperfections' (a sign of genuine hand-work) and royal blue Finnish felt boots bought by his father on a geo-thermal energy fact-finding trip to Helsinki. In boring financial terms his ensemble comes to approximately £230. Specially seated behind his mother, he glides off into a lead-poisoned bicycle lane on his way to a multi-cultural nursery school which promises lots of 'elemental play' (water and sand).

For fun, Child Green eats Hedgehog brand organic potato crisps (available in yoghurt and cucumber flavour) and wholefood imitation Smarties made with natural colours at 70p a quarter to stop him being hyperactive. At his fourth birthday party Child Green began to know his was different when his jelly did not wobble. This is because it was made from floppy agar-agar instead of rubbery animal gelatine ('poor animals' hooves and horns'). Even on the way to nursery school comes the first public duty of the day. CLONG, THONK. Pausing briefly on the pavement beside a huge green dome with round holes in it ('bott-le bank') his mother lifts the previous day's supply of domestic glass bottles from her wicker bicycle basket and, feeling rather good about it, drops them in.

Whether it is bicycling, recycling, the cycle of the seasons, personal bio-rhythms or a no-growth economy, Greens like things to go round and round, including talk. Several months before Child Green was born, for example, his parents had sincerely discussed the ecological consequences of what nappies he should wear. Disposables (of course) merely added to the torrents of demon plastic municipal waste. Soundly made of cotton, Harrington's traditional terry squares could be re-used by subsequent children, passed on to others, recycled into dusters, then floorcloths, down to bits of handy cloth for bicycle-chain readjustment. *But*, as the Greens explained over a carton of convenient Pampers, in those days the Ecover Company (of Meerle, Belgium) did not *make* a biodegradable detergent. Washing terries would have meant putting phosphates into the water system *every single day*. As with other religions, even amateur Green-ness requires the constant and minute inspection of conscience on every aspect of personal conduct.

After a week of the blinding headaches which usually mark detoxification, Green Man no longer needs tea or coffee. Pretty lively on fruit juice and muesli, he laces up big friendly shoes shaped like Cornish pasties and cycles off to his rather successful business, the Mountain Hi Ioniser Company. This is a classic 'right-on' business. Outside, the shop is painted dark cabbage green with a hand-painted fascia showing very pointed snow-topped mountains in the manner of a Japanese print.

Inside, on a few simple wooden shelves sit a selection of small utterly silent plastic boxes which you plug in to charge the air with negative ions. No heavy sales talk is necessary. Between the boxes piles of low-key leaflets explain how ions (electrostatically-charged molecules) are found in such naturally exhilarating places as waterfalls, the seaside and mountains. Greens love silent, pure, mildly futuristic things which *clean* the universe and make animals and people feel well ('negative ions are the vitamins of the air'). Inside Mountain Hi, the Green Man sits all day reading *The Buddha's Ancient Path* by Piyadassi Thera (Kandy, 1974). Although he looks slightly 'blissed out', car ionisers are now so popular that soon he will be opening branches of Mountain Hi in Totnes and Bath.

Despite being consciously non-competitive as people, Greens are nevertheless curiously successful in small businesses. From the outside their business premises usually look the same – a low-key sludge-painted door, a few stickers in the window ('NUCLEAR POWER NO THANKS' or 'MY OTHER CAR IS A BICYCLE') and perhaps a few giant sunflowers or peace rainbows painted on external brickwork.

Green Man and Woman learned to do urban painting in the mid-Seventies when, after a four-year self-sufficiency stint in Wales, they discovered that neither goats nor chickens observe public holidays. Returning to London and signing on (those were the days), they painted enormous flowers or Krishna and the Milkmaids on the side of a very run-down house near Neal Street as their share of a short-life housing commune. Inside, a tremendous amount of I-Ching, aromatherapy (lavender is good for almost *everything*) and lying in bed went on ('They can't come down just now, they're meditating'). They also experienced Tibetan Applause – shaking one's hands in the air after a particularly moving musical performance because Western clapping 'breaks the communal energy'.

After youthful years of saying 'right-on', Green people try to pursue what is called a 'right livelihood'. That means 'conducting business as if other people mattered' and not causing animals or the environment harm. Throughout the Eighties, the Mountain Hi Ioniser Company became part of a flourishing alternative economy built round organic farming, vegetarian restaurants, 'peace food' grocers, macrobiotic importers, wholefood bakers ('try Paul's tofu cake'), non-animal tested cosmetics and specialist dairying. This can range from genuine cottage industry ('Sheep's Milk Yoghurt – From Ewe To You') to the Green country house whose Jersey herd appears on the boxes of Grand Ice-Cream. On top of all this there is homoeopathy, British ethnic handknits, pleasant herbal quackery, perfume distillery, renting videos of Hindi films (rather chic), intermediate technology (making windmills or skirting-boards for people), the second-hand Aga business, bicycle shops, in which *Zen and the Art of Motorcycle Maintenance* became a Green reality, and 'spiritual tourism'. That means leading small packaged tours to ashrams, along ley lines or to virtually any non-Christian spiritually charged place.

From the late Sixties to the late Eighties, the Greenish generation has somehow managed to stay 'alternative' and to maintain a voluntary simplicity within the confines of the 'Dirty Economy'. Annually, Greenish people now look forward to TOES (The Other Economic Summit) founded in London in 1984 as an enlightened version of the Club of Rome.

In his light and well-observed book, *Spilling the Beans* (Fontana, 1986), Martin Stott defines Greenish people as the lucky generation. They are the post-war 'baby-boomers' for whom was devised the Welfare State, the economic boom of the Fifties, and the Sixties expansion of higher education. Having benefited as young people from a politically more generous climate, they can emotionally afford to do with less, or to appear to do with less. 'It is an amusing paradox,' he writes, 'that these "anti-consumers" are now an identified and targeted trend among advertising and marketing agencies who correctly see them as sceptical consumers: innovative and influential, in some cases even trendsetters (e.g. in preventative health care). They are open to new products, but will not accept change for the sake of it, and will not succumb to the pressures of advertising.' Through them, in fact, consumption now carries a radical ethical dimension. Greenish people believe that through enlightened consumption, agriculture can be reformed, world food resources more fairly redistributed and the nature of capitalism changed from within. One major problem is the packaging of organic foods for large-scale retail outlets. The use of cling-wrap and plastic foam trays is ecologically at odds with the idea of reducing petro-chemically based consumer waste.

In a busy supermarket, Green Woman shops through a fog of global concern. Even buying five pounds' worth of basic groceries takes at least an hour because every close-worded label on tin, jar or packet must be minutely read for ecological and ethical nuance. Anything with an 'E' on it (the EEC food additives code) is back on the shelf in a flash. E is for filth. Then come the more agonising Czechoslovakian bottled gooseberries (not after Chernobyl); Israeli avocados (not after Gaza); Japanese-packed tuna (more lead in them than a pencil); and free-range eggs – a TRIUMPH for the Huddersfield-based non-stop pressure group Chicken's Lib. (Free-range salmon will be a cause of the Nineties.) Vaguely worrying about the Panama Canal drying up, she loads her bicycle basket and cycles on.

Next Green Woman drifts into Peace Wholefoods whose taped in-store music moves with peculiar ease from Celtic fringe bands to Mozart, to the famous record of whales mating (OOOOOOH) under the Antarctic ice. Here Green Woman buys a curried aduki-bean burger for lunch; a six-week-old copy of *Greenline* (to catch up on the spring debate 'Are Green Socialists the Same as Socialist Greens?'); and several pounds of rather muddy, misshapen but utterly-delicious-and-well-away-from-Trawsfynydd Welsh organic carrots. Moving towards the check-out she spots delicious unsalted cashews imported by Anti-Apartheid Trading with the minimalist label 'NUTS TO BOTHA'. On a scrubbed counter staffed by soft-voiced slightly remote co-operative shareholders, the local ozone protection petition is waiting to be signed ('We have *never* had an aerosol in the house').

Although the age of the Greenish generation is on average 35, their influence in Britain has dramatically crossed the age barriers. A recent Gallup survey for the Realeat Company (a genuine 'right-on' business) showed that 35 per cent of the British population now claims to be eating less meat or none at all. Run by Gregory Sams, the very successful Realeat Company is developing the ideologically contentious area of vegetarian convenience foods. It supplies, for example, wholesome mixes to which you add water (and possibly an egg) to shape them into Vegeburgers or Vegebangers. (Whether one should eat 'animal-shaped' meatless products is the vegetarian Schleswig-Holstein question.) Recently, the Realeat Company moved into vegetarian mass catering by supplying meatless 'Vege Menu' dishes principally for middle-class school meals. This is because, according to its 1986 Gallup survey, one in three children under the age of 16 is vegetarian.

Green Grandmother is appearing too. Up in the North Riding of Yorkshire, Laura Green looks down at the slice of lemon fizzling in her lunch-time gin-and-tonic, now knowing that its skin contains enough pesticides to stun a horse. Although not given to silly artistic flights, sometimes even the garden now strikes her as faintly surreal. Is Nature the way it seems to be?

Aged 60 she is an environmentalist rather than a Green (there is a difference). Increasingly the rather horrid news in a patchwork of small newspaper paragraphs underlies her daily life. (If it appears in the *Telegraph* it *must* be true.)

'Nirex . . . the radioactive waste disposal authority has designated the North York Moors as geographically suitable for N-dumps around Whitby.' . . . 'Cumbrians Opposed to a Radioactive Environment (Core) said today, "The admen pushing nuclear power are down there, Cumbrians are living with it up here."' . . . 'toxic run-off in 1980–85 meant that 1,000 km of British rivers were downgraded' . . . '200 grammes of plutonium are unaccounted for at the Nuclear Studies Centre at Mol, Belgium' . . . 'the proportion of *foreign* nuclear waste to be reprocessed in Britain will rise from 4–65 per cent in the next ten years . . . More than 3,000 tonnes will be from Japan.' *From 4 to 65 per cent!* How *can* one be a patriot, the children argued, and see one's country turned into the cloaca of the world? It all seemed to be getting completely out of hand.

Down in London, Green Woman cycles back with packs of cling-wrapped organic carrots, arriving home to a ringing 'phone. It is Laura Green absolutely ticking about N-dumps in the North Yorks Moors – and are they *really* burying *Swiss* municipal waste in Bedford? In that soft and faintly remote Green generation voice her daughter explains the problem. 'This is not "polite and tidy Britain", Mummy. It's Widow Twankey's Nuclear Laundry.'

5 March 1988

Chapter 6
TOWN AND COUNTRY

*'If England is two nations, how come we've
ended up in the wrong one?'*

FOX-HUNTERS, UNITE

Raymond Carr

The campaign against fox-hunting may provide future historians with yet another example of the Jacobin effect. A sect of fanatics, replete with the self-righteous moral superiority and ruthlessness that comes from a conviction that their cause is just and that history is on their side, through organisation and persistence can force their will on the course of events as the Jacobins did in the French Revolution. Immune to boredom and the discomfort of hard benches, they stuck it out, sitting up late to push through committee resolutions when their opponents, susceptible to human weakness, had gone off for a drink or to bed. I am not suggesting that Mr Richard Course is the Robespierre of the League against Cruel Sports ready to send fox-hunters *en masse* to the guillotine; but as its Executive Director he is a fine exponent of Jacobin techniques. His 10,000 crusaders and fanatics may succeed in banning fox-hunting in this country.

What is the passion that excites and inflames the members of the League against Cruel Sports and the activist wing, the Hunt Saboteurs? All would answer, like Bentham, that animals are sentient beings with rights and that the law should not 'refuse its protection' against wanton cruelty inflicted on any sentient being. But no one who has studied the social and political history of fox-hunting and its adversaries can doubt that much of the passion of the antis is fuelled by class prejudice. Fox-hunters are under fire, not so much for what they are supposed to do, but for what they are supposed to be. To the great 19th-century radical Cobden fox-hunting was a 'feudal sport'; a recent president of the JCR of that great nursery of MFHs, Christ Church, described it as a 'bourgeois' sport – bourgeois being a more 'fashionable' synonym for evil than 'feudal'. That heroic lady, Jilly Cooper, after a day spent with the Hunt Saboteurs spraying hounds with aerosol and blowing hunting horns concluded it would be honest to call them the 'Anti Blue-Blood Sports Brigade'.

To defend themselves against the accusation that they are a collection of snobs in fancy clothes fox-hunters have trotted out an argument that goes back to the 18th century: that fox-hunting is 'democratic', that dukes and chimney sweeps are equal in the sight of a stiff fence, that

Welsh miners have a pack of foxhounds, etc. Beating about for ammunition to meet an absurd charge that the affluent should be prevented from amusing themselves in public is an absurd occupation. Like all sports, fox-hunting is only open to those who can afford it. It's true that, in spite of the braying of upper-class voices at smart meets, those who can afford it are no longer confined to the nobility and squirearchy. But even hordes of car followers do not make hunting democratic.

What is a humane way to control a population of vermin – beautiful vermin, but vermin nonetheless? To put it brutally, what is a good way of killing foxes since foxes *must* be killed? Here I think the balance of the argument lies with the fox-hunters. I wouldn't argue that foxes enjoy being chased by hounds, but at the end of the chase they are either killed instantly – usually their backs are broken by hounds – or they get away. The alternatives to hunting suggested by the antis are shooting or gassing. Having had to shoot foxes I can't say much for the efficacy of the first method, and no one, I imagine, conceives of gassing in a hole to be a pleasant form of death. The antis must answer this question fairly and squarely, and they don't.

All our relations with the animal world are riddled with paradox. The rational hunter becomes a conservationist, preserving the animals he hunts. Portugal's democratic revolution gave every citizen the right to shoot: the result was the slaughter of 3,000 wild partridges on one estate, leaving three or four brace behind. Without foxes having been preserved by a hegemonic landowning class for hunting purposes they would have vanished from some parts of England – indeed even respectable masters imported bag foxes from Germany and Russia in the early 19th century. To a fox-hunter death except by hounds is a terrible social mid-19th-century solecism. That great autocratic MFH, Thomas Assheton Smith, was once observed to pale over the newspaper at breakfast: 'The ladies present, supposing some great European calamity had occurred, hastily asked him what was the matter, when he replied, looking over his spectacles: "By jove, a dog fox has been burnt to death in a barn." '

Preservation of foxes is, by antis, regarded as shameful. How terrible to preserve animals in order to kill them. But then, how obscene to breed animals in order to eat them. Sensible fox-hunters should accept the objections of vegetarians. Self-denial on grounds of moral consistency deserves reward.

Fox-hunters should stop inventing arguments about the 'democracy' of the hunting field, etc. They should acknowledge that they go hunting because they enjoy it – to those who have once tasted its excitements there is nothing in the world that can replace it – and that they are, as Christopher Sykes argued, infected with a kind of madness. A time-worn apologia is that hunting stops these madmen doing anything worse, freed by their exertions, as one mediaeval enthusiast wrote, from 'imaginations of fleshly lust'. Tired out after a hard day in the saddle you go to bed, presumably alone. An equally time-worn accusation is the old puritan charge that hunting debases those who practise it; but, as *The Times* has argued, to stop hunting because it is bad for those who hunt is 'to invade the sphere of the individual conscience'.

Nor should fox-hunters be browbeaten by puritans and progressives who dismiss them as brute beasts, unreconstructed High Tories or worse. How can one listen to the nonsense spouted in the Berkshire Council debate about abolishing fox-hunting on council land: 'Hunting shows the sort of thinking that leads to concentration camps.' Supreme silliness is reached, as one might expect, among radical philosophers in the US: foxes' tails are phallic symbols and to hunt is to engage in a 'masturbation fantasy'.

The antis – particularly the League against Cruel Sports – are well funded and well organised to achieve their aim: to legislate fox-hunting out of existence. Hence a contribution of £80,000 to Labour's campaign funds on condition that the party pressed for the abolition of hunting. Labour lost in 1979 and fox-hunters breathed a sigh of relief. But they counted without Mr Course, who reminded Labour local councillors of his investment. Five local councils have expressed their determination to stop fox-hunting on council-owned land. Existing tenants cannot be forced to ban fox-hunting; new tenants, presumably, will have to accept leases which forbid it, just as 19th-century landlords put clauses in their leases forcing tenants to allow hunting – and were roundly abused by radicals as tyrants. What a turn-up for the books!

Labour has been fixed by cash as well as conviction – the TGWU has declared fox-hunting 'distasteful to the British way of life'. The Liberals and the SDP, as heirs to the radical tradition of Cobden in British politics, will be just as bad if not worse. The whole tactical weakness of the blood sports lobby is precisely here: a pressure group of 10,000 antis can kill the enjoyment of millions by playing on the fear of being caught out opposing what is presented as a progressive, humanitarian crusade. To oppose blood sports is electorally safe provided coarse fishing – a proletarian sport with TV coverage – is left untouched. Fish, perhaps, are not sentient beings.

Fox-hunters of Britain, unite. Your case is sound. Go into battle, your banners emblazoned with the words of Trotsky: 'Hunting acts on the mind as a poultice does on a sore.'

31 July 1982

THE LAST OF THE SQUIRES?

Hugh Montgomery-Massingberd

Even so uncompromising a pessimist as Evelyn Waugh had to admit in 1959 that his evocation of the past glories of aristocratic life in *Brideshead Revisited*, written fifteen years earlier, was 'a panegyric preached over an empty coffin'. The English aristocracy, he observed in the preface to the revised edition of *Brideshead*, 'has maintained its identity to a degree that then seemed impossible'. This is still surprisingly true today as far as the greater aristocracy is concerned. They have managed their large landed estates so professionally and ridden the heritage hobby-horse so skilfully that one can be reasonably optimistic about their chances of survival. It is the squirearchy, the dutiful, stay-at-home breed of smaller landowner, that is an endangered species. A memorial tablet erected in a Gloucestershire parish church in 1961 by a son to his father describes him as 'the last of the squires'.

Traditionally the squires are defined as the 'landed gentry', that untitled aristocracy which is so peculiarly British a phenomenon. 'I'll ha' no lords or courtiers in my vamily,' says Fielding's Squire Western. 'They have beggared the nation,' observes this bucolic sportsman, 'but they shall never beggar me.' A myth grew up in Victorian times that the peerage originated with Tudor upstarts and Georgian borough-mongers whereas the untitled landed gentry tended to have longer descents and had steadily refused titles through the centuries. In fact, though there are some notable examples of squirearchical dynasties with the proud distinction of being descended in the male line from a mediaeval ancestor who took his surname from lands which they still hold (Fulford of Fulford, Gatacre of Gatacre, Plowden of Plowden, etc.), the great majority of these families acquired their lands in Tudor or Stuart times, or even later.

Although the untitled squirearchy certainly form the majority of the lesser landed families in the make-up of the aristocracy, one must also put most of the baronets in this group as well as not a few peers of moderate means and rustic tastes. The point is that the only significant division that has existed in Britain between the greater and the lesser aristocracy is not related to titles but to wealth. Sorting out the sheep from the goats, families with enough of the right stuff to be of national importance tend to form one group; families of only local importance the other. A century ago a landowner in England would have had to own upwards of 10,000 acres and certainly more than 5,000 to be in the wealthier group. At the opposite end of the scale, the smaller country squires who were the typical landowners in the less wealthy group would have owned estates of under 5,000 acres; in many cases not much more than the 1,000 acres which used sometimes to be thought of as the minimum required to qualify as 'landed gentry'.

Capital gains tax and capital transfer tax have done much to offset the spectacular rise in land values which had given the chronically hard-up squires new hope. ('You understand the position,' said one landowner to his nephew when making over the family estate to him recently. 'You're a millionaire on paper but you can't afford a bicycle.') The problem of maintaining a country house has been growing ever more acute with inflation; indeed the present tax system seems particularly loaded against the smaller seats of the squires as opposed to the stately show-places. Unlike the great territorial magnates, the squires cannot spread their resources and avoid this taxation which now seems set to destroy the continuity of ownership in the countryside.

There are now about 2,200 'family estates' in England, Scotland and Wales. Over three-quarters of these are under 5,000 acres in extent and about half come within the 1,000 to 2,000 bracket. Significantly, only about 15 per cent of the 1,600 existing English family estates have survived in the same ownership over the last hundred years. The individual county averages for the survival rate range from 6 per cent for industrial or suburban counties, such as Surrey, to 25 per cent for a few of the rural areas like Devon and Shropshire. In Norfolk, for instance, although some 120 family estates remain, there have been 40 demolitions of country houses this century and the break-up of some 110 estates. It is melancholy to record that one now has to subtract up to about 20 every year from the total of family estates.

Turning from statistics to what may just be regarded as 'well-bred sentiment', it is painfully sad to see the disappearance of so many 'illustriously obscure' squirearchical families from their beloved seats. They go unnoticed and unmourned. The hard-faced modern 'Conservative' view, as typified by Michael Heseltine, is that if such long-established families cannot manage to maintain their houses adequately, then good riddance to them. But this gradual chipping away at the fabric of rural society can only be regretted. It might be argued that there is nothing new about the lesser landowning families slithering down the greasy pole, but the trend is depressingly one-sided. Although there are some 400 comparative newcomers among the English family estate-owners who have put down roots over the last century, one can be sure that very few of the families who are now giving up the ghost will be succeeded by potential squirearchical dynasties of the future.

In fairness to Mr Heseltine, he has shown a proper concern for the preservation of buildings, but the families who live in them should also count for something. In Japan, I believe, the owners of historic properties are themselves classified as ancient monuments; a similar scheme over here could have diverting possibilities. The so-called 'national heritage' was created by private owners and the squires' contribution should not be forgotten. Being less exposed than the magnate class to the corrupting influence of too much cash, the squires have always been associated with the best gentlemanly values. One likes to think of the ideal squire carrying on the role of unpaid local administrator (started by Queen Elizabeth and officially stopped by Queen Victoria), presiding over a pocket of rural contentment and stability. This paragon looks after the village on the estate – where his ancestors built the parish hall, presented the playing fields, etc. – and contributes largely to the upkeep of the church. When a trendy parson invited everyone to bring their favourite pets to church for an absurd 'Animal Service', the local squire threatened to bring his bull.

These traditions, with all their overtones of feudalism, paternalism and *noblesse oblige*, are happily still not quite extinct; though one fears the exigencies of estate management are the main concern of the modern squires as they struggle to pass the place on to the next generation. One is, alas, much more likely to encounter mere technocrats of the land among their number than people living up to the aristocratic concept of the 'Complete Man' by being scholars, public figures and patrons of the arts as well as sportsmen.

31 July 1982

WIZARDS AND CHEESE

Richard West

Wells, Somerset

Although northern Somerset has been made into something called Avon, under the Heath-Walker local government Act, nobody here respects the change, especially in its effect on Somerset County Cricket Club. They no longer play at Wells, but an old man told of matches he once had seen here: 'Do you remember Wellard? I've seen him hit four sixes and two fours in one over.' And now Somerset has in its side the two best cricketers in the world, Viv Richards and Ian Botham. 'Botham hit one six out of the ground,' the same man said, 'and it fell in a shop. Botham went round to the shop to apologise – of course he was insured – and the shopkeeper just wanted him to autograph the ball.'

Oddly enough Botham comes from Lincolnshire, which is not a first-class cricket county, while his friend and flatmate, Richards, comes from Antigua in the West Indies; just as another West Indian, Clive Lloyd, is now a hero of Lancashire. Counties get the cricketers they deserve, and I was glad to read recently that the great Pakistani Imran Khan had gone to play for Sussex from Worcester. 'I couldn't bear to live in that town, so dreary and unappealing,' he told the *Mail on Sunday* and now when he plays there they boo him out to the crease. Worcester is one of the most defiled of the cities of England and also returns to Parliament the unspeakable Peter Walker. A county like Worcestershire, which incidentally was merged by Walker with Herefordshire, does not deserve a cricketer like Imran Khan.

The recent success of Somerset's cricket has served to increase the local pride that one finds in other pleasant counties like Lincolnshire, Dorset and Warwickshire. Often this pride is shown in outright hostility and contempt for post-industrial dumps like Liverpool, Sheffield and Birmingham, which, we are told by sentimental socialists, represent the 'real' England. In fact, I believe, if it ever did come to confrontation between the North and South (a popular fantasy of the middle-class Left), the South would prove stronger. In Wells, as in all the pleasanter parts of England, one sees thousands of refugees from the dumps of England. 'One can't help feeling sorry for people in Birmingham and the rest,' said the same old gaffer who was discussing cricket, 'stuck in those high-rise flats.'

Two local men who saw me holding a copy of Boswell's *London Journal* started a conversation on Dr Johnson and what he thought of the Scots. They were well informed and curious, in a gruesome way, on some of the ghastly crimes that always seem to be happening in Glasgow: a woman raped and razor-slashed by a gang; a dental mechanic murdered almost at random; a man whose leg was cut off in the street by people with a machete. One of these young men said: 'I went to Glasgow once and I didn't dare go into a pub. I was told it wasn't safe.' The intense distrust of Scots is just as strong today as it was in Boswell's time, when two kilted officers who appeared at a play were booed and pelted with apples. When Scotland plays England at football at Wembley, all central London shuts

its doors against the tartan invaders. Our national anthem's now controversial references to the enemies of the monarch – 'Confound their politics, frustrate their knavish tricks' – referred specifically to the Scots who
were once again threatening us with war.

Strangely enough, the English remain incurably amiable towards the
Irish, in spite of the bombs they plant here. Only a few weeks after the latest outrage in Hyde and Regent's Parks, one hears very little anti-Irish
feeling. This must infuriate the IRA.

Wells is a self-sufficient town. Women residents say there is no need
ever to go to Bristol or Bath to shop; my wife says that Wells is cheap and
good value for clothes, leather goods, pottery and above all needleware,
knitting and embroidery – the kind of shops that no longer exist in the
cities, where rates are prohibitive. In Wells there are few of the chain
stores that infest most English towns and cities. Most of the wealth here
comes from tourists to the cathedral and of course agriculture: Cheddar
cheese is the best known local produce. Wells also shares some of the
trade from nearby Glastonbury, a reputedly holy place which attracts
thousands of seekers after the Holy Grail, Druids, astrologers, real food
fanatics, survivalists, born-again Buddhists; in short, more freaks to the
square mile even than southern California.

Wells is also popular with the followers of that strange modern cult for
re-fighting the Civil War in elaborate mock battle. The Sealed Knot, as
they call themselves, were due to perform a two-day Siege of Wells. All
over England now you see the recruiting signs of the Sealed Knot – for
instance, one asking for men for 'the Parliamentary Regiment of the Lord
Sayes and Seles Bluecoats'.

Wells Cathedral, this year celebrating its 800th anniversary, is impreg-
nated with memories of the Civil War. On seeing a banner inscribed with
the name of 'Bishop Ken' I thought for an instant that this must be one of
the trendy, left-wing cathedrals like Stepney, where 'Bishop Jim' pre-
sides; or Liverpool, where most of the clergymen are known as the Revd
Sid, Russ, Stan or Len. But Ken, I recalled, was the surname of one of our
most famous clerics and Bishop of Bath and Wells in the reigns of Charles
II and James II. Thomas Ken (1637–1711) was one of the chaplains to
Charles II and made himself famous in 1683 when, on the eve of a royal
visit to Winchester, he refused to allow the royal harbinger to appropriate his prebendal house to the use of Nell Gwynn, saying that 'a woman
of ill repute ought not to be endured in the house of a clergyman and
especially the King's chaplain'. Oddly enough, this action impressed
rather than vexed King Charles; when Bath and Wells needed a bishop

soon afterwards, he declared that no one should have the see but 'the little black fellow that refused his lodging to poor Nelly'.

Bishop Ken attended the King's death-bed; later that year he sat with Charles's illegitimate son, the Duke of Monmouth, on the eve of his execution for leading the West Country revolt (in which Wells Cathedral was damaged). Although a Tory, Bishop Ken denounced the Romish practices of the next King, James II; he was one of the seven bishops sent to the Tower. He fell out again with William III and in 1691 was deprived of his see. In his will Bishop Ken declared: 'I die in the holy Catholic and apostolic faith, professed by the whole church before the division of East and West; most particularly I die in the communion of the church of England, as it stands distinguished from all papal and puritan innovations, and as it adheres to the doctrine of the cross.'

The poor old Church of England today is torn not only between the papists and puritans, but between the patriots and the pacifists, the Tories and liberation theologians, homosexuals and feminists, partisans of the Book of Common Prayer and dozens of weird new liturgies; even between those who believe and those who do not believe in what Bishop Ken called the doctrine of the cross. The Church of England is now much attacked by the Conservative Party, the party that eagerly carried out the destruction of England's even more ancient system of justice and local government.

Bishop Ken said that the Church of England was 'both in her principles and constant practice unquestionably loyal'. But loyal to whom, or to what? That is the question now.

18 September 1982

NOTEBOOK

Alexander Chancellor

How does one deal with the outbursts of irrational anger which one so often encounters in London nowadays? Recently, as I was driving to work, a taxi driver drew up beside me and pulled down his window. So I amiably wound down my window to hear what he had to say. 'Are you a c—— or something?' he asked, to my amazement. I replied that I wasn't, that this was clearly a case of mistaken identity. 'Yes you are,' he insisted, 'you're a f—— c——.' By now he was spitting with rage and looked as if he might explode. I hadn't the faintest idea what on earth I could have done to provoke such fury. So I just smiled patronisingly and told him what an unhappy little man he must be if he made a habit of addressing people in such a manner. This was probably a mistake, for he looked as if he might easily kill me. However, I am told it is reasonably safe to provoke taxi drivers by laughing at them, because they know that if they resort to violence, they will lose their licences.

30 October 1982

RECOMMENDED

Jeffrey Bernard

The main trouble that I find with the majority of pub and restaurant guides and columns is that they're too damn nice about the establishments they sample. There are roughly 4,000 pubs in London and how many of them are *really* any good? Ten? Twenty? Well, hardly any more. Admittedly I'm eating and drinking in ever-decreasing geographical circles, hemmed in as I am by not having expenses as your staff hack has, but even so I doubt whether a trip north to Hampstead, west to Notting Hill, south to Camberwell or east to Wapping would pay any sybaritic dividends. Space invaders and unimaginative chefs are ubiquitous. And so, of course, are 99 per cent of the bloody customers. But take L'Escargot in Greek Street. It lives on a phoney reputation created largely by magazine plugs. And why? Because Eleanor the maitresse and late of Bianchi's, is a very nice lady whom no food writer wants to upset. Neither do I. The fact remains that it's a rip-off patronised by really dreadful people, as is Langan's Brasserie which is now also beyond the range of my pocket. Peter Langan may have – and did have – the style to extinguish a kitchen fire with champagne but how could you stomach even good food seated in the same room as the sort of people who are about to present breakfast television? Perhaps, if food writers had to pay for their grub out of their own pockets and not expenses, we might hear a different story.

As perceptive readers of this column probably know, the Coach and Horses and the vodka therein comprise my psychological life jacket, but not even Norman's perfect. A space-invader wanker himself, he's also got an unpleasantly noisy fruit machine and he's got a sawn-off barrel containing bottles of wine at one end of the bar, which impedes social intercourse there and which has damn nigh ruined that corner of the pub. To the regular such trivia are important. The bar staff have lapsed into putting the ice into your glass with their fingers and I don't know where their fingers have been. I stopped using the rather charming Carlisle Arms up the road because the barmen handed you your glass by the rim and I didn't know where their fingers had been either. But Norman picks up valuable house points for different reasons. Not only is the Coach a clean pub – with excellent French bread incidentally – but Norman can understand and appreciate the veracity of being called a prick. He is one of the very few who can take as well as dish out.

What worries me is that we're going to get some very nasty fallout from the French pub when Gaston retires. What's odd is that Gaston's pub should have attracted so many creeps, since he's one of the best guvnors ever. Whether it is the publican or the customers who make a pub is something of a riddle. But anyway, speaking as a man who spends some time in pubs and safe in the knowledge that no one will take the slightest notice of what I have to say, I can recommend two or three. I say safe because there's nothing screws up a restaurant like a recommendation from a Maschler or a Parkinson. It makes for staff complacency. But as to that riddle of guvnors or customers making it all happen, the best landlords I know, apart from the aforementioned Norman and Gaston, are Dave Potton of the Duke of York by *The Spectator*, his brother, Malcolm Potton of the Prince of Wales in Hampstead Road, Roy England of the White Swan in New Row and Vince Marshall of the Swiss in Old Compton Street. You can keep your wine bars.

As for food on my manor I suppose the Gay Hussar is as good or better than anywhere. I also like the Soho's Friend in Meard Street and the Karlywah opposite the Coach – two oriental places that you can get out of without being beaten up by the waiters. What a pity you can no longer get out of Wheelers without getting beaten up by the bill.

15 January 1983

THE BEAUTIES OF BELFAST

Gavin Stamp

I first visited Belfast at the height of the troubles in 1973. After a short journey from the ferry at Larne in a battered train filled with frighteningly jolly Orangemen, I emerged from York Road Station to see an appalling vision of destruction with scarcely a building standing in the vicinity. I assumed that the IRA bombs had been even more destructive than I had imagined. Quite wrong: the destruction had been caused by the City Council's bulldozers. It was the result of 'planning' and the same swathes of demolition could – and can – be witnessed in Liverpool or Manchester where the explanation was just the same: over-optimistic, non-sectarian urban renewal planned in the 1960s.

Belfast certainly bears the scars of and faces problems created by the last fifteen years of violence, but the city, past and present, is essentially comparable with the industrial cities of the north of England. Like Leeds or Bradford, say, Belfast is a Victorian city and, like them, Belfast has fine and remarkable buildings amidst much Victorian dross. And, like Leeds and Bradford, it has managed to survive 1960s planning with something individual and characteristic intact. The city's worst moment, in fact, was in 1941 when, in four nights of German bombing, over 56,000 houses were damaged or destroyed. Few English cities took such a battering.

Belfast is a most congenial and much underrated city. Unlike Dublin, it is not an English city. Ulstermen created it and Ulstermen can take pride in it. There are a few buildings by foreign architects – the Academical Institution by Soane, the Opera House by Matcham, churches by Butterfield and Clough Williams-Ellis and Brumwell Thomas's City Hall – but the real character of the city and most of the important buildings were created by local men. Given the nature of Ulster religion – fragmented and sectarian – Belfast has more places of worship per acre than any English city, and possibly more than Rome or Florence. When Charles Brett published his indispensable and authoritative *Building of Belfast* in 1967 (now, alas, out of print) there were 265 places of worship in the city – and 589 pubs. Despite bombs and attrition, the number of both cannot be significantly less today.

Precious little is left of Georgian Belfast. The few terrace houses that have survived the bombs and bulldozers are mostly derelict. It is from the early years of the reign of Victoria that a substantial architectural legacy survives and it is with some of these buildings that we meet the first of Belfast's several superlatives.

The Palm House in the Botanic Gardens is one of the earliest as well as one of the most beautiful of early Victorian glass and iron structures. The first part was erected in 1839 and is the work of the architect Charles Lanyon and the Dublin engineer Richard Turner, who later created, with Decimus Burton, the great Palm House at Kew – the Belfast conservatory's only peer. In 1971 this Palm House stood rusting and neglected with most of its glass smashed. The restored Palm House was reopened a fortnight ago. Better late than never: and it is hard to think of another recent restoration where money has been so well spent.

Belfast came into its own in the mid-Victorian decades, when its architecture was dominated by two names. The principal one is that of Sir Charles Lanyon, an engineer and architect born of English parents who established the architectural profession in Ulster. He designed most of the public buildings the growing town needed in the 1840s, 50s and 60s. The Queen's College – the core of the University – is red-brick Tudor Gothic and the Crumlin Road Gaol naturally castellated, but most of his buildings, such as the Assembly College and several splendid banks, are in an exuberant Renaissance style. Best of all, perhaps, is the Custom House of 1857, whose noble exterior is rich in sculpture and decoration. Lanyon closed his career by becoming an MP.

Lanyon was joined by the Ulster architect W. H. Lynn, who eventually set up on his own and carried on until the end of the century. On the 'mainland' – as too many Ulstermen distressingly refer to it – Lynn designed Chester Town Hall in Victorian Gothic. He was responsible for Belfast Castle, one of many essays in Ulster in Scottish Baronial which emphasise the province's roots. He also designed the Venetian-style building in Donegal Square whose elaborate roof, destroyed in the last war, is currently being restored. This Ruskinian design was admired by Oscar Wilde, who visited Belfast in 1884. Lanyon's and Lynn's only real competitor was William Barre, who designed the Ulster Hall, dominated by a prodigious organ, and the Albert Memorial Tower, a Gothic structure now conspicuous for its Pisaesque lean.

Following the achievement of city status in 1888 and the failure of Gladstone's Home Rule Bill and the sounding of the cry 'Ulster will fight and Ulster will be right!', Belfast, as the capital of potentially beleaguered Protestant Ulster, attempted to establish its cultural and political independence from Dublin. In architecture this was achieved, paradoxically, largely by English architects and not by local men.

In 1895 the Grand Opera House was opened. This was designed by the greatest of theatre architects, Frank Matcham, the creator of the London Coliseum and the Buxton Opera House. Diagonally opposite the Opera House in Great Victoria Street and directly opposite the horrible Europa Hotel (on the site of the old Great Northern railway terminus for Dublin) stands another jolly building dedicated to entertainment: the Crown Liquor Saloon. Combined with the civilised licensing hours, the interior is a drinker's dream with its coloured tiles, stained glass and wooden partitions. I cannot think of another late Victorian pub which is as good.

Rather different in character is one of Belfast's two symbols of civic pride. A city must have a cathedral, so the Georgian St Anne's Church gave way to a lugubrious neo-Romanesque structure designed by Sir Thomas Drew and W. H. Lynn, begun in 1898 and still not finished. Transepts completed in 1981 to an interesting design fail to alleviate the chilly Protestant gloom of the building. Much more successful is the building which really gives identity to the city: the City Hall. To the dismay of many, a competition held in 1896 was won not by a local architect, but by young Arthur Brumwell Thomas from London. The right choice was made, for Thomas filled Donegal Square with a vast Edwardian baroque composition, finished off with a great dome in the manner of Wren. The interior is properly municipal and impressive, with a fine marble staircase under the dome and many good, grand rooms.

The traveller by sea from Belfast to Liverpool (a threatened pleasure these days) is reassured to find standing at Pierhead what appears to be a smaller replica of Belfast City Hall. This is the Mersey Docks and Harbour Board building, designed by Arnold Thornely. By a curious coincidence it was Thornely who came to design the Parliament House at Stormont, opened in 1932, after the original architect, Ralph Knott, the designer of the County Hall in London, had died of drink. Thanks to partition in 1921, Belfast now has Britain's only example of monumental Beaux-Arts planning, for it is with New Delhi and Canberra that Stormont must be compared. At the end of a vast, rising, axial avenue, punctuated by a statue of Edward Carson in a dramatic Lenin-like pose, stands Thornely's stern classical block, with giant portico and raised blank attic above.

If the monumental stone exterior is a little frigid, the interiors are fine and it is sad that they cannot easily be visited. But Stormont is unloved because it is a building of unfashionable date and style, because its vast, neat grounds are too remote from the city centre and because the buildings are associated with imposition from London. Stylistically, nothing could be more wrong, for the Stormont Parliament House is not at all like Westminster but is a version of that stripped Beaux-Arts Classicism which is is utterly American – and republican – in character.

The preservation of historic buildings in Belfast has benefited from central government control. Before 1972 not a single building in the city was listed; since that date two-thirds of Belfast has been surveyed by the Historic Monuments and Buildings Branch of the Department of the Environment, Northern Ireland (although if it was in England the whole city would have been covered decades ago). The City Council now has no power in the sphere of architecture and planning as both preservation and development are handled by the DoE.

Today in Belfast many of the best buildings have been and are being carefully restored and no more road plans seem to be threatening the city centre. It is not churches or conservatories which are the chief worry for the future in Belfast, it is ordinary houses. To the visitor, what seem most typical of the city are the Victorian two-storey brick terraces which came right in to the city centre. Thanks both to urban renewal and sectarian violence, far too many of these have been bulldozed or stand forlorn, with their windows and doors bricked up. Their inhabitants have been obliged to move further out, to dreary post-war, Harlow-style housing estates where, today, most of the violence takes place. In England, the old terrace houses would be bought and restored by young middle-class professionals; it is Belfast's peculiar tragedy that 'gentrification' has been inhibited by the threat of IRA bombs.

21 May 1983

IN SEARCH OF ENGLAND

Roy Kerridge

Where can the real England be found? My Quest for the Spirit of England began at Wantage, where in the year 849 Alfred the Great was born. From there I hoped to walk, in easy stages, 30 miles or so along the Ridgeway path, said to be the oldest road in Britain. My destination was Avebury, which was England's capital only three and a half thousand years ago.

I found Wantage, on a Saturday evening, to be an agreeable red-brick market town, its streets crammed with a surging mass of smart young people roaming from pub to pub in search of excitement. The whole town seemed to be given over to the young. Deafening disco music from the Swan drowned the chimes from the church opposite, and I wondered if these happy, unreflective youngsters were the 'unemployed youth' of whom I had read so much.

In the fading light, the anguished features of King Alfred, depicted on a statue, gazed across Wantage's market square, but offered no clue. Beneath the monarch these words had been inscribed, 105 years ago:

> Alfred found learning dead and he restored it.
> Education neglected and he revived it.
> The laws powerless and he gave them force.
> The Church debased and he raised it.
> The land ravaged by a fearful enemy from which he delivered it.

From the bottom of my heart there swelled a mighty cry: 'Come back, Alfred!'

You may say that no fearful enemy ravages the land, but having seen the ancient church of Wantage quail before the blasts of rock music from the Swan, I know otherwise.

On the bus to Wantage I had overheard two Berkshire farm boys with rich local accents describe English customs to a bemused American couple. 'Funny, Oi'm the only one o' moi family doant loike beer,' one lad of ten ruminated. He lived with his grandparents in a tied cottage, and boasted of his skateboard, BMX bike and the motor-bike and tractor he was allowed to use on the farm. To his great pride, his mother was being married for the third time that very week. 'Moi mum's gettin' married tomorrer, but that's only the second toime,' his older friend chimed in a trifle jealously.

Smiling all over their pink plum-pudding faces, the two boys alighted near a farm-track and waved the Americans a long goodbye. Perhaps this explained the prosperity of Wantage youth – each one may have had two or three fathers sending pocket money.

Now, it appeared, Wantage was no longer in Berkshire. 'We've been demoted to Oxfordshire,' a middle-aged man told me sourly.

Next day a fox paused and gave me a quizzical look as I toiled up the hill towards the Ridgeway, my pyjamas, alarm clock, towel and electric razor stuffed in a plastic bag. It was a hot day in the lowlands, but up on the hilltops a cool breeze restored me, and I strode along, greeting other walkers and listening to the twitterings of meadow pipits and corn buntings.

In pagan times, we Ridgeway travellers would have been pilgrims to the great temple at Avebury, with many sacred sites to detain us along the way. One of these, the White Horse of Uffington, I was eager to see, and made a detour down the hillside to do so. I was almost standing on the horse before I saw it, for the white curving scars on the hill suggested broken paths rather than the sacred beast of the Atrebates, a Celtic tribe. This was because the strange beaked head of the animal stretched on a long neck over the brow of the hill. As a whole, the horse was visible only at a distance, but I made up for this disappointment by finding the head and standing defiantly in its jaws. The habit of putting beaks on horses and other animals is typical of Iron Age art. What would the Atrebates have made of a platypus? The connection between horses and dragons in English folklore may stem from literal-minded Saxons examining fanciful Celtic art, for a beaked horse certainly does look reptilian.

Below me, the sudden, stark contours of flat-topped Dragon Hill suggested a man-made earthen pyramid among the serene sweeps of natural scenery. Here it was that St George is said to have fought the dragon. Again dragon and horse collide, not necessarily unseating poor George, for many unravellers of myths have decided that our national hero was once himself a horse. The knightly saint took the place of a horse-god when Christianity came, and we are a People of the Horse. Possibly the god's name resembled George's, and today's cry of 'Gee-up' may once have been 'Gee-orge'.

Despite these magic mysteries, the White Horse Hill had no eerie sense of Celtic twilight about it, but was a jolly spot, alive with weekend picnickers, mums, dads and children. The England it represented was that of John Bull, and the fact that this hill was chosen of all others as a place to sit in the sun and watch young people play attests to the potency of the horse-god's spell.

Uffington Castle's circular earthwork marks the site of the Ridgeway, which I regained once more, travelling on to Wayland's Smithy, a long barrow set in a clump of trees beside the path. A burial place of Neolithic men, the mound became a smith-god's forge for the Saxons, just as Bronze Age hill forts became Saxon burial grounds. Latterday Saxons told tall tales of Wayland and his smithy until the modern era, when the overgrown mound with boulders tumbled around its cave entrance was tidied up by the Department of the Environment and the gifted archaeologist Stuart Piggott. Although I admire Professor Piggott, who writes as well as he digs, I feel a tinge of regret that in future no awestruck children will peer into black depths between the brambles, ready to run at the first sign of a spark from the smith's fire or the 'chink' of his hammer, perhaps supplied by an obliging stonechat.

Far from being an open track showing my silhouette on the skyline, the

Ridgeway rolled up and down between hawthorn bushes. Now the path grew wilder, corrugated with grown-over tractor grooves. Walkers returned to their cars, and the trail became a grassy, shadowy green lane. A gipsy trailer stood at an angle to the deep ruts I was hopping along, but nobody was home. Later I met the swarthy incumbent, and we gave each other long suspicious stares. So gloriously white had the hedges now become that I felt I was walking among Christmas trees laden with snow. Where the Ridgeway became a thorny, flowery rabbit tunnel, difficult to walk along, I came across a weathered wooden sign reading 'Wiltshire'.

Hours later, having crossed a motorway, I was still walking, now up the side of Liddington Hill, where some say that King Arthur defeated the Saxons. Just as each age reads its own preoccupations into Stonehenge, from amphitheatres to temples to computers, so King Arthur has descended from being a mediaeval monarch to a Dark Ages freedom-fighting guerrilla leader.

The sun had set long ago, and in the failing light I shushed my way through the long grass away from the Ridgeway to the haunted Iron Age fortress of Liddington Castle. Looming battlements of earth and stone rose above a grassy moat and enclosed a weed-covered circle where, if myths are true, the dragon standard of the Celts once flew. The young Richard Jefferies, a great hero of mine, used to sit dreaming under the rim of this earthwork, gazing down at his parents' farm. Now the sun's last red gleam across the horizon was reflected in the glow of Coate Water, the reed-fringed lake that appears in so many guises throughout the author's works. Jefferies must have lingered on the magic hill until far later than I, knowing every stile and footpath of the countryside, even in pitch darkness. In his day the lights of Swindon would have seemed further away and of a more wholesome hue than lurid orange.

Over my hazardous descent to the insensitively placed M4 motorway, my confusions of direction, my succession of lifts from tipsy teenage motorists and my eventual arrival in Swindon Old Town, where I banged up a surprised guest-house keeper and demanded admission, I will draw a veil. Suffice it to say that the helpful young people of Swindon seemed to regard me as a quaint old Wiltshire character, and one insisted that I ask for a cell in the police station for the night, 'or else you'd only have to pay money'. However, I had tried this ploy once in Huntingdon, only to be told that the cells were full of drunks.

Never for a moment doubting that Jefferies's old home would be sacred ground and Swindon's pride, with scarcely a blade of grass altered since the author had lived there, I unwittingly rode past it on a bus next day and had to walk back through the featureless housing estate it had become. Coate Water was now 'Coate Water Country Park, Barbecues and Mini-Golf' and abounded in asphalt and notices reading 'No Access Except for Yachting Personnel'. Jefferies's farmhouse home, now the Jefferies Museum, showed whitewashed empty rooms with neon lights and shiny pine floorboards. It would have been a far better tribute to Richard Jefferies's genius to have left Coate House as a working farm, amid unspoilt countryside, let to a farmer who had never heard of the author of *Bevis*.

I found Swindon Old Town, with its two parks, quite a restful place to stay before travelling on to Avebury. Soon I was high on the windswept downs, with all Wiltshire to my right and left, and Liddington Hill standing in the distance like a green Table Mountain. Two walkers approached, and to my delight one of them proved to be *The Spectator*'s television critic. I should have known the Ridgeway wasn't long enough to prevent *Spectator* writers from bumping into one another. At once I began to hector him about the non-appearance of a contribution of mine to the scandal-sheet he edits, while he goodnaturedly fended me off with his stick. He went on his way and I on mine, but two great forces such as these (Ingrams and Kerridge) cannot meet without causing apocalyptical changes in the temperature, climate and atmosphere. A strange fog descended and a light drizzle sprayed across my spectacles.

Now I appeared alone in the universe, walking for ever along a Ridgeway, with Wiltshire invisibly below me. I nearly trod on a crow, which flew from beneath my feet and joined another on a wire fence ahead. As I walked on, the crows flew ahead, leading the way. I heard traffic, but instead of a road I found two shepherds rounding up their flock by driving tractors at them and honking, rather as the police were said to have controlled rioters at Toxteth. Soon all the sheep were pressed together amid wattle hurdles without casualty. The rain lifted, and I walked down the hill to Avebury.

To my surprise the road ran through a gap in tall Celtic defences spread with buttercups. The village was inside the fortress, as in ancient times. Rings and avenues of great stones jutted lopsidedly here and there, and I found a bed for the night at Hollis Cottage, where kindly Mrs Jane Lees takes in visitors. This delightful old house, which I suspect was partly built from one of the broken-up sacred stones, was full of unexpected corners and inglenooks, with a minstrels' gallery of sorts, where a staircase had replaced the old ladder and a trap-door.

'When I was a girl we had knowledgeable ladies and gentlemen come to see the stones,' Mrs Lees told me, 'instead of just school parties who only see them because they have to.'

However, next day I was pleased to find that one of these school parties had been supplied with an assorted rag-bag of Victorian dress to put them in a historical mood. Kate Greenaway maidens gravely walked beside boys who looked like extras from *Oliver!* Today's Avebury has as many visitors as in its heyday as the sacred centre of England. Its Manor House, built from the ruins of a Benedictine monastery by Sir William Sharrington on the proceeds of an embezzlement from the Bristol Mint, was closed to a grumbling bunch of tourists because the present lady of the manor had gone shopping. One sacred site stands outside the main ring of stones: the village church. Here, to my annoyance, I found the Jerusalem Bible was in use, and Jehovah was referred to as Yahweh.

I dare say the Hebrews of old *did* call God 'Yahweh', as the moderns insist, but in the English language the name merely suggests 'Yah boo!', the cry of 'with-it' clergymen rebelling against authority without realising that *they* are authority. 'Jehovah', on the other hand, suggests Jove-like majesty, a nod to the pagan past by no means out of keeping with the beauties of Avebury. That evening I walked along the turfy ramparts looking down at the strange grey boulders on the other side of a moat where in the Bronze Age water might have gleamed, making Avebury a sacred Isle of Avalon. Mediaeval castles appear to have evolved from such ancient forts and temples. In the distance, the strange man-made pyramid of Silbury Hill presided over the birth of the River Kennet, a weed-clogged ditch of water hurrying on its way to reach Newbury in time for the races. In its shallows I watched a water rat, a round-faced miniature beaver, felling water plants at the stem and then munching them up leaf by leaf.

Old England and its ways and waywardness have all but vanished, though its outward appearance is preserved by the National Trust and the Department of the Environment, with labels to tell us what everything means. Soothed, we look at it and then go home. Only as night falls and we glance up at the darkening hills and the misshapen long barrows and mounds upon them, do we feel that somewhere there is something more. The old gods may have the last laugh, or Jehovah, or, I hope, St George.

13 August 1983

USER-FRIENDLY SWINDON

Gerda Cohen

Speeding by train to Swindon through the raw expectant mist of early March, you know the odour: a brisk triumphant smell of burnt toast on little plastic trays, manoeuvred down the aisle by youngish men drenched in the confident tang of Eau Sauvage body lotion. It's all happening here: upturn Britain, computer people on the go, going mainly and rapidly along the Slough–Bristol axis which holds our bright future. From the train window, admittedly, it might seem drab: trading estates, picket lines of dwarf conifers, neo-rural housing flashing a denture grin of clapboard through Berkshire, Wiltshire – but a grin of success. Here in the First Class fug, how buoyant it felt. Young computer managers bent forward in conversation. Except it was hardly conversation. Rather a curious, throttled exchange of micro-speak: 'How are your JC85s?' 'Oh, great, repeat orders from Hull. How's your semi-custom video circuit?' 'Oh, great, sort of gone without trace into the QL micro.'

Both men opposite me worked in Swindon. They seemed such nice, ordinary people despite their palpable technical superiority that I ventured to ask if they liked Swindon. 'Great.' 'Oh, great, we relocated from Luton, and Tim here – Tim, isn't it? – relocated from Slough. Bit iffy in Slough.' They laugh agreeably. 'No ethnic situation in Swindon' – they laugh again – 'but further from the airport.' Tim said his only problem was driving to the airport. 'You see they've got this roundabout, actually it's a cluster of mini-roundabouts, about the largest cluster in Britain, leading to the M4 . . .' But hope was at hand. A youthful company named Clean Acres Aviation plan a commuter airline for Swindon. 'It's the fastest-growing town in Europe,' they told me as we slid alongside the platform. 'Enjoy your day!'

A quite astonishing number of purposeful youngish men poured into the raw mist at Swindon. Above and opposite the station rose the offices of Hambro Life Assurance. In fact the railway seemed embedded inside Hambro Life. 'That don't worry me,' remarked the station supervisor, parading his platform in a kindly, rotund way, 'they keep the wind off.' Mr Roberts blew a long blast to send the InterCity off, and took me through his station. 'Come along, my lovely, up them stairs. Never been here before?' He couldn't credit it. 'Well, my lovely, better get started.'

Beyond Hambro Life swung cranes at work on office blocks, many complete, sleek, glazed as impenetrably as anti-glare monitor screens in nightmare black or cyan green. I wondered who would rent all that office space. 'Computer firms,' said Mr Roberts, impassive, 'lots moving in.' He wasn't sure why. 'Cheaper than London, and people behave theirselves. You had to, see, or you'd be out of a job in Swindon. Everyone used to work for the Great Western. Swindon *was* the Great Western. They had 15,000 men in the loco works, and on the carriage side, that's where the Oasis Leisure Centre is now. They built a nice pool when the carriage side shut down. Well, go for a swim, my duck, and there's good shops.' Affable Mr Roberts pointed me past the desolate wind-bitten shrubs with their labels still on. Neat signs led away from the silent loco sheds to the Brunel Plaza. One couldn't get lost. Everyone was helpful, trotting along in the bitter cold, rather porky, friendly, their kind, lard-colour faces lifted to the glitter beyond. It's all happening here: upturn Britain, even a new bus station planned.

Meanwhile, admittedly, the old and poor were queuing for buses in the cold mist. But once inside the Brunel shopping Plaza, it's perpetual shock-price summer, perpetual shiny acres of bonanza buy, leafed around by foliage varnished so green you think it must be plastic. 'Marks and Spencer ivy,' said a kind plump cleaner dusting the leaves, 'you can't go wrong with M an' S.' Except for her slow Wiltshire approval (or had I heard her before in a TV commercial?) it's like being trapped inside a perpetual TV commercial, an infinity of cat food in a pedigree yawn. Yet oddly the whole place felt hushed, dead. There was hardly a sound beyond the dismal mechanical hum of travelators, taking you up to a vast glade of frozen chips, a hecatomb of freezer fun. No denying, the Brunel Centre is big, 'bigger than Birmingham' said a comfortable old body going up the travelator.

'Oh that's right,' confirmed the pretty girl at Information, 'that's right,' she told me, so glad and eager, 'it really is the largest scheme of the kind in Britain, more than five hectares of traffic-free shopping – sorry about the hectares – all created and run by Thamesdown.' Thamesdown? I thought we were in Swindon.   'Oh no,' she corrected me forgivingly, 'Thamesdown replaced Swindon in 1974.' To prove this, she gave me a map of Thamesdown, like a digital green puzzle with flashing diagonals and numbers. Underneath this puzzle was a key, 'towns and villages of Thamesdown'. Digit ten on the far left turned out to be Swindon. A polygonal black circuit of lines and dashes bounded the whole. It could have been Upper Volta. 'Oh sorry,' she cried, 'that's Thamesdown borough boundary, you can't get fields and hedges and things onto a computer.'

'Actually,' put in a young couple leafing through the brochures, 'it's lovely countryside. Unspoilt.' Whereas Liverpool had unspoilt countryside some way off. They had just moved here from Liverpool, a keen, good-looking couple, he in microwave, she a radiotherapist. 'We've found a lovely bungalow in Freshbrook, it's a new village, exclusive but not posh at all.' They burst out laughing. 'D'you ever watch *Brookside*? Daft! Maybe this new village – it's a housing estate really – took the idea off telly. "Freshbrook" . . . bet they got it off Channel 4. People down south expect us to say "flipping heck" all the time.' Of course they had sold their bungalow in Liverpool (Knowsley, to be precise) and left good jobs for better – otherwise, well, they couldn't have moved away. 'Firms want staff with experience, cuppla years at least. They don't want kids out of college.' As for moving home, 'if you're in a council flat, you're stuck'. Unemployed council tenants could forget about Thamesdown. But the right sort were spoilt for choice: executive Costa Brava type by the golf course, neo-rustic in the western development area with its chic Carrefour superstore and new super leisure centre rapidly nearing completion.

'Would you care for a view, my duck?' The duty officer in the Brunel Plaza took me up in the lift, twenty storeys high. 'Fresh air,' he breathed at the top, a big quiet man with teeth like neolithic flints. 'Name of Reeves,' said he, 'quite a few Reeves in Swindon.' He pointed far below to a cramped railway terrace: 'That's where we live, nice size garden.' His bulk looked crushed into the navy blue uniform. 'I used to work at Pressed Steel,' he added. 'I'm lucky to get another job. Air-conditioning, uniform . . . At night, I come up here and look at the stars.'

We gazed out at the town, its persistent cranes creeping over the mild and undistinguished face of Wiltshire. 'Burmah Oil, Nationwide, W. H. Smith, used to be rough grazing. My uncle kept pigs.' The sun came out, hesitant through misty blue like a hyacinth. 'They took our allotment,' said Mr Reeves mildly, 'for a trading estate. Course we need work, but where's the jobs? Done by computer.' Down in the Brunel Plaza, plastic sky filtered through plastic pleasure domes. Hesitant spring could not enter. No risk of rain spoiling that hard fake glitter. Even the indoor plants had a rubbery summer sheen. 'Aren't they lovely?' asked a waitress bent watering them, let off for a lunch break from the suicide blue pool of terylene. 'Aren't they gorgeous? Not a mark on this begonia.' Her homely, piggy features were lit up, whorehouse pink, by the crude strip lighting.

'Lovely place altogether,' agree a youngish couple, slim, likeable as

Torvill and Dean. 'We're moving here from Preston, just bought a *gorgeous bungalow* in a village, Highworth, a new estate covered in lovely Cotswold stone,' the young wife rattled on, her husband silent and happy. 'English and him don't get on,' she told the waitress, 'I have to do all the talk, he's a programmer for ACT, they've got a lovely place at Highworth. And now we've bought this bungalow, 80 per cent mortgage – what *more* can you want?'

They are so friendly, simple, the waitress and these bright migrants of new Britain, I could weep. Something brutal and desolate about Swindon, some underlying fraud of the telly-bred generation, defies analysis. Of course I don't weep. I enjoy a giant defrozen slice of Black Forest gâteau at Woolworths' cafeteria, amid waving plastic ferns and fire-proof lingerie.

28 April 1984

RACING WITH THE COLONEL

Simon Blow

Cheltenham

I have been staying for the races with a friend of my late father. The two men had fought side-by-side during the last war, although Johnnie – as my father always referred to him – was several years his senior. Colonel John Musgrove has lived for many years in a stone Cotswold house, about the size of a small manor, some ten miles from the racecourse. I had not seen him since I was a child, and all I remembered of him was that he shook his head a great deal while talking and was of a big build. Then, out of the blue, a few weeks ago, he telephoned me: 'I say, do come for Cheltenham, old boy.' He told me that he had been thinking of my father, and wondering what had become of me. I have always felt at home with people like Colonel Musgrove, so I went.

At dinner after my arrival, the Colonel was soon into a variety of family stories dealing mainly with estates lost, divorces, and dissolute heirs. Colonel Musgrove was well versed in matters of landed property, who was related to who, and 'good' or 'bad' bloodlines. As the discussion deepened, it brought on a great deal of the head-shaking that I'd remembered. 'Well, I'm not a bit surprised they got into such a mess. Everybody knows that the blood on his mother's side is really quite appalling.' And when we turned to politics he was brief and to the point: 'You really can't trust any of them today – they're all so totally dishonest.' By the end of the evening we had settled back into the scandals of Profumo, Thorpe and Parkinson, which drew the following statement from him: 'You know, there are two things which have destroyed this world: sex and religion.'

During my stay I came to realise that away from the dark polished furniture and Lionel Edwards watercolours that gave his house its distinctive flavour, Colonel Musgrove felt the threat of a world in which he was not at ease. A universe of concrete motorways and fierce red-brick shopping precincts – which have gutted nearly every county town – gave him a visible sickness. 'I just don't know how you young people manage,' he would say, repeating it. There were aspects of Musgrove that reminded me of Evelyn Waugh's Pinfold, who 'abhorred plastics, Picasso, sunbathing, and jazz – everything in fact that had happened in his own lifetime'. For Johnnie Musgrove belonged to an era when things had been properly made – namely, his suits, his hunting clothes, and his car. However, he could still protect himself from the hideous new world that encroached on every side by wearing suits cut in the early 1950s, and continuing to drive an upright silver Bentley from around the same period.

Once at the racecourse the Colonel and I made our way towards the members' enclosure. He had a few comments to make about the new stands opened only a year or so ago. He informed me that it had turned Cheltenham into an Oxford Street department store. 'Quite impossible to find one's friends,' he said, clearly used to a Cheltenham that was socially no more than an enlarged point-to-point. Then he led me to a seafood bar placed in a surviving section of the old cream and green stand. But now it was not only for the gentry, but contained a fair mixture of racing's punters.

As Colonel Musgrove attacked a plate of cold lobster at the stand-up table, somebody next to him gave a tug at his brown woolly scarf. 'Lend it to us, will yer,' said a man with a pug-dog face and the letters L-O-V-E tattooed on the fingers of one hand. 'Lend us yer scarf,' said the man again. 'No,' said the Colonel firmly. 'Come on, be a sport. Didn't anybody ever dare you to do something?' The pug-faced man, who was hiccuping through a pint of beer, pointed out his two friends, the darers. 'Will you please go away,' the Colonel insisted. 'Sorry, I'm a bit drunk,' the man now suddenly confessed. He then lurched back to his friends muttering: 'I never much liked your kind anyway.'

Disentangling himself from this encounter, the Colonel took me to a quiet patch of grass outside the bar where others of his kind seemed to have found a little haven of peace. Most wore the traditional dress of the Cheltenham gentry: a rather loud check suit, permissible for the meeting, and a black bowler. Quite a few, though, wore trilbies and many of the young were bare-headed. Colonel Musgrove wore a bowler. The talk of Musgrove and his friends was whether anybody had seen somebody called Monica, and who might win the Gold Cup now that Burrough Hill Lad had been taken out of the race.

I drifted away from the Colonel's group at this point to see something of this legendary race-meeting for myself. As with so many equestrian events nowadays, Cheltenham has gone commercial. The meeting is no longer in an idyllic setting flanked by the wild Cotswold hills as in the famed Munnings painting. From the new paddock you now look down to a network of blue and white tents where companies and shops advertise or sell their wares. The only civilised tent is held to be the Turf Club's awning, where members and friends have often been known to disappear for the whole afternoon. But the new Cheltenham was redeemed for me by the presence of a brass band that played adjacent to the paddock. On their red tunics they advertised Amoco petrol, but their melodies were thoroughly English. 'D'ye ken John Peel' broke into 'A Nightingale Sang in Berkeley Square'. They were the sort of melodies that I imagined Colonel Musgrove might hum continually to himself.

I never gathered very much about the Colonel's personal life, and it was not my business to do so. There had been one wife who had died soon after their marriage, but he did not speak of her. Like many in his mould, the Colonel played his cards of personal feeling close to his chest. But he did not lack for a social life. Apart from that first evening alone, we were out the next night, and the night after that he gave a dinner party. His friends were the local gentry and their wives, with the odd dowager thrown in. They lived in the county and had a delightful air of innocence about anything beyond it. 'What fun to write!' a lady said to me, as she clasped her hands deep into the lap of her blue silk evening dress. 'Do you work with your imagination?' They too, it seemed, were able to obliterate the horrors of the modern world. Over the port one evening, the conversation veered from the qualities of Montgomery as a leader, to those required to make a first-class huntsman.

On Gold Cup day, I lost the Colonel after what had become our habitual seafood lunch. I had gone to place a bet for the big race and the crowds were so thick, that when I returned he was nowhere to be seen. A friend took me into the Turf Club, for I wondered if he might be there. It was filled with ruddy-faced young men – some wearing cavalry twills – and ruddier-faced older men, all talking very loudly. At the sides of the young men were girls who on other days would have been wearing huskies. And there were also some people popping champagne bottles a little too noticeably. I did not think the Colonel could be happy in this company. No, the Colonel was not here.

Eventually I found the Colonel. The main race was over and the crowds had begun to disperse. I spotted his large form rising upwards from his highly polished broad, brogue shoes, his feet spread a little apart. He was standing silent and transfixed before the Amoco brass band. They had moved into 'The Teddy Bears' Picnic' and I noticed how one brogue of the Colonel's was lightly tapping. His head was now not so much shaking as nodding, and the several chins with it. It was a most touching sight to see Colonel John Musgrove, formerly of the famous 'O' Battery, Royal Horse Artillery (generally known, for speed into action, as 'the Rocket Troop'), tapping the time to this nursery tune. But whether it reminded him of the parade ground of his own nursery long ago, were, of course, questions I was unable to ask.

23 March 1985

CONSERVATIONIST MENACE

Auberon Waugh

For most of us, the 1960s ended 15 years ago, on 20 June 1970, with the emergence of Mr Edward Heath and Mr Peter Walker at the nation's helm. A new horror had arrived to replace the old rubbish. Peace, love and organic farming made way for the new spectre of salvation through efficiency. Gritty modern methods and an unsentimental abrasive approach to all problems were the order of the day. After a few years of that, we all saw it was a dreadful mistake. Grocer Heath was put in a corner in the dunce's cap he has been wearing ever since and Peter Walker, having destroyed the English counties, is allowed to exhibit himself from time to time in some ridiculous pose or other – torturing badgers or sticking up for Edward Heath and Old-Fashioned Toryism –as a terrible example to us all.

The new message, as we all know, is Salvation through Greed. We must simply eat and drink our way out of the problems of overproduction inherited from the Grocerist deviation. But even as we opinion-formers, trend-setters and Thatcherite groupies buckle down to our patriotic task, we are aware that other parts of the country are dragging their feet. There are still farmers and small businessmen out there grocerising, as they should have done in the 1970s, just as there are still country cottages where middle-aged hippies sit around calling each other 'man', smoking pot and hoping to get magical vibrations from some disused silage pit or beet store which they have identified as an ancient burial ground. We may have moved on, but others have chosen to stay behind at various stages of the odyssey.

Irritated as we may be by those institutions which seem immovably stuck in the Sixties, like the Catholic Church, there is something distinctly endearing about people like the Prince of Wales who suddenly appear to have discovered that confusing decade a quarter of a century after everyone else. His latest outbreak is against farmers who despoil the countryside in the interests of agricultural productivity – or 'greed' as it was more fashionably called before 'greed' became a cheer-word. He was speaking to an agricultural college near Newton Abbot last week in his role as Duke of Cornwall.

'Fascinating places, wetlands, moorlands and hedgerows have been lost, often in response to greed,' he said. 'We have come to look on the land as an almost endless source of increasing income . . .'

Of course it is absolutely true that many farmers, left to themselves, will behave like pigs, leaving horrible plastic sacks all over the countryside and putting up hideous metal barns and grain-dryers as well as tearing up hedgerows and chopping down trees. Other farmers prefer not to live in a pigsty and keep their hedgerows and trees, at some cost to themselves. Until very recently, the Government was paying farmers to plough up moorland and pull down hedgerows. It was called land reclamation and improvement. Now, in some cases, it pays them not to do so and leave the land untilled. That is called conservation. I do not see how any great issue of morality is involved. It rather depended on how many people were going to be fascinated by a particular piece of wetland, as against the rather larger number who might have had to pay an extra penny on their loaf of bread for allowing a sedge warbler to warble on his own patch – possibly delighting the soul of some bearded creep hiding behind the reeds, possibly not.

The Prince of Wales urged farmers to develop new skills, specifying tourism, light industry and forestry, in order to discourage them from destroying what is called 'the environment'. This would seem to confirm the countryside in the role of recreation area for townspeople – who are themselves exiled from the countryside by their own greed for money – rather than as an area dedicated to agriculture and its own pursuits. The farmer's role is to show misty-eyed townspeople his sedge warblers and possibly serve them a cream tea afterwards. It does not seem to occur to these bird-fanciers and nature fanatics that they are as much a pest as the voles, rabbits and squirrels they admire, and that any farmer who took his job really seriously would poison their cream teas as surely as he pours cyanide into a wasps' nest.

Two developments show the way the wind is. The first is the decision of an elderly judge in Bristol Crown Court to allow the League Against Cruel Sports an injunction against the Devon and Somerset Staghounds from trespassing on one of the 33 plots of land the League has bought on Exmoor for no reason except to exclude the hunt from them. There is no law of trespass which farmers can invoke against animal sentimentalists wishing to gape at their own countryside.

Even worse than this is what has been happening in Orkney. There a quango called the Nature Conservancy Council, hand in glove with the Royal Society for the Protection of Birds, has declared vast areas of agricultural land virtually out of bounds for farmers: no cattle may graze there and sheep only under the most stringent conditions. They now control vast tracts of land all over the islands. In addition to 13,000 acres on the island of Hoy, another 7,000 acres have just been declared a Site of Special Scientific Interest in order to protect some 400 black-backed gulls and 800 skuas. When these wretched gulls – not to mention the 30,000 pairs of guillemots, razorbills and other pests – kill lambs, the RSPB, driving around in Land-Rover Safari Trucks and green wellies, talks of a 'management problem'.

Dr John Francis, the Nature Conservancy Council Director for Scotland, says that his objective is to 'ensure that our natural heritage of flora and fauna, animals and plants, is maintained as fully as possible . . . for the future of the community at large'.

What community, one wonders, and what future? Orkney has a shrinking population of some 17,000 humans, 75,000 beef cattle. Its only important industry is the raising of beef on poor land in a poor climate. When, in saner times, the Navy used the north of Eday as a gunnery range, it killed many cattle (and paid suitable compensation) but did not succeed in frightening away the birds. Now the birds are being given the run of the island for their own fatuous pursuits and the cattle are being driven off.

'Despite misunderstandings great stress is placed on the fact that we must work through a voluntary approach and that is very much the central remit of our structure,' says Dr Francis. 'The alternative would be statutory controls.'

13 April 1985

OUT TO LUNCH

Jeffrey Bernard

I spent last weekend in Scotland at a perfectly splendid three-day house party or, to put it accurately, a *castle* party. My wrenched ankle kept me off the grouse moors but I did manage to dispatch a couple of clay pigeons. There was a fantastic firework display put on by professionals and there were two Highland pipers. There was salmon and champagne and the only thing that jarred slightly was a man saying that he thought I was 'hard work'. Well of course I'm hard work before opening time and you shouldn't expect much change out of a man before 11 a.m. But it's very pretty, Scotland, isn't it? What I must do in future though – if I do have any future in castles and formal gardens – is to resist and curb the habit of gravitating to the servants' quarters and passing the time of day in the kitchens. It isn't inverted snobbery and I rather suspect I might have had an amazing sexual experience when a boy, behind a green baize door. In the end only a fool could prefer downstairs to upstairs. And I have a fool right here now sitting behind me. Draped in her Greenham Common garb and looking like a walking jumble sale she has drawn herself up to her full majestic height and declared that it is 'disgusting' that I should have spent a weekend in a castle. If I had cried off going to Scotland it wouldn't have erased world poverty or eased the tension between East and West, but She who would raze castles to the ground doesn't comprehend.

But what a dreadful journey home on the train. British Rail stung three of us for £45 for lunch. The vegetables were tinned and tasteless and my steak was curled in a way that reminded me of one of Charlie Chaplin's shoes. How a so-called food expert like Prue Leith can be officially connected with British Rail is rather odd and can't do her restaurant much good. Norman should be put in charge of the catering. I've had better meals of the nursery variety in the Coach and Horses than I have had on trains, although my friend Charlie says the food in Wandsworth Prison is even better. Perhaps he and Taki will one day honour us with an Egon-Ronay-type guide to food in the nick. I shall do the same for the great British hospital lunch. And talking of food reminds me of a strange story I heard from a fellow guest in Scotland. She told me that during the war she was in an air raid shelter in a blitz when she stopped an old lady from leaving it. She asked, 'Where do you think you're going to?' The old lady said, 'I've left my false teeth at home and I'm going to get them.' She was told, 'Come back, they're dropping bombs, not sandwiches.'

But more seriously, back in London I find that Robert Maxwell is about to halve my wretched income. Could this be the end? Can you get Supplementary Benefit if you weekend in castles and dally in saloons? I doubt it, although I think it's wrong. As I think I've mentioned before, Tom Baker has the solution. He says doctors should be permitted to write you out prescriptions for money. But She says, 'You are a rat to think like that.' She would have us in sackcloth and ashes and She says that come the revolution She will make sure that if I am not to be shot I will certainly end up working in the Cherry Blossom boot polish factory. Such anger. But isn't it odd that these people *never* refuse a dinner?

31 August 1985

I'M BACKING BRIXTON

Zenga Longmore

Brixton! The heart of the New Black Renaissance. No black British artists, writers, poets or actors can be taken seriously unless they live in

'You will all walk round London after dark.'

Brixton. For this reason Brixton has occasionally spread to Kennington and Camberwell. There was even a case of it stretching to Thornton Heath.

I myself, a black actress, can flatter myself by saying that I actually *do* live in Brixton, and wouldn't dream of living anywhere else. How could I? What other part of London can you walk down the road singing to yourself at the top of your voice, and not even receive a second glance? When you're indulging in a one-man argument over whether to buy the yams or the sweet potatoes, instead of being carted off to some cell or other, you get a kindly word of advice from an old man, 'Sweet potatoes look a whole heap of nastiness darlin', likkle yam'll do you more good.'

Yes, anything goes in Brixton. When you've locksed your hair up, and found it looks too ridiculous for words, Brixton is the only place to wear it with pride, and even get the odd 'Stay sweet, Sis!' or 'Whappen daughter!' shouted in your direction.

Brixton's market is the best in London. There is no style of wig that cannot be bought here, from afro to Lady Di, and there is no obscure Nigerian vegetable that you will not see on the stalls – yes, even egusi. You can buy your Fulani batique material to the accompaniment of the latest soca record that blares from the next shop. If Rasta crowns are your cup of tea – then Brixton is the place to find them in all shapes and sizes. While we're on the subject of Rasta bonnets, a word of advice in your shell-like. Leather ones are for the gentlemen of more advancing years, woolly ones for the lefties who work in rights centres, and the tall felt ones are for crooks and dealers who drive E-Type Jags and own a gold chain for every tribe of Judah. The floppy black caps are to be worn on those leisure days when you hang out with your posse on the Frontline, enjoying your can of Tennants. Don't be fooled by the women who wear Rasta caps; far from being Rastas, they are merely polytechnic students in disguise.

Leaving Rastafarian headwear aside for the moment, shall we talk of Brixton's nightlife? What can I say? There is something for everybody. Sinatras for the soul boys, the Fridge for the trendies amongst you, and myriad blues parties for all you reggae freaks. To enjoy a blues party at its best, you need to be under 20 and female, but there are seldom any complaints (except from the next-door neighbours).

Now we come to the seedy side of Brixton life, the vile corrupt side that no one has dared print until now . . . *health food shops.* Yes, I'm afraid to say the trendies have swept upon us, cursing us with a plague of vegetarian restaurants. These restaurants are crammed to bursting point with skinny, spiky-haired men and women, drooping over cabbage leaves, and so resembling the vegetables they eat that it is practically cannibalism.

These people are creeping into Brixton so insidiously that I wouldn't be surprised if you don't hear of another riot in the near future. If you're white, and you disagree with these people's so-called 'sound' ideology, they label you pernicious and evil. If you're black, they pity you, and think you're stupid but misguided. In trying to guide blacks, they swarm upon us, selling us unreadable magazines, scattering left-wing book shops in their wake, and whining at us in unnatural cockney accents about our oppression. Jamaican housewives will suck their teeth in scorn, as copies of *Militant* are thrust under their noses, by a pasty-faced girl who screeches: 'Basically, you're unaware of insensitive policing!' Although these people like to be seen in Brixton's veggy cafés for the all-important 'cred', there is one place they will not be found, and that is the Atlantic pub.

When all's said and done, the Atlantic pub is where it's at. Be there or be square. With two sprawling bars, it caters for the true Brixtonian. It is the only pub in Brixton where you can find every conceivable form of Rasta crown. Singing with the jazz band there is always a wonderful experience for me, for the simple reason that it never matters whether I am in good or bad voice, because no one takes the blindest bit of notice. Couples will argue, old men will shout at themselves, and young men, who perhaps have had one over the eight, will laugh uproariously at nothing at all. All the while, I'm on stage, lamenting (and very tunefully too if I may say so) over my man who's done lef' me. When the number's finished, if I order the ones standing nearest to applaud, then I'll get applause, if not, I'll step off the stage with queenly dignity and continue the debate about Margaret Thatcher with my friends at the bar.

If, however, you're the more conservative type, who views an absence of etiquette with horror, then there's still a place for you here in Brixton. You will gain many hours of quiet satisfaction sneering at everyone, from behind your net curtains, in one of the maisonettes near Herne Hill, where Brixton becomes suburban. You can go to the library and curl your upper lip at the dungareed women, who sprawl on the floor reading *City Limits*, then you can ask one of them in a loud voice where to find the latest Roger Scruton. Your trump card can be to offend the stall holders by picking up a plantain and snorting – 'Aggh! What's *that*? You don't eat it, do you? It looks *obscene*!'

So you see, whoever you are, and whatever your inclinations, Brixton is most certainly the place for you. You know it makes cred!

20/27 December 1986

TALE OF THE UNEXPECTED

Alice Thomas Ellis

I was wakened quite late the other morning, or rather afternoon, by an awful little bird sitting on a topmost bough making a noise like an unoiled hinge. Musical it wasn't. He was very small and a bit yellow and I must ask Janet (who knows about these things) what the little horror is called so I can put his name in a drawer.

We were staying in the country for a few days because I had just heard from an editor asking if I had finished the project on which I am engaged. There is nothing like those words for reminding one that one had better make a start, so we shot off to meet Gladys Mary who is helping me with the said project.

We arrived in a blizzard and didn't take our coats off for the first two days while the house gradually warmed up. Then one evening we were just relaxing and thinking about going to bed when the third son and Neil had the sort of experience we could all do without. They were in the barn enjoying an innocent and bracing game of ping-pong when suddenly upon their ears fell the fearful words 'Evenin' all', followed by the sound of size twelves on the barn steps. The ping-pong ball froze in mid-flight, the words 'I never dunnit' hung unuttered on the air and the two of them stared wildly around wondering if there was any evidence they should fling a hasty tarpaulin over. I ask myself if policemen have this effect on families other than our own.

The boys led the officers of the law across to the house where I, in my turn, nearly suffered cardiac arrest, since I always first expect them to tell me that somebody has died. It must be very thankless being a policeman. After the initial shock I found myself pondering shiftily whether I should hide the Scotch behind a chair leg, and whether smoking was illegal in one's own sitting-room. It was reassuring to see one of them accepting a fag from the son, but I restrained myself from asking ingratiatingly whether they were permitted to drink on duty.

The reason for their unexpected presence was that four teenagers on a Duke of Edinburgh Award Scheme or something had failed to return to base at the correct time and were wandering around somewhere up on the moors. We left all the lights blazing to guide them down, should they drift our way, and crawled off to bed, where I found I couldn't sleep. Then the ghosts started talking downstairs. Last time I heard them they were all men, but this time I could hear a woman's voice too. I strained my ears to try and distinguish words, but this isn't possible, and anyway they indubitably speak in old Welsh.

Next day Gladys Mary said she had heard them too. Gladys Mary is quite amazing. She had worked solidly all day on 'my' project while I had spent half the afternoon in exhausted slumber. She had written an article in bed until about 3 a.m. with the ghosts all gassing away downstairs; then she got up at the crack of dawn, hit the ground running and I wouldn't be at all surprised if she'd written a poem before breakfast. What's more, she'd driven miles to get to us, traversing the Berwyns in the snow. I wish I knew where she got her energy.

We heard the helicopter plying to and fro in search of the lost teenagers, but then came the cheerful news that they'd teamed up in the pub over on the other side, so I had another nap to celebrate, wondering how many of the ghosts got that way by finding themselves benighted up on the mountain. I was once told by the oldest inhabitant, of a previous owner-occupier who rode into the village on his horse and never returned. The horse came back but he was found floating face down in the stream. From the tone of the account I gather that this had happened yesterday, but it transpired that the granny of the granny of the granny of the oldest inhabitant had told him about it. Time, while not precisely standing still, does tend to lounge around a bit here. There had been a suspicion that the drowned man had not died an accidental death – some talk of sheep rustling and bad feeling – and I wondered who had had the task of enforcing the law in those far-off days and whether they had said 'Evenin' all'. Perhaps if I bone up on my Welsh, burnish up my courage and come down one night to join the talking ghosts I shall find out. I am pretty sure that, in view of the impression they made, the shades of our two policemen will continue to alarm generations to come should they chance to be playing ping-pong in the barn as night thickens.

12 March 1988

WHERE THERE'S MUCK

Dominic Lawson

Mr Henry 'Hank' Valentino is one of the victims of the international waste disposal business. Over the past 11 years he has spent $7 million in a fruitless attempt to export Philadelphian municipal sludge to the Third World. He has tried Haiti. He has tried Bermuda. He has tried Guatemala. He negotiated a deal with the Turks and Caicos, only to see the government arrested and its replacement ditch the project.

Mr Valentino's problem is one of image. The sewage export business stinks. 'What would you say, sir, if I told you that I was going to export my sludge to your country?' 'I would say "I don't want your shit," Mr Valentino.' 'Sir, that is exactly my problem,' replied the president of Applied Recovery Techniques. 'Everything is going fine, and then someone stands up at an ambassadorial cocktail party, and says what you just said.'

The sad truth is that, although Mr Valentino would not claim to be motivated by altruism, his plans might well be in the best interests of the countries which have spurned him. Philadelphian sludge, spread out at a depth of 18 inches under the Haitian sun, will dry, and can then be scooped up and sold back to the US for a dollar a tonne as fertiliser ('It smells kind of sweet,' says Mr Valentino).

But Central American politicians have a different interpretation. Colonisation was bad enough. They do not want to be colon-ised as well. Perhaps they also believe those who say that the US eastern seaboard waste disposal industry is one of the Mafia's favourite routes for laundering 'dirty' money.

The reason why Mr Valentino and other entrepreneurs are attempting such stunts lies in the US domestic situation. Following years of catastrophic unregulation of the disposal of toxic waste, particularly by the chemical industry, the Americans – such a reactive people – have turned against the idea of landfill for any form of waste, however innocuous. Hence the absurd spectacle over the past 18 months of two barges of sewage, one from Long Island, the *Bark*, the other from Philadelphia, the *Khian Sea*, sailing the high seas around the Caribbean in search of a home. Like the *Flying Dutchman*, neither has yet found a final resting place. But, unlike W. C. Fields, they would rather not, on the whole, be in Philadelphia.

Under American law an exporter must notify the US Environmental Protection Agency of any plans to export hazardous waste, and prove to the EPA that the importing government has given its assent. At the beginning of the decade the annual number of such shipments was about 30. Mrs Wendy Grieder of the EPA told me last week that in the first three months of this year she has received 400 export notifications.

Perhaps one of them is for the shipment of part of Philadelphia's 100,000-tonne stockpile of incinerated sludge to the United Kingdom. Mr Bruce Gledhill, Philadelphia's deputy streets commissioner, told me that a British company had recently approached him with an offer to take the sludge off his hands. It would not be the first time that a British company had become involved with plans for the export and recycling of the Philadelphian sewage. Mr Valentino's consultants are none other than our very own Thames Water, and, according to Mr Valentino, Thames were to operate the sewage farms planned for the Turks and Caicos.

Until very recently the idea of exporting American garbage to the UK would have seemed risible. But last month Environmental Data Services revealed that a new company called Power Water and Waste (PWW) had devised plans to ship two million tonnes a year of Boston household garbage to Cornwall. In 1986 the UK imported 130,000 tonnes of non-hazardous waste, so the PWW plans are of a different scale altogether, and equivalent to ten per cent of the indigenous domestic waste stream.

Mr George Harrison, a director of PWW, claims that the garbage could be landfilled in Cornwall at a price, including transport, of about $60 a tonne, or half what it costs the Boston authorities to barge it to Ohio. The British newspapers which followed up the ENDS report played up the story as a case of Britain on the verge of becoming a global dustbin and obtained the necessary horrified quotation from local authorities.

Yet, like Mr Valentino, PWW, acting commercially, may also be acting in the interests of those who would spurn the waste. PWW's plans have been devised by Mr George Pritchard, previously the co-ordinator of Greenpeace's anti-nuclear campaign. The idea is that the waste will be placed in a 25-acre polyethylene bag in one of the many poisonous cavities left by the tin-mining industry in the North Downs area near Redruth. The decomposing waste will, after several years, generate enough methane to sustain a 25-megawatt power station, enough to keep the 50,000 population of Redruth and Camborne in electricity. PWW aims also to take care of all of Cornwall's waste of 200,000 tonnes a year, and to take responsibility for the poisonous waste streams from what remains of the Cornish tin-mining industry.

Mr Pritchard, a Cornish resident and former tin-miner, claims that his venture will create 550 jobs in an area where a quarter of the workforce is unemployed. The 1,100 containers shipped in every week will be a particular benefit to the almost defunct Falmouth docks.

This promise of a local gravy train (or whatever else the Bostonians put in their rubbish bins) might save PWW from the fate that befell Shanks & McEwen, Britain's largest landfill waste company, when it attempted to import incinerated household rubbish from Zurich and dispose of it in Bedfordshire. In February Bedfordshire councillors rejected the plans following an outcry in the local press. Mr Gower Keeling, Bedfordshire's waste disposal officer, is an unrepentant advocate of the plan: 'Shanks & McEwen were forced to reject ideal waste. It wouldn't rot, doesn't smell, and doesn't attract vermin. Our own waste is verminous and much more dangerous. The press in England is alarmist. We have an open door policy in this country and it should remain. The origin of waste is irrelevant. But I must do what the councillors say even if I don't agree with it.'

Mr Keeling's problem is that the excavations of the London Brick Company (owned by Hanson Trust, which also owns 20 per cent of Shanks & McEwen) has left Bedfordshire with about 100 million cubic metres of unfilled brickpit. For the past 20 years Bedfordshire Council has struggled to fill these hideous cavities, in an attempt to reclaim the land desecrated by London Brick. The Bedfordshire clay is an ideal impermeable base for a refuse dump, according to Shanks & McEwen's managing director, Mr Roger Hewitt, who describes the cavities as 'bathtubs in the ground'.

But Britain's biggest landfill company has now turned against the idea of importing waste, and Mr Hewitt now describes deals such as the one devised by Power Water and Waste as 'waste management in the interests of the US, not waste management in our own national interest'. It is difficult to avoid the impression that Shanks has abandoned imports for reasons more closely allied to PR than to logic. International markets are created by arbitrage, the theory that something is worth more in one local market than it is in another. In this case the market would be based on an arbitrage in aesthetics and the British belief, quite contrary to that of the Americans or the Swiss, that landfill is the most suitable method of disposing of the vast bulk of wastes.

It is also an arbitrage in price. Landfill is about four times cheaper than incineration or treatment, and the UK, unlike any other country in the developed world, is an advocate of the codisposal of household and industrial waste. That attitude – endorsed by government – of 'let nature do the work' is far cheaper and easier than the continental approach, which is to separate domestic and industrial waste, and often subject the latter to chemical treatment.

The market is also created by differences in geology. That is why the US has for years exported waste to Canada whose ranges of impermeable pre-Cambrian rocks are seen as a safe dumping ground. So it is natural for Holland, where the water table is about a yard below the soil, to export waste for landfill in countries such as Britain, the site not only of massive clay pits, but of many other extractive industries.

It is also an arbitrage in different needs for the same currency. Which is another way of saying that Eastern Europe, and especially East Germany, is a major importer of waste. The East German government earns about 160 million deutschmarks a year by taking two million tonnes a year of West German waste. The East Germans dump the waste at the inappropriately named Schoenberg site, just across the border from the West German town of Lubeck. According to Uta Bellion, Greenpeace's anti-waste campaigning co-ordinator, 'From the waste site you can see Lubeck's church tower. The groundwater stream from Schoenberg is going back across the border to West Germany and the people of Lubeck are screaming.'

According to Bellion, 'Apart from the Eastern bloc and the Third World, the UK is the only significant importer of waste.' Mr Harvey Yakovitz, who monitors trans-border waste shipments for the OECD, claims that as the West Germans are becoming squeamish about waste crossing their territory: 'A lot of waste which used to head for East Germany is now turning right around and heading for the Channel.' Over the three years to 1986 UK imports of hazardous waste grew from 5,000 tonnes a year to 53,000 tonnes a year (or about four per cent of the domestic market). And some provisional estimates of 1987's imports range as high as 200,000 tonnes.

Yet the phrase 'waste import' is in economic terms a complete misnomer. It is in fact an export which looks like an import. Waste management is probably Britain's fastest growing invisible export, and it is in these terms that it is defended by the British Government. 'We are a world leader in disposing of waste,' says Lord Caithness, the Environment Minister. 'The flow of waste into this country is not a bad thing.'

The most graphic illustration of the foreign currency potential of waste 'imports' is provided by British Nuclear Fuels. According to Mr Neville Chamberlain, the chief executive of BNFL, 'We stand to gain foreign currency revenues of about £2.7 billion, mostly from the Japanese, in return for reprocessing spent fuels from their nuclear power stations.'

Since 1976 BNFL has signed contracts which require that the senders of the waste take back (probably by aeroplane) not just the processed uranium and plutonium (which they want), but also the high-level radioactive waste (which they assuredly do not want). BNFL already has a temporary home for this most hazardous of wastes on its Sellafield site on the edge of the Irish Sea. Called the 'Store', and the size of four double-decker buses, it must also qualify as the least desirable detached property in Britain.

But the signs are that the Japanese are beginning to wonder why they pay trillions of yen to BNFL if they also have to go to the expense of finding a permanent home themselves for the most lethal waste product of all. BNFL fears that Japan might therefore construct its own nuclear reprocessing plant. The only way to pre-empt such a move and thus avoid the loss of its most important contract would then be for BNFL to offer to keep all the high-level radioactive waste which results from the reprocessing. That would really test how much popular 'green' opposition this Government is prepared to endure in its defence of the great cause of foreign currency earnings from waste management.

The decision by Mrs Thatcher to appoint Lord Caithness as successor to another member of the upper house, Lord Belstead, suggests that she at least does not consider the environment a matter of such burning importance to the electorate, or its representatives, despite her occasional litter-gathering forays in St James's Park.

Not surprisingly, the noble succession of British environment ministers have not found it easy to get a place in the legislative queue.

One reason why European waste producers will often prefer to export their waste across the Channel to Britain is that certain waste which would be designated hazardous in Europe is defined as 'not special' by the British authorities. A gungy mixture of solvents and heavy metals is one example. This is in part because the 1980 Public Health Act (Special Waste) does not mention the effect on the environment in its strictures, but only the effect of waste on human beings. In July 1987, on the *Panorama* programme, 'Not in My Back Yard', Lord Belstead conceded that this was a significant weakness in UK legislation and said, 'We must bring in legislation to include the environmental element . . . I am absolutely determined that we should do something about it in the near future.' But nine months later Lord Caithness still cannot say exactly when such legislation will be brought in.

The infinite variety of ways in which countries define hazardous waste is at once at the heart of both the growth of the international trade in waste and also the attempts, chiefly by the EEC, to regulate this trade.

Mr Yakovitz describes his attempts to formulate a definition agreeable to all as 'like stacking billiard balls in a high wind'. The Germans refer to 'special' waste, the Dutch talk about 'difficult' waste, the French speak of 'toxic and dangerous' waste, the US legislates against 'hazardous' waste while the Australians speak only of 'intractable waste'.

In 1984 the EEC – concerned at the way in which the 41 barrels of dioxin which caused the Seveso disaster simply got lost within Europe, and turned up in a Parisian slaughterhouse – promulgated legislation designed to control the burgeoning market in waste across frontiers. Their starting point was that since waste was a commodity, it would be against the Treaty of Rome to interfere with its free trade within European member states. The Germans, with teutonic logic, attempted – without support – to argue that since the waste itself was of a negative value, it was not a good, and therefore need not be freely traded. Eventually the EEC came up with rules which would standardise and regulate the trade in waste within Europe. But, vexed by the problem of definition, so far only Belgium and Denmark have put the enabling legislation through.

The EEC legislation has thus not only been useless in regulating the trade, but has actually encouraged its proliferation. This is because many companies had believed, for no good reason, that the trans-frontier shipment of waste was either illegal or at least seamy. But the legislative framework devised in Brussels in 1984 gave a certain spurious respectability to the trade, and the publicity surrounding the negotiations opened many entrepreneurs' eyes to deal-making possibilities.

Hence the rise of the international waste broker, a man who need know nothing about waste, but who simply puts the producer in touch with a disposer. The one-man waste brokers tend to have the grandest names. One such is 'Global Transport and Trading', based in Northwick, Cheshire. Others have more descriptive names such as Etna Waste (based in Kennington, London), or Belgium's largest waste broker, Destructo. Mrs Heliane De Vliegere, Destructo's chief executive, would not speak to *The Spectator* about her business. But her assistant, after explaining that 'Mrs De Vliegere thinks you might not write what she wants you to write', vouchsafed that Destructo's revenues have grown at a rate of 50 per cent in each of the last four years.

Mr Philip Butler of Etna Waste was more forthcoming. 'We are no different from stockbrokers. They find people who want shares. We find people who want waste.' Mr Butler, however, does far more business in East Germany than any city stockbroker has ever done. For the producer of waste a broker is a real joy, because he will often take on the legal obligation to dispose of the waste properly. Outside the US, which operates a rigorous 'polluter pays' policy, the waste producer can forget about his waste, once he has transferred legal title.

The latest waste broker to join the market is *The Spectator*, albeit unpaid. I let slip to Mr Henry Valentino (he of the fruitless 11-year quest to ship his Philadelphian sewage to the Caribbean) the tale of Power Water and Waste, and its plans to take Boston's refuse to Cornwall. 'You mean they are exporting our waste to the UK? I'd never thought of that,' said Mr Valentino. He asked me for PWW's telephone number, and in deference to this new, rather anal version of the special relationship, I gave it to him. 'God bless you,' said Mr Valentino.

9 April 1988

NUCLEAR POWER? YES, PLEASE

Andrew Kenny

I am a vegetarian and therefore a supporter of nuclear power. I became a vegetarian 20 years ago because I believed that the farming and slaughter of animals was cruel and because I thought it was a shameful waste of food to take the grain that could feed ten people and give it to a beast to produce only enough meat to feed one person. My reasons in short for turning to vegetarianism were respect for man and nature. These are precisely my reasons for turning to nuclear power.

Rather late in life I changed careers, became an engineer and joined an electricity utility. They required me to spend one and a half years at a coal station before I could join the nuclear section. My stay at the coal station shocked me and greatly increased my zeal for nuclear power. I have taken a vow to myself that if I ever have children I shall not allow them to grow up near a coal station (I shall be perfectly happy for them to grow up near a nuclear one). But distance from coal power is not enough to escape its menace.

I support nuclear power for one reason only: that it is cleaner and safer than any other practicable large-scale source of electricity. The best way to see this is in the question of waste. In the case of nuclear power, a small amount of uranium is dug out of the ground, refined, passed through a nuclear reactor, stored and then returned to the ground again. The original uranium lying in the ground is mildly dangerous in that it emits a radioactive gas, radon, that naturally seeps out of the ground sometimes causing lung cancer. The nuclear waste is dangerous in the short term but in the long term, because of its shorter half-lives, it is less dangerous than the ore it came from. In the case of coal power, a huge amount of coal is dug out of the ground, passed through a coal furnace and converted into dangerous substances which are then either poured into the atmosphere for plants and men to breathe or dumped onto ash tips, leaching their poisons into the watercourses. The original coal is quite safe. The coal wastes are very dangerous, and unlike the nuclear wastes, many of them remain dangerous forever.

Nuclear power produces only one form of pollution, radiation, and only two possible dangers, cancer and genetic disease. Even in these it is overshadowed by coal. Large amounts of radiation can certainly cause cancer but low levels of radiation are a natural and inescapable fact of life. Soil, milk, stone, wood, flesh – these are all radioactive and with the sun they give us a 'background radiation', which is massively larger than any radiation received even on the doorstep of a nuclear station. Certain regions of the Earth, because of their geology, have abnormally high background radiation, thousands of times higher than that emitted by a nuclear power station, but no unusual rate of cancer has been seen in any of them.

Coal, too, is radioactive and, having heard that a coal station routinely emits more radiation than a nuclear one, I put radiation badges on the workers of our coal station and measured the levels there. Sure enough, the radiation next to the coal station was twice as high as that next to our nuclear station, but this was a trivial result as the levels were both very low and the higher altitude of the coal station would have had an effect.

Far more serious are the chemical cancer agents from the coal station. In the short time I lived in the small township at the coal station, two people, one the power station manager's wife, died grim deaths by cancer. Their deaths are doubtless of no statistical significance, but the carcinogens in the coal wastes are a hard fact. They include organic carcinogens such as nitro-samines and benzopyrenes and, worse, heavy metals such as cadmium and arsenic. Cadmium is normally locked safely into the coal but when the coal is burnt in the furnace the cadmium vaporises, turns into tiny particles, passes through the smokestacks and spreads through the atmosphere to settle finely on the ground where it dissolves in water, enters human tissue and causes cancer. Cadmium has a half-life of infinity. It remains dangerous until the end of time. When Chernobyl's ruined reactor has become less radioactive than the soil in your back garden, when the Pharaohs' mighty pyramids have crumbled into sand, when our sun has become a Red Giant and boiled our oceans dry, the cadmium from your local coal station will still be as deadly as on the day it left the smokestack.

Radiation in large amounts is known to cause genetic damage in animals, especially the hapless fruitfly, but the curious fact is that it has never been observed to cause genetic damage in human beings. The first generation of survivors after the bombs on Hiroshima and Nagasaki were minutely studied but the babies born to them showed not the slightest increase in abnormality. Now coal power stations emit many chemicals, such as the polycyclic aromatic hydrocarbons (PAH), known to cause genetic defects in animals. It is likely that they do the same in humans but this is not yet known. Those cartoons of two-headed children, so liked by the anti-nuclear brigade, apply at least as well to coal power.

By every measure the death rate from coal power is much larger than the death rate from nuclear power. Per unit of energy extracted, coal mining claims more than ten times as many deaths as uranium mining. Far worse are the civilian casualties. Study after study into the deaths caused by coal pollution agree that the figure is about 50 deaths per medium-sized coal station per year. This figure is necessarily tentative because coal pollution is diffuse and insidious in its effects. It translates into 25,000 deaths per year in the United States and 1,700 deaths per year in the United Kingdom. The World Health Organisation estimates that the Chernobyl accident may cause 1,600 premature deaths over the next 30 years. Thus coal power in the United Kingdom kills more civilians in one year than Chernobyl will kill in 30. And Chernobyl is the only civilian nuclear accident ever to claim a life. Three Mile Island killed nobody, injured nobody and exposed the nearest civilians to radiation less than one tenth of one dental X-ray.

The direct human casualties from coal power, although far larger than from nuclear power, are dwarfed by the devastation coal causes to the environment. Acid rain, caused by sulphur oxides (Sox) and nitrogen oxides (Nox) from coal stations and other burning of fossil fuel, has already caused vast damage to the planet's lakes and forests and the damage is spreading. Even more ominous are the future consequences of the millions of tons of carbon dioxide that coal stations pour into the atmosphere. The 'greenhouse effect' has been much in the news recently and the strange weather the world has experienced this year may or may not be due to it. The global weather system is very complicated and very finely poised, and it is difficult to make short-term assessments. But what is absolutely certain is that the fragile balance depends crucially on the amount of carbon dioxide in the atmosphere and that amount is rising inexorably. We are sliding towards some immense change, perhaps a catastrophe. The human race is threatened by several rising trends – the population growth, the demand for resources – but of all the graphs of doom none gives such apocalyptic warning as the rising level of carbon dioxide. The future of our civilisation may well depend on reversing it. Nuclear stations produce not one drop of acid rain, not one breath of carbon dioxide.

There is no such thing as a clean coal power station. A 'clean stack' simply means that the visible pollution, the dust (smoke), has been removed. But most coal pollution is invisible. Only a minority of advanced coal stations have chemical scrubbing and even these only attempt to reduce the sox and nox. None try to remove the heavy metals. It is impossible to remove the carbon dioxide.

The most fanatic antagonists of nuclear power are forced to admit that its safety record is without equal in power generation. But, they cry, what if the really big nuclear power disaster happens? The really big disaster will not happen because it cannot happen. No nuclear power accident can match the damage done by the routine operation of coal power stations. The superb safety record of nuclear power in the West is not because of any superhuman diligence by nuclear engineers – indeed many of them were hair-raisingly sloppy in the early days – but because the designs they have chosen are intrinsically safe. Chernobyl happened because the RMBK reactor was not intrinsically safe. Nuclear power, unlike any other large industrial process I can think of, offers itself to inherent safety. There are nuclear reactor designs now on the drawing board in which safety is entirely passive: human operators will control the reactor only while it is running within safe limits; if it deviates from the limits, the laws of nature will overrule the operators and shut the reactor down safely. Nuclear power, safe now, offers yet more safety in the future.

Then the inevitable question: if nuclear is so safe, why is it so feared? Why is there such hostility against it?

The first and obvious reason is the link with the Bomb. Natural uranium contains 0.7 per cent of Uranium 235. To make a bomb you need at least 90 per cent. Nuclear power reactors have less than six per cent, which is why it is physically impossible for them to explode like an atom bomb. It is sometimes thought that nuclear power is the veil behind which governments make nuclear weapons; if so it is a transparent veil, which any nuclear inspector can see right through. Weapons grade fuel can be made through two routes: enrichment of Uranium 235, a conspicuous, difficult and enormously expensive process, or production of Plutonium 239 in a production reactor, different from a power reactor and much simpler. A nuclear power programme is more a hindrance than a help to any country bent on making nuclear weapons. Indeed, the spread of internationally approved nuclear power under the supervision of a Non-Proliferation Treaty that gave full access to nuclear power technology in return for opening their facilities to international inspectors would be the best way to deter countries like Israel, Pakistan, South Africa and India from developing nuclear weapons.

The usual explanation for the witch-hunting in the 16th and 17th centuries is that in a time of change and new knowledge people sought certainty by chasing a recognisable demon. Today, in an age of space-shuttles and computers, where the average housewife in London or businessman in New York has an understanding of the natural universe that is little different from that of prehistoric man, nuclear power seems mysterious and therefore a suitable object of dread. Witch-hunting soon becomes institutionalised. In the 16th century, an ambitious clergyman knew he would not help his career by declaring suspected old ladies harmless; and he would do it a power of good by burning them. Similarly the modern witch-finder, the investigative journalist, knows that he must keep denouncing nuclear power even if he realises it to be quite safe – which, to be fair, given the stupendous technological ignorance of modern journalists, he probably does not.

A paradoxical reason for the fear of nuclear power is its unique ability to take precautions. Precautions scare people. An ambulance parked conspicuously on the beach and marked 'shark attack unit' would frighten bathers rather than reassure them. Nuclear power is able to take precautions and does so; coal is unable to take them and does not. When you have been working near the reactor, you are scanned for radioactive contamination because it is so easy to do so; when you have been working in a coal mill, you are not examined for particle penetration of the deep lung tissue because it is difficult to do so. It is quite easy to collect and store nuclear waste and so it is done. It is impossible to collect and store coal waste and so it is not done. The nuclear safety measures are highly visible and make people nervous.

There are passionate and articulate pro-nuclear voices within the nuclear industry but these voices are deliberately silenced by the industry itself. This was my biggest surprise on entering it. But it is easy to see why. The best argument for nuclear power is simply a comparison between its dangers and the dangers of all competitors, including the renewable sources, but mainly coal. (If you look at any pro-nuclear book you will always find it compares dangers. If you look at anti-nuclear books you will find they ignore most dangers of coal, such as cancer.) Nuclear stations usually belong to utilities, such as the CEGB, which make most of their electricity from coal. The dangers of coal are much greater than those of nuclear but less well publicised and of course the utilities want to keep it that way. When I first joined our nuclear section, I was asked to write a publicity blurb to attract young people to a career in nuclear power. I did so, and included a comparison between nuclear waste and coal waste. My blurb was published in full, except that all reference to coal waste was removed. Some people suspect that the power utilities are covering up a big secret about nuclear power. They are right. The big secret is that nuclear power is very much safer than coal.

Indeed if I were an engineer in the CEGB, I would be in trouble for this article. This is why I am coyly avoiding naming my country or utility. If privatisation in Britain were to mean the nuclear power stations becoming independent of the coal ones and competing against them, then the proponents of nuclear power would be free to go onto the attack and the British people would soon hear what the people in the industry already know, that coal stations are ecological time bombs.

For me, and I am not alone, the most wonderful artefact of our civilisation is the steam locomotive and I am sure that coal's magnificent machines will remain in the folk memory of our race long after they have been condemned to scrapyards and museums. There is nothing in nuclear power that can match the romance and splendour of the coal age. Nuclear power is a bit of a bore but it has arrived, perhaps at the eleventh hour, to offer us salvation from looming ecological disaster. If we do not take up its offer, our grandchildren and their grandchildren will neither understand us nor even forgive us.

11 February 1989

Chapter 7
FAITH AND CHARITY

NOTEBOOK

Alexander Chancellor

Like so many churches nowadays, the church of St Laurence at Affpuddle in Dorset possesses a Visitors' Book which lies open on a chest-of-drawers next to the vestry. There is a pencil beside it to encourage the shy or the idle, and each page includes a column headed 'Remarks'. I wandered into the church last weekend and was arrested by one of the first 'remarks' I saw. 'Something from Aladdin's cave!' it said. How odd, I thought. It is certainly a charming little church, mostly 15th century and some of it earlier, but striking more for its simplicity than for any pantomime glitter. So I read on. 'Old and nice.' Yes, that seemed more appropriate. So did 'Plain but sweet', though I didn't care for the patronising tone. 'Artistic.' (I suppose so.) 'Intimate.' (Small, certainly.) 'Not changed in 20 years.' (Good heavens, I should hope not.) The largest number of visitors to the church found it 'Peaceful', 'Restful', and things like that, though one found it merely 'Cold'. 'Cold but interesting', wrote another more encouragingly. I was surprised by how many people were obsessed with the church's smell; I sniffed around but could find nothing unusual. However, I read several entries saying things like 'Smells lovely', 'Smells beautiful' before coming across the reason for all this excitement: 'Smells of Pledge'. There were those who did not seem to realise they were in a church. 'Beautiful grounds,' wrote one, referring presumably to the graveyard. But the oddest by far of all the comments was the single word 'Useful'. I offer this to the vicar as the text for his next sermon.

20 September 1980

EASY-GOING

A. N. Wilson

The Alternative Service Book 1980 *(SPCK/Cambridge)*
Since the new liturgies started to be foisted on us by the ecclesiastical
bureaucrats – somewhere in the year 1549 – it has been hard to know
whether to blame them more for their own shortcomings, or for the vitri-
olic, frequently ignorant protests they inspire from the conservative
ranks.

The present collection of new services, 1292 pages, bound together in
attractive plasticette, has already inspired more hysterical objections
than almost all the previous prayer-books, from 1549 to 1928, put
together. The objections have been on grounds of language, theology,
tradition, or because of the innate anti-clericalism which is so healthy a
feature of English life. The new rites have been called donnish, lower
middle-class, too Catholic, too Protestant, too short, too long, too ugly.
With such enemies, what book needs a friend?

Whether we accept its publishers' implication that its appearance is
the most important event since the Reformation, there will be, doubtless,
some extravagant clergymen who are going to buy it, so that most of us,
from time to time – at country weddings, or during the sermon at evensong – will find ourselves flicking through its pages and trying to find out
whether it yields anything odder or more fascinating than the Tables of
Kindred and Affinity, and the Thirty-Nine Articles, the Commination
against Sinners or The Churching of Women, which beguiled many a
day-dreamy hour in the old days while a voice droned on from some eagle
or pulpit.

Needless to say, the aforementioned items are not in the new book,
which is meant as a supplement to, not a replacement of, that of 1662.
The new church, heralded in by the new book, is going to be altogether
easier-going than the old one. If we may judge by the words it deliberately
omits, it is no longer necessary for baptismal candidates to renounce the
Devil, or to believe in the Apostle's Creed. The married need no longer
avoid fornication, nor need communicants be in love and charity with
their neighbours. Confirmation, always rather dull in the past, is to be
enlivened with the use of oil, as in various foreign rites. Criminal ordi-
nands will be pleased to note that their congregations are no longer asked

if any of them know 'any impediment or notable crime in any of these persons'; and that, having been made priests, they may also be called Presbyters, as in Scotland; or, if celebrating the Communion, 'the President', which has quite a ring of the White House (or of the Mothers' Union) about it.

The number of occasions when they can celebrate the Communion is almost countless. Gone are all those Sundays after Trinity which seemed the quintessential season of the old Church, to be replaced by Roman-sounding Sundays after Pentecost. In addition to the old Prayer Book Saints' Days, there are masses for St Joseph, St Mary Magdalen, and All Souls' Day; as well as Votives for Social Responsibility, for Civic Occasions, for the Blessing of an Abbot, or, simply, For Any Saint.

If you are wondering what sort of saint the compilers of the book had in mind, you have only to turn to the calendar at the beginning to see that it includes John Bunyan, James Hannington (Bishop of East Equatorial Africa), Josephine Butler (Social Reformer, Wife, Mother) and John Wyclif. Sometimes the committee has been swayed in a papalist direction and we find included in this motley list the names of Francis de Sales and St Teresa of Avila. Sometimes the Low Church have won the day and we are bidden to commemorate William Tyndale, or Thomas Cranmer. How little they would approve if we invoked them as saints. But, if we are not meant to do so, what are they doing in a list which includes Thomas More and St Patrick? Sometimes the committee evidently reached deadlock at lunchtime; what else could explain grotesquely euphemistic and ambivalent groups such as 'Saints and Martyrs of the Reformation Era'?

On a brief calculation, it would seem that, if you went to Communion only half as often as this book recommends, you would find yourself going two or three times a week. The old book suggested a minimum of three times yearly – once a week for priests. The Communion was considered too serious a thing to be received without rigorous preparation and self-examination. The danger is great, it taught, 'if we receive the same unworthily'. And, if the conscience could not be quieted by solitary self-examination, we were meant to seek absolution from some 'discreet and learned Minister of God's word'.

All this appears to have gone. Anglican congregations nowadays, like Roman ones, must enjoy the liturgical equivalent of 'chips with everything'. It is impossible for any occasion to pass, from an induction to a harvest festival, from a funeral to a synodical meeting, without some clergyman wishing to do what is called 'placing it in the context of the Eucharist'. Just as, in social life, 'calling' has gone out, and we all have to slave away cooking meals whenever we visit each other's houses, so it is hard to go to church, even in the evening, without some amiable clergy-

man, probably rather high church, getting up behind the altar and celebrating the communion service.

Do we all want it so often? And if we have it so often, will it not diminish our sense of its power and importance? In the Roman Church, the frequency of masses in the past did not mean that the faithful received communion any oftener than the Anglicans. Now, members of both denominations are gobbling round the altar rails as frequently as each other. Or
rather, the remnant of these denominations who still go to church. I
remember an old Roman priest saying to me when the new rites came in,
'Now, we only get the goody-goodies coming to church.'

Those who feel unworthy to receive communion, but a desire to worship God, will in future have to stay away. That is sad. Perhaps, too, those
with a strong sense of the Real Presence of God in His sacrament will feel
inhibited from attending frequently at services where there is so much
jollity and munching. High Mass, Matins, Evensong and Benediction –
the services of the church which were pure praise, have vanished, or are
vanishing. The new Service Book bids the worshipper 'pursue all that
makes for peace and builds up our common life'. Good. But there will be a
few empty places beside him, as he turns to shake hands with his neighbour. And not all those that stay away will do so for frivolous reasons.

29 November 1980

'50p to play this video of us singing a carol.'

MORE TRAVELLERS' TALES

Auberon Waugh

Stuck in a first-class railway carriage for seven hours between Paddington and Taunton on Friday, I fell into conversation with my neighbour, as travellers are wont to do. She was a little old lady from Aberdeen who turned out to have a whole bottle of brandy in her suitcase.

She said she was the daughter of a fisherman, drowned at sea. Her mother worked gutting herrings in a freezing factory until she was 65. Her husband, whom she planned to join in Plymouth, was a fishing captain. On his rare moments on shore – in Aberdeen – he was also captain of the local lifeboat. In their home was a buzzer: within three minutes of the buzzer being sounded, the lifeboat, fully manned, was charging down the ramps into the sea.

At least I think that is what she said. She was also president or chairman of the Scottish women's branch of the Lifeboat Institution, or something of the sort. And she was *furious* that the widows and orphans of the Penlee lifeboat were to receive such huge sums of money as a result of public hysteria. It would ruin their lives, she said with passion. Of course they should receive something – perhaps £50,000 held in trust for the children, with the income available to the widows. But when sums like £250,000 were being given out to each family, they simply would not know how to handle a bonanza on this scale.

Another member of our party – I think she owned and ran a hotel in Plymouth – claimed that the Mousehole widows had acknowledged this and proposed to give some of their jackpot to build a social centre for lifeboatmen or something of the sort. The lady from Aberdeen shook her head. In the blunt accents of the far north, she said that once they had got the money, they would not give a penny back. She knew these seafaring folk. They would spend it all, and be left more miserable than before. Many of the widows would remarry, and who would have the money then? It was wrrong, wrrong, wrrong . . .

Obviously she would have won any argument on any subject, after the bit about her ten-shilling-a-week fish-gutting widowed mother. In most first-class carriages, I imagine, she would have carried the day on the point of whether £250,000 was too much for a working-class family. People with aching social consciences do not usually travel first class. If they were discussing the matter in second class, it would have been to repeat, with little compassionate whining noises and much tongue-clicking, the opinion shouted from every single newspaper in the country, and echoed by our drivellingly inept Attorney-General, that the widows and orphans should receive every penny subscribed, without remission of income tax, capital transfer tax or any of the other diabolical inventions which politicians have contrived to torment the rich.

For my own part, I held no very strong view on the matter. As someone who has nearly always enjoyed good luck, I could scarcely grudge the widows and orphans of brave men a windfall of this sort. My first appearance on television was as a grinning urchin at the scene of the Lynmouth flood disaster. I was eating a banana. There, public sentiment ran so strong that any farmer who lost a chicken was able to claim about £60 for it. The government of some friendly country – I think it was Ghana – sent a boatload of bananas to relieve their distress, and these were handed out to all on the scene, including sightseeing ghouls like myself. Bananas were still rather a luxury then – I don't suppose the sailors' orphans in Aberdeen saw many – but I got one. No wonder I was grinning.

It is true that Aberfan made me slightly queasy, as Welsh villagers squabbled over what grotesquely inflated sum they should receive in compensation for their lost kiddies, but this was probably just hatred of the Welsh. They should have *paid* the Coal Board for saving them so much money. Princess Margaret gave them a good lead by sending them teddy bears instead of money, even if she was a little late. And I was nauseated by the thalidomide episode, but chiefly by the self-righteousness of the *Sunday Times*, demanding ever more huge sums of other people's money to compensate for a misfortune which might have befallen any of us. This vulgar identification of human tragedy with huge sums of money was something one should resist, I felt – but obliquely, perhaps, rather as a lonely sniper will pick off random enemy targets without any clear idea of his contribution to the total war effort, or even any certainty that others are still waging it.

But nobody who lives in the modern world can grudge the football pool winner, even if some forms of winning the football pools may involve the death or mutilation of a loved one. There is simply too much money floating around. Tens of millions of pounds are spent on a road improvement scheme, or a new comprehensive school to replace better buildings in a better school already existing, or to change the name of half a dozen ministries after some government reshuffle. If some of this money did not occasionally fall off the back of the state juggernaut into the lap of an undeserving proletarian, public resistance to the society which politicians have created for themselves would be that much sharper. As Lord Hailsham might say (if he can still speak), our beloved national institutions would be at risk. The ordinary educated private citizen may not give a tinker's curse for any of Lord Hailsham's institutions – the Houses of Parliament, the Inns of Court, the Lord Mayor and Corporation of the City of London – but so long as they can keep the Hailshams of this world happy and occupied and out of our way, it would be a foolish man who urged their destruction. The increasingly obtrusive activities of such would-be Hailshams as Michael Havers, Tony Benn and Erin Pizzey suggest that all is not well in the world of 'leadership' people.

But the chief lesson of Mousehole must surely be that there is still an enormous amount of spare money floating around in the private sector. All this talk of cash shortage is so much hot air, or at most applies only to a small part of the population. No doubt a few penniless old age pensioners were so taken up in the general hysteria that they sent a crumpled, Kit-e-Kat-stained £5 or £10 note from their pitifully inadequate pensions as a sincere token of some profound emotion. But the majority of the money *must* have come from the indulgence of a passing whim. Nobody can seriously have supposed that the widows and orphans were going to starve. Gifts were the emotional equivalent of buying a box of chocolates. A better and nobler way of spending money, of course, but in terms of instant satisfaction very much the same.

The full measure of this spare cash is something which neither the newspapers nor television will ever discover, unless we are prepared to look into our own private arrangements for survival. Another of my companions on Saturday was an insurance broker, with an office in one of London's less favoured suburbs and another in Taunton. He had the jovial, impenitent air of a self-made man, and I hope he will not take it amiss – since I see in him a new friend for life – if I suggest he was slightly plumper even than the average New Briton in the street. Hearing that I lived some miles from Taunton, he offered to drive me through the blizzards and the ten-foot snowdrifts to my home, saying he had a special 19-gear, four-wheel-drive automatic vehicle which he brought out only in snowstorms. Normally he drove a Rolls-Royce like everyone else. A guest at my house identified it as a machine made by General Motors for use in the deserts of the Middle East, costing about £17,000 at the time. On the way, he asked his wife if his six-inch-thick rope was in the back. In some alarm, I asked him what he wanted it for. He replied that he always carried one in a snowstorm in case he met someone stuck who needed a tow. My conclusion was that Britain is still a rich, caring, sensible nation. But you have to be stuck for seven hours in a first-class railway carriage to discover this important fact.

16 January 1982

LEAVING YOUR MIND BEHIND

Roy Kerridge

Bhagwan Shree Rajneesh, leader of the Orange People, is no ordinary Indian guru. The things that other priests either forbid or forgive, he insists on. Sannyasins, or followers, are expected to drink, smoke, swear and indulge in casual sex.

Some friends of mine had 'taken sannyasin', no doubt surprised to learn that their normal behaviour was in reality a Holy Meditation, and they had been issued with Indian names, every boy a Swami and every girl a Ma. Few, if any, Indians join the cult, which takes its nickname from the orange clothes once worn, sold at the Bhagwan Boutiques. The uniform is now maroon red, and perhaps one day sannyasins will be known as Purple People. I was urged to spend a weekend at Medina, formerly Herringswell Manor, the cult's stately home in Suffolk. Bhagwan now lives on a ranch in Oregon, but he is supposed to be at Medina in spirit, where he sits invisibly in a sacred easy chair.

It was a fine spring evening when I set out for Medina, and I swung jauntily along beneath an avenue of beech trees, my pyjamas in a plastic carrier bag and a song on my lips. Soon an eerie mock-Tudor water tower loomed before me like a turret on a fort. A stud farm for racehorses adjoined Medina, convincing me more than ever that this was really a case for Jeffrey Bernard. Dusk fell before I reached the late Victorian manor house, built for the racehorse magnate whose heirs no doubt huddled beneath the water tower.

In the hall hung a notice reading 'Leave Shoes and Minds Here'. I took a firm grip on my mind and proceeded. Marred only by large photographs of the bearded Bhagwan everywhere, the interior was a model of opulence and good taste, with leather-bound chairs, oak panelling and potted ferns in hanging baskets. Before long I was signed up for a course in Self Experience and shown to my room, where a mattress and blankets lay on the floor. 'There's a disco tonight in the Omar Khayyam pub next to the Great Hall,' I was told, so I went along to see.

Squeezing into the packed room, where the bar did a roaring trade, I saw the red-clad sannyasins leaping wildly about, while others cuddled in corners. I looked round for Bernard Levin, said to be a convert to this cult, but could not find him. A record player boomed out a song called 'There Ain't Nothing Like a Gang Bang'. Altogether it was a scene of debauchery only equalled by every other disco I have seen on any Friday night in any town anywhere in Britain. Whatever happened to the waltz?

One or two of the young men looked arrogant and sensual, but most of them were mild and may have been scholarly before they had left their minds behind. There was no intellectual life in Medina as far as I could see. Everyone took for granted that they must do everything Bhagwan wanted, as if he were Jehovah to their Chosen People.

Preparing for bed, I found that there was a communal bath and shower room, where naked couples larked around splashing each other. A spiv I know in Brighton runs a mixed sauna, and I now realise that if he called it a Meditation Retreat he could treble the entrance fees.

'I've got these red marks – it's the acupuncture,' a bearded young man told me. A blonde girl without a stitch on walked past us, but he never batted an eyelid. 'When they tear the pins out, it tends to hurt a bit.'

Next morning I and nine others sat on cushions while our Self Experience teacher instructed us in Dynamic Meditation. We were a mixed bunch, mostly in our thirties, and included a freckle-faced housewife from Lowestoft, a fat bald man with a curly black beard and a childish face, who later confessed to being 'infatuated with all women', and a tragic yet defiant-looking girl whose short spiky hair somehow accentuated her Edwardian drawing-room features. Everyone except myself had been there before, and some worked there.

Our teacher also had an Indian name, but I shall call him Dave. He looked like a Dave somehow, wiry, tough and bearded, the sort of person you see tinkering with a motorbike while rock music blares from a transistor. From the beginning I regarded him as an enemy. His lecture on the Dynamic Meditation, which turned out to consist of snorting, screaming, barking, standing in silence and finally dancing, was peppered with four-letter words. Spoken deliberately, they sounded very odd, and I later found that a Bhagwan tape of therapeutic effing-and-blinding was being offered for sale in the Medina shop.

After the snorting, 'breathing outwards with the whole body, but not inwards,' came the screaming. We were issued with blindfolds, but I insisted on keeping my spectacles on underneath, claiming that they were an integral part of my Self. This was uncomfortable, but as the blindfold was kept askew, only Dave and I could see what was going on. He told us to do whatever we felt like. Everyone at once rolled around on the floor screaming and savagely fighting the scattered cushions. Picking up a cushion, I hurled it at Dave's head and scored a bulls-eye. Turning in surprise, he copped another cushion right between the eyes.

The Edwardian girl was having a severe fit of hysterics, having taken on two cushions at once, but another well-aimed cushion soon snapped her out of it. Dave ran over to me. 'You're supposed to do whatever you like in relation to yourself, not to others,' he hissed.

After this Meditation came an Awareness Walk. Forming into couples, we were sent out into the beautiful grounds, with orders to speak non-stop for half an hour apiece on whatever we were aware of at the moment. I was paired with the sad-eyed Edwardian girl, who had a sensitive nature, and was chiefly aware of buds and unfolding leaves on the trees in the woods. Every sentence was supposed to begin with 'I am aware of ...' but she kept forgetting and exclaiming 'Oh look, these buds are dark on one side and pale on the other!'

A botanist was lost when, in her own words, she 'fell in love with Bhagwan'. If society had not crumbled, and we were Edwardians, she would have enjoyed pressing leaves and painting in water colours. When it was my turn, I became Aware of a dear little house in the undergrowth, made from discarded cinema screens by the Medina children, and we ended up sitting cosily inside while I entertained my companion with shadow pictures on the screen walls. This was an art I learned years before from the *Children's Encyclopaedia*. Good old Arthur Mee never lets you down, and the Encyclopaedia is still a guide for any circumstance.

After this idyll came a vegetarian lunch, and then we confronted Dave once more. This time we were formed into couples again, and from his aggressive four-letter chat, with references to 'your lover', it appeared that converts were being enticed to take further and more expensive courses by the promise of sensual delights.

I had to dance with the freckled Lowestoft housewife, whose absent husband was 'not interested in religion', and probably imagined her to be praying and fasting. Then we were blindfolded, spun around and told to find one another. Many of the Bhagwan's 'meditations' were pretentious versions of childhood games, and after Blind Man's Bluff came Cosmic Pass the Parcel, Therapeutic 'Simon Says' and Neo-Reichian Musical Chairs.

'You have a Psychic Bond with your partner, and can find him or her blindfolded across a crowded room,' Dave announced. 'You will probably be friends for life, or else enemies. Embrace when you find one another, and remember, when you are together once more, you are at Home.' I waited impatiently while my blindfolded partner embraced someone else, not very flattered to note that she later identified me by sniffing.

Dave told us all to remove the blindfolds and sit on the floor facing our Psychic Partner. Each had to ask the other, 'Who are you?'

'My name's Roy, a bloke, aged 40, brought up near Wembley,' I told the freckled one, who asked the question first.

'What do I do now? He keeps giving the wrong answer,' she asked Dave anxiously.

'Just keep on asking,' he advised, but I could do no better. Then it was her turn, and I saw, with admiration, how the job ought to be done.

'I am Truth, I am Space, I am Mystery,' she began in her East Anglian accent. 'I am Me. I am You. I am Silence. I . . . I am getting a little confused, actually. I'm always confused for two months after I leave here, and then I feel wonderful and come back again.'

'Don't you think it just takes two months for the effects to wear off?' I inquired, but she didn't think so. The dancing and leaping about gave her considerable pain, and I wished she would go back to her husband. I tried to imagine their home life together.

He: 'Could I have some toast, dear?'

She: 'I am Time! I am the Universe! Gerrit yourself, you gurt idle oaf. I am All-Knowingness . . .'

Muttering 'That's a lot of squit!' and other Lowestoftian expressions, he slams his way out of the house and enrols for a course of Self Realisation with the glamorous Ma Prem Anandibear (formerly Doreen). So the fabric of the home is being destroyed.

No more was said of the Psychic Bond after this, and we were all partnered with others later on, for more soul-searching questions. Most of the girls seemed to want a varied sex life and a steady partner at the same time. Bhagwan's substitute for marriage was called a 'relationship' and seemed insecure and impermanent. Many of the girls had haunted, spinsterish expressions. I felt very sorry for them, but could no more rescue them from Medina than I could from Fairyland. In old legends, Fairyland seems delightful at first but once you have eaten the food you can never leave, trapped in a false world of 'fairy glamour'. What seems to be a prince is really a hideous goblin, just as what seems to be the beloved Bhagwan at night turns out, in the morning, to be a stranger from Harlow New Town.

After their meditations, sannyasins sat talking of times when they had actually seen Bhagwan drive by in his white Rolls-Royce. A party of starry-eyed day visitors was shown around by an Orange guide, in stately home fashion, and I was able to slip a girl a note reading, 'Beware – Never Come Back.'

'Take a risk and have a treat,' Dave urged us at the end of the first day. 'For example, if you want to ask Ma Deva Geeta to go to bed with you, then just ask her! Take a risk and have a treat!' Ma Deva Geeta, sitting crosslegged on a cushion, looked down modestly.

My chosen risk was to break into the children's house, where I found the well-cared-for infants bouncing on their bunk beds in pyjamas. As a treat, I hope for all concerned, I told them bedtime stories. Unwittingly I won the gratitude of their parents, who seemed worried about leaving them in a commune of their own all day. Young housemothers cared for them, and their school seemed the equal of anything I had seen in the outside world.

Next day we had Sufi Whirling, which turned out to be spinning round and round until you fell to the floor unconscious or retching. My Psychic Partner of the previous day ricked something and was taken to the doctor sobbing in agony. Observing all through my 'blindfold', I took two spins and sat on a cushion, my fingers in my ears to drown the deafening, reverberating sound of Music of the Spheres apparently played on heaps of scrap metal.

'The Beginning drives you crazy,' Bhagwan intoned sepulchrally from a tape recorder. To conclude our course, a Sufi Dance was held, which would have surprised any ancient Persian philosophers present. A Bhagwan band played square dance tunes and we had to sing a ditty beginning 'I'm Just a Cosmic Cowboy'.

That night, sipping vodka in front of a log fire, I made small talk with a Swami and his Ma, a sannyasin couple who had been together for some years. Their sons had learned to read from hippie comics. While the man talked of his heyday in the late Sixties, his Swedish girl friend looked at me curiously. 'I should like you to go to bed with Swami and me tonight!' she commanded. This rather stunned me, but Swami nodded in agreement. What would Jeffrey Bernard have done? Before I could decide, the girl suddenly had a row with her Swami, and rushed out of the room.

So ended my course in Self Experience. As the Bhagwan himself remarks: 'How can you seek yourself? You are already that.'

8 May 1982

LETTERS

The Bhagwan factor

Sir: I should like to clarify a few very misleading points that Mr Kerridge made in his article of 8 May. First, Bhagwan Shree Rajneesh does not insist or expect that anyone should drink, smoke, swear or indulge in casual sex, as Mr Kerridge stated. Bhagwan does not offer any dogma whatsoever – no particular activity is expected of anyone, and his followers are free to choose to live as they choose, not as Bhagwan chooses.

Second, many Indians have become followers of Bhagwan. Recent figures for India suggest that there are well over 50,000 Indian sannyasins, far more than in England.

Third, the statements that 'there was no intellectual life at Medina, as far as I could see' and 'everyone took for granted that they must do everything Bhagwan wanted' seem to be an attempt to persuade the reader that the members of the Medina community are all stupid or duped. Bhagwan's followers do not put much value on abstract intellectualisation, this is true, but the 75 adults who live at Medina hold between them some 25 first degrees, 15 higher degrees (including four PhDs) and numerous diplomas and certificates. Each one of them has chosen to be with Bhagwan out of his or her own free will and is free to leave whenever he or she chooses. Most choose to stay – but Mr Kerridge has made no attempt to understand what it is that draws these people to Bhagwan. Yet he must have had every opportunity to do so.

People stay with Bhagwan because of the love, the joy and the acceptance that they find in his presence, and in the communities of his followers – qualities that are rarely experienced in our society. Mr Kerridge's article remained in the journalistic world of doubt and cynicism, and gave no hint of whether he was any richer at the end of his weekend of 'Self Experience' than he was before.

Swami Anand Veetmoha
Press Officer, Medina Rajneesh,
Herringswell,
Bury St Edmunds,
Suffolk   *22 May 1982*

THE POPE AND HIS PRINCELING

Peter Ackroyd

Canterbury

The pilgrims arrived in Canterbury, carrying their fold-up chairs in plastic Sainsbury bags; strange rumours on the train from London: 'You can't get into town without a permit. They say they've stopped all the cars for three miles . . . They've taken the door off the cathedral.' 'They' hadn't, in fact, but it was encased in scaffolding as if in danger of crumbling. Inside, the primarily Anglican congregation settle down in anticipation: lots of waves and smiles, clergymen clutching their tickets with that benign, slightly silly, expression which clergymen always seem to have.

When I was a boy, we entered church with a certain atavistic awe as if we were going into an echo-chamber of strange rituals and sorrowful renunciations. I can still recall the silence when the monstrance was shown to the people, and we were forbidden to look at it. We would sing hymns like 'Faith of our father, holy faith, we will be true to thee till death' – and then there was something about 'prisons dark' and flames. But that is the faith the Pope leads – here, in Canterbury Cathedral, the atmosphere was mild and comfortable, exuding the sort of muted satisfaction which one might find at a flower show.

But then the Pope arrived. They greeted him, with fanfares of trumpets and loud applause, like a returning king. It was described in the newspapers as 'moving' but it was more odd than anything else; the enthusiasm seemed out of place and somewhat extravagant – like the sound of applause in an English cathedral, like the scarlet of the cardinals' robes and the Pope's cape which seemed almost pagan beside the sombre greys and blacks of the Anglican clergymen. (There is a passage in Nathaniel Hawthorne about scarlet as the colour of blood and of desire.) It was a highly theatrical occasion.

The papacy itself is the supreme emblem of religion as theatre, and there is no doubt that the present Pope fills his role to great effect – the impassive countenance, the deliberate economy of his gestures, the way his voice rises in blessing or in denunciation; when the Archbishop of Canterbury mentioned Poland, he tilted his chin upwards and gazed sombrely at the vaulted roof. Beside him Archbishop Runcie seemed a plaintive and whimsical figure, with a tremulous voice – the voice of the mad aunt who is allowed downstairs at tea-time.

One had only to witness the scenes at Southwark Cathedral to recognise the extraordinary power of the Pope. The sick and the dying stretched out their arms to clutch at him, and they wept when he anointed them with holy oil. It is a primitive faith, perhaps – the 'laying on of hands' is an archaic ritual quite un-Christian in origin – but it is a mark of the significance of this man that he can still embody such faith. It is a matter of semantics only whether you describe his power as 'spiritual' or 'political', since we are dealing here with responses which reach beyond that division; and, more importantly, it is not a distinction which the Church, or the Pope, can in fact acknowledge. When the crowds wave their banners and shout 'We Love You', they are paying homage to a man who enunciates principles which must have a marked effect in the temporal sphere and whose purpose is to affect the disputes and procedures of the political world. When he travels to Argentina, he will no doubt speak of the dangers of communism and the perils of too close a relationship with the Soviet Union – is that a political, or a spiritual, stance? The question is meaningless.

When Pope John Paul describes his journey to England as a 'pastoral visit', he means quite simply a visit to the people. His is an unashamedly populist stance – he is addressing the people over the heads of their rulers, and reminding them of the principles and perceptions which may be at direct variance to the professed aims of those rulers. In his first minutes in England he called for 'peace' in the South Atlantic and, in Coventry on Sunday, he castigated those who use war as a method of resolving international disputes. It may be couched in the language of eternity but the message is a quite specific one – that the British Government has erred in a fundamental way, that it has abrogated those values which people come in their thousands to hear him confirm. It might be called an 'interference' in the affairs of government except that the Pope feels himself obliged to interfere in such a manner:

> 'To condemn kings, not serve among their servants,
> Is my open office.'

These are the words of Thomas Becket, from Murder in the Cathedral, a man of authority who stood out against the State and who sought a martyr's death. Perhaps it was fitting that it should be at Becket's shrine that the Pope prayed on Saturday.

Just as it is misleading to separate the 'political' from the 'spiritual' role of the Pope, so it is wrong to divorce the 'pastoral' and the 'ecumenical' aspects of his visit. They are part of the same mission. The Pope is claimed to be, after all, 'Christ's Vicar on earth' and so by definition he is the pastor of all peoples, whether they choose to recognise the fact or not. His 'flock' cannot be limited to the Catholic community – he is God's representative, and God has no constituency. So it was that, in his Canterbury sermon, he declared that he brought to the Anglican communion 'the good will of all who are united with the Church of Rome, which from earliest times was said to "preside in love"'. He could not have made it plainer: he had come to reclaim his own.

It was doubly unfortunate, then, that the present Archbishop of Canterbury should seem so palpably the smaller figure, a princeling who has erred but who may by a mixture of toughness and, for him, face-saving diplomacy be allowed to return to the fold and bring England, 'the dowry of Mary', back with him. If the Anglican church decides to move towards 'unity', the tenets of its faith are not so strongly held or clearly defined that they can withstand the moral authority of such a man as the Pope or the faith which he has used both as a shield and a weapon against those who doubt the Catholic Church's role.

But there is something else to be said. Although the Pope and his Church deny any real separation between spiritual and political affairs, there is no doubt that we all live as though one existed. It was perhaps fortunate that the Pope arrived during the war in the Falklands; that crisis, and the attendant emotions which it has elicited in the country, have demonstrated as nothing else could, the limits of the Pope's actual authority – the boundaries, if you like, of his spiritual appeal. In confrontation with the undoubted nationalistic convictions and fervour which this dispute had evoked, his power fades – and it fades in precisely that area where, by contrast, the Anglican faith grows stronger. Archbishop Runcie, after all, supported the sending of the task force, and in so doing he confirmed the role of the Anglican Church as the spiritual arm of the State. A vulgar but not inapposite analogy might be made between the Pope and the EEC. The Anglican Church's identity is essentially the identity of the nation – the country's interests are also its interests. Only if we were to lose, or neglect, that identity and those interests would the Pope's compelling message also seem to be a compulsory one.

5 June 1982

IS THE CHURCH DEAD?

A. N. Wilson

Emerging from the cool of the cathedral, a flurry of black-habited nuns waddled sweatily into the scorching sunlight of the cloister courtyard, keeping custody of the eye as they passed a Franciscan friar, impervious to the heat and reading a newspaper. An Italianate scene, but enacted at Christ Church Oxford on Friday last. Had any of the canons of Christ Church alive in 1833 witnessed it, they would have assumed that their college had been visited by a party of continental ecclesiastics, and no words would describe their incredulity if they learnt that all these visitors, so fantastically arrayed, were protestants of the Church of England.

Oxford was full of pilgrims and sightseers, come to celebrate the 150th anniversary of an Assize Sermon, preached by John Keble at St Mary's. This famous homily protested against the suppression of ten Irish bishoprics, and by implication attacked the religious indifferentism which had allowed the passing of the Catholic Emancipation Act of 1829 and the Reform Bill of 1832. It was a high Tory counterblast to the perils of radicalism and, read today, it seems as quaint as the utterances of Archdeacon Grantly.

The monks and nuns had been swanning decoratively about Oxford all week for a conference; and on Thursday 14 July, the very anniversary of Keble's sermon, one of them advanced into the pulpit where it was preached to deliver his own attack on 'National Apostasy'. This was Archbishop Trevor Huddlestone, the Mirfield firebrand and scourge of apartheid. Keble had seen any diminution of the authority of the Church of England, the unique representative of Christ's Church in this land, as a symptom of secularism. Huddlestone was applauded by his congregation for bemoaning the 'parochialism' of the national church. 'If the Church of England is not free to be the Church, it is better that it should die.' He finds ecumenical dialogue with other churches 'wearisome'. 'It is interfaith ecumenism – the recognition that dialogue between Hindu and Christian, Muslim and Christian, Buddhist and Christian must have priority', words which would have given Keble apoplexy.

On Friday night, the faithful thronged to St Mary Magdalen's Church, whose north aisle was built to commemorate the Protestant martyrs of the Reformation, to hear a very different sort of prelate preach a very different sort of sermon. The building was packed, and the air was heavy with incense and after-shave lotion, as the Bishop of London stood in the pulpit in his high Roman mitre. He spoke of the 119th Psalm, which had been the prayer of Our Lord, and which was dear to the fathers of the Oxford Movement. The Psalm, like the Movement, is a call to personal holiness, obedience to the laws of God. He spoke with scorn of those modern churchmen who think that they can 'discern the will of God' by sitting on committees and discussing such questions as the lawfulness of divorce with no reference either to Scripture or to the traditions of the Church. One felt that, though he would have been surprised, not to say scandalised, by the bishop's outfit, Keble's bosom would have returned an echo to Graham Leonard's words.

After the mass, there followed an all-night vigil of prayer in St Mary Magdalen's, with the Holy Sacrament exposed in a monstrance which had belonged to Lord Halifax. On Saturday morning, another blazingly hot day, everyone trooped to the University Parks for an open-air mass, con-celebrated with 200 priests clad in curious Mexican-poncho-style chasubles, by the Archbishop of Canterbury. The local papers had been predicting crowds of anything up to 100,000, but I have seen the Parks more crowded for cricket matches. Optimists said there must have been 2,000, but most of them were clergymen. The order of service, inevitably, was from the Alternative Book, and the musical accompaniment was largely from *100 Hymns for Today*. There was a faintly pathetic attempt to recall the atmosphere of last year's papal jamborees – one even noticed a faint Polish accent creeping into Dr Runcie's locutions – and the crowd clapped his arrival with a slightly giggling sense of how English they were being. He preached an intelligent, somewhat Muggeridgian homily, contrasting the illusory hopes of happiness held out by the modern liberal creed and the joy which was theirs who trod the Way of the Cross. The Eucharist followed, the altar groaning with dozens of chalices. (A man next to me, brought along by his pious wife, exclaimed, 'He surely isn't going to drink all that!') Then the Bishop of Oxford read out a friendly message from the Vatican. When the last Mexican poncho had disappeared from the park gates, the scene became pure Barbara Pym, with toothy curates marshalling their bus-loads of doting crones for cheese-rolls and orange squash.

These Anglo-Catholic celebrations lacked any of the sunny confidence of the centenary celebrations of 1933, when crowds flocked to the White City Stadium for a splendid baroque High Mass celebrated by the Bishop of Colombo. All three Oxford sermons this week seemed to admit that the steam has gone out of the Movement. Though to outward appearances the Church of England is very like the Church of Rome, the chances of viable unity are surely very slight. The Bishop of Rome can easily post off bland telemessages to the Bishop of Oxford. But would he really admire Dr Rodger for turning a blind eye to nonconformist ministers presiding at Anglican altars in his diocese? Would the Pope be able to absorb into his communion a church which last week authorised the remarriage of divorced persons; which takes a wishy-washy line about abortion; which is about to admit women to the order of deacons and which is in communion with those who ordain women to the priesthood? And what of the Anglican Evangelicals, who would view the high mariolatry of Anglo and Roman Catholics with abhorrence? What of the Anglican theologians who, having discarded any belief in the Incarnation or the Trinity, seem to have abandoned belief in God Himself? One thinks of Belloc's comment that to speak of the union of the Church of England with the Church of Rome is like talking about the union of the Carlton Club with the Club of Hercules; you are using the same word for two things quite different in kind.

The example and words of John Keble and his friends led to an enormous enrichment of the National Church, and no one can contemplate with cynicism the saintly lives of the Anglo-Catholic slum priests, nor the founders of the Anglican religious orders. But the cost of all this 'revival' was that the National Church, reasonably cohesive when Keble preached his sermon, broke up into an ill-fadged collection of sects and parties. Before the Tractarians, every member of the Church of England held roughly the same beliefs, accepted the same liturgy and ceremonial. Nor could it be said that a Church which nourished William Law, Samuel Johnson, Bishop Wilson of Sodor and Man, or Keble himself was devoid of spirituality or divine grace. The history of the Oxford Movement over the last 150 years has seen the development of that spirituality in lives of high sanctity and practical goodness. But it has also been a story of lunatic sectarianism, squabbles about incense, obsession with vestments, and a bitchiness unparalleled since the days of Queen Anne and Sarah Duchess of Marlborough.

Keble's sermon raised a mare's nest. It also raised an idea of holy and divine society on earth, coherent in doctrine, unified in its liturgy and ordinal. It was an idea which changed the life of Keble's greatest disciple, John Henry Newman. And when the Pope's telegram was read out to the crowds on Saturday, there must have been many who thought of Newman's lonely years at Littlemore and his submission, having met no Roman Catholic and attended no Catholic worship, to the ultimate logic of the Tractarian position.

An Anglican friend wrote to Newman some years after his secession to

Rome and boasted to him of how 'advanced' the churchmanship had now become in Anglo-Catholic circles. He described a High Mass, with deacon and subdeacon. Newman replied affectionately but added, 'Let me hear no more nonsense of deacons and subdeacons. Tell me about the Church of England I know and love.' That Church of England, which Newman had learnt from Keble how to love, was dealt a mortal blow by Keble's sermon. But it was not until our own day, with the destruction of the Book of Common Prayer, that it died completely, and forever.

23 July 1983

GREAT SIGHS OF TODAY

John Osborne

When I mention religion, I mean the Christian religion; and not only the Christian religion, but the Protestant religion; and not only the Protestant religion but the Church of England. Tom Jones

About ten years ago, I resumed regular church-going after a long lapse. It was doubtless feeble of me not to have done so before but, although I was aware that I had never properly abandoned my faith, I did not want to subject it to the derision of a couple of frivolously rabid churchless wives. There are times when I feel God needs protecting from the likes of me. He doesn't deserve it, nor bringing Him into the house on the wintry boots of a lone visit to Evensong. Even now, my present, devout Geordie companion snaps at me each Sunday around noon: 'Are you talking to God this evening or not?' If I am locked in the passages of some hardy gloom, I say no.

It's a good question. If I have nothing jolly or interesting to offer, I don't see why I should waste His time. Or mine. One can anticipate the smarmy sky-pilot's objections to this. 'God doesn't mind you boring Him. You see, God loves bores like everyone else.' Just so.

Apart from my own doctrinally invalid sensibilities, there was a much more preposterous block to Evensong. In three openly dishonest words: the Alternative Service Book. When I moved away from London and, I hoped, its picket Evangelicals, its mob of reverse-collared social workers, all in an aggressive funk about the fiction of living in a multi-racial society and other loving Christian cant I looked for the rigour and spirit I had resisted so fiercely as a Bradlaugh-like Victorian atheist teenager.

I had urgently read *The Freethinker*. I had refused confirmation at my rather cranky boarding school, and was subjected to weekly grillings by the chaplain, as nasty and bullying a clergyman as you'd meet in a dozen General Synods. Why is it that so many clergymen seem unfeeling for others, unlike, say, professional soldiers who are often such Christian gents? They grind on about absurd, insoluble abstractions like the Third World and put up prayers for them, while ignoring their own parish loners, who may be suffering spiritual murder without complaint or comfort.

I have never myself sought comfort, except in its strictest theological sense, and I don't expect to be treated like some punk on probation. It is tricky to talk of faith or God to an unbeliever. So it is with your ASB clergyman. Bishops find it an embarrassment. It is like talking to a homosexual about sex, or love, even.

No one asked us if we wanted to live in Humberside, Avon or Tyne and Wear. We were told. As we were with ASB and NEB. Legislation by contemptuous stealth. Only bureaucrats or loons can be vigilant all the time. Not human beings, who get drunk, forget the day of the week or fail to recognise their ex-wife.

When the Marquess of Hartington was asked what was the proudest day of his life, he replied that it was when his finest pig won first prize at Skipton Fair. My only similar success is that, after ten glum years, I was instrumental in restoring the Book of Common Prayer to Evensong in my parish church. As the local paper put it: 'The decision was taken because some church members have expressed reservations in recent months about the use of the yellow booklet for all services.'

It's a puny achievement and is advertised as being celebrated at 18.30 hours. The hi-de-hi of the squalling Family Service at 9.30 hours is as unassailable as pub lager. Matins is no more. Yet it is still an amazing reward from the time when I found myself facing three guitar-playing Polyslobs after the Second Collect and hearing, even more painfully, 'When I was a child, I spake as a child . . .' translated into: 'When I grew up, I had finished with childish things. Now we see only puzzling reflections in a mirror, but then we shall see face to face.'

Many of us have made our Great Bores lists of vindictive and provocative clerical vandalism, some even more offensive because of their very slightness. This, for Ash Wednesday: 'Jesus told a parable which *aimed at* those who were sure of their own goodness and *looked down* on everyone.' The language of housemaids and Open University. ('And he spake this parable unto certain which trusted in themselves that they were righteous and despised others.' Original.)

I have been to Evensong in about a dozen cathedrals during the past three years. With their glass front doors, their dinky shops, cafeterias, blackmailing notices, they all seem to use the RSV, boomed over in microphones to careless strangers. Worcester, York (one of the worst super-church-markets), Durham (and what to come?), Exeter, Salisbury, Chichester (very Habitat), Belfast and even Canterbury had all blandly succumbed to this born-again philistinism against which there seems no appeal.

The Turks of the ASB and RSV – such Nalgo names – have been politic and crafty, implying that it is all a matter of secularist aesthetics, irrelevant to the card-carrying worshipper. They are threatened by what is both inaccessible and open to mystery and enduring contemplation. Their committee-style graffiti give them licence to bluster and overbear. Most ordinary parishioners are intimidated by their unfeeling priests. They seem unempowered to argue with their titanic prognoses, just as they would feel with their GPs, and the Revd Rons and Teds inside their authoritative frocks know it all too well. Their flock is frightened almost unto death of being accused of the unchristian sin of dowdyism.

When I complained about Corinthians i.2. to the incumbent of the time, he looked astonished. 'Nobody's ever complained before,' he said. They didn't know how to, being used to harangues and harassment from these ungodly social workers with their collars turned the same way as their trousers should be. Many of them – like this one – are ex-airline pilots or car salesmen and computermen, rather like the new Tory MPs. Well, I did, for once in my faint-hearted life, persevere, and last summer the vicar promised me that those scraps of Series 3 booklets would be forever dumped. Thanks be to God and amen.

How did I win my equivalent of the pig at Skipton Fair? The answer, crudely, is blackmail, the one consummate gift still pursued and respected by the Church of England. The church needed a new roof. After the unease of years, plus a few stickers on cars and the feigned threat of unrenewed covenants, the murmurers found the tongues that had been taken from them.

It's only a beginning and it's not first prize. Doubtless I shall have to take my own King James Bible if I am again asked to read the lesson. The local newspaper notes that: 'The vicar hopes that churchgoers will revive the practice of taking their own prayer books to service in case there are not enough to go around.' But it's reassuring that with so little political resolve, skill or experience, so few can achieve as much.

One of my favourite passages in the Litany began: 'O God, Merciful Father, that despiseth not the sighs of a contrite heart, nor the desire of such as be sorrowful . . .' I think I was truly born with a contrite heart, an impatient though *not* a guilty one. So there, for the moment it is: Great Sighs of Today.

22 December 1984

GETTING AWAY FROM GOD

John Stewart Collis

We hear a great deal nowadays about the need for religion, even the need for a new religion – as if anything could be more absurd. And, of course, the phrase 'a Revival of Religion' never dies. 'Youth' is particularly taken up with this. The religion is going to help you to 'find yourself' or 'your identity'. There are plenty of fake saviours on hand – never have there been so many as in our day when the great official religions have lost their authority to such an extent.

I don't see much point in 'the Young' flattering themselves on their concern for religion, nor anything admirable in the way in which they hand themselves over to quacks of every kind. Often the 'saviours' are just psychological and psychiatric quacks, who are the worst of all, and seem to be multiplying every day.

What should they do? Go in for education. Learn to read. Take up solid study in history and anthropology, and then, or at the same time, concentrate upon the marvel of natural phenomena. They will find that they can do without the supernatural. If this is not enough for them, then surely their spiritual needs can be satisfied by the Catholic Church. It provides everything they could possibly need, including glorious buildings in which to attend imaginative rituals and hear magnificent liturgies, hymns and psalms. And if the difficulty of taking doctrine literally is too difficult for them in these modern times, they can still take it symbolically. In this sense the Mass is as real as the sunset and can enrich the soul as much as a personal mystical experience; and indeed, on that plane, it can be a religious experience, to be repeated – not too often, but whenever the inspiration is really needed.

In any case, all who have an ear for literature can continue indefinitely to glory in the Bible and Prayer Book. Unfortunately, most of the clergy are against this. They wish to scrap the Bible and Prayer Book. At present they have no power to ban it, but they wish to shelve it. In fact, they have already produced a substitute which they actually call the New English Bible. The idea behind the thing is that the Authorised Version may be at times a little difficult to understand. So let us make it plainer, they have said, more consonant with modern speech. Now we will bring it *nearer* to the man in the street.

In this they are mistaken. They do not bring it nearer. They make it *farther* off. We read the words, 'Come unto me all ye who are weary and heavy-laden and I will give you rest.' We may well rightly think that these words, though translated, could have been spoken ten thousand years ago. Indeed, they speak to us over the centuries in a miraculous way. If, instead of those words, we read: 'Not to worry. Everything will be all right. Come round to me and I'll help you to relax', we *know*, the simplest person knows, that they are modern words used only in our own day. They could never have been spoken by Jesus. His words are not brought nearer, they are quite simply *annihilated*. True, the phrase above is not what is substituted in the New English Bible. I invented it in order to make my point really clear.

Take a genuine and rather mild example of what has been done. 'A voice crying in the wilderness' has been changed to 'A voice shouting in the desert'. In the first version we have a phrase of outstanding appeal, if not terribly easy to define, save by stressing the obvious that the very 'crying' (which we take at once as 'crying out') is a verb of imaginative appeal and the noun 'wilderness' still more so. The overtones or undertones in the sentence are wonderfully evocative. 'Shouting in the desert' conjures up nothing, evokes nothing more than an angry oil man whose car has stuck in the sand.

In a quiet, though devastating critique of these translators, Robert Nye referred to them as 'serious and responsible men' by way of being polite. But seriousness is no passport to an understanding of art. These men, in the literal sense of the word, are illiterate – that is to say, they do not know what literature is. To them the destruction of a work of art is not noticed. If there was a public for it they would give us Shakespeare in verbal modern dress, with the same seriousness and sense of responsibility.

But these men are not only illiterate, they are so stupid that they could not see the pit that lay open before them. Of course this and that passage of the Bible are obscure and the language perhaps a bit too archaic, and it would be quite right to explain it and have footnotes in modern usage. But they could not see that as soon as they had decided to alter whole passages they would be faced with the necessity of altering *every* passage. For if they didn't do so and kept passages of the Authorised Version which were perfectly clear as well as beautiful, those passages just would not fit with the prosaic version. So every sentence had to be lowered. You couldn't say 'crying in the wilderness', you had to lower it to 'shouting in the desert'. You couldn't say, 'the lilies of the field, they toil not, neither do they spin, but Solomon in his glory was not arrayed like one of these', you had to take the poetry away in order that the terrible prose of the new version would not appear as tawdry as it is.

There is no department in the modern scene where the lust for violence and destruction is not evident. The clergy cannot very well hack down our cathedrals to make way for council houses; that wouldn't find full support.

But they can satisfy their feelings by destroying the Bible, with the added knowledge that it is amongst our greatest works of art.

22 December 1984

'Smoking or non-smoking?'

SAINT BOB

Alexander Chancellor

Should Bob Geldof be knighted or given the MBE? Should he be awarded the Nobel Peace Prize, or should he not? These are tricky questions which I am glad I am not called upon to answer. Mrs Thatcher's problem is the more difficult. If she gives him nothing, she will be hounded by the popular press until the next election and probably lose it. If she gives him a mere MBE – the honour Harold Wilson thought appropriate for the Beatles – she will be hounded hardly less. But if she has him knighted, she will appear opportunistic (and he ridiculous).

The Scandinavian notables on the Nobel Peace Prize Committee have an easier problem. They are ridiculous anyway, and Mr Geldof would be a worthier recipient of the award than several past winners, including Dr Kissinger and Mr Begin. At least he has not yet started a war. But the committee could be deterred from canonising any further Irish idealists by the disasters which befell the Ulster peace women after they received the prize.

Bob Geldof is an improbable saint. He has a lean and hungry look and is also, quite clearly, a tremendous bully. During the early stages of the *Live Aid* spectacular on BBC2 last Saturday he was furious that more money wasn't coming in from the people of Britain. Banging his fist on a table with disturbing violence, he commanded us to telephone various numbers immediately and pledge everything we could to the starving of Africa. I was so frightened that I called all the different numbers in London, only to find them permanently engaged. Finally I tried a number in Scotland, trusting in the Scots to be less easily hectored into parting with their money, but that was engaged as well. It was cruel of Mr Geldof to threaten us so without giving us the means of redemption.

All credit to him nevertheless for getting these vain, self-obsessed pop stars to entertain the world for free. And they did a terrific job. Wembley and the JFK stadium in Philadelphia pulsated with energy, and the miraculous to-ing and fro-ing between them by satellite made it more exciting still. The success of *Live Aid* has been taken as a tribute to the altruism of youth. Perhaps rightly so, but it is also amazing how old many pop heroes are. Saturday's stars included Mick Jagger and Paul McCartney, both over

40, and a very grey-haired group called The Who. It is a tribute to the broad-mindedness of the young that they continue to idolise such people.

20 July 1985

DIARY

Christopher Booker

I recently had occasion, in the space of four days, to visit three of Britain's great cathedrals – York, Salisbury and Wells. Each of these mighty buildings presented a striking scene of bustling activity. In Wells we enjoyed an excellent lunch in the new restaurant in the cloisters, and found the nave filled with the sounds of a tuner preparing a grand piano for that night's concert. In Salisbury the colourful scene included a visiting choir practising for Evensong. At York we had the chance to visit the workshop where Peter Gibson and one of the world's leading teams of stained glass experts are painstakingly reassembling the thousands of pieces of mediaeval glass cracked and splintered in the fire; while in the Minster itself, at the sound of St Peter's great bell at midday, the thronging crowds of tourists were momentarily silenced for a short informative speech of welcome and prayers from the pulpit. Not all the changes which have come over Britain's cathedrals in recent years may be to everyone's taste, such as the shops selling tea towels and the plastic boxes demanding entrance fees. But in the past decade or so many of these incomparable buildings have again become centres of spiritual and cultural life, in a way which would have once seemed unimaginable.

21 September 1985

'On the seventh day he got up late and washed the car.'

WHAT THINK THEY OF CHRIST?

Andrew Gimson

The Spectator Poll
THE SAMPLE

The 151 respondents were drawn from the City, business and industry, the trade unions, press and television, the universities, the law, medicine, the arts, the Civil Service and the Houses of Parliament. For this Poll only, the clergy were excluded. Field work was carried out by the Harris Research Centre between 19 and 28 November 1986.

Most of the British believe in God, but only one in ten goes to church with any frequency: that is confirmed by every poll on the subject, except for ours. The Spectator Poll, conducted among people holding senior positions (see above), did indeed show 74 per cent believing in God, comparable to the 79 per cent given in a poll of the population at large published in last Sunday's *Sunday Express*. It was, however, remarkable to find that nearly two-fifths of our respondents claim to attend church at least three Sundays in four, of whom well over half prefer traditional forms of service, and just over half the Authorised Version of the Bible.

This is an extraordinarily high figure for a church attendance by modern standards, even when we take into account people's capacity for wishful thinking. The energy which has helped to make those in the sample successful in their careers is likely to show itself in anything to which they set their minds, including religion. Religion may also possess greater social importance for them than for society as a whole. But maybe – a theory which seemed worth testing – they actually believe.

Certainly they still wish the churches to perform their rites of passage. Of our 151 respondents, 135 have been baptised and 108 want a church funeral, while 87 per cent of those married had been so in church, at least on the first occasion. Perhaps most interestingly, nine in ten of the married people had had, or intend to have their children baptised. A picture begins to form of a group more Christian than had been supposed.

Moreover, those who describe themselves as Christians give strong assent to certain traditional dogmas, some of which the Bishop of Durham has recently questioned. No fewer than 86 per cent said they believe that Christ's miracles actually happened. The figures for belief in other dogmas were:

	per cent
That Jesus is the Son of God	85
The Trinity	82
Heaven	81
That prayer can alter events on earth	80
That Christ's body rose from the dead	69
The Virgin Birth	64
Hell	55

Roman Catholics were notably more attached to the last three of these dogmas than anyone else, but otherwise the main fluctuation, across all denominations, was between those who go to church regularly and those who go seldom.

When we came to examine faithfulness to particular churches, the answers were far less reassuring, at least for the Church of England. Having established that three-quarters of the poll believe in God, 15 per cent are agnostic and 11 per cent atheist, we asked which denominations they belong to: 42 per cent said Anglican, 19 per cent other Protestant churches, 13 per cent Roman Catholic, and 24 per cent described themselves either as lapsed or as without religious denomination. There were also two Jews and a Hindu.

Those with an Anglican upbringing were much more likely to have lapsed than people of any other denomination. Only 55 of the 82 childhood Anglicans remain so, compared to 18 of the 19 Roman Catholics, and ony five of the Anglicans who left have joined other churches, though four others still believe in God. What is more, among those Anglicans who remain, six said they were agnostic and two declared themselves atheists. Anglicans are also least constant in their attendance at church: only 42 per cent of them claim to go at least three Sundays in four, compared to 54 per cent of other Protestants and 75 per cent of Roman Catholics.

And although the Christians had shown themselves so orthodox when asked what the Church should say, what dogmas it should uphold, this was balanced by overwhelmingly liberal opinions about what the churches should do. Just over half of our 151, Christians and non-Christians, think the churches 'should uphold traditional teaching regardless of social trends', but only one in ten opposes the remarriage of divorced people in church, only 13 per cent oppose the ordination of women. These are both cases where the churches are under enormous pressure to follow social trends, and a majority of their own members wish them to do so, except in the Roman Catholic church, where opinion is evenly divided. On female ordination, one man spoke for many in our male-dominated sample: 'The whole male-dominated interpretation is now an outdated idea.'

The idea that the monarch must be an Anglican is also outmoded, even among Anglicans, 55 per cent of whom think that if Prince Charles became a Roman Catholic, he should still be allowed to succeed to the throne. Only a quarter of all respondents disagreed with that.

It would seem, indeed, that while people are favourably disposed to the clergy, and are often prepared to assent to the abstract propositions they make, they are neither willing for the churches to constrain their behaviour, nor even very interested in what they have to say. Most people regard a clergyman's social work as more important than his spiritual or sacramental duties: 'His work in the parish, visiting, his counselling, his comforting work. His visibility in the parish itself – not his sermons or what he does in church,' as one respondent put it. Very little anticlericalism could be detected: 71 per cent hold the clergy in very or fairly high regard, the Archbishop of Canterbury attaining a rather lower individual score of 64 per cent. Only four people would be 'not at all pleased'

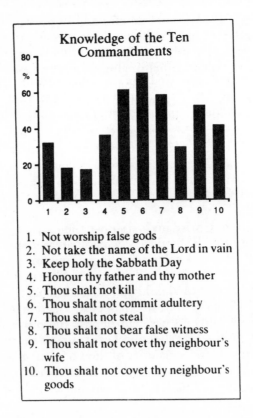

Knowledge of the Ten Commandments

1. Not worship false gods
2. Not take the name of the Lord in vain
3. Keep holy the Sabbath Day
4. Honour thy father and thy mother
5. Thou shalt not kill
6. Thou shalt not commit adultery
7. Thou shalt not steal
8. Thou shalt not bear false witness
9. Thou shalt not covet thy neighbour's wife
10. Thou shalt not covet thy neighbour's goods

if one of their sons became a clergyman, only eight would be 'not very pleased', though more would be surprised. Politeness underlain by indifference seemed to govern most replies. If Burke was right to say, 'Nothing is so fatal to religion as indifference, which is, at least, half infidelity,' then the churches have great cause for concern.

Nor is religious knowledge at a very high level. Readers may be amused to try these questions on themselves, their families or friends:

What were the gifts presented by the three wise men?
(83 per cent knew this: gold, frankincense, myrrh)
Why were Mary and Joseph travelling to Bethlehem?
(74 per cent: to register for the tax census)
How many of the Ten Commandments can you name?
(see adjoining table for the individual 'score' of each
Commandment: the most memorable were those about
adultery (70 per cent), killing (61), stealing (58) and not
coveting your neighbour's wife (52), the least memorable those
about bearing false witness (29), blasphemy (18) and keeping
the Sabbath (17). Only a quarter of people could manage more
than half the Commandments, including only 31 per cent of
Christians, though 55 per cent of Roman Catholics.)
What did Christ say were the two great commandments?
(42 per cent: love God and love your neighbour)
What event in Christ's life does the Communion service
commemorate?
(73 per cent: the Last Supper)
Who was mainly responsible for writing the Book of Common
Prayer?
(28 per cent: Cranmer)
What day does Easter Day commemorate?
(87 per cent: the Resurrection)
Who said the following:
'Forgive us our trespasses'?
(80 per cent: Christ)
'He hath put down the mighty from their seats and hath
exalted the humble and meek'?
(16 per cent: Mary)
'The Word was made flesh and dwelt among us'?
(31 per cent: St John)
'Am I my brother's keeper'?
(21 per cent: Cain)

For purposes of comparison, it is worth quoting an earlier survey, though the historian who cites it warns that it should not necessarily be taken at face value (England was, for example, changing from Latin to English as the language used in church):

> When in 1551 the new Protestant Bishop of Gloucester carried out a survey of the diocesan clergy he found that of 311 there were 171 who could not repeat the Ten Commandments, 27 who did not know the author of the Lord's Prayer, and ten who could not repeat it. (Keith Thomas, *Religion and the Decline of Magic*)

We have not asked the present Bishop of Gloucester to try these questions on his clergy, though we hope he may be inspired to do so, but can add to the results given above that only 11 of our 151 laity could mention all the Ten Commandments, while 22 could or would mention none.

But even if our own age does not have a monopoly of religious ignorance, ignorance is surely greater than would have been found a generation ago, and greater not only because learning by heart is less fashionable, but because the subject itself is considered less important. A surprisingly strong outward appearance of Christian belief among leading people in Britain is not accompanied by inner commitment. We found only a dozen who read the Bible daily, although a quarter say they pray daily, and most, including 12 of the 22 agnostics, pray in times of crisis: 'In difficult times, for inner peace,' one said. Another said: 'It is someone to talk to.' A third declared: 'Results come from prayer. When I need help with a problem, it's the asking and acceptance that gives help. I always have a positive response.'

In examining prayer, we had again stumbled upon evidence of faith among a larger minority of our elite than anticipated, but confirmation that for most Christianity is only taken seriously as a matter of last resort. The experience of an Anglican church where 25 people regularly worship but over 50 are on the flower rota, is more characteristic. This ability to support the church, but not by being Christian, is perhaps best summed up in the remark attributed to Lord Melbourne: 'While I cannot be regarded as a pillar, I must be regarded as a buttress of the church, because I support it from the outside.'

13 December 1986

GODFORSAKEN

Kingsley Amis

My grandparents were Baptists of the Denmark Hill Community in south-east London. My parents, who first met in chapel there, moved eventually away from the chapel and towards the church, like not a few English Nonconformists of that era, but by the time I started taking notice of such concerns they no longer visibly practised any religion. When I was a boy they took me to a few services, at Easter and at Christmas and on Armistice Day, but they never gave me religious instruction, told me to say my prayers or anything like that. This was policy much more than laziness; my father, laughably as I once thought, considered himself a rebel in these matters, an emancipator.

What I missed at home I was given at school, in the measure then prevailing: morning prayers, weekly Scripture (I got a credit in the subject in School Certificate) and, when the war transformed us from daily grammar school into boarding school, Sunday chapel. I had less in the way of religion than some of my contemporaries – no parish and no Sunday school – but more than others – Greek Testament in the Classical Sixth and, a less superficial experience, the chapel choir. This I joined entirely for musical reasons, or so I would have said then. But I must also have been drawn to what was on offer besides the music, and come to be familiar with it. Choir practice is in itself an unregarded form of religious training.

Except in detail, I have described the common experience of many thousands of my age-group and those younger. It would hardly have been worth recounting if large parts of my subsequent experience, beliefs and attitudes were not also common, as they surely are, and connected with it in all sorts of ways, as they must be. Something, at any rate, has made me an unwilling unbeliever, one with a sense of deep and continuous attachment to the Christian religion, a fascination with its doctrines and its and their history, and an inquisitive interest in the Church of my country and its doings and sayings.

My belief is not uniform. Notions of God's omnipresence, of his knowing everything I think, of my ability to reach him through prayer, even of my being a part of him, I feel I could accept if I could accept other things, anterior things. But I have no belief in the existence of God, not the first beginning of one, not a shred, and never have had as far back as I can remember – not no belief in him as all-wise, all-loving, all-powerful, difficult as these might be to acquire, just no belief in him as an eternal supreme being. How could the idea of such an entity be believable? Logic will not help and the rest is poetry at best: 'I believe in order that I may understand' – 'It is believable because it is absurd' – 'I believe because it is impossible' (Augustine? Tertullian?) – a lamentably discouraging and frivolous remark, the more so for its quibble between it-as-belief and it-as-thing-to-be-believed.

But there the belief under discussion was of course not God as a general concept but the Christian God and all the immense structure of Christianity. Once more I feel I could take the second step as soon as I had taken the first, and accept a God who became man. But how can all the rest be accepted, every piece of it, and if just one piece, even the smallest, can be dropped, then why not others, why not all? I will never understand how and why not, until I believe, and I know well enough by this time that belief does not come by looking for the answers to questions. Faith is evidently not an explanation or a discovery but a gift.

One principle I can accede to is that human beings without faith are the poorer for it in every part of their lives. But many of those in that condition are far from being entirely pauperised, indeed are decidedly rich compared to the truly godless, those who know and care nothing about God at all. To us who were brought up or partly brought up as Christians but who cannot believe, a world without religion in it would nevertheless be as sad and dreadful a place as a world without art. In fact it would be a world in which art as we have known it might become impossible to create, and great tracts of existing art would for certain become fatally impoverished.

English poetry is such a tract. Specifically religious poetry in English is on any reckoning one of its great beauties. To read such poetry from the outside, with only a swotted-up knowledge of the religion in it, is to experience a bloodless simulacrum of it. Something ominous can be learnt from imagining what it would be like to have read a poem of George Herbert's, as it might be 'Redemption' ('Having been tenant long to a rich lord'), with no more than footnotes for illumination. This is doubtless an extreme case, but from beginning to end English poetry as a whole has been shaped by religion, constantly reflects it, looks back to it often when it seems furthest away. I imagine it would not be hard to make out similar cases where other arts are concerned.

We in this country, not uniquely, may be entering a world without religion, by which I mean a world without Christian belief. Any attempt to hatch such a thing by direct means, as we now know, will go wrong. This would have been the worst cruelty of the communists, because irreparable, but the attempt has been their most ludicrous failure.

What will bring it off, in this country, is the Church of England itself, out of no malice to anybody, in a general honest thought and common good to all, assisted by a number of less attractive qualities like stupidity, cowardice and – is there a polite word for it? – flattery, sycophancy, desire to appease *bien-pensant* sentiment at almost any cost.

I pass over for now the atrocities the Church has inflicted on the Bible and Prayer Book, though it is very much part of my argument to suggest that the total effect, or at any rate the strongest effect, of these is to help to render unbelievable the doctrine in and behind the original texts. 'The Lord be with you, And with thy spirit': that clearly means something, even if we cannot at once paraphrase it. 'The Lord be with you, And also with you' means nothing, can be forgotten. The motive for the assault is possibly less sinister: by destroying its special language, to damage the status of Christianity as something special in itself, something partly detached from the things of this world.

From the progressive point of view, the trouble with Christianity is that like other religions, but unlike modern systems of belief, it is pervasively élitist, indeed it has given us the word 'hierarchical'. Although open to all, it imposes rules, difficult rules, and introduces a struggle in which some succeed while others fail. (Think of that!) Most people in it stay ordinary sinners, a very few become saints, who are regarded as much more exalted than anybody else. Parsons or priests, once called 'men of God', know more and know better than the laity, and have or had a special dress to show their difference, accentuated on those (increasingly rare) ostentatious special occasions. Above priests come archbishops and popes. And above them . . .

What makes the Archbishop of Canterbury most uncomfortable is his sense of being above other people and knowing more and better than they do. To tell them what he knows, especially what he knows about God, and how in the light of that knowledge they ought to lead their lives, would be authoritarian of him, or at best paternalistic. Better to keep quiet about all that. As he put it in his gloom-spreading interview with Bernard Levin in *The Times* recently: 'If we are to have a free society, which is essential if love not power is going to rule the world, then we can't have some people – people who believe in God – in a position to order other people what they should believe and how they should behave.'

His Grace's embarrassment is fascinatingly highlighted in a point of grammar. To talk of some people telling other people what they should believe sounds too harmless and commonplace. To talk of some people ordering other people to believe this, that or the other sounds daft, not what anyone ever does. So he coins a totally un-English construction and talks of some people – people who believe in God – being 'in a position to order other people what they should believe'. But of course 'we can't have' the first lot of people *in a position* to order or tell another lot of people anything at all. What, then, according to the Archbishop, should the Archbishop's position be?

Faced with all the difficulties of being a clergyman in a free society, most of them understandably shy away from the élitist propounding of doctrine (never the easiest of options) and settle down to discussing 'values'. Here at least Jack's view is as good as his master's, and all can agree that compassion and peace, for instance, are what to believe in. More popular than the Trinity, and much more fun, what with speaking out against Mrs Thatcher and demonstrating against the Bomb.

In a free society, in a liberal society, in a secular age, in sceptical times – however the clergy characterise the times, their nervous consensus is that the Church must move with them. Any Christian in the old-fashioned sense, and anybody in my own position, is likely to feel that this must be wrong. Let the times move as far as they like, the Church should stand still as it has done in the past. Or rather, things having gone as they have, it should move back to where it was before and preach the Christian religion, at whatever price in incomprehension, indifference and hostility, and wait for the times to return to it if they will.

It may be asked – I ask myself – by what right I lay down the law to a Church I have never embraced. Well, as an Englishman, I still call it and think of it as my Church. More important, it is my grandchildren's Church. I have said that faith is a gift, and so it is, but it requires a living religion to prepare its recipient and to invest it with meaning. A living religion is in turn inseparable from a living, believing, practising Church. Since I want my grandchildren to live in a society in which the Christian faith is still possible, I am surely within my rights in demanding the continued existence of the kind of Church that safeguards that possibility. Unlike many other human institutions and practices, but like a language and like literature, its most intimate associates, a religious belief, once no longer current, is dead and gone for ever. (Some years ago I wrote a novel on that theme.)

The early Christians foresaw the Parousia or Second Coming as the return of Christ in glory, either to judge the living and the dead and to terminate this world, or to rule it in person for a thousand years. Just as likely it will be much as before, and with everything to do over again. If so, the chances are not bad that there will still be the Jewish religion to build on, as before. But I gather that 'the prevailing Christian tradition' has opposed speculation on the time and manner of the Second Coming. I am sure that this is one part of that tradition that the contemporary Church has unswervingly followed. It has enough trouble with the First.

18 April 1987

Chapter 8
THE MEDIA – AND THE ARTS

'I've been voted nonentity of the decade.'

HOPEFUL

John McEwen

Few artists honestly believe that their efforts and methods are adequate to these urban and technological times, but in the continuing absence of a philosophy that will once more make a common purpose of science and art – that ultimate dream of post-industrial man – the Seventies have seen them pursue their priestly way undaunted as before, a motley horde (at least in England) of Leavisites, socialites, parasites, Trotskyites and acolytes in their train. After the hype and spivvery of the Sixties – and, it should also be recognised, its enthusiasms and optimism – it was not surprising to find our innate puritanism reasserting itself. For the disaffected a moral purpose was to be found in turning art into an adjunct of the social services. There were contrary signs of a return to silk slippers by the end of the decade, but nevertheless we face the perils of such earnestness in the Eighties without the irreplaceable Beachcomber to pull us to our senses. No more artistic memories of Parisian days in the rue des Odeurs Incroyables, of the painter Souris with his loud laugh and flashing smile, of shared brimless straws and bowls of soupe (soup) with Munet, Minet, Meenet and all the other heroes of those dear, dead days. Beachcomber always complained that, latterly, reality had invariably upstaged his fictions. He was uprooted from the *Daily Express* at about the same time as the Tate's purchase of a pile of bricks became the modern art scandal of the decade.

The bricks proved instant starbore material, and still do. Only a week ago two ladies were finding a Van Gogh masterpiece preferable to them at the Academy's current post-impressionist extravaganza. Vanity of vanities! Awaiting round the corner like a time-bomb was an anarchist jape of the 1880s. A 'picture' by Alphonse Allais in the form of a blank piece of paper entitled: 'First Communion of Anaemic Young Girls in the Snow'. The bricks were, of course, no joke. They were a monument of logic, a perfect illustration of Tom Wolfe's thesis in *The Painted Word* that, without a theory to go with it, no one can *see* what they are looking at today.

The jargonauts of the art world thundered on, of course, as deafeningly as ever. Whole issues of magazines were dedicated to incomprehension, and statements like the following abounded: 'The role of Cézanne's objects I think might usefully be called "syncategorematic".' Apparently Cézanne, if he heard the word 'academic', would rise from the table and leave the room tearing his hair. And Constable was accused of being a bad artist because his pictures did not give an honest enough account of labouring conditions in the early 19th century. An argument that, if accepted, boded ill for the reputations of Phidias, Leonardo, Duccio, Michelangelo, Piero, Giotto, Cimabue, Raphael, Titian, Giorgione, Botticelli, Mantegna, Poussin, Jackson Pollock and everyone else, with the possible exception of Hieronymus Bosch and the Brueghel clan.

Such severe levelling was however met with a renewed interest in the élitist activity of painting – so far to no very startling result – and an academic turn for the romantic. All sorts of movements and figures, banished for one dogmatic reason or another, were tenderly reconsidered. In a secular world, as Robert Rosenblum, the American critic, pointed out in his book *Modern Painting and the Northern Romantic Tradition*, many artists could be seen to have searched for the sacred. There were important exhibitions of Puvis de Chavannes and Symbolism in Paris and a sublime scene of the arctic by the 19th-century American painter, Frederick E. Church, was sold this autumn for 2.5 million dollars, the third greatest price ever paid for a picture. A similar shift is currently discernible here in the eclectic nature of the post-impressionist selection, a show whose popularity may well take the Academy out of the red. It is a mood contradicted by the totalitarian gloom of the Tate extension, finally opened in May after 40 years, the work of yet another member of the intellectual élite at Cambridge in the Thirties. It is a mood that offers some hope for the Eighties.

5 January 1980

THE NEW ENGLISH LITERATURE

A Spectator *Leader*

The award this week of the Booker prize to William Golding, for his novel *Rites of Passage*, marks the welcome recognition of an English novelist whose writing has characteristically been more praised than read. In contrast to the political machinations which have turned the Nobel Prize for Literature into a home for lost but no doubt deserving causes, this year's Booker jury have paid a proper attention to actual merit and achievement. Although the Booker awards tend to receive neither the attention nor the publicity which surround other literary prizes, such as the Prix Goncourt, it can confidently be stated that the novels awarded the Booker prize have been consistently interesting and substantial.

Matters were not always so; in the late Sixties and early Seventies, it was peculiarly difficult for an Englishman to be anything other than slightly awkward and apologetic when confronted with the energy and expansiveness of American and European writing. There was Saul Bellow, Joseph Heller, Philip Roth – the litany of names was endless – and it seemed that America was the new empire; and that those of us who had the good fortune to share its language were in the position of itinerent minstrels and scholars finding patrons wherever we could. In Europe, also, the pursuits of the 'avant-garde' and the more avowedly political writers produced a literature that seemed both sharp and timely: a reminder, if any were needed, that the novel itself could be an exploration of contemporary circumstances rather than a nostalgic exhumation of the past.

In England, however, there was no distinctive avant-garde in the Seventies: the self-conscious exploration of 'alternative forms' could hardly be taken seriously at a time of great economic and social unrest. It was difficult, also, to imitate our American contemporaries: they were living off the fat of a culture which was, in any case, over-weight. Instead, we turned in upon ourselves. We were forced to confront an economic decline which seemed to be the symptom of some larger national distress. Modish aesthetic theories, and the ambitious rhetoric of the Americans, both seemed peculiarly ill-equipped to help writers and artists who were surrounded by decay and by a hopeless self-abnegation within the nation itself.

But out of this struggle with local circumstances, with the idea that our society and indeed our whole social history might have to be re-examined, has come a literature which is now strong and easily recognisable. It has been said of mainstream British fiction that it is too domestic, too narrowly class bound in its preoccupations. Now it is certainly true that in most English novels there is a deliberate smallness of scale – but it is a smallness full of resource. In effect, the achievement of the contemporary English novel has consisted of a refusal to countenance rhetoric, or modish theories of language, as ways of describing reality. In the best of recent English fiction, there has been a genuine attempt to register the actual reality of contemporary circumstances. Just as our national identity has itself been slowly redefined, so the novel itself has taken account of changing circumstances and become harder, less conventional in its preoccupations.

We are not suggesting that there is any easy correlation between economic circumstances and cultural ones. But it can be said with some confidence that the peculiar and distressing circumstances we have lived through – and which we are still living through – have changed our notion of ourselves in radical ways. Conventional wisdom is seen not to be wisdom at all. English novelists have assisted in this process by, as it were, stripping the veils off the language. Reality in the contemporary English novel is now presented as uncomfortable and demanding. As a result, it has become less entranced by conventional habits of narration and description. It could be said that our writers have made a compact with smaller truths, but these truths are human truths and they evoke our society with a rare clarity. The Booker prize this year has been awarded to a major English writer – but, more than that, he is a writer of world stature. It is time we proclaimed such things; there is a renewal and self-confidence in English writing which needs to be understood and appreciated. It is as if we were learning to say to ourselves, and our writers were saying for us – look, we have come through!

25 October 1980

IN SEARCH OF WILLIAM REES-MOGG

Byron Rogers

Ten years ago I was a reporter on *The Times*, and he was my editor. I caught sight of him once or twice. The paper's library was on the same floor as its corridor of power and I would look up over the cuttings as Mr William Rees-Mogg, then in his early forties, glided with a preoccupied air towards his private lavatory. I felt like a man in a fairy tale, peering out of a thicket. In three years I did not meet him once.

But I saw rather more of his predecessors, whose pictures lined the walls. National newspapers do not always commemorate their editors, having parted with so many of them on bad terms. But not *The Times*. Since 1817, when Barnes was appointed, there have been just ten of them (and 14 Popes, as Rees-Mogg once reminded his reading public).

We talked much of Mr Rees-Mogg in the news room, for few of my colleagues had met him. The news editor, it was said, had once taken a holiday in Somerset to gaze, like a plane spotter at an Iron Curtain air field, at the Palladian outline of what was then his editor's country house.

We knew that he was Catholic, that he had grand houses in London and the country (travelling between which occupied much of his time), that he had married his secretary on the *Sunday Times*, and that he had a large family. But we had few clues to his character. In 1966 he had written 'A Letter To My Newborn Son' in the *Sunday Times*, of which he was then deputy editor. His career, it is sometimes said, was influenced by two articles, of which this was the second. The first, in the Oxford undergraduate magazine *Isis*, was in praise of the *Financial Times*, a newspaper which Rees-Mogg joined on leaving university. The Letter to his son was a statement of traditional English values. A year later its Canadian proprietor offered him the editorship of *The Times*.

Those seeking to denigrate him found in The Letter the equivalent of those ships, bursting with good things, that were so conveniently wrecked in the lagoons for Robinson Crusoe and the Swiss Family Robinson. They return to it profitably again and again.

There is, for example, that famous passage at the end in which Rees-Mogg compares life to 'a great Cathedral on some Northern hill . . . The fog may shroud it, changes of history may pass by, sometimes bats may fly in and out of its thick pillars. But the cathedral remains, century after century, standing for what it stands for, a solid and permanent truth.' Rees-Mogg has always experimented with metaphor, but never more dangerously than here. One wonders what his son will make of his advice. 'I hope you will have a long and happy life, and that you will never be Prime Minister, a much over-rated job,' writes a man who has fought two elections without success. 'It is, I think, a great mistake to become very rich unless you have the gift of making money and cannot help yourself.' 'When you are a boy, cricket matters,' he says. And among his values he includes 'land and Rembrandt and country houses'.

In 1978 William Rees-Mogg was made High Sheriff of his native county, Somerset, and the gossip columnists rushed to their social registers. The Moggs have lived in Somerset since the 13th century, Rees being added to their name in the 18th century when a Mogg heiress married a Welsh clergyman who was also chaplain to Butcher Cumberland. Welshmen on the make have a habit of acquiring hyphens. But Fleet Street editors seldom become High Sheriffs. William Hickey said thoughtfully: 'Minor gentry can improve their position in this way.' The *New Statesman* was appalled. 'Amateurism', it said, 'is the curse of our ruling élite.' Others were overjoyed, particularly *Private Eye* in whose pantheon of comic heroes Mr Rees-Mogg has long been included (having passed his Common Entrance, a successful prosecution of the magazine for libel).

He continues to fascinate many people, not least his staff. 'I think he still lives in his prep-school,' says one colleague. 'A clever schoolboy, who got into newspapers. But underneath that vague academic air there is a very hard and ambitious journalist. He is a much more sensational editor than his predecessors.' And *The Times* can be very sensational. Eleven years ago it warned its readers that 'a small army of militant extremists' was planning to take over key installations in Central London. Later it disgraced the memory of a dead Cambridge don in the belief that he was the Fourth Man. But when the real Fourth Man turned up, he was given lunch at *The Times*. You never know what to expect of Mr Rees-Mogg's paper.

His own leading articles are a far cry from the wary essays written by his colleagues. William, said one of them, likes to come to conclusions. And these are often, as when he writes about gold, the opposite of safe, establishment conclusions. His love of metaphor can bring triumphant results, as in this passage on James Prior: 'It is more as though he were a sloth, or some other modest and short-sighted animal, feeling his way forward through dense undergrowth, turning aside to avoid a rock on one side and a puddle on the other, and always with an alert sense for the presence of predators.' He is capable of dictating leaders like this off the top of his head, a facility which awes some members of his staff.

He is in fact much liked by his colleagues, many of whom have now met him. They admit that he is awkward, and that he has no small talk. But they like his sense of humour, the discovering of which seems to surprise them. And he is a forgiving man. A journalist who publicly attacked him during the 1979 closure in a letter to another newspaper is still working at *The Times*.

He chastised the *Times* journalists (rightly, as it turns out) for threatening the paper's future with their recent strike, but now they regard him as their best hope for the future. He is a great survivor. Mr Rees-Mogg has also survived something else. In his novel sequence *Alms for Oblivion*, Simon Raven has a character called Somerset Lloyd-James. Raven was at Charterhouse with Rees-Mogg, and could not have made the inspiration for his character plainer. Lloyd-James starts life on an economic daily. He is a Catholic. He knows a great deal about money. He has a speech defect, a lisp (Rees-Mogg uses the Welsh 'll' sound). But Lloyd-James is described as 'manifestly not a gentleman but a howling shit'. He is a crook and an opportunist. He frequents a golden-hearted whore called Maisie who is obliged to dress as a nanny or a school matron before Lloyd-James can rise to the occasion. He is also, the novelist makes clear in later books, warily widening the gap between the character and its original, a bachelor, a Tory MP and, ultimately, a suicide.

'He's a horrible character,' says William Rees-Mogg. 'But, no, it doesn't distress me. I don't feel it has anything to do with me. Raven just took certain aspects of my character and built something around them. At Charterhouse we were all ambitious, and we were all jockeying for minor positions. But one thing it did tell me about myself was that I was noticeably greedy as a boy.'

His door in the first floor corridor of *The Times* is the only one without initials on it. A notice says 'The Editor' and, beneath it, a smaller notice, 'and Bernard Levin'. That double act, according to Mr Auberon Waugh, is the most remarkable thing in English journalism. Mr Levin uses the outer office where the secretaries sit.

William Rees-Mogg is now 52, and serenely at anchor in that middle age which he has been accused of aping since school. He is greyer and heavier than when I last saw him from behind cover, but still looks younger. He defended his acceptance of the position of High Sheriff. One has to be deeply embedded in a county, he said. He was the President of the Mendip Society, and on the committee of the Wells Cathedral Appeal. His family has been there for some time, as clergymen, solicitors, small landowners. They had been involved in the North Somerset coalfields.

We talked about his predecessors on *The Times*. He admired Delane, who had known the inner circles of government. Barnes he considered 'a good knockabout Radical journalist'. I recalled the memorial to Barnes in the *Times* library which says: 'The nation found in him a mind familiar with our native manners and institutions, and acquainted through every grade with the fabric of our social system.' I asked Rees-Mogg if he thought such a description could apply to himself. He said he felt it referred in part to Barnes's active Bohemian life. His own experience was not so wide, but he had a much better knowledge of the world outside Britain. Alas, for a moment I heard the echo of Frank Harris admitting that while Christ went deeper he, Harris, had a wider experience of life.

Did he think he was cut off from most of his contemporaries by money and by character? He said he mixed more in Somerset, where he led a more relaxed existence. Yes, he could talk to working men. He had fought two elections in a Northern industrial city, and had got on well with them. He tries not to dine out more than twice a week, and then 'usually in the company of people whom it is valuable and interesting to know'.

No, he did not at all regret having written the famous letter to his son. He had been much teased, but advice of that kind was easily parodied. It still represented his point of view. On the Cathedral metaphor he was grandly defiant. He quoted Dr Johnson on Swift, 'The dog would never try a metaphor'. Anyone who wanted to write interestingly had to use them. Then he grinned (he has an attractive grin); it had certainly given the wits a field day.

He does not like the second half of the 20th century, though to a journalist, he says, it can be fascinating. He looked mildly around his office, at the steel chairs and the thick leather couches. 'This is my office and every bit of furniture in it is hideous.' He has often been mocked because of the rocking chair, accused of affectation, of aspiring to the Kennedy touch. The truth may be simpler: the chair could be the one piece of furniture that he likes. A more direct man would have had the room cleared. Mr Rees-Mogg continues to sit there, rocking away, writhing gently, beneath pictures of comic violence from the 18th century. He is fond of the 18th century. But 'land, Rembrandt, country houses'? Great artists, he said, communicated great sanity, but he was no longer so sure about country houses. Another man, the scion of a food-canning family, now resides at Ston Easton.

He outlined his days: the family breakfasts in Smith Square (Rees-Mogg, say his friends, is very good with children), the 10 a.m. arrival at *The Times*, the mornings of conferences, especially those with his leader-writers, and then lunch. He spends two hours at lunch, and four out of five of them are working lunches.

'I do have a small number of long-standing acquaintances, but inevitably a large number of friendly acquaintances. It is part of my profession to have them, and part of theirs.' That is to say, he knows many strangers. Then there are the afternoon conferences, the discussion and writing of leaders and then home at 7.30 p.m. The first edition of the paper is delivered to his home at 10.30 p.m., and he rings through to discuss it.

He spends quite a lot of his time on the leading articles; an hour when he is not writing them, two hours when he is. *The Times*, he says, depends on serious analysis and judgment. He delegates more than any other Fleet Street editor, and rarely appoints staff. But does he meet them? He stopped and grinned, as though anticipating the next question. 'I'm very sorry I didn't meet you,' he said. But it was different now. He met most members of staff a month or two after their arrival.

The Times, he said, was still influential because over 80 per cent of Members of Parliament read it. He talked, with some distaste, of the 20th century and brought up a theme familiar to readers of his leading articles, its lack of limits. In the 18th century men had recognised limits, and had operated philosophically within them. Even the old wars had been fought within limits.

Later, at an editorial conference, he sat in his rocking chair as low voices discussed the world's events. Quietly he thanked each speaker. He was told of sieges and hostages and trade unions and sports scandals, and nodded without comment, like a galactic emperor for whom there is nothing new under the suns. But I heard little of it. I was still reeling from his last polite inquiry. 'I feel very guilty at not meeting you, you know. Er . . . what exactly did you do?' It could have been mischief.

1 November 1980

NOTEBOOK

Alexander Chancellor

Michael Heath, our cartoonist, was rather late at *The Spectator* on Tuesday. He had been walking in the vicinity of Fleet Street, minding his own business, when a pretty girl stopped him and asked him if he drank lager. He replied that there was practically nothing he did not drink. 'Come with me,' she said; and off they went together on a longish walk that ended in a stark upstairs room filled with trestle tables, just behind St Bride's. There a row of girls were interrogating a row of boozy gentlemen. Heath had fallen into a den of market researchers. His escort sat him down and asked him a lot of foolish questions about how much he drank, what kinds of lager he preferred and how he responded to an advertisement that was flashed before his eyes. The normal reward for undergoing all this was a pint of a mysterious new brand of lager, its identity carefully concealed from those present. Heath, however, was unlucky. Halfway through the interrogation, she asked him about his occupation. 'I'm a cartoonist,' he said; and she tore up the questionnaire and threw it into the wastepaper basket. 'We don't want journalists,' she explained. But could he, he pleaded, just taste the lager before he went? The answer was a firm and contemptuous no. This seemed a bit much. He had wasted half an hour of his working day in a most disagreeable manner. He appealed to a higher authority. Just one glass? The reply was still no. Tramps and prostitutes are treated with greater compassion.

11 July 1981

BOOKER REVISITED

Paul Johnson

There is an air of desperation about the attempts of the literary establishment to turn the Booker prize into a major event, as though sheer publicity will somehow pump life into the dying British novel. Malcolm Bradbury, the hardworking and conscientious chairman of the judges, did a little too much protesting. 'This year has been a vintage year, one of extraordinary fictional riches,' he told the *Bookseller*. 'I happen to think myself,' he said in his speech at the award ceremony, 'that we live in an extraordinary and innovative age of fiction.' If this were really true, would he feel obliged to say it? And of course when he gets down to particulars, the hyperbole seems – well, hyperbole. 'The age of Günter Grass and Peter Handke, Samuel Beckett and Jorge Luis Borges, Italo Calvino and Gabriel Garcia Marquez, Claude Simon and Alain Robbe-Grillet, Saul Bellow and Thomas Pynchon . . . will be looked back on as a major time of creation and invention.' That may possibly prove accurate. But for the novel to live, and still more to reoccupy its central position in cultural life, future accolades are no substitute for present, paying readers. When I saw that list, I wondered how many novels by the writers on it had actually been bought by, say, those who voted for the absurd Bill Pitt in Croydon last week, the same kind of people who, a century ago, might well have had a bust of Dickens in their parlours as well as a shelf of his stories.

Literary prizes have multiplied in Britain because the substance of the battle has been lost. Bradbury thought it a 'disappointment' that 'this year media coverage of the short-list was initially thin, jostled out by bigger stories'. But what sort of 'coverage' was he expecting? Hardly long, argumentative essays, advancing the merits of one or another of the contenders. What he meant, presumably, was gossip-column paragraphs, based on 'inside stories' of how the minds of the judges were shaping up. A pity if we've come to the point where leading novelists and their mentors have to rely on this kind of attention to keep the circus going.

Novelists no longer occupy an important place in our society. Their doings are not much regarded. Their views on contemporary problems are rarely sought. However high they stand in the hierarchy, their new books are no longer events. The novel is being pushed to the margin of literature. Sales are pitifully small. Only the waning optimism of publishers keeps them risking scarce resources on first novels which will not sell 1,000 copies. Of course the writers are to blame; nobody else. They treated their readers with contempt. It is now being returned with indifference. A huge chunk of the regular, middle-class, novel-reading public, which once automatically bought new Bennetts or Maughams, or not so long ago Waughs and Greenes, paying cash over the counter, has simply vanished without trace. It is no use blaming inflation. There is plenty of money about for pleasure.

The fact is that novelists neglected their market. They thought they could dictate to the reader. But the novel is a popular form of literature or it is nothing, and that implies a two-way traffic of taste. So now novelists are retreating into the subsidised sector, seeking refuge in Arts Council grants or as 'writers in residence' at universities, New Towns and big-spending Labour boroughs, or desperately struggling round the prize-trough. But the subsidised sector won't last. As the individual paying customer disappears, the pressure from taxpayers, ratepayers and shareholders to reduce, and then end, the handout is bound to increase. As the BBC has learned, to keep the licence you have to keep the ratings. Even in literature the customer's rights cannot be indefinitely denied. The market always wins in the long run.

The moral was neatly pointed by the conjunction of the Booker award and the enormous success of the television serialisation of *Brideshead Revisited*. It is a very long time since a novel has been so much talked about among the masses of middle-class educated people who once formed the novel-buying public. And of course the merits of the serial are precisely those of the novel: a powerful, well-constructed story, sharply defined characters, dialogue that lives and a narration which communicates pleasure in words as well as images. The series succeeds precisely because the novel itself is a solid piece of brass-and-mahogany work, fabricated by a great artist but one who remembered he was also a craftsman, serving the user.

Television, like the old novel, gets into the home in a way the cinema never did. The thought occurs that, just as the monthly part-work, in the 1830s, introduced a new epoch in the development of the novel and made the universality of Dickens possible, so television offers novelists opportunities which, so far, they haven't even begun to explore. It is one of the very few things that sells books in this country. Novelists, instead of reacting defensively and retreating into their subsidised bunkers, might seek to discover imaginative ways in which they can conquer this beckoning marketplace.

What they should not do is give vent to the fury displayed by Martin Amis in an attack on Waugh and *Brideshead Revisited* in last week's *Observer*. Amis writes novels with titles like *Dead Babies* and seems ill at ease when a major theme is tackled, in this case the operation of divine grace on wayward people. He had clearly missed the whole point of the book. What made me sad was the realisation he had done so because of an almost total ignorance of Christianity. He exposed himself rather like poor Rex Mottram, someone (to quote Waugh) 'only this ghastly age could produce'.

31 October 1981

LOST FACE

Richard Ingrams

I commended ITN's newsreader Selena Scott a week or so ago for avoiding the pitfalls which have brought about the collapse of Angela Rippon and Anna Ford. But, oh dear, no sooner were the words out of my mouth than the woman goes and makes a prize idiot of herself. The occasion was *A National Salute* (ITV), a fairly appalling three-hour-long entertainment, a kind of combination of the Royal Tournament and the Royal Variety Performance put on at the Coliseum on Sunday in order to raise money for the South Atlantic Fund. It began with the incongruous figure of Lord Olivier in dark glasses and a beard reading from what looked like a menu card, introducing us to the men and women who had won the great victory, though it turned out afterwards that very few of the soldiers and sailors who then marched proudly onto the stage had been anywhere near the Falklands. There followed the usual old ragbag of tatty comics, magicians and singers, interspersed with moments of banality and embarrassment, the most memorable coming when Frank Finlay, representing Sir Peter Hall and the National Theatre, read out a prayer by St Francis. It all came to a grisly finale with the company and the audience led by Dame Vera Lynn singing 'Land of Hope and Glory' under a large cardboard replica of the Union Jack. This song is tolerable when rendered at the last night of the Proms by flag-waving students but sung in earnest by the grown-ups struck a discordant and distasteful note. As

Christopher Booker has written, the Falklands victory relied on a very strong element of luck. One or two better aimed Exocets and it could all have ended very differently. This is something that needs to be remembered before we all get too carried away. It was after the theatricals were over that Selena Scott and her colleague Michael Nicholson fell flat on their faces. As the guest of honour, Prince Charles, shook hands one by one with members of the cast these two nincompoops kept up a commentary of such incompetence that it ought to be shown again as an example of how not to do this kind of thing. For a start, unlike Prince Charles who seemed to know exactly who everyone was, the ITN duo hadn't got a clue. 'All those familiar faces!' gasped Selena, but she couldn't put names to any of them. One man with a beard was said to be John Mills when he clearly wasn't; Denholm Elliott, whom even I can recognise, was called Donald Sinden by Michael Nicholson, but the most infuriating thing of all was Selena's repeated cry of 'If only we could hear what they are saying!', when if the two of them had just kept their mouths shut, we could have heard every single word.

24 July 1982

ENGINEERS' CORNER

Wendy Cope

'Why isn't there an Engineers' Corner in Westminster Abbey? In Britain we've always made more fuss of a ballad than a blueprint . . . How many schoolchildren daydream of becoming great engineers?' –
Advertisement placed in *The Times*
by the Engineering Council.

We make more fuss of ballads than of blueprints –
That's why so many poets end up rich,
While engineers scrape by in cheerless garrets.
Who needs a bridge or dam? Who needs a ditch?

Whereas the person who can write a sonnet
Has got it made. It's always been the way,
For everybody knows that we need poems
And everybody reads them every day.

Yes, life is hard if you choose engineering –
You're sure to need another job as well;
You'll have to plan your projects in the evenings
Instead of going out. It must be hell.

While well-heeled poets ride around in Daimlers,
You'll burn the midnight oil to earn a crust,
With no hope of a statue in the Abbey,
With no hope, even, of a modest bust.

No wonder small boys dream of writing couplets
And spurn the bike, the lorry and the train.
There's far too much encouragement for poets –
That's why this country's going down the drain.

23 March 1985

DESIGNS ON THE MARKET

A profile of Sir Terence Conran

When it was announced last week that the National Economic Development Office is to investigate the standard of design in British manufac-
tures, it came as no surprise that Sir Terence Conran was to be involved.
Owing, above all, to the popularity and influence of his Habitat shops
with a wide public, he has become the prince of designers. Knighted,
wealthy and very powerful, Conran has made the leap from the world of
business to that of official culture; he has succeeded in his ambition to
become an insider. It is a phenomenon which, in theory, would not have
displeased Prince Albert and Sir Henry Cole, who, long ago, were concerned about the quality of design of British manufactured goods and
who established what became the Victoria and Albert Museum as an
exemplar and a remedy.

The significant difference, however, between Prince Albert's day and
our own is that in the 19th century there was no doubt about the quality
of workmanship of British goods. Today there is, and 'design' has become
a sort of cosmetic, a matter of superficial styling to make goods more
attractive in appearance and therefore more saleable to the

undiscriminating. The ambitious type of young man who, a few years back, would have gone into the BBC or become an advertising copywriter aspires to be a 'designer', a fashionable 1970s figure wearing designer spectacles with coloured frames, refining the minimalist design of an angle-poise desk lamp.

Sir Terence Conran is both a creator and a product of this phenomenon, but he owes his present power to his undisputed brilliance as an entrepreneur. The creator of Habitat took over Mothercare – with its 500 shops – in 1982. In 1983 he acquired the chain of Richard Shops. Conran has expanded abroad: there are shops in New York and Paris. Another coup was the acquisition of Heal's, the once-famous store in the Tottenham Court Road which had a deserved reputation for well-made, well-designed furniture earlier this century. Sir Terence evidently thinks of himself as a new Ambrose Heal, but he is more of a Gordon Selfridge, in truth more of a businessman than a real designer – a 'creative retailer' as he styles himself. A few months back full-page advertisements were taken in newspapers to persuade Debenham's shareholders of the merits of the Conran-Burton takeover bid (ultimately successful). 'Either one of these two men could turn Debenhams around', read the caption under photographs of two remarkably sinister-looking characters. Sir Terence chose to appear, not like a 'designer' but as a smooth, ruthless, 'godfather'-like figure, buttoned into an executive suit and above the modest claim that he is 'arguably the most influential designer that Britain has yet produced' (Adam? Morris? Mackintosh?). It was an image which, to students of Conran's rise and rise, rang true.

To his credit, a good story is told against Conran. 'What is a plagiarist?' asked the eight-year-old daughter of one of Conran's oldest friends. 'I am,' said Conran. He could scarcely deny it. Fiona McCarthy, in her study of the history of British design, long ago pointed out that the Habitat style as 'design' was 'phoney: a brilliant and timely commercial pastiche' of what readers of the *Architectural Review* were encouraged to admire over 20 years before – white enamel ironware, simple earthenware jugs and the rest of that look which is a fusion of the late Arts and Crafts movement with Scandinavian puritanism. Conran's success, and it was, at the time, undoubtedly deserved, was to make a rarefied, rather highbrow taste available to a much wider public: 'I am interested in selling good design to the masses.' Conran's career shows, yet again, how driving ambition combined with careful plagiarism is irresistible in Britain.

Terence Orby Conran was born in Esher in 1931. What celebrities choose to include or omit in their *Who's Who* entry is always highly significant. In Conran's case, his famous marriage to Shirley Pearce, who quite matched him in ambition and who, in truth, has brought quite as much lustre to the name of Conran, is simply dealt with by the cryptic '*m; two s.*' before '*m*. 1963 Caroline Herbert', while no mention is made at all of his parents. A little more information is vouchsafed in the tedious hagiography published last year by Barty Phillips, *Conran and the Habitat Story*: his father was an importer of gum copal. Conran was educated at Bryanston – which he apparently left under a cloud – and then studied textile design at the Central School.

In the early 1950s, Terence Conran was one of several struggling young artists and designers in the then *avant-garde*, Bohemian world of the King's Road, Chelsea. Nor was he the only one to succeed: Mary Quant and the late Laura Ashley were of the same generation, all pioneers of Swinging London. Conran first attracted notice as the co-founder of the Soup Kitchen in 1954, which, by its contrived simplicity, so lived up to its name that on the opening night it was taken over by tramps. But his principal work was as a commercial designer and as a salesman of modern furniture. To both a younger and an older generation, the litany of complaint by Conran against the austerity and stuffiness of post-war Britain seems greatly exaggerated, but conventional continental modern ideas were certainly striking in London. Conran made furniture and plant stands strongly influenced by the style of the Festival of Britain. One of his early 'designs' was the 'Homemaker' plate, decorated with icons of the Fifties – a rubber plant, an amoeba and a coffee table (with wooden balls at the end of its metal legs); another was the conical cane chair on a metal frame. The cane part was simply imported from Madeira, to the fury of Lord Roberts's Workshops for the Blind who complained of being undercut.

Conran's great moment came with the opening of the first Habitat store in 1964. It was, in his own words, a 'shop for switched-on people' who included, in the early days, John Lennon, Julie Christie, Vanessa Redgrave and Kingsley Amis. Habitat was undoubtedly right for the time and successfully catered for the impecunious, upwardly mobile young middle classes who wanted modern-looking objects. Conran did for furnishings what Barry Bucknell did for panelled doors and banisters. Habitat was also successful because it obviated that tiresome matter of aesthetic choice. The key was pre-selection, the presentation of a consistent image, in Conran's own words, a 'pre-digested shopping programme' of Habitat-style goods. This image was also remorselessly sold in a series of books which illustrated that fashionable idea of the minimal, the stripped, the informal, which, in the text, cleverly echoed the puritanical ideas of Morris and Voysey. In *The House Book* of 1974 the deliberately ungrand interior of Conran's country house, Barton Court, near

Newbury, was illustrated: 'Comfort, controlled casualness, flexibility and prettiness: the Conrans' living room scores high on all the important priorities without being over-designed.'

'Controlled casualness', along with that neophilia which is again being embraced by Margaret Thatcher's Britain, may well be the key to the Sixties. What is remarkable is how little the Habitat look has changed over the years. There is a hint of restrained luxury in Habitat today and the now taken-over Heal's is intended to be more up-market, but the stripped pine and primary colour look is still sold and still bought, both by now ageing but still denim-clad couples who bought their first coffee table 20 years ago and by a younger generation to whom the Sixties have a revivalist glamour. Whether Conran actually stands for good design is, however, another matter. Not for nothing has the chain long been known as 'Shabitat', full of goods which, by being near copies of British or French designs, never seem to work as well as the originals. Nor do they have the craftsmanship of modern Italian designs. Conran cares little for the consumer. His Mothercare chain, intended presumably for pregnant women, is notorious for providing no lavatories or nursery facilities for its customers.

There is another aspect to Conran which explains his continuing success. He appeals to that type of Englishman who is enamoured of things French, worships French *cuisine* and who holidays in the Dordogne. This element of exclusive *chic*, once known only to those, in the Fifties, who could afford to go on continental holidays – Conran first went to France in 1954 – informs much of the Habitat style. As one keeper at the Victoria & Albert remarked exasperatedly: 'Conran labours under the illusion that he is the only person ever to go to France.'

That keeper should know: Conran is a trustee of and a power within the V & A, anxious to leave his mark. One mark has been left in the form of the Boilerhouse Project, opened in 1981. When the Project itself moves to the new Conran empire at Butler's Wharf, Rotherhithe, the V & A will be left with a strange, white-tiled basement, more reminiscent of an operating theatre than a museum of design. The Boilerhouse was established by the Conran Foundation, a charitable trust, to promote interest in modern industrial design as a significant element in 20th-century history. Exhibitions have been held of Ford Sierra cars, vacuum cleaners and, more recently, of plastic bags. Wiser heads advised against the idea of an exhibition of machine guns as examples of style and design.

Critics of the Boilerhouse accused Conran of endowing it to promote his own stores and wares. They were wrong. What the Boilerhouse has done is to promote the respectability of Design and, thus, of Conran himself. He is now a force within the official cultural world, the world of museum trustees, the Design Council and the whole structure of grant-giving art bureaucracy. Conran is an empire builder. Apart from the disastrous episode of the Ryman merger, his commercial empire has grown and grown. Soon the Conran influence will be in every high street. Like all great and inspired businessmen, there is a touch of megalomania about him. He is also a bit of a bully.

What, however, worries many people is that a man with undoubted expertise in the realm of marketing and styling should now set himself up as an arbiter of taste, an adviser to a great national museum. It was curious earlier this year how desperate Sir Terence was to deny a rumour that the fashionable High Tech designer, Eva Jiricna, had been hired to style his planned Debenham chain: the great populariser must shun the precious. It is also that Sir Terence's taste in design seems very limited, as the rather dated Boilerhouse shows. Even admirers were shocked when he proposed to remove the 1930s non-reflecting, curved glass windows from Heal's, for commercial considerations seemed more important to him than the retention of a feature which was both stylish and rare. On his own admission, Conran has no interest in painting or in music. Apart from making money, his only enthusiasm is that of the professional Francophile: cooking and wine.

There are further goals to be achieved. C. H. Reilly, the architect and teacher, received a knighthood at the end of his life but his son, the writer and design bureaucrat, Paul Reilly, has been made a peer. Baron Conran of the Dordogne cannot be far away, honoured for his service to British design and commerce. Whether Sir Henry Cole would really approve is another matter.

16 November 1985

FOR WHAT WE ARE ABOUT TO PERCEIVE

Sebastian Faulks

Every now and then a word is misused so badly that it becomes a major public hazard. We all remember the 'situation' epidemic of the mid-Seventies which now seems mercifully to have passed. But there is a new menace, and one that, instead of being derided by the press, is being taken up by them. It is impossible to turn on the radio now without continuously hearing the word 'perceive' and its noun 'perception' being used in a new and brutal way. In the space of about a year, the meaning of the word has been turned through very nearly 180 degrees. Where it used to mean 'see clearly, apprehend, *se rendre compte*', it is now used by politicians, pundits, interviewees and the press to mean 'view subjectively, believe, suppose, see partially or mistakenly.'

The misuse is so widespread that one already feels self-conscious about using the word in its proper sense: 'Jane Austen's gift of perception ...'; 'Trevor Brooking's skill and perception in midfield...'; 'He was able to perceive the weakness of the enemy and act upon it...' Whenever the word is correctly used, it has the sense of truthful, accurate, indeed unusually acute apprehension.

But consider recent usage. 'What we have to do is try to improve the black community's perception of itself ...'; 'the BBC's perceived independence ...'; 'Neil Kinnock is not only perceived to be a nice chap, he really is a nice chap!' In each of these examples the word carries a connotation of inaccuracy, wrong-thinking, and subjective or blurred ideas. In the first example the speaker is not implying that black people have a correct view of themselves which needs to be improved; in the second he is not saying that the BBC is rightly thought to be independent and applauded for it; in the third, most extreme example the speaker implies that fact and perception are almost directly opposed. You can take it for granted, he is saying, that if the public 'perceives' something, it is probably wrong. Given the actual meaning of the word, this is a logical nonsense.

I first heard it used in its new sense by a council officer in Bradford in May 1984. He worked in one of the newer disciplines, where respect for language is not a priority, and I assumed, rightly or wrongly, that he had picked it up from the closed world of sociology where simple things are often given long names to make them sound more important and more worthy of salaried inquiry. It was not until this summer that it reached epidemic proportions on the radio and, to a lesser extent, in newspapers. What is sad is that it is not only the rougher hacks who are doing it.

Gordon Clough, the gravelly, slightly impatient presenter of *The World At One* is one of the worst offenders. This is disappointing, because everything else about him is first-class. The Kinnock example quoted above comes from the journalist Edward Pearce, who is generally thought to be a good writer. (Quite a different thing from being perceived to be a good writer.) Michael Charlton's recent Radio 3 interview with Jimmy Carter on the arms race could have been subtitled 'Mutually Perceived

Destruction'. On *Any Questions?* on 26 October a young American asked the panel: 'Is there any difference in the way that America and Europe view the Soviet threat?' The presenter, John Timpson, took the question and 'improved' it. 'Thank you. Our first question,' he told the panel, 'is about perceptions of the Soviet threat.' Which of course is exactly what it wasn't about. The torture of the English language that took place over the next seven or eight minutes as the panel took their cue from the chairman was awful to hear. In the *Times Literary Supplement* of 18 October 1985 Maggie Gee, the novelist, wrote: 'Because Vonnegut is popular, he is not perceived as experimental. It is not just a question of how he is perceived and presented; Vonnegut has made some very different stylistic choices from Burns.' The first 'perceived' means 'believed to be' or 'thought of as'; the second 'perceived' makes it clear that the writer thinks the word has something to do with mistaken reading and distortion. (The words after the semi-colon do not bear close inspection, either, but that's a different problem.)

It is a bad misuse for several reasons. First, it is pompous. Second, it is unnecessary, since there are so many words (viewed, thought, seen, believed, supposed, etc.) to choose from, and any one of them can give a finer nuance in the required context. Third, it diminishes the language: 'perceive' in the proper sense has no exact synonym, and if the word is to be hijacked off to an area of meaning already well served, then the range of expression open to us is, however minutely, reduced. Fourth, it is just

'*Our son has programmed us out of his life.*'

wrong: perceived doesn't mean what these people want it to mean. It is especially irritating when journalists and politicians of some standing can throw away the acquired verbal habits of 50 years and change the meaning they give to a word overnight, just because the next man has done so.

When people used to talk about 'confrontation situations' and the like, the press were quick to pour scorn on them, and now the usage is limited to the very, very dim or to the jocular – 'Did you get into a group sex situation?' has a pleasantly dated and sarcastic spin to it. The campaign against 'hopefully' used in the sense of 'with any luck' as opposed to 'with a song in one's heart' has been less successful. This is partly because the abuse may have met a genuine need; there certainly does not seem to be a single word that covers the meaning it has now acquired. Dr Robert Burchfield of the *OED* and others defended its use.

With both of these words the press did its best, and a scoreline of won one, lost one, is not too bad, especially when one considers that there are strong arguments for the new use of 'hopefully'. But 'perceive' is a different matter. The press appears to be leading the assault, not holding out against it. Just how a solecism escapes from an enclosed world and is foisted on the general public is something of a mystery (advertising is possibly one route); but until the mystery is solved, it is worth remembering that when Aldous Huxley wrote about his drug experiences in *The Doors of Perception*, he did not mean to imply that there was anything false in the reality he encountered. He did not call it 'the Doors of Supposition'.

21/28 December 1985

OPEN THE DOOR, RUPERT

Miles Kington

'I am going to the new *Times* building in Wapping today,' I told my loved ones.

'Be careful!' they cried. 'Take out insurance! Learn unarmed combat! Don't take any valuables with you!'

It's curious how the image of the News International offices has already taken on military and warlike overtones. 'Fortress' is the word constantly used. Mr Murdoch's enemies no doubt think of Fortress Wapping as something like Hitler's Bunker, the last stand of the forces of evil, with all sorts of war crimes going on in there. Mr Murdoch is likely to see it as more like a Foreign Legion fort, a haven of civilisation surrounded by the howling rabble of unbelievers, a romantic symbol of knowledge facing ignorance. But I simply saw it as a place I had to get my copy to.

I have been a freelance writer for *The Times* for 20 years now, and though I've always enjoyed writing for it, I've never enjoyed trying to get my copy there. 'Phoning it in is lengthy and causes misprints, especially if you write a humorous column, as I do. Posting it is too dangerous for words: the internal messenger service at *The Times* in Gray's Inn Road was so unpredictable that the staff warned me not to use it, either for mail or taxi delivery. One member of the staff, as an experiment, once sent many memos to himself from all over the building. Some came at once, several took days and one took a week.

My solution to the problem was simple and ingenious. I moved to an address two doors away from Philip Howard, the literary editor of *The Times*, and gave him my copy to take in when he went to work in the morning. But now even this foolproof plan has temporarily broken down, because last week Philip continued going to Gray's Inn Road where his books were, not to Pennington Street, Wapping, where my copy was needed.

'It will be nice to see you,' said my sub-editor on the telephone; 'come inside when you get here and I'll show you round Brave New World. Make it 2.30.'

It wasn't at all like a fortress when I got to Wapping, more like a Second Division football ground with some high fences, a bit of barbed wire and a lot of waterlogged grass. Half a dozen pickets stood stamping their feet, and half a dozen policemen loitered up the lane. None of them tried to talk to me.

'I have an appointment with one of the editors of *The Times*,' I told the man behind the glass, inside the gate.

'Do you know their extension number?'

I did. I told him. He dialled it.

'Sorry, sir. They're out to lunch.'

'That's impossible. They're waiting to see me.'

'Well, he's left the out-to-lunch notice on his 'phone.'

'Can I go in and find someone else?'

'Sorry, sir.'

'Well, can you 'phone someone else if I give you their name and get clearance from them?'

'Sorry, sir. I don't have a list of names of editorial.'

I decided, desperately, to go straight to the top.

'Will you ring the editor's office for me?'

'Sorry, sir. I haven't got the number.'

I went straight back up the lane, foolish and furious. The pickets glanced at me approvingly: someone who had not entered. A young woman came over to talk to me.

'Hello, I am a Dutch journalist and I am here to do a story on *The Times*. Please, are you a writer? Ah, good. Well, please I would like to meet someone from inside the building.'

'Believe me, sister, so would I,' I told her.

I went to see a friend who has an office in Wapping High Street (highly interesting part of the world, by the way – my friend says he'd far rather work there than Fleet Street) and came back to Murdoch Towers at 3.45. I asked the mystery doorman to ring my editor again.

'Sorry, sir. He's still out at lunch.'

I debated whether to ask the pickets for advice on how to get in. I was just going to talk to them when a grand car drove out of the building, and all the pickets shouted 'Heil Hitler!' There in the car sat Rupert Murdoch. Maybe if I threw myself under the wheels and stopped the car, Mr Murdoch could arrange to get my copy in through the front gate, I thought rapidly, but not rapidly enough; he had gone before I fell forward.

The light was beginning to fade now and I didn't want to stand around all day outside the newspaper that employed me but wouldn't let me in. So I went home, and have tried to telephone *The Times* ever since. It has always been engaged. I have written a letter to my man in *The Times*, enclosing copy and asking him to ring me, but so far no answer. So I am writing this piece for *The Spectator* to attract his attention, as one last desperate attempt to get in touch with him.

George, if you read this, could you give me a ring? I want to go on writing for you. Thanks.

And if Mr Murdoch is reading this, I think you're doing a grand job but there seems to be a weak link in your new set-up. I suspect you've put the old internal messenger service in charge of the new front gate.

8 February 1986

ILLITERATE VERNACULAR

Gavin Stamp

Post-Modernism may well seem a wonderfully self-contradictory concept. To be Post-Modern can have no meaning except as a response to the peculiar cultural conditions prevailing in the 20th century, for until the ideal of modernity was invested with absolute moral values, 'modern' merely meant up-to-date, fashionable. Renaissance writers referred to the Gothic as 'moderna' since it had succeeded Roman Classicism, for instance, and when Lord Palmerston dismissed Gilbert Scott's Gothic Revival design for the Foreign Office by saying that he wanted something 'more like modern architecture', he meant Italianate and was merely expressing a stylistic preference.

But by the fourth decade of this century, modernity ceased to be a matter of inevitability and fashion; it became the immutable, absolute expression of the *Zeitgeist* of the modern world. Siegfried Giedion, Nikolaus Pevsner, Henry-Russell Hitchcock and others decreed that the spirit of the age permitted no deviation from the mechanistic, cubist and planar style of white architecture evolved on the Continent in the 1920s. This Modern Movement succeeded in establishing a half-century-long dominance as orthodoxy, but not even Pevsner's strict condemnation of 'the craving of architects for individual expression' and 'the craving of the public for the surprising and fantastic' could prevent a reaction. And when the Modern Movement was seen to have often catastrophic social and functional failings, the demand of the public for something different and more interesting could no longer be resisted. The result was Post-Modernism. The Modern Movement, of course, enjoyed a similar dominance in other fields but, as far as I know, there is not, yet, a distinct Post-Modern music, or sculpture. Architects seem peculiarly attracted by -isms and orthodoxies.

Post-Modernism is, however, a more precise phenomenon, which does not, strictly speaking, embrace those other reactions to Modernism, such as the pedantic Classicism of Quinlan Terry or the brick 'neo-vernacular' which has proved so alarmingly popular since the demise of high-rise public housing. Post-Modernism has become a distinct style with a recognisable vocabulary of motifs; it alludes to the past but tradition is interpreted with a modern inflection, with a conscious or unconscious illiteracy and, most tiresomely, with irony. The essential distinction, indeed, between Pre- and Post-Modern architecture is that lessons are not properly learned, that historical elements are never used correctly. This is to show that its practitioners are still modern, that is progressive, at heart. Post-Modernism is a whimsical fusion of past and present which could only flourish in the intellectual void left by the collapse of the Modern Movement. Back in 1978, the high priest of Post-Modernism, Charles Jencks, prophesied that 'we might see an architecture emerge that is quite similar to the Neo-Queen Anne and Edwardian of eighty years ago'. This has happened; Post-Modernism has become a style which is as eclectic, if not as charming, as the 'Queen Anne' which sprang up after the collapse of the Gothic Revival; I also suspect that it will be as ephemeral.

The origins of Post-Modernism undoubtedly lie in the writings and buildings of Robert Venturi, the American architect who was recently commissioned to design the National Gallery extension in London. In 1966, Venturi published *Complexity and Contradiction in Architecture*, a highly influential little book, full of illustrations of historical parallels, which contained such apparent heresies as 'I am for richness of meaning rather than clarity of meaning . . . I prefer "both – and" to "either – or", black and white, and sometimes gray, to black or white.' In his built architecture of the 1960s, however, Venturi seemed to learn more from American pop culture than from his heroes, Borromini, Hawksmoor or Lutyens; his buildings were still thin, flat and spare. True, there were historical motifs, but they appeared superimposed; they were not done straight but with *irony* for, as Tom Wolfe acutely observed in *Bauhaus to Our House*, Venturi was not a true apostate; he was still part of the self-regarding, avant-garde 'compound' of intellectual, anti-bourgeois architects – *Complexity and Contradiction*, after all, was published by the Museum of Modern Art in New York.

Irony is all-important. That Post-Modernism is usually discussed in linguistic terms is significant, for Charles Jencks, the tireless promoter and interpreter of the phenomenon, is exclusively concerned with semiology, with the conveyance of meaning in architecture. Mr Jencks, also an American, is a witty and intelligent commentator as well as an occasional architect. He loves to categorise, to distinguish between Post- and Late-Modernism, to define Free Style Classicism, Radical Eclecticism and Adhocism in architecture. In 1977 he published the most significantly titled *The Language of Post-Modern Architecture*, a book hugely influential on students and young architects which is now in its fifth edition. Jencks applied semiological ideas about signs to architecture and he concluded that the failure of the Modern Movement was the failure of a mode of architectural communication: the Modern Movement died because it was dumb. The linguistic analogy explains why Post-Modernism is the ambivalent style it is, for it 'speaks on two levels at once: to other architects and a concerned minority who care about specifically architectural meanings, and to the public at large, or the local inhabitants, who care about other issues concerned with comfort, traditional building and a way of life. This Post-Modern architecture looks hybrid ...' In short, it is a less arid architecture, which enables its adherents still to feel morally and intellectually superior to their clients and to the general public.

Now the linguistic analogy is far from new in architecture – Sir John Summerson, after all, wrote *The Classical Language of Architecture*. The trouble is that Post-Modernism is not only not a precise language; it may also have nothing to say. More to the point, a building can have two windows above a central door and so be a 'face house' and so humane, familiar, but this does not affect whether it is well or badly built, whether it is efficient and watertight, whether it is pleasing or ugly; in short, whether it is good or bad architecture.

But Charles Jencks remains convinced that the purpose of architecture is to convey meaning and that this is best achieved through symbolism. In his latest book, *Towards a Symbolic Architecture*, he notes how 'several of us in different countries, now grouped under the Post-Modern banner, have been making modest efforts towards a symbolic architecture'. What is impressive about Mr Jencks is that he has the courage of his convictions, for most of this lavish volume is devoted to the illustration and interpretation of his own 'Thematic House', the extraordinary conversion of a humble Holland Park terraced house into a central monument of Post-Modernism. Even Mr Jencks, however, concedes that a symbolic architecture is difficult when we live in an age that has no consistent system of belief and set of values. The conditions that enabled a mediaeval cathedral to be a popular didactic work of art and craftsmanship have long passed, so the Jencks House is left to symbolise the obvious: the passage of time – there are rooms for each of the four seasons and a spiral staircase with 52 steps.

But why bother? Jencks observes that when he takes guests around the Thematic House, 'I notice that whether they like the building or not, many' – and here I know he is thinking of me – 'regard my explanations as either reductive or superfluous.' Superfluous, I am afraid: the spiral stair would still be impressive even if it had only 51 steps. It has all been done before. W. R. Lethaby wrote a book in 1891 called *Architecture, Mysticism and Myth* which encouraged Arts and Crafts architects to make their designs all the more elaborate through recondite, occult symbolism. Lethaby's friend, Weir Schultz, made St Andrew's Chapel in Westminster Cathedral have a vault like the sky and a floor like the sea, with marble inlaid with sea creatures. But this is not the reason why it is beautiful.

Symbolic architecture can easily degenerate into pretentiousness. It is best when it is a simple joke, as with the symbolic 'egg cups' - representing breakfast - on Terry Farrell's TV-am studio in Camden Town. Lutyens was the master of the architectural joke, but his were not symbolic statements but mannerisms, such as the pilasters which have bases and capitals but disappear into the rustication in between (as on the Midland Bank in Poultry in the City). The Thematic House is naturally full of Post-Modern Classical jokes. A good one is in the kitchen, which has a Doric entablature-cum-shelf - the metopes are gaps for teapots, etc., while the triglyphs are made of wooden spoons.

Post-Modern Classicism has become, therefore, a whimsical misuse of Classical elements. Certainly a distinct style can be detected, characterised by the perverse and non-structural use of mouldings, columns reduced to cylinders, and a penchant for the semi-circular gable and a strange segmental shape with a stepped bottom which is a motif Jencks claims as his own - the 'Jencksiana' - having evolved it in about 1975. Many of these elements can be found in the work of Piers Gough, a young architect of real wit who designed the jacuzzi in the Jencks House, and in the increasingly huge schemes of Terry Farrell, a resourceful planner who is an accomplished exponent of 'contextualism' - working with existing urban fabrics (perhaps the most positive aspect of Post-Modernism) - and who abandoned the harsh language of 'High Tech' for that of Jencks. Farrell was responsible for many of the best features of the Thematic House; that he is designing skyscrapers to straddle London Wall and office developments to loom over Charing Cross Station shows that Post-Modernism is thoroughly acceptable to planners if not to all architects.

The most vulgar elements in the Thematic House - monumental chimney-pieces which support fat tubes, or columns, supporting busts - were designed by Michael Graves, an American architect responsible for much of the language of Post-Modernism. Graves began as one of the East Coast 'Whites', a coterie of architects who developed an utterly esoteric language from the style of the early Modern Movement. Pretentiousness to the point of obscurity is the essence of these heroes of the architectural schools, whose careers were made by teaching and drawing rather than by building - Tom Wolfe, that unerring deflater of pseudery in architecture, quotes Graves speaking about 'a level of participation that involves the reciprocal act of ourselves with the figure of the building'. Then Graves went Post-Modern, not in built work but in charming, abstracted drawings in crayon, depicting arches and keystones in pastel shades which soon became highly regarded and very expensive.

It is no accident that the principal interpreters of the rhetoric of Post-Modernism are all American. It is difficult, I think, for Europeans to appreciate just how seriously American architects take themselves. Charles Jencks made a television film in 1983 – also published as a book – called *Kings of Infinite Space* in which Frank Lloyd Wright and Graves were compared as significant architects who have kept architecture as an art. Mr Graves did not demur, but the only comparison I found convincing was in terms of the two men's squalid private lives – Graves seems almost proud of the number of women who have divorced him. It seems to me, however, that Frank Lloyd Wright was a very great architect who developed a personal language which was based far more upon materials and structure than it was on any symbolic iconography. Graves's Post-Modernism, on the other hand, is all iconography: the buildings themselves are thin, flat, and tawdry. Nor is this quality exclusive to Graves.

Charles Jencks hopes that 'we are only taking the first step in the Post-Modern tradition, a beginning where art, ornament and symbolism are starting again'. I would be more optimistic if I felt that Post-Modernists were trying to learn other lessons from the past, about Commodity and Firmness as well as Delight, which were understood well by the Edwardian Pre-Modernists as well as by the Renaissance. Architecture is more than cosmetics. The essential bankruptcy of Post-Modernism is shown by James Stirling's two alternative designs for redeveloping Mappin & Webb's for Peter Palumbo, each with an arbitrary external treatment of overscaled columns and arches which bear no logical relationship to the interior. All we can be thankful for is that these designs are not loaded with pretentious symbolism. No wonder architectural students are returning to the Modern Movement. *Plus ça change . . .*

2 August 1986

DOMINGO - FREE FOR SOME

Frank Johnson

In the next century, social historians should be able to make something out of the first night last week of Covent Garden's new production of Verdi's opera *Otello*, with Placido Domingo. Over three million unemployed at the time: on day of performance, leader of the Opposition accused Prime Minister of being too mean to pay enough to make sure old people did not die from freak cold suddenly gripping country: yet other people paid from £2 (for a seat from which little can be seen save the wigs of the performers) to £40 (for a seat from which quite a lot can be seen, unless view blocked by wigs of audience): Grand Tier boxes (from which disproportionately little can be seen of performance, but which command perfect view of auditorium) going for £160: yet first night and all four subsequent performances over-subscribed tenfold: also, lots of people managing to get in without paying anything at all (of us, more later). The performance was sponsored by Morgan Grenfell, famous money-lenders of the period who, on the very night of the show, were in disgrace for something complicated to do with famous tavern-keepers.

Furthermore, although the premiere took place amid that bitter weather, people queued on the pavements all the previous night for return tickets which never came, or for the mere 65 seats kept back for sale on the day of the performance, or for standing room. Others queued from six in the morning, only to be disappointed.

The production came at a difficult time for the much-loved, but much-hated, institution in which it took place. For years, the people who ran the opera house had been denounced for putting on stuff which was too unimaginative for most of the time and which had an excess of imagination the rest of the time.

Much of the population thought the opera house cost them too much. A minority, mainly in the capital, all agreed that a triumphant *Otello* had become essential to the institution's survival. To the Royal Opera House, Covent Garden, then, on the fateful night of 13 January, 1987!

As we neared the theatre, people in the streets held out banknotes – the traditional sign of despair among the ticketless. Burly men, of coarse manners, lurked in the freezing doorways – the hated touts. No lovers of late Verdi, they! More like the desperate *bravos* of the Maestro's early and middle periods, such as Sparafucile, the professional assassin who approaches Rigoletto in a darkened Mantuan street, and offers his sword for any service. ('Signor, a moment, you see before you a man who bears a stalls ticket. £300 and it's yours, guvnor.'). In the foyer, *tout Londres* greeted one another with shrieks and cuddles. As the house lights went down, the Prime Minister slipped into the seat in the Royal Box, next to Sir Claus Moser, the house's sorely abused chairman. After the interval, she was seated next to Lord Drogheda, the previous chairman.

Further along the box, distributed among less famous faces who might have come from Morgan Grenfell, or its less controversial clients, was Mr Denis Thatcher. Sitting through late Verdi, one of the ones without decent tunes, not so much as 'La donna è mobile' in sight, Mr Thatcher was performing not the least of his many services to his country.

Only a fraud would accuse him of philistinism. Reservations about late Verdi have become perfectly respectable in recent years. I wanted to burst into the Royal Box and reassure Mr Thatcher: 'I quite agree with your critique of *Otello*, Sir. I see you subscribe to the view of Italy's foremost authority on Verdi, the late Gabriele Baldini – prefigured by our own George Bernard Shaw, of course – that by *Otello* Verdi had been unduly influenced by Boito's intellectualism, a view now shared even by modernists such as Berio.' But the Special Branch made that impracticable.

As for the performance itself, the audience was in formidable voice, if a little lacking in ease in the higher register. 'MAHV-allous, isn't it,' City editors assured arbitrageurs in the interval.

A lot of people were there who had paid nothing: guests of Morgan Grenfell, guests of corporate seat-holders. But what about the critics' guests? Why should critics need a guest to help them get through a night such as this? And what were the critical credentials of some of the critics – those from glossy magazines, and the pops? Affectionately, I greeted one such friend who had scarcely been known to pay for his opera tickets for nearly a generation. Also jumping the queue free were officials of other subsidised arts institutions, such as museums and theatres. Then there were the free tickets for the diary columns, and the arts editors. I know. I was in on one myself. It was a perfect occasion on which to ponder the rise of the Freebocracy. As in the ancien régime, access to privilege and the sweets of life is gained in our time, not by possession of vulgar wealth, but of offices – some of them mythical.

The guests of Morgan Grenfell and the other corporations, though less knowledgeable about opera than some among the Freebocracy, were at least occupying seats for which the opera house, and therefore the taxpayer, had been paid. Also, the bankers had paid for part of the show, so they had a right to give seats to any old brute and his wife – some of whom might well become opera lovers as a result. The remedy is in the opera house's own hands.

At the end of the evening, Sir Claus was seen to cover his face with relief the moment the cheering brought reassurance that triumph had been secured. Mr Thatcher betrayed no sign of his ordeal. Addressing the cast on stage afterwards, the Prime Minister was reported as denying the evening paper diary's report that she did not like opera. The subsidy seemed safe for the time being.

24 January 1987

POETIC PAINS

Anthony Daniels

Dr Johnson thought it was easier to say what poetry was not than to say what it was. He had, of course, the inestimable advantage of living in the 18th century.

With my exiguous poetical education, even I appreciate that, for example:

> Full many a glorious morning have I seen
> Flatter the mountain-tops with sovereign eye

is poetry. About the following, heard recited by a vagrant poet at Speakers' Corner above the raving of a Palestinian fanatic and the impassioned rationality of a British Humanist Society missionary, while a man with a sandwich board warning of the seven deadly proteins (peas, lentils, etc.) threaded his way through the audience, I am not so sure:

> Quarter past six! Quarter past six!
> And still the bloody fucking bastard of the bus doesn't come.

Was it poetry? And if it wasn't, what of the anthologised words of Ian Hamilton Finlay?

> Green Waters
> Blue Spray
> Grayfish

Anna T
Karen B
Netta Croan

These days, it is just as difficult to say what poetry isn't as to say what it is.

I started out on my investigation of the poetical life of London with the assumption that educated and literate people (like myself) no longer felt constrained to keep up with the poets of their day. I asked several of my friends, literate to a man, to recite some lines of any post-Eliot poet, and with the exception of some stuttered Betjeman, there was a deathly hush. I concluded that latter-day poetry was of consuming interest only to a tiny minority of hardened literati.

Yet London is teeming with poets. Every night of the week there are several poetical events. But the unacknowledged legislators of the world are no more united than the acknowledged ones. They live in myriad small circles which scarcely intersect. Some, moreover, are hermetically sealed. The Black Women's Writing and Creativity Workshop at the Greenwich Council for Racial Equality would not speak to me because I was white (and a man).

Of course, poets have certain traits in common. Generally, they do not dress well. They do not arrive on time. Their squabbles when they congregate make *Dallas* seem like the Vienna Boys' Choir. They tend to be earnest.

Numerically speaking, the most important poetic events are the writers' workshops which abound at the periphery of slums. They take place in dismal rooms in near-derelict municipal buildings, venues also for hatha yoga classes, anti-rape seminars and English lessons for Turkish immigrants. They are obviously important in the lives of their participants. There is something desperately sad about them.

Many were founded with the intention of giving the inarticulate a chance to be heard, an opportunity to develop their powers of self-expression. There are still a few genuinely working-class poets among them, people who have struggled – quite often late in life – against a lack of formal education, a limited vocabulary and syntactical inflexibility. They have a wealth of experience on which to draw, but their imagination rarely takes flight. They do not realise that all over the city are people producing identical work.

For the most part, however, these workshops have been taken over by intellectuals on the fringes of working-class life: teachers, community workers and so forth. They are all 'committed'. They believe themselves free of convention but they have certain attitudes and beliefs in common. They are hostile to poets who have sullied themselves by publication by 'establishment' publishers. They do not study classical poets, whom they regard as mystifiers and misleaders of the toiling (but poetry-reading) masses. They are all but unanimous in their belief there is a conspiracy afoot to prevent them from being published, except in cyclostyled format or in small editions subsidised by local councils. (There is a vast *samizdat* in England too.)

They are convinced it is the subject matter of their verse that makes them unacceptable to capitalist publishers, too hot to handle as it were. It is a perfect psychological antidote to failure. They do not understand the tedium of poetry as *agitprop*, of poems which are merely pamphlets cut up into short lines.

Of the Brixton riots one poet writes:

> And Brixton is a woman wasted, shot in the back
> Squeezed to her knees by lawless law-men.

Even the deepest personal feelings are subcontracted to a Cause, in the case of the above poet (a teetotal transvestite schoolteacher, who described himself as simply a man who wore skirts), that of demanding that every man allow his femininity a chance:

> My sex
> Isn't narrow or one-eyed
> Like a fist to the jaw
> Doesn't slam the door
> Or jump into the driving seat.

Into this world of causes, claimants' rights, etc., no complexity, irony, ambiguity, melancholy, joy, tragedy or even love is ever allowed to enter. It was all the more surprising, therefore, to meet in one of the groups a poet, introduced to me as an anarchist bus driver, who had what I can only call a poetic vision of the world. I am no real judge of such matters, but his use of language struck me as original, and unlike the others he was broad-minded enough to have an affection even for what he did not approve of.

His idea of poetry did not meet with general approval. It was insufficiently political. A discussion ensued. He did not agree Shakespeare was great because he represented a rising class. There *was* such a thing as poetic genius. The others retorted it was wrong to think of poets as geniuses, they were merely exemplars of social tendencies. But even here they could not allow themselves to be honest. If only they could have seen themselves extracting their most recent compositions from their plastic carrier bags, trembling with passion and anxiety, and heard their own voices quivering at each line of their latest masterpieces, written but yesterday in the launderette, *then* they might have believed in the theory of poetical genius. Significantly, only the anarchist bus driver was collecting his work for a proper publisher.

I went to the offices of one of the largest publishers of poetry, the very epicentre of the conspiracy against the nation's poets. There I met one of the poetry editors, himself a well-known poet, and the man in charge of poetry marketing. Poetry *marketing*? Had the era of the hard sell come at last to high art? In a word, yes.

Surveys, he said, had shown that at least 70 per cent of the population had tried to write poetry at some time in their lives. Sales of mainstream poetry in Britain were running at £7 million a year (of which his company accounted for a quarter). Certain poets now sold 35,000 copies of their new collections. The print run of a book by a previously unpublished poet was 4,000, compared with 2,000 for a novelist. Two new books of poems had reached the bestseller lists this year. Past poets sold in editions of scores of thousands year after year. At that moment, if I could have bought shares in poetry, I would have.

Poetry publishing had come through a very bad patch, the marketing man continued. For a long time poetry had been treated like a rare and fastidious orchid on the verge of extinction. To survive, it was thought to need careful sequestration from the public plus liberal subsidies. First a poet received a subsidy for a book, then it became absolutely vital he sold *less* than 500 copies, to justify the subsidy. Subsidies were as habit-forming as heroin. Eventually someone realised there was money to be made out of poetry, and before long poets were barnstorming the country like election candidates, reading their work to packed audiences. One famous tour allegedly took place by helicopter. It didn't, but all the razzamatazz and associated publicity sold thousands of copies.

I looked at the poetry editor for signs of distaste at this vulgarity. He was smiling and nodding his head enthusiastically. I imagined him parachuting into Wembley Stadium where 100,000 sonnet-lovers greeted him with rapturous applause.

I asked whether commercial considerations determined the content and style of what was published. But the poetry editor's freedom was absolute in this regard, and he took the view that if it was good, it would sell. The marketing came later. I asked him what he meant by *good*. 'If I like it. If I find it arresting.' As for the conspiracy against the poets, he received nearly 2,000 unsolicited poetical manuscripts a year, and he read every one. Under the circumstances, he was remarkably normal.

Poetry readings fall naturally into several categories. I missed out altogether on the phenomenon of Punk poetry which, from the reports I received, consisted largely of young men shouting insults at their listeners and even spitting at them. I gather Punk poetry does not transfer very successfully to the printed page. The best exponents of this avant-garde form were (I was told) Atilla the Stockbroker and Joolz.

Rather up-market, I attended a reading by Molly Parkin and her daughter Sophie in an SW3 pub. Miss Parkin was advertised as a 'bawdy bardette'. The local intelligentsia flocked in, pale young men and ladies straight from Garsington. In front of me sat a formidable lady with a piratical black eyepatch, who kept repeating 'Marvellous! Marvellous!'

The Misses Parkin had a supporting cast of two poets, the first of whom dressed for the occasion like an editor of a small-town American newspaper in the 1940s. The dispute at Wapping had inspired him to write a Kipling-style ballad, about 'Murdoch and his team of foreign spivs'. Unfortunately, he read it in an assumed Yorkshire accent, a symbol no doubt of his solidarity, but geographically and sociologically inaccurate. One line suffices to illustrate his analysis of the events: 'Coz we're only simple printers, see.' The audience was much moved.

The second of the supporting poets was a Welshman with a fine turn of phrase, a minor Dylan Thomas, whose description of what he called 'a force ten hangover' was splendidly graphic. 'I go out in search of another head as others go out for a loaf.' His political viewpoint soon revealed itself, expressed with some talent:

> Sloane noses in the air,
> The Tory Party at breath

The audience laughed, but a little nervously. They all read the *Guardian*, of course, but some of their best friends came from Sloane Square.

Then it was the turn of the bawdy bardettes. The younger Miss Parkin, in ochre satin and matching turban, looked as though she had escaped from a production of *Il Seraglio*. Her mother's appearance, on the other hand, reminded me forcibly of a palmist I once consulted at Battersea Funfair. ('You'll be educated,' she had said. 'It'll take a long time.')

It became apparent in the course of their recitation that all that was necessary to enthral the audience was a sufficiently smutty poem. When Miss Parkin (senior) mislaid one of her poems and said 'Oh fuck it,' the audience rocked with laughter as though a Wildean *bon mot* had been uttered. I came away with the impression that our bourgeois intelligentsia were a craven and spineless lot.

Of *real* poets I do not feel able to write. I attended readings by well-known figures, and it seemed to me they were well-known precisely because they are better. (Please don't ask me what I mean by better.) But occasionally even so accomplished a poet as Fleur Adcock descends to the bathos of right-thinking and turns a *Guardian* editorial into verse:

> I write in praise of the solitary act:
> of not feeling a trespassing tongue
> forced into one's mouth . . .

Generally the standard is high, however, as why should it not be? After all, there are 12 times as many Englishmen alive as in Shakespeare's time.

But whether anyone in a hundred years will recite the verse that is written now is a question as open as whether anyone then will go around humming Stockhausen. For my own part, I heard nothing that gripped my heart like Shakespeare or Keats, but when it comes to modern verse:

> Don't ask what it was all about
> I haven't got a clue.

7 February 1987

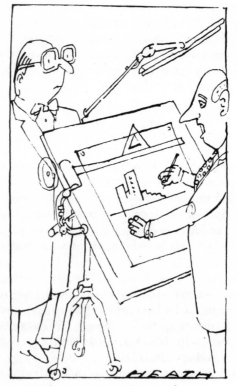

'Mind you, I'm not too keen on the way
Prince Charles is designed, either.'

THE NEW EDITORIAL AMAZONS

Paul Johnson

It would not surprise me if, in 50 years' time, perhaps even in 30, the British newspaper scene were dominated by women. This will be achieved not by feminist militancy but by personal success stories. Fairness between the sexes (the word equality should be dismissed with contempt) is brought about not by ideological nonsense or ridiculous bodies like the Equal Opportunities Commission but by getting real women into actual jobs and allowing them to show how well they can do. One Thatcher is worth regiments of Kate Milletts and Gloria Steinems. When I was an editor I was not keen on publishing Women's Lib material but I had women correspondents in New York, Moscow, Berlin, Paris and Jerusalem and brought in one of the first women leader-writers. That seems to me then, and still seems now, the right way to do it.

There is a continuing need, however, to give women positive encouragement. Journalism is still a man's world: you have only to peer into the newsroom of a national paper to see that. Young women in particular can do with a helping hand, through such institutions as the Catherine Pakenham Memorial Prize. Catherine was the youngest daughter of an exceptionally gifted and competitive family and found it hard going to match up to her elders. She had just, to her intense delight, achieved her first real success, a job on the *Telegraph Magazine*, when she was killed in a car accident. Her parents and the *Telegraph* set up the prize, awarded annually to the best piece of journalism by a woman under 30. It has been an outstanding success in encouraging and discovering talent, with many of the prizewinners becoming stars in national journalism. It is now sponsored by the *Evening Standard*, an appropriate choice, for the *Standard* has long had a reputation for promoting women writers, of the calibre of Valerie Grove and Maureen Cleave. The *Standard* is owned today by Lord Rothermere's group and the presentation of the 1987 prize last month was made in Northcliffe's own office, now painstakingly restored, a spectacular chamber of ormolu, rosewood and Napoleonic symbols. I could not help thinking: what would the old monster have thought of this occasion? The answer is not in doubt: he would have strongly approved of it. For Northcliffe sought talent, whatever the cost and provenance.

Indeed it is the archetype press tycoons, despised by the feminists as promoters of male-inspired stereotypes, who are now taking the lead in pushing women up the ladder. I have often complained in this column that, whereas women writers were now common, men remained in almost exclusive possession of the positions of power on newspapers. That is no longer true. Quite suddenly, women are being given key commands. This month, for instance, women take over as news editors of two of the most important regional dailies, the Southampton *Southern Evening News* and the *Leicester Mercury*.

More significant, however, was Rupert Murdoch's decision, last summer, to appoint Wendy Henry to edit the *News of the World*, which with a circulation of over five million is Britain's biggest-selling paper and a top money-spinner in his empire. This adventurous decision seems to have proved a commercial success. It has brought a response from Robert Maxwell, who has given the editorship of the rival *Sunday Mirror* to Eve Pollard. She, like Henry, is young but hugely experienced, in magazines as well as newspapers. She has had a hand in Murdoch's *Elle* as well as Rothermere's brilliant *You*, and I take it that her appointment means Maxwell has decided to give the *Sunday Mirror* what it so badly needs, a colour magazine.

What we are going to see, in fact, is a struggle between two journalistic Amazons for the top position in the Sunday tabloid market. The *News of the World* starts out with a commanding, some would say unassailable, lead of two million copies, and with all the psychological advantages of self-confidence, panache and (not least) money-power which such success produces. By contrast, the *Sunday Mirror* is low-spirited and in danger of becoming demoralised. But that gives Pollard the opportunity to stamp her own personality on the paper and to pilot it in a new direction. What I shall be looking for is two things. First, does she recognise that the Age of Sleaze, which dominated tabloids in the 1970s and most of the 1980s, is now on the wane – the failure of the first Bonk paper being a portent? In short, there is not much future for the *Sunday Mirror* as a mere me-too paper tagging behind the *News of the World* with the same formula of sex, royalty, television soap stars and privacy-invasion. Second, can she give back to the *Mirror* the characteristics which once decisively differentiated it from its rival: a political soul, a fiery conscience and a campaigning spirit? If so, this struggle for the new title of Queen of the Nationals is going to be well worth watching.

Meanwhile, up market, where higher and more progressive values are supposed to prevail, there is no sign yet of a corresponding breakthrough by women. Lack of talent cannot be the answer, with journalists of the calibre of Polly Toynbee and Mary Kenny around. I suspect the reason is a lingering conviction that women are not suited to write about politics and finance, with which the qualities must principally concern themselves. That is nonsense. The *Mirror*'s Julia Langdon is an excellent political columnist, as was Nora Beloff of the *Observer* in her day. As for money-making, this is an area where women are now achieving the most rapid progress, both as doers and analysts. One of the smartest journalists I have met for a long time, for instance, is Amity Shlaes, now a big wheel on the European edition of the *Wall Street Journal*. The truth is there is now nothing to stop a woman editing a quality national, except prejudice.

23 January 1988

DURABLE BRILLO PAD

A profile of Andrew Neil

The host of bruised journalists hoping to see Andrew Neil tumble out of the sky and land flat on his back are in for another season of disappointment. Neil has lost none of the powers of abrasive endurance so brilliantly encompassed by his *Private Eye* nickname, 'Brillo Pad'. Only 39, and currently doubling as editor of the *Sunday Times* and chairman of Rupert Murdoch's Sky TV venture, he is still on the advance. Neil is a future-lover, entranced by gadgetry, and rarely moved by the past, other than for an occasional gloat. 'I have never hidden my hatred of Fleet Street,' he once said. 'I'm delighted to have played a major part in its demise.'

It is hard to imagine any journalist who actually worked in Fleet Street expressing such a hostile view, however much they might detest the print unions. The place was deep in sentiment, inhibiting every reforming move. Neil had no problem, never having worked for a national newspaper before Murdoch appointed him to the *Sunday Times* back in 1983. On arrival the new editor was the third youngest member of the editorial staff.

At the time old *Sunday Times* hands, recruited in the high days of Harry Evans, saw Neil's appointment as a gratuitous humiliation exercise on Murdoch's part. His role, it was thought, was to give a hard time to the journalists who had previously given the proprietor a bad time by threatening to haul in the Monopolies Commission when he took over the *Times* and *Sunday Times*.

This was shallow thinking. Murdoch is not averse to revenge, but he always keeps a cold eye on the balance sheet. And to achieve his designs at the *Sunday Times* and in Fleet Street he needed not just an outsider, but a rank outsider. Someone a bit like himself.

Though born on opposite sides of the planet, Murdoch and Neil have a lot in common. Both espouse right-wing radical views and couple them with blunt utterances. Neither is particularly keen on the English, especially the softies from Oxbridge in its Establishment. And both, while possessed of powerful intellects, are averse to intellectuals. A *Sunday Times* leader, with Neil's thumbprint, spoke of Britain's intellectuals, 'wandering aimlessly between Islington and the Groucho Club'.

America is greatly admired. Murdoch is its most famous non-native citizen and Neil is refreshed by its energy – 'a great source of ideas and adrenalin for me'. In their dressing style and personal carriage both have a touch of the Hollywood gangster, though Murdoch leans to Bogart, while Neil is more the double-breasted Cagney.

Neil was brought up in Paisley in the west of Scotland where his father worked as a town and country planner. By all accounts he was precocious politically. Where the other paperboys used to siphon off comics for home reading, Neil would salt away a surplus issue of *The Spectator*.

At Glasgow University, where he read politics and economics, Neil's cudgelling style soon impressed itself on the Tory Party. The young man attracted loud applause from the faithful at the 1970 Conservative Party conference when he urged the Government to desist from willy-nilly wage increases and take on the unions, even at the risk of a general strike.

He was an active chairman of the Federation of Conservative Students, enlivening its annual revue with a sketch entitled 'Parliamo Glasgow' which Neil presented in impenetrable Glaswegian. On graduation, he immediately landed a job in the Tory Party Central Office. Peter Walker, then the Environment Secretary in the Heath government, took a shine to the young Scot with an extraordinary capacity for hard work and employed him on housing problems.

It was good experience, but Neil was not one of nature's backroom boys. In 1973 he joined the *Economist*, then being moved and shaken by the editorship of Alastair Burnet. Neil learned the trade, seeing service in Ulster, America and the House of Commons. In the year before he was plucked away by Murdoch, Neil worked as the *Economist*'s home editor. It was not national newspaper experience, but it was as good as. And Neil had another crucial area of expertise.

One of Neil's earliest articles for the magazine had dealt contentiously with social issues in Scotland. He was invited to join a television debate on Scottish problems and the camera somehow took to his rough-hewn features. Television work began to flow and Neil wound up presenting *The Risk Business* for BBC and *Look Here* for LWT. But his was more than a front-of-house interest.

The diversity of American television enchanted him and Neil persuaded the US anti-trust consultancy, National Economic Research Associates, to let him set up a British branch to campaign for the deregulation of television. One of the first people Neil approached was Rupert Murdoch, a man known to have satellite longings in him even then. They then strayed onto the subject of Fleet Street.

As editor, Neil was always way ahead of his detractors. While the gossip columns wittered on about his bachelor status, deeply unconfirmed, and the significance of the 'Norwegian Wood' jingle on his answerphone – 'I once had a girl, or should I say she once had me' – Neil was already formulating plans for Fleet Street, fingers curled round the end of the rug.

Within four months of taking over, Neil had already quietly persuaded Eddy Shah of the wisdom of outflanking the print unions by starting a national newspaper with the new computer-based direct inputting technology. Thereafter, even more quietly, Murdoch was drawn into the idea of printing all his British titles (the *Times, Sunday Times, News of the World* and *Sun*) in one plant, using the same labour-shedding new technology.

Things could hardly have worked out more sweetly. While the print unions stood poised, hammers raised, over Shah's *Today* mousehole, the Wapping elephant came thundering by.

Wapping was Neil's finest hour as a technocrat but his most perilous as a journalist. In the period between his arrival and Wapping – little over two years – more than 40 front-rank journalists left the paper, ranging from Hugo Young, arguably the best political writer of the decade, to Don McCullin, unquestionably the best war photographer of the time. But there was a certain hard logic to it, as the editor fashioned a paper in his own image. Young expressed the liberal sentiments Neil did not much want to read, and McCullin took the kind of pictures of Third World suffering that he did not want to see.

But the earlier outflow was as nothing to that after Wapping. *Sunday Times* journalists peeled off in all directions to join the picket line, to prop up *Today*, and most of all to climb aboard the *Independent*. Ian Jack, a fellow Scot thought to be close to Neil and the best writer on the paper, left with the parting words, 'I felt if I were to carry on walking through picket lines I had to have something to believe in, to walk in to. It has stopped being an intelligent newspaper.'

Name-calling Neil could stand, but as the newspaper's circulation headed briskly down towards the million mark it had passed 20 years earlier, his position did begin to look vulnerable. A vote of no confidence in his editorship by the journalists actually inside Wapping was narrowly headed off.

The end of the industrial dispute in February 1987 gave Neil the freedom to expand the journalistic supermarket at his disposal. Neil, from his American experience again, is disposed to the creation of a newspaper best picked up with a fork-lift truck. And his commercial instinct has been right. As the sections have multiplied, the circulation has risen past the 1.3 million he inherited to within hailing distance of 1.5 million, an all-time high.

The newspaper has improved. It is now so big that the editor cannot breathe so heavily over its entirety and the main section, once cluttered by ad-pulling specialisms, now has scope to address more general issues.

With his newspaper base secure, Neil has been able to explore the satellite propositions that first brought him together with Murdoch. Wishful thinkers among Neil's enemies believe that Murdoch may be tiring of his protégé and that the improbably difficult Sky job may be designed to give him his come-uppance. But given that Murdoch has offered himself as scapegoat for the main flaw in the enterprise – the conspicuous absence of dishes – this seems hardly likely.

More troublesome for Neil perhaps, as newspapers start to move out of the era of dramatic technological change and back conceivably to journalism, are the question-marks over his editorial standards. The most recent embarrassment has been over the paper's coverage of Thames Television's 'Death on the Rock' programme. Three *Sunday Times* 'Insight' reporters involved in the story have expressed disquiet about how their material was used to fashion an anti-Thames, pro-government case.

This calls to mind one of Neil's earliest investigations into the plight of Eddy Shah when locked in combat with the print unions in Warrington. The copy produced was colourful and Neil got to meet Shah, but Peter Gillman, the top 'Insight' reporter working on the story, quietly climbed off the back of the newspaper. He had difficulty matching what came out with what he had put in.

'Insight', the newspaper's investigative unit, was high on Neil's hit list when he took over. It was founded in the Sixties, not one of Neil's favourite decades, and went on steadily winning awards through the Seventies. Neil bizarrely regarded it as 'a state within a state' and a vehicle for the 'hard Left', yet the enterprise, if not the personnel, survived. There is no question now of its operating as a state within a state, the only uncertainty is about what it is the vehicle for.

25 February 1989

Chapter 9
ALTERNATIVE HEALTH

'Monsieur wants a second helping?'

PUT OUT MORE FLANS

Evelyn Daube

When it comes to food there is a war on: nouvies versus the regionalists. What sweet relief it is to go to a house where someone bangs a joint of meat in the oven, boils a few vegetables anglaise and lets you get on with it.

The other day I offered seven people a Christmas pudding which had marinated in its own brandy since last September. There were a few nouvies among them who stared at it glumly. They had been expecting Perrier water sorbet with three hand-culled strawberries on the side. Like many a smiling hostess before me, I looked down the table and thought buzz off the lot of you.

Nouvelle cuisine has undermined many robust traditional dishes both in France and England. Nothing debases faster than food. Whatever its earnest origins, NC now means dining in a dragged, ragged room full of Fulham anorexics. It means octagonal plates and having to say 'How lovely' before the waiter will go away. It is a chef arranging five smears of

'Waiter! There's meat in my soup.'

fish pâté on a plate ah so because food is like a haiku. It is a gherkin spread out like a fan or a thin pastry case shaped like a flower with a dot of mango gloop in it. NC means looking at food without the obligation of eating it ('*Nouvelle*, Alice,' 'Alice, *nouvelle*'). It means five blobs of puréed veg on your side plate and a bill for £72 for three plus VAT. It means you need your head examined.

30 June 1984

THE BIG SLEEP

Jeffrey Bernard

Did you read or hear about the man who killed himself while trying to commit suicide the other day? Apparently this man, in an attempt to hang himself, climbed up a tree to attach a rope on to a branch and fell and broke his neck. Then there was the drunken motorist who was stopped by the police who asked him to take a breathaliser test. He ran away from them and inadvertently fell over a cliff, killing himself. A little longer ago, I'm told that the fire brigade were called out to rescue a kitten which had got stuck up a tree. They successfully rescued the animal, bringing him down to earth, and then the fire engine reversed over pussy, finally flattening him. Delightful stuff. Father Time must surely be about to join the great band of the unemployed. It makes one realise how delightfully uncomplicated lemmings are.

What worries me though is the amount of people who are making no attempt whatsoever to kill themselves when it should be, of course, their priority. I myself have to own up to a certain amount of lethargy concerning my own suicide which seems to be taking an age, but then I always did like to take things easily. Falling out of trees, over cliffs and beneath fire engines is far too sudden for me. I think though that Ruby is slowly talking me to death.

Ruby is a local barmaid who some call 'nurse'. She's middle aged, looks rather like Harpo Marx and she gets a taxi to and from work although she only earns £1 an hour. She lives on Bounty Bars and crisps – don't they all? – and she moans from opening time till closing time. I say she's talking me to death since I actually fell asleep at 11 a.m. the other morning when she was on at me, and I wasn't even tired. Does the tsetse fly lurk in Lambourn? Half an hour later I actually dozed off while standing in a queue in the dry cleaning shop. The women ahead of me spent 20 minutes discussing their forthcoming coffee morning and all of them with those fixed benign smiles on their faces just like Ruby has. I suddenly realised that I'm hypnotised by them and that's why I keep dropping off.

It's very odd. You know the way girls up till the age of 20 or so can't help giggling all the time; well, women who don't feel they're in direct competition with men, that is, housewives who've suffered brain damage from having been married to boring men for too long, they plod through life with the fixed smile. Age silences the giggle and then the paralysis of the smile sets in. There are men too in the Lambourn valley who can play the sandman just as effectively. I came closer to the grim reaper than I've ever been before the other day, when a relative of Ruby's got me nodding off at a table in the pub car park. This is what I get a hell of a lot of.

*'Good Lord! Isn't that Jenkinson? I thought
he was drinking himself to death.'*

'Plenty of work about for you, Jeff? No? I should have thought you'd be doing very well. But it's the same for all of us really, isn't it? And, you mark my words, it's going to get a lot worse before it gets better. I mean there just isn't the money about any more, is there? Mind you, it's all right for some, I dare say; farmers and suchlike. No, when you think what a pound's worth today, well. Funny though, I should have thought those magazines and things you write for, I should have thought they'd pay very well. No? Of course, you know what you ought to do? I'll tell you. You should write a book. I'll tell you what. If I could write I'd sit down and write a book. God, the stories I could tell. Still, Fleet Street's cutting its own throat, isn't it? I'll say one thing for Mrs Thatcher though, she's nobody's fool. Tell me, Jeff, what do you think of her? Oh you don't. Well we're all entitled to our views aren't we. One man's meat and all that. Oh well I suppose we'd better have one for the road, eh. Your usual I take it? Righty ho. By the way, Jeff, something I've always meant to ask you. You've met Lester Piggott haven't you? What's he *really* like?'

Now a few months ago, at this point, I would have simply screamed with the pain of it. But, this time, I fell asleep again. I'm beginning to think that off a tree, over a cliff or under a fire engine would be preferable after all.

6 September 1980

THE MEDICAL REVOLUTION

Brian Inglis

Six weeks ago I wrote an article, 'Medicine and the media', criticising the press, radio and TV for their chronic subservience to the medical profession. Even before it had appeared in *The Spectator* Ian Kennedy had begun his Reith Lectures on the theme of 'Unmasking Medicine'. *Panorama*, too, had sought to do its own unmasking, by sowing doubts about the ability of doctors to ascertain whether patients are really dead, before transplanting their organs: the resulting controversy showing just how tired the BBC, from the Director-General down, has become with the medical establishment's assumption that it has a prescriptive right to have such issues presented only in the way it wants them to be presented.

The medical establishment's reaction, amounting in some instances to paranoia, provided a topical justification for the thesis Kennedy propounded in the first of his lectures: 'We must become the masters of medicine, not its servants.' Ironically Kennedy has taken the doctors' side on the transplant issue, on the ground that the programme was unfair. Perhaps it was; but for the establishment to demand not just the right to reply, but the right to have what amounted to control of the programme, raised doubts, as the *New Scientist* put it, 'about their genuine intention to participate in an honest debate'.

As it happens, there has just been an example of what can happen when a member of the medical establishment is given the right to reply unfettered. Following a *Man Alive* programme which had shown a particularly horrendous breast cancer operation, a surgeon was allowed time to criticise the programme; and he denounced it as dishonest, on the ground that the operation is not now employed. This was simply untrue; extended radical mastectomy has been widely used here, and although the fact that it is ineffective as well as mutilating has been clear from the mortality statistics for some years, there are still surgeons who subject patients to it. But as this surgeon had not informed the *Man Alive* production team that he proposed to challenge their research findings (taken, incidentally, from medical sources), nobody was ready with a rebuttal; viewers were left with the impression that the early programme *had* been dishonest.

Yet perhaps not; viewers, too, are showing signs of mistrust of the medical profession and its spokesmen. General practitioners used to stand high in the public's esteem; no longer. Citing a poll which has revealed that the proportion of patients who trust their doctors has slipped from over 50 per cent to under 40 per cent in a single year, a writer in *World Medicine* – himself a GP – has sadly admitted that 'the image of the GP has reached its lowest ebb'.

Why is it, the writer asked, 'that patients who were once ready to put their lives unquestioningly into the hands of their GP now wouldn't buy a used car from him?' The answer, or part of it, has emerged in these Reith Lectures. The medical profession, Kennedy shows, has become an anachronism, for much the same reasons as the cavalry became an anachronism. Doctors are selected and trained to diagnose and treat diseases on the basis of a medical model. But the diseases of our civilisation require a different, psychosocial, model; and the profession is not geared to make the change.

This is not the fault of the National Health Service. As Professor Archibald Cochrane has recently pointed out, it is the most cost-effective health service in the world, 'the best of a very bad lot'. It is the most cost-

effective because it has avoided 'payment per item of service', which
encourages a proliferation of unnecessary and expensive forms of treatment ('That any sane nation, having observed that you could provide for
the supply of bread by giving bakers a pecuniary interest in baking for
you, should go on to give a surgeon a pecuniary interest in cutting off
your leg', as Bernard Shaw commented, 'is enough to make one despair of
political humanity').

The existence of the NHS protects us from the worst consequences of
professional rapacity; but it does not protect patients from the kind of
professional myopia which has preserved extended radical mastectomy
in spite of the evidence. Doctors in general, and surgeons in particular,
tend to offer the same types of treatment whether they are paid for it or
not – they merely offer it more frequently if they are paid. And what they
are offering, Kennedy argues, is largely irrelevant to what we, the public,
need.

We need a medical service which would primarily be concerned with
prevention. The service we get is almost entirely concerned with the
treatment of diseases which have *not* been prevented: a 'curative science
in which the model of the doctor is that of the engineer-mechanic curing
a sick engine'. That well over two-thirds of the funds available for the
NHS should go to hospitals is an indictment of modern medicine: 'If pre-
ventive medicine, school health care, and general primary care meant
anything, hospitals would be far less needed.'

Take heart disease, the chief killer of our time. There is disagreement
over the interpretation of the evidence, but nobody now disputes that the
chief risk factors are psychosocial rather then medical: cigarette smoking, excess of animal fat in the diet, lack of exercise, and a 'Type A' personality, competitive, stress-prone.

Inevitably, the medical profession concentrates on the only major risk
factor which can be medically treated: high blood pressure. But high
blood pressure, as a number of eminent cardiologists have insisted, is not
a disease. It is a stress symptom. Artificially to lower it by taking drugs is
foolish – and dangerous. But in the main, cardiologists concentrate upon
it, and upon treating the unfortunates who have had heart attacks; wherever possible bringing them in to coronary care units, in spite of the fact
that independent surveys have shown that the chances of recovery are
rather less, in such units, than at home.

What, then, can we do to make ourselves once again the masters of
medicine, not its servants? Kennedy's plan is to enlist consumerism to
the cause: the consumer, in this case, being the patient. Patients must
learn not to do what the doctor orders unless they feel that they have
been fully and fairly briefed about the drug, or the operation, so that they

can make up their own minds. And it is time to end the convention whereby doctors are allowed to police themselves, which has enabled them to resist any audit of the methods they use (if there had been such an audit, extended radical mastectomy would long since have been discarded).

But if, as Kennedy's survey reveals, the medical profession is an expensive anachronism, why should consumers waste their time wrestling with it? Surely it is more likely that, as the *World Medicine* writer suggests, they will vote with their feet; if the trend indicated by the poll continues, 'GPs may wake up one day to find that, while their heads are full of pompous pride, their waiting rooms are empty'.

In my experience, a growing number of GPs are far from feeling either pomposity or pride about their work; they are increasingly uneasy about it. Partly this is because they realise that their largely hospital-orientated training is ludicrously irrelevant to primary care in the home; partly because patients are becoming increasingly suspicious of modern drugs.

But consumerism cannot do anything to alter medical education; it is controlled and run by hospital specialists, umpires who are incapable of accepting the radical reorganisation needed if GPs are to be trained as GPs, with the psychosocial rather than the medical element predominant. And if consumerism is going to shy away from drugs, it is going to shy away from doctors, too, because they have become so hooked on drug-prescribing that they find great difficulty in kicking the habit.

The medical establishment has so insulated itself from the realities that it does not seem to be aware of the shift in the public's attitude. 'The climate of opinion has changed,' Tony Smith, deputy editor of the *BMJ*, wrote recently – but went on to claim that the change lies in the fact that 'the public has come to understand that effective medicines carry some (albeit small) risk'. In my experience, the precise reverse is true. People are becoming more worried about side effects; more mistrustful of stories about 'break-throughs', like interferon; more inclined to go to osteopaths, homoeopaths and acupuncturists, who are enjoying an unprecedented boom largely, they will tell you, because of the prevailing disillusionment with modern drugs.

Although he mentions Illich in passing, Kennedy does not reveal how far he, a lawyer, has taken his study of his predecessors in this field. He makes no mention of Rene Dubos, who sounded an early warning that medicine was taking a wrong path over 20 years ago; or of Eliot Freidson, whose impeccably-documented *Profession of Medicine* won him the American Sociological Association's award for 'having contributed in an outstanding degree to the progress of sociology'; or of Rick Carlson, also a lawyer, who covered ground similar to Kennedy's in *The End of Medicine*;

or of Bernard Dixon's *Beyond the Magic Bullet*. What these books showed is that consumerism is not going to provide enough effective prevention. If it is to be introduced, it can only be introduced by taking it out of the hands of the profession.

20 December 1980

IMPERATIVE COOKING: BELOW THIRTY-TWO FAHRENHEIT

Digby Anderson

No sooner is it British Summertime than Harold Stephenson holds his first dinner party with drinks 'outside'. I don't mind the rain too much but I do not enjoy sitting in Harold's garden staring at his Volvo. He keeps it there. If you want to see plants, you have to go to the kitchen. There are trailing green things in hanging baskets, yuccas on the sill, flowers on the draining board, and a cutlery drawer full of secateurs and soggy green stuff. For all I know there's a pond in the larder. The same perverted principle operates upstairs. There are not books in Harold's 'study': they're all in the lavatory. In my more charitable moments I suppose all these misplacements are part of a regressive chain caused by the deep freeze. That occupies the garage.

Josephine Stephenson says it's invaluable. She cannot think how she ever managed without it, especially when entertaining. She tells us her secret. We 'imagine' the casserole we're eating was prepared that afternoon – not so. Once every ten years, she buys a Volvo bootload of beef, a sack of onions, and a catering-size stock cube. Then she makes a huge stew and freezes it in aluminium containers which hold enough for six persons; 'I expect you've wondered why we are always six for dinner, now you know'. Not to be outdone, Harold has converted the garden beyond the Volvo into a vegetable patch in which he grows stringy runner beans. These he overboils and freezes in eight-pound bags. We eat them with the casserole.

You still want a freezer? You, unlike the Stephensons, will use yours sensibly. You will have to do three things. First, move, as far away from a good fish shop as you can. There are delicious varieties of fish which are nearly always sold frozen: red mullet, snapper, tuna. So, if you can find a house more than two hours' drive from a fishmonger who sells them, if, then you might have found a justification for keeping your own frozen.

Or you could buy an acre and keep pigs, poultry and rabbits. We had lovely pigs. One, the Borough Surveyor's Office, drank beer ullage and ate the plastic washing-up bowls in which he was given food. Some animals, ducks, did freeze well. The pigs, who, plastic bowls apart, lived off scraps and potatoes, certainly tasted better than bought pork even when frozen. But there again, if you can be bothered to keep them, you can be bothered to salt them, turn them into salami, raw ham or bacon. The 20th century is unique in inventing a method of preserving which adds nothing to that preserved. Think not only of charcuterie but of those Italian peppers, artichoke hearts and aubergines bottled in oil or wine vinegar and then think of a bag of Harold's frozen stringy beans.

Or you could develop a liking for outings. Deep freezes provide Puritans who need one with an excuse for an outing. Try 'Sacred and Game', 'St Bartholomew's Eve' and 'Harbour Lounge'. 'S and G' is an early winter morning drive to Norfolk, accelerated pilgrimage to Our Lady of Walsingham and ransack of butchers' shops for stewing partridge, hares, pheasants and wild duck. 'St Bart's' involves finding an egg farm which keeps hens in deep litter. Once the hens' laying average falls (age 18 months plus) the farmers sell them cheaply. Wring the necks, pluck them 'hot' (much easier), hang them for a few days, gut and clean them. 'HL' is no more than hanging about the harbour and buying from the fishing boats the fish the English are too stupid to want. Cuttlefish is usually free. Local restaurants only want crab claws, so the backs, with the excellent dark meat, can be had for next to nothing. Other customers are usually inept and have to ask the fishermen to clean their fish (always cod) so there are always cod heads free. We always return with a sack of fish and miscellaneous ingredients for a fish stew.

The Puritans' reasoning seems to be this, that a deep freeze allows you to buy more on these outings and 'save' more to justify them. Once we took a man with us who talked all the way about how much it 'would' have cost if . . . It quite spoiled the thing. Forget the freezer: better bring home the day's plunder, have two or three splendid meals and give the rest to friends (who have their own outings and bring you their different plunders).

That leaves the distant fish shop as the only reason for any self-professed cook owning one of these frightful things. I'm as fond of mullet as the next chap but not if it means Iris Murdoch in the lavatory, Oasis in the kitchen and an advanced safety-touting chassis on the croquet lawn.

27 April 1985

WHY I DON'T FEEL WELL

Anthony Daniels

Around the year 1900, according to some historians of the subject, a momentous change came over the practice of medicine: for the first time a visit to the doctor was as likely to be beneficial as harmful. According to the same historians, another such change occurred 30 years later. At long last doctors had a statistically unequivocal chance of doing their patients more good than harm.

These momentous changes went unnoticed, however, for the popularity of medicine had never depended on its efficacy. People had been bled and purged for hundreds of years without detecting the absurdity of these treatments. Exquisite were the torments inflicted on patients in the name of therapy, yet provided they were prescribed with authority and brio, they were submitted to gladly.

Paradoxically, it is only as medicine has become more firmly scientific that people have begun to question its value and even turn their backs on it. Every Sunday newspaper carries stories of medical malfeasance, new diseases which medicine cannot cure, or dangerous side-effects of commonly prescribed drugs. Furthermore, there is a revulsion against the mechanistic premises of modern medicine. People want to be treated as 'whole' human beings, not just as broken legs, failing kidneys and so forth. They are turning increasingly to alternative medicine which, as everyone knows, is wholesome, natural, effective and cheap. Who does not know of a chronic case of something or other who, having found no relief from orthodox medicine, has been cured at once by a naturopath, acupuncturist, homoeopath, vedic practitioner, chiropractor, herbalist, spiritual healer, reflexologist or other fringe practitioner?

Even doctors are losing their nerve. For fear of appearing intolerant or arrogant, they are beginning to accord alternative medicine new respect, on the grounds that forty million Frenchmen can't be wrong. They forget their own history.

The scale of the intellectual effort required to give medicine as scientific a basis as some of it now enjoys is insufficiently realised. Every schoolboy knows, for example, that malaria is caused by a microscopic parasite spread by the bite of a certain genus of mosquito; but few appreciate the years of painstaking endeavour it took to make this vital discovery from a position of ignorance. More importantly, the liberating effect of a naturalistic attitude towards disease is not emphasised, for cultural relativism is all the rage: if tribal Africans believe infectious diseases are caused by evil spirits, their views are to be given weight with those of microbiologists.

The efforts of the great pathologists and bacteriologists of the 19th century, however, did no more than lay the foundations for the scientific practice of medicine. They made it possible but not inevitable. One has only to read medical textbooks published before the Second World War to appreciate first that doctors were even then powerless against many of the diseases which we are now able to take lightly, and secondly that their prescriptions (of diet, inhalations, ointments, bed rest and so forth) were often without any scientific basis whatsoever. Indeed, reading the confident assertions of the much-honoured and fashionable physicians of the time, it is clear they did not understand the need for scientific validation in the first place. They regarded their raw, unstructured but ten-thousand-fold experience as quite sufficient in itself.

Only very late in the day has it been understood that to prove the efficacy of a treatment is actually quite difficult and not a matter of mere reflection on the cases one has seen. A treatment has to be compared with the natural outcome of the disease, or another treatment of known efficacy. Furthermore, the strong placebo effect has to be taken into account and methods devised for distinguishing between this effect and the true effect of the treatment under investigation.

Let me illustrate the point. When I worked in the Gilbert Islands, I found a widespread belief that the local traditional healers were especially skilled in treating jaundice. The reason for this was not difficult to discern. The commonest cause of jaundice in the islands was infectious hepatitis, which was very common indeed. It is known that at least 99 per cent of all cases of infectious hepatitis resolve spontaneously; but since nearly every case in the Gilbert Islands was treated by a traditional healer, it was believed the local medicine was highly effective.

The great majority of ailments that afflict mankind are similarly self-limiting. Furthermore, many of them are susceptible to suggestion. It would be very surprising, therefore, if there were a method of treatment that was *not* able to claim its successes. It would have to be positively murderous to fail completely.

Alternative medicine is not, on the whole, troubled by such intellectual scruples. The evidence in its favour is still the testimonial and the anecdote.

To read books written by alternative therapists is to regress to the 18th century, or beyond. I went to an 'alternative bookshop', where I found an entire section devoted to alternative medicine. (It was opposite Black Women's Writing and near Radical Politics – that is to say, Chile, South Africa and Nicaragua. Is there, I wonder, some psychological connection between these disparate subjects?) Browsing, I soon discovered the basic tenets common to most alternative therapies.

First, modern industrial society is unnatural and therefore uniquely unhealthy: 'We pollute ourselves and our surroundings, and in consequence suffer from disease . . .' It is entirely overlooked that, from the point of view of life expectancy and freedom from epidemic disease, modern industrial society, whatever its other problems, is the healthiest that has ever existed.

Second, orthodox medicine has failed: 'The man in the street is becoming more and more discontented with drug therapy and conscious that it leaves much to be desired.' There is here a complete failure to understand that knowledge is always provisional, and however much is known, there will always be much left to be desired. Systems which claim full and final knowledge are charlatanry.

Third, orthodox medicine does not heal 'the whole man', unlike alternative medicine. 'The basis . . . is rational in that it treats the whole man . . . and there are no side-effects.' The whole man is here an unproblematical concept. Neither is it explained how advances are to be secured once the analytical methods of science are abandoned. It is assumed also that somewhere within the phenomenal man – the man who pays his mortgage, the man who shouts at his wife – there is the True Man who, like God, is without attributes.

I chose two books at random from among the hundreds available. (It does not seem to worry devotees of alternative medicine that the multifarious theories are mutually contradictory.) The first was a short guide to homoeopathy, now in its third impression.

We are treated to an exposition of the Law of Similars, upon which the whole system rests. The founder of homoeopathy, Hahnemann, discovered that quinine, a cure for malaria, could produce in a healthy man symptoms not dissimilar from those of malaria itself (the considerable differences are not mentioned). From this, he jumped to the strange conclusion that any substance which produced symptoms reminiscent of a disease could cure that disease. He also discovered that the more dilute a substance, the greater its effect, since more of its 'energy' had entered the solvent.

We go on to learn about the *Miasms*, Psora, Syphilis and Sycosis. Psora is quite serious:

> [it] has, through the centuries, polluted the human bloodstream
> through hereditary transmission ... Psora is invisible ...
> Suppression by application of ointments, the use of x-rays, etc.
> ... has forced it inwards ... Psora, in fact, affects every function
> and has numerous stomach and bowel symptoms ... The patient
> is always hungry ... he craves sweet things and sour things ...
> [he] often suffers spots before the vision ... The face often has a
> triangular appearance ... [he] dislikes washing ... he quite
> happily endures dirty shirts.

When a sufferer from Psora misguidedly unites with a sufferer from
Syphilis (eccentrically defined) the outcome is tuberculosis.

As for smallpox vaccination:

> [it] is the father of ... erysipelas, impetigo, psoriasis,
> morbelliform rashes, some forms of gangrene, erythemas,
> roseola, papular and pustular eruptions ... urticaria, eczema,
> dermatitis ... lupus vulgaris and many others.

There is no mention, naturally, of the elimination of smallpox from the
world.

The second half of this instructive work is devoted to case histories. A
Backward Girl, I Don't Feel Well, Difficulty in Walking, Headaches,
Almost a Nervous Breakdown, Skin Trouble on the Hands, Back Trouble,
A Case of Dirty Unmanageable Boy, Misshapen Head, etc., all successes
for homoeopathy, some dating back to the 19th century.

Finally, we are reminded that George V was very keen on homoeopathy.

Turning now to *The Seven Levels of Healing*, one derives much useful if
surprising information: 'It is not generally understood that the power of
healing manifests in different rays which correspond directly to the rain-

'It's much more than just a token guinea pig.'

bow.' The red ray, or vibration, '. . . draws poisons, builds up red corpuscles, stimulates arteries, sluggish menstrual discharge and the autonomic nervous system'. For those suffering from a lack of vitality '. . . a simple remedy is to wear red underclothes'. The purple ray on the other hand 'is good for headaches and for some people can be a slimming aid'.

There is interesting anatomical information too:

> Seven vital centres are situated down the spine from the top of the head to the sacrum and are known as *chakras*. These seven main chakras are attached to the spine by cords which have roots and the general appearance is that of flowers . . . At the core of every chakra is a black and white hole . . .

At first sight it is curious that people who reject orthodox medicine, with its comparatively powerful intellectual infrastructure, should accept uncritically such a farrago of nonsense. But alternative medicine appeals to the millenarian and the messianic in modern man, which is not otherwise catered for. It is the search for certainty (*Happiness is Junk-Free Food*, according to the title of one book) in an uncertain world. It is displaced religion.

I do not say that herbalists and others do not effect genuine cures; only that, to prove it, they will have to adopt the procedures of orthodox medicine. In doing so they will lose their attraction. Alternative medicine is not worthy of the fashionable respect it receives.

20 September 1986

DAVE, DAVE,
DAVE, DAVE
AND DAVE
————
ALTERNATIVE
LAWYERS

INDEX